The Academic-Practitioner Divide in Intelligence Studies

Security and Professional Intelligence Education Series (SPIES)

Series Editor: Jan Goldman

In this post–September 11, 2001, era there has been rapid growth in the number of professional intelligence training and educational programs across the United States and abroad. Colleges and universities, as well as high schools, are developing programs and courses in homeland security, intelligence analysis, and law enforcement, in support of national security.

The Security and Professional Intelligence Education Series (SPIES) was first designed for individuals studying for careers in intelligence and to help improve the skills of those already in the profession; however, it was also developed to educate the public on how intelligence work is conducted and should be conducted in this important and vital profession.

1. *Ethics of Spying: A Reader for the Intelligence Professional*, edited by Jan Goldman. 2006.
2. *Communicating with Intelligence: Writing and Briefing in the Intelligence and National Security Communities*, by James S. Major. 2008.
3. *A Spy's Résumé: Confessions of a Maverick Intelligence Professional and Misadventure Capitalist*, by Marc Anthony Viola. 2008.
4. *An Introduction to Intelligence Research and Analysis*, by Jerome Clauser, revised and edited by Jan Goldman. 2008.
5. *Writing Classified and Unclassified Papers for National Security*, by James S. Major. 2009.
6. *Strategic Intelligence: A Handbook for Practitioners, Managers, and Users*, revised edition by Don McDowell. 2009.
7. *Partly Cloudy: Ethics in War, Espionage, Covert Action, and Interrogation*, by David L. Perry. 2009.
8. *Tokyo Rose / An American Patriot: A Dual Biography*, by Frederick P. Close. 2010.
9. *Ethics of Spying: A Reader for the Intelligence Professional*, Volume 2, edited by Jan Goldman. 2010.
10. *A Woman's War: The Professional and Personal Journey of the Navy's First African American Female Intelligence Officer*, by Gail Harris. 2010.
11. *Handbook of Scientific Methods of Inquiry for Intelligence Analysis*, by Hank Prunckun. 2010.
12. *Handbook of Warning Intelligence: Assessing the Threat to National Security*, by Cynthia Grabo. 2010.
13. *Keeping U.S. Intelligence Effective: The Need for a Revolution in Intelligence Affairs*, by William J. Lahneman. 2011.
14. *Words of Intelligence: An Intelligence Professional's Lexicon for Domestic and Foreign Threats, Second Edition*, by Jan Goldman. 2011.
15. *Counterintelligence Theory and Practice*, by Hank Prunckun. 2012.
16. *Balancing Liberty and Security: An Ethical Study of U.S. Foreign Intelligence Surveillance, 2001–2009*, by Michelle Louise Atkin. 2013.

17. *The Art of Intelligence: Simulations, Exercises, and Games*, edited by William J. Lahneman and Rubén Arcos. 2014.
18. *Communicating with Intelligence: Writing and Briefing in National Security, Second Edition*, by James S. Major. 2014.
19. *Scientific Methods of Inquiry for Intelligence Analysis, Second Edition*, by Hank Prunckun. 2014.
20. *Quantitative Intelligence Analysis: Applied Analytic Models, Simulations and Games*, by Edward Waltz. 2014.
21. *Handbook of Warning Intelligence: Assessing the Threat to National Security—The Complete Declassified Edition*, by Cynthia Grabo, 2015.
22. *Intelligence and Information Policy for National Security: Key Terms and Concepts*, by Jan Goldman and Susan Maret. 2016.
23. *The Handbook of European Intelligence Cultures*, edited by Bob de Graaff and James M. Nyce, with Chelsea Locke. 2016.
24. *Partly Cloudy: Ethics in War, Espionage, Covert Action, and Interrogation, Second Edition*, by David L. Perry. 2016.
25. *Shattered Illusions: KGB Cold War Espionage in Canada*, by Donald G. Mahar. 2016.
26. *Intelligence Engineering: Operating beyond the Conventional*, by Adam D. M. Svendsen. 2017.
27. *Humanitarian Intelligence: A Practitioner's Guide to Crisis Analysis and Project Design*, by Andrej Zwitter. 2018.
28. *Reasoning for Intelligence Analysts: A Multidimensional Approach of Traits, Techniques, and Targets*, by Noel Hendrickson. 2018.
29. *Counterintelligence Theory and Practice, Second Edition*, by Hank Prunckun. 2019.
30. *Methods of Inquiry for Intelligence Analysis, Third Edition*, by Hank Prunckun. 2019.
31. *The Art of Intelligence: More Simulations, Exercises, and Games*, edited by Rubén Arcos and William J. Lahneman. 2019.
32. *Weaponized Marketing: Defeating Radical Islam with Marketing That Built the World's Top Brands*, by Lisa Merriam and Milton Kotler. 2020.
33. *Shadow Warfare: Cyberwar Policy in the United States, Russia and China*, by Elizabeth Van Wie Davis. 2021.
34. *African Intelligence Services: Early Postcolonial and Contemporary Challenges*, edited by Ryan Shaffer. 2021.
35. *The Academic-Practitioner Divide in Intelligence Studies*, edited by Rubén Arcos; Nicole K. Drumhiller and Mark Phythian. 2022.

To view the books on our website, please visit https://rowman.com/Action/SERIES/RL/SPIES or scan the QR code below.

The Academic-Practitioner Divide in Intelligence Studies

Edited by
Rubén Arcos
Nicole K. Drumhiller
Mark Phythian

ROWMAN & LITTLEFIELD
Lanham • Boulder • New York • London

Published by Rowman & Littlefield
An imprint of The Rowman & Littlefield Publishing Group, Inc.
4501 Forbes Boulevard, Suite 200, Lanham, Maryland 20706
www.rowman.com

86-90 Paul Street, London EC2A 4NE, United Kingdom

British Library Cataloguing in Publication Information Available

Library of Congress Cataloging-in-Publication Data

Names: Arcos Martín, Rubén, editor. | Drumhiller, Nicole K., 1980–editor. | Phythian, Mark, editor.
Title: The academic-practitioner divide in intelligence studies / edited by Rubén Arcos, Nicole K. Drumhiller, Mark Phythian.
Description: Lanham : Rowman & Littlefield, [2022] | Series: Security and professional intelligence education series (SPIES) ; 35 | Includes bibliographical references and index. | Summary: "To a significant extent both the profession of intelligence and those delivering intelligence education share a common aim of developing intelligence as a discipline. However, this shared interest must also navigate the existence of an academic-practitioner divide. Such a divide is far from unique to intelligence—it exists in various forms across most professions—but it is distinctive in the field of intelligence because of the centrality of secrecy to the profession of intelligence and the way in which this constitutes a barrier to understanding and openly teaching about aspects of intelligence. How can co-operation in developing the profession and academic study be maximized when faced with this divide? How can and should this divide be navigated? The Academic-Practitioner Divide in Intelligence provides a range of international approaches to, and perspectives on, these crucial questions"— Provided by publisher.
Identifiers: LCCN 2021055275 (print) | LCCN 2021055276 (ebook) | ISBN 9781538144466 (cloth) | ISBN 9781538196175 (pbk.) | ISBN 9781538144473 (epub)
Subjects: LCSH: Intelligence service—Study and teaching. | Intelligence service—Methodology. | Academic-industrial collaboration.
Classification: LCC JF1525.I6 A26 2022 (print) | LCC JF1525.I6 (ebook) | DDC 327.12—dc23/eng/20220206
LC record available at https://lccn.loc.gov/2021055275
LC ebook record available at https://lccn.loc.gov/2021055276

Contents

Figures and Tables

FIGURES

TABLES

Figures and Tables

FIGURES

TABLES

Acknowledgments

Rubén Arcos, Nicole Drumhiller, and Mark Phythian

This book would not have been possible without the support of a great number of people, including those who have worked to facilitate the networking opportunities which allowed the editors to meet and collaborate.

As a start, we'd like to thank Stephen Coulthart, Larry Valero, Damien Van Puyvelde, and the faculty and students from the National Security Studies Institute at the University of Texas, El Paso who hosted a dialog on "The Role of Social and Behavioral Science Research in Intelligence" in March 2017. As participants burned the midnight oil, networking after hours at Rosa's Cantina, we first established a plan to develop the International Online Intelligence Hub (IntelHub), which brings together scholars and practitioners from across the globe to engage in collaborative discourse on issues relevant to the study of intelligence. This online collaboration between the School of Security and Global Studies at the American Public University and American Military University, School of History, Politics and International Relations at the University of Leicester in the UK, and Rey Juan Carlos University in Spain has allowed the IntelHub to host speakers from all over the world to present on a wide variety of topics relevant to the study of intelligence. Later, in 2018 the editors came together again in San Francisco during the International Studies Association's annual convention, where they developed the plan for this book.

As we discuss in this book, international forums like those hosted by the University of Texas, El Paso, the annual meeting of the International Studies Association, and the events organized by the International Association for Intelligence Education (IAFIE) (both in the US and in Europe), play a vital role in the continuing development of the intelligence studies field. So too do the opportunities provided by organizations like the Center for Asymmetric

Threat Studies (CATS) in Stockholm, where Lars Nicander and his colleagues have made such a valuable contribution over several years in bringing together practitioners and academics. Without such opportunities this book would not have been possible.

In addition to those who host opportunities to dialog on intelligence studies topics, we would also like to thank those individuals who are actively engaged in those discussions. This book would also not have been possible if it was not for those practitioners and scholars whose works came before this and provided inspiration for a dialog on the academic-practitioner divide in intelligence studies. Their research and scholarship have helped to further develop the field. In particular, we want to thank all of the authors who have contributed to this volume—each of them part of this wider international conversation about the study of intelligence—for their valuable contributions, which we hope will serve as a springboard for continuing thought and collaboration around the core issues represented here.

Finally, we would like to thank all those at Rowman & Littlefield who have helped in the development of this book. Specifically, we'd like to thank Jan Goldman, April Snider, Megan DeLancey, Rebecca Anastasi, Dhara Snowden, and our anonymous reviewers. Managing a book project during the COVID pandemic comes with its own set of special challenges and we want to thank each of you for your efforts in seeing this through from initial idea to finished product.

Navigating the Academic-Practitioner Divide in Intelligence Studies

Rubén Arcos, Nicole K. Drumhiller, and Mark Phythian

This book is a product of sustained engagement on the part of the editors and individual authors with crucial questions about the nature of intelligence studies as an academic project and its relationship to the profession of intelligence. As in several other areas with clear policy and practitioner relevance, such as security studies and international relations, for example, when it comes to intelligence, questions arise concerning the inevitable divide or gap between the worlds of government and policy, on the one hand, and academia, on the other, as well as how far both sides should seek to build bridges to facilitate regular and mutually beneficial contact across it. The premise of this book is that, for the reasons we set out below, this is an opportune moment to take stock of the question of the academic-practitioner divide as it relates to intelligence and to facilitate discussion of its nature, to what extent it is inevitable, and how far it can and should be mitigated.

It is also essential to closely examine the idea of the "divide" itself; how far are we faced with a single divide, and how far is the academic-practitioner relationship more complex than this image might suggest? As we set out to show in this chapter, the academic-practitioner divide in intelligence is multifaceted, with stark lines in the sand over different components that make up the field and the way it is or should be taught. Nevertheless, within this landscape, the question of secrecy constitutes a fundamental line of demarcation. There are clear divisions among those working as intelligence practitioners and those teaching/researching intelligence topics on the importance of secret information, and the degree to which the classified nature of (some) data in the intelligence field inhibits the ability to study intelligence-related topics effectively. A second division that comes to light is specific to who should or can best teach intelligence-related subjects. Some are of the position that little can be learned from intelligence studies faculty who lack a prior employment history with a three-letter agency or other organization that conducts intelligence. Others are of the position that faculty members without direct intelligence work experience can add value to the field, develop its conceptual underpinnings, research and explain aspects of its history, address problems of practice, and effectively teach intelligence-related topics.

Still others are of the position that the "ideal type" of faculty member would be one with prior experience working within an intelligence community who also has teaching and research experience and can walk in, and speak to, both worlds. A third point of departure, stemming from the question of who should be teaching intelligence, is what specifically should intelligence education encompass? Under this divide are questions surrounding the differences between the provision of training and education. What should be the purpose of teaching or studying intelligence? Should intelligence curriculums be designed with content that serves job fulfillment needs? To what degree should curriculums provide education on intelligence policies, practices, successes, failures, and a critical evaluation of them? In other words, how narrowly should "intelligence" be understood for these purposes? How much focus should be placed on carrying out research and conducting studies on intelligence-related topics? Another area that could be considered a fundamental division is over who sets the agenda for intelligence-based research. Here questions arise over the kinds of questions asked and how questions are framed. While both academics and practitioners work on intelligence-related topics, their agendas differ, they seek different answers to similar questions, and their deadline requirements are different.[1]

UNIVERSITIES AND INTELLIGENCE: CONTOURS OF THE RELATIONSHIP SINCE WORLD WAR II

However, before embarking on an examination of the divide and approaches to mitigating it, it is useful to begin by sketching something of the history of intelligence-academic relations, including the history of cooperation and exchange and the issues that have arisen. Historically, the relationship between universities and intelligence organizations has been varied. For British and US intelligence organizations, universities were often looked to as talent pools in the early establishment of organizations like the Central Intelligence Agency (CIA), General Communications Headquarters, MI5, and MI6.[2] In several national contexts, it has been one of cooperation, with universities providing expertise and personnel for intelligence organizations, albeit in secret.[3] It has also been one of suspicion, with universities at times regarded as sites of radicalism whose spaces nurture potential challenges to the state and need to be monitored.[4] In the globalized higher-education market of the twenty-first century, it is also one where intelligence advises universities on securing their research secrets from possible theft by third parties[5] and against foreign interference.[6] Over the past thirty years or so, the relationship has also become more open and extensive, developments driven by the rise of the profession of intelligence and its rapid globalization and, in response, the almost equally rapid growth of academic courses delivering intelligence education across a number of countries within a globalized higher-education environment.

Shared Interests

The United States was perhaps the first country to recognize the potential contribution that academia could make to the national intelligence effort and develop a basis for utilizing it. In 1941, William Donovan recommended to then president Roosevelt that in developing the foreign intelligence service, there was a need to "draw on the universities for experts, with long foreign experience and specialized knowledge of the history, languages, and general conditions of various countries."[7] During the Allied war effort, both social scientists and natural and physical scientists, drawn from the United States and beyond, collaborated with the US military; however, the latter's achievements, including the development of the atom bomb and radar, led to social science contributions going largely unnoticed.[8] During this time, psychologists and anthropologists would focus on predicting national behavior, while researchers and faculty in communications focused on coercion tactics.[9] As Mark Solovey has noted, "During World War II and the Cold War, the expertise of psychologists, psychiatrists, and professionals in related areas seemed especially relevant to military and intelligence operations. Psychologists proclaimed that their work was perhaps more valuable than military hardware in winning the allegiances of foreign governments and peoples."[10] This perspective gained the attention of US foreign policy experts focusing on communism and attempts to shape political-ideological mind-sets.

Following the Second World War, academics—social scientists in particular—sought to continue their partnership with the military in order to enhance their "public respectability and scientific legitimacy."[11] This desire for partnership was to some degree driven by the desire of the social sciences to be respected and taken as seriously as the hard sciences. Much as with the hard sciences, "the military took a special interest in social research that appeared to be rigorously scientific" and could further contribute to its Cold War goals, while containing the seeds of later controversies.[12]

Between 1955 and 1959, we see additional examples of universities such as Michigan State University contracting with the CIA to provide cover to agents in South Vietnam.[13] In 1956 the CIA established the Asia foundation to fund anticommunist academics in Asian countries to recruit them as agents.[14] Additionally, a joint project between MIT and Cornell focused on the training of the Indonesian military that would later end in a military coup.[15]

One massive collaborative effort (with a whopping $6 million budget) between social scientists and the US Army in 1964 was Project Camelot.[16] Project Camelot sought to improve a knowledge gap specific to understanding revolutionary movements' development, behavioral dynamics, and counterinsurgency tactics.[17] During this project, Latin America was a key center of research focused on studying how and why conflicts in the region arose and how the United States could anticipate them.[18] Other proposed field research areas included a few countries in the Middle East, Asia, Europe, and Africa.[19] One participant stated that this effort was the equivalent of the Manhattan Project for the social sciences, while another reflecting on the proposed expansion of the original Camelot proposal stated that the research effort would be similar to putting a person on the moon.[20] However, in 1965 the political tide began to change as opposition to the Vietnam War swept across college campuses. As a result, academia became a key battleground for discussions of state abuses of social science and the role of the United States in the international arena.[21] Project Camelot ended up coming under fire when an anthropologist misrepresented the project to colleagues in Chile and concealed the US military's financial investment in the research.[22] As a result, the anthropologist fell under suspicion of being a US spy and was subsequently banned from returning to Chile, his country of origin.[23] Following this incident, the Chilean government denounced Project Camelot as "an attempt against the dignity, sovereignty, and independence of states and peoples and against the right of the latter to self-determination."[24] This incident resulted in increasing international outcry and culminated in Project Camelot's cancellation. Though Project Camelot was canceled, the United States also had other counterinsurgency projects under way with social scientists, including Project Troy (something that would spark the development of MIT's Center for International Studies), Project Simpatico, Project Revolt, and Project Michelson.[25]

Following the controversy and attention surrounding Project Camelot, additional fallout emerged in Thailand with the release of an emotively titled article, "Anthropology on the Warpath in Thailand," where anthropologists researching the Tribal Research Center in Thailand were accused of transferring knowledge to Thai and US military intelligence.[26] Heated debate emerged within the academic community, with proponents both for and against academic and government collaboration. As the accused researchers were from the United States and Australia, the American Anthropological Association and the Australian Association of Social Anthropologists advised against and openly opposed contractual agreements between academic researchers and governments.[27] By mid-1972, the controversy had run its course, and though it sparked divides within the academic community, no conspiracy among governments was revealed.[28]

Moving into the mid-1970s, academics in the United States started distancing themselves from the government due to strained relationships resulting from what might be called mission focus. Concerns stemmed from intelligence collection on groups and individuals on college campuses that had a perceived radical slant. One such project run by the CIA was Project Resistance, which collected intelligence from colleges and some high schools across the United States.[29] Domestic surveillance programs like this served as a wedge between academic and government collaboration. Given the changing political tide,

> the Church-Pike congressional inquiry into domestic spying, the fatal over-reaction of Ohio National Guardsmen at Kent State, FBI illegal monitoring of the civil rights movement, and other developments prompted many academicians publicly and stridently to distance themselves from any cooperation with U.S. intelligence, particularly the CIA. Agency (and military) recruiters were banned from or spurned on campuses, professors were excoriated for contracting or consulting with intelligence agencies, and "intelligence" seemed to have become a four letter word.[30]

In the 1980s, relations between academics and government intelligence services warmed due to the intensification of the Cold War and the need for information on the Soviet Union, its allies, and a range of Third World states, as instability and revolutions impacted the national security picture.[31] However, toward the end of the 1980s and into the 1990s, another shift occurred, causing US college campuses to again distance themselves from the intelligence community. Some of the developing perceptions for why the communities should not mix included "the belief that secrecy was antithetical to academic freedom; efforts to recruit professors and students; and the IC's assumed long-standing role in undermining democratic movements around the world."[32]

However, the September 11, 2001 (9/11), terrorist attacks on the United States had a transformative effect on the academic-practitioner relationship, most immediately and most extensively in the United States, but then gradually and to varying degrees in a number of other countries. In the United States, following several years of immediate post–Cold War downsizing, the 9/11 attacks provided the impetus to recruit and train the next generation of intelligence officers required by the enormous public-private enterprise that constitutes the US intelligence community.[33] The partnerships that developed here and in other countries encompassed internal security (e.g., identifying and countering "radicalization" among those groups judged most susceptible to this) and foreign intelligence. As in the earlier Cold War era, the scope of these relationships gave rise to controversy in specific areas.

In 2005, academics from the social sciences and other fields partnered with the US military to develop a new counterinsurgency, or COIN, doctrine.[34] Then in 2006, academics and practitioners were brought together in a workshop where they would produce a new COIN field manual, where "nation building and nonmilitary actions aimed toward the local population remained at the heart of the new doctrine" but now included a key focus on human rights.[35]

The US Army and Marines established human terrain teams in 2007, made up of military forces and social scientists from political science and anthropology fields designed to enhance the knowledge of operational forces in Iraq and Afghanistan.[36] During this time, debate would emerge among anthropologists surrounding the ethics of such uses of social science. Though the intended goal was to minimize the need for deadly force ultimately, the perception within the academic community was that social scientists were being used to identify and kill targets.[37]

For example, another US government–initiated research endeavor, Minerva, was developed and offered upward of $50 million over five years to researchers seeking to study Chinese military and technology, the documents captured during the Iraq War, the impact of religious and cultural change in Islam, terrorist organizations and ideologies, as well as national security, conflict, and cooperation broadly defined.[38] Reminiscent of Project Camelot, the collaboration between social scientists and the US government came under scrutiny during Minerva—for example, concerning selection issues specific to the grant-funding allotment and the ethical challenges surrounding the militarization of knowledge production in academia.[39]

THE DEVELOPMENT OF INTELLIGENCE STUDIES:
TWO LITERATURES

Throughout this history of academic-intelligence engagement, cooperation, and tension, as intelligence gradually professionalized during the Cold War era, so it began to develop its own specialist literature. This involved reflections about the purpose, role, and conduct of the intelligence organization and the individual intelligence professionals within it. Almost in parallel, another intelligence literature was being developed, written from outside intelligence organizations by academics who grasped the importance of thinking about the questions that arose from this most secret profession. In this, we can see that intelligence generated two complementary yet separate literatures. Once again, the United States was the site of the earliest and most significant developments. This section maps out the contours of these developments as a prelude to our focus on the question of the academic-practitioner divide.

As early as 1942, the political scientist Harold D. Lasswell wrote on the intelligence function in an article titled "The Relation of Ideological Intelligence to Public Policy." Lasswell reported that "a canvass of the existing literature reveals that very little systematic and unified treatment has been given to the intelligence function."[40] As communications studies pioneer Wilbur Schramm wrote on Lasswell, "When World War II started he answered the Government's call for expert help. During the war years he directed a research project at the U.S. Library of Congress studying 'world revolutionary propaganda' not for a book but for real-world policy guidance."[41] This experience led Lasswell to reflect on the organization of intelligence. For example, in a 1943 "memorandum on personal policy objectives" that sheds light on the intelligence aspects of his research agenda, Lasswell wrote,

12. As a policy adviser I hope to aid in perfecting the intelligence function in our society. By the intelligence function I refer to the process of making available to those who make decisions the facts and interpretations designed to improve the rationality and morality of their judgments. During the present war I have had unusual opportunity to experiment in this direction, and to become acquainted with difficulties to be overcome. 13. An adequate intelligence function should clarify goals and appraise them not only in terms of expediency but of morality; it should clarify alternatives of action; it should provide pertinent information about trends and causal relations. If I am to perform a policy advisory function I must keep myself informed of the major trends of world development and the advances of science; I must think creatively about ways and means of accomplishing future results; I must operate with explicit conceptions of the common good. To some extent I have been involved in the criticism of policy, or the guidance of research, in connection with several agencies, such as the U.S. Department of Agriculture (analysis of the administrative effectiveness of the Farm Security Administration), the U.S. Department of Justice (detection of enemy and subversive propaganda), the Library of Congress (War Communications Research, available to the Federal Communications Commission, and the war information agencies of the government), General Education Board (The Rockefeller Foundation; self-appraisal and program of communications research), etc.[42]

We can see the wartime experiences of Lasswell and several other social scientists and historians as a foundation for the production of the professional intelligence literature. The single most important figure in this is Sherman Kent, who taught history at Yale University, where he had been awarded a doctorate in the subject before joining the Office of Strategic Services (OSS) in 1942. Taking advantage of the space afforded by a postwar return to academia at the National War College, he wrote his seminal book, *Strategic Intelligence for American World Policy*, published by Princeton University Press in 1949.[43] By the mid-1950s, Kent was becoming aware that as intelligence professionalized and took on a number of the characteristics of a discipline it still lacked one that was core: a specialist literature that could inform thinking about the profession and guide practice.[44] He warned that

> as long as this discipline lacks a literature, its method, its vocabulary, its body of doctrine, and even its fundamental theory run the risk of never reaching full maturity. I will not say that you cannot have a discipline without a literature, but I will assert that you are unlikely to have a robust and growing discipline without one.[45]

He drew a parallel between the emerging profession of intelligence and the centrality of a specialist literature in other professions:

> Consider such disciplines as chemistry or medicine or economics and ask yourself where they would be today if their master practitioners had committed no more to paper than ours. Where would we be if each new conscript to medicine had to start from scratch with no more to guide him than the advice of fellow doctors and his own experience? Where would we be in medicine if there was nothing to read and nothing to study, no text books, no monographs, no specialized journals, no photographs, no charts, no illustrations, no association meetings with papers read and discussed and circulated in written form? Where would we be if no one aspired to the honor of publishing an original thought or concept or discovery in the trade journals of his profession?[46]

The crucial difference between the context in which Kent was operating and seeking to develop a specialist literature and the professions he compared it to here was, of course, secrecy. Kent was advocating the development of a literature that, to realize its full potential, required the oxygen of open debate, with propositions widely disseminated and readily available for others to critically review. In his vision,

> The literature I have in mind will, among other things, be an elevated debate. For example, I see a Major X write an essay on the theory of indicators and print it and have it circulated. I see a Mr. B brood over this essay and write a review of it. I see a Commander C reading both the preceding documents and reviewing them both. I then see a revitalized discussion among the people of the indicator business. I hope that they now, more than ever before, discuss indicators within

the terms of a common conceptual frame and in a common vocabulary. From the debate in the literature and from the oral discussion I see another man coming forward to produce an original synthesis of all that has gone before. His summary findings will be a kind of intellectual platform upon which the new debate can start. His platform will be a thing of orderly and functional construction and it will stand above the bushes and trees that once obscured the view.[47]

Many intelligence professionals in the United States took up Kent's call. As a result, a number of significant contributions to an emerging literature were published in the following decades, a significant number of them in the in-house journal *Studies in Intelligence*, which progressed quickly to being published on a quarterly basis. A number of the pieces published focused on specific areas of tradecraft, such as the use of hotels,[48] but these were published alongside episodes from intelligence history (for example, Benjamin Franklin's private secretary in Paris as a British spy), a particular focus on intelligence in the Second World War, and the CIA's own, emerging history.

However, the vision set out by Kent was, in many ways, for something more than a technical professional literature. Moreover, the key issues that he suggested should be a focus of this literature (first principles of intelligence—"what is our mission?"; how are we going about our mission—"what is our method?"; the importance of arriving at definitions of key terms)[49] had, in a liberal democratic context, an importance to people outside of the closed world of intelligence. What the mission of intelligence was, how agencies went about it, and what they understood key terms to mean were not issues that just affected intelligence organizations; they all had the potential to have a wider impact on the state and society more generally.

Other notable professional contributions to the literature during this period were made by George S. Pettee[50] and Willmoore Kendall, with his article reviewing Kent's strategic intelligence book,[51] who together with Sherman Kent formed a sort of triad labeled by Roger Hilsman as "the academic observers." As noted by Hilsman in his book, *Strategic Intelligence and National Decisions*, which itself represents a significant contribution to the academic intelligence literature, this label of "academic observers," justified by the fact that the three of them came from the academic world, should not "obscure the fact that all three have also had considerable service in intelligence."[52]

Already in 1948, Colonel Ralph I. Glasgow, writing on planning and intelligence, referred to the intelligence process as collection, evaluation, interpretation of information, production, and dissemination of intelligence.[53] A decade later, General Washington Platt published *Strategic Intelligence Production*, with one group within this process—intelligence production officers and those dealing with them—as its target audience.[54] In the preface to the book, Platt claimed that the body of his book "points out how much intelligence production has to learn from the social sciences," while at the same time, "social scientists could perhaps learn something in their turn from the point of view and methods of the humble intelligence worker," as well as business executives.[55]

The professional literature continued to develop in the following two decades, not just via the pages of *Studies in Intelligence* and *World Politics* but also via key works such as Allen W. Dulles's *The Craft of Intelligence*,[56] Klaus Knorr's "Foreign Intelligence and the Social Sciences,"[57] and Harold L. Wilensky's *Organizational Intelligence*.[58] Cynthia Grabo wrote a major contribution to the professional intelligence literature and particularly to warning intelligence between 1968 and 1972.[59] The *Handbook of Warning Intelligence* was classified secret and was not fully published until 2015. It was intended, in Grabo's words, for "desk analysts and their immediate supervisors, and for use in intelligence training courses, [and] it is hoped that it will be of benefit also to higher-level intelligence personnel, and those at policy level who are dependent on the intelligence process for strategic warning."[60] Another highlight in this strand of analytic literature is Clauser and Weir's *Intelligence Research Methodology: An Introduction to Techniques and Procedures for Conducting Research in Defense Intelligence*.[61] Following this, the collection of articles written by Richards J. Heuer Jr. between 1978 and 1986 were published in a single book, *Psychology of Intelligence Analysis*.[62]

The production of academic research on intelligence and intelligence agencies, besides helping in gaining understanding of this function and its role in security and international relations, also helped unveil epistemologies underlying intelligence practices and theorization from scholars. The critical review by Willmoore Kendall of Kent's *Strategic Intelligence*, besides being one of the first "controversies" identified in the field, or as Jack Davis put it, "the Kent-Kendall Debate of 1949,"[63] unveiled a series of assumptions relating to what Kendall called "the general theory of the intelligence function."[64] This included the wartime conception of intelligence-dominated intelligence as an aggregation of knowledge on foreign entities under a "regional breakdown" approach; intelligence driven by the logic of absolute prediction (as opposed to contingent prediction), in which "the course of events is conceived not as something you try to influence but as a tape all printed up inside a machine; and the job of intelligence is to tell the planners how it reads";[65] and an empirical conception of the underlying research process leading to the oblivion of theory in favor of an empirical conception of social science research.

By this time, the professional literature had been joined by an academic literature, analyzing intelligence from the outside rather than reflecting on it from within. The experiences of Vietnam and Watergate heightened awareness that excessive secrecy could harbor practices that existed in tension with liberal democratic norms and expectations and acted as a spur for US academics to explore the secret world of intelligence. Even more importantly, the study of intelligence as a social science project in the United States during the 1970s and into the early 1980s was stimulated by revelations arising from the Church Committee inquiry into domestic surveillance in the United States,[66] the nature and role of covert action in a democratic polity, and how this should be regulated.[67] This "season of inquiry" experience demonstrated how a proper concern underpinning the study of intelligence was the relationship between intelligence, the state, and the broader society—or, if you like, between power, knowledge, and secrecy—and not simply about intelligence as a process. One notable academic pioneer in the United States was Harry Howe Ransom, who, in the context of these developments, asked how intelligence performance should be evaluated. By this, he meant on behalf of the public. He proposed several basic questions that should be asked as a starting point in looking to understand intelligence policy:

- What was the CIA supposed to be when it was created by Congress in 1947?
- What did it become, and why?
- What has been the nature and quality of its performance?
- And what ought to be the future structure and functions of a national intelligence system within the American democratic framework?[68]

Hence, by the late 1970s, the study of intelligence was being undertaken both in-house, as a means of developing the profession of intelligence, and from the outside by academics, but with, at least in part, a different focus—as a form of oversight and accountability.

In practice, the production of the textbooks, monographs, and journals that constitute the specialist intelligence literature has required cooperation with academics. In a sense, this was inevitable if the field was to flourish. As Sherman Kent had himself asked as early as 1955, "How is such a literature to be written if most or all of the potential authors are practicing members of the profession, already burdened with seemingly higher priority tasks?"[69]

Today, then, we have arrived at a position where the literature on which the study of intelligence rests combines contributions by academics, practitioner-academics, and practitioners. Hence, the development and testing of ideas in this area is a joint endeavor. Practitioners draw on academic ideas and combine them with their own perspectives, analyses, and reflection. Academics draw on practitioner analyses and reflections and use these to confirm prior assumptions and develop their understanding about specific organizational processes. Both draw on the increasing volume of publicly available information that is generated in an era when oversight and accountability bodies regularly investigate and report on issues, and when postmortem inquiries produce detailed reports along with the primary evidence underpinning them. Both academics and practitioners use these to develop and illustrate their analyses of intelligence organization and practice.

Intelligence Studies after 9/11

It is useful to pause at this point in our discussion of the development of academic intelligence studies to reflect further on the impact of 9/11 on the shape of, and demand for, intelligence education. After 9/11 the intelligence community within the United States was charged with rethinking how it carried out its intelligence practices. The 9/11 Commission called for the creation of a new intelligence function that dealt with capacity building between intelligence community stakeholders and also academia.[70] Given the renewed attention and increase in financial resources, the study of intelligence in the 2000s entered an "adolescent" phase, with growth in the literature "in terms of sophistication and abstraction, [including] much additional emphasis on key intelligence concepts and theories."[71] Scholars interested in researching intelligence were specifically interested in understanding the overall placement of intelligence within the national security apparatus of the state. In addition to this are interests in understanding the "organizational structure of intelligence agencies" and their vulnerability to politicization.[72] Topics of intelligence oversight and overreach, privacy violations, insider threats, and torture came to acquire a new salience resulting from the post-9/11 intelligence and security climate. However, the impact of 9/11 was felt within the United States and across the globe. This ripple effect can also be seen to have made an impact on intelligence studies within the United Kingdom, France, Germany, Spain (hit by train bombings in Madrid on March 11, 2004), Scandinavia, Australia (the October 2002 Bali bombings killed 88 Australians among the 202 dead), and beyond. For example, after 9/11, "French politicians and the general public in France [were] more aware of the role that intelligence plays in national security," and thus its study was "rediscovered" as a vital decision-making tool for leaders in foreign policy and international security.[73] As with France, in Germany, renewed attention was given to the study of national security matters and the role that intelligence can play in avoiding terrorist attacks across the globe.[74]

The origins of the post-9/11 expansion of intelligence education in the United States can be traced back to the latter part of the twentieth century. The integration of "intelligence" as a subject within the public university setting first occurred in the 1980s.[75] However, the history of US government personnel obtaining degrees in security and intelligence studies dates back even farther, to the 1960s, with intelligence program and course offerings by the Defense Intelligence Agency's in-house school, the National Intelligence School, and the National Defense Intelligence College (currently the National Intelligence University).[76] In the early to mid-1990s, we begin seeing "intelligence" as a formal degree term. Early adopters included Mercyhurst College (now Mercyhurst University) and American Military University. For Mercyhurst, their first intelligence concentration was offered in 1992.[77] The concentration was developed by Robert J. Heibel, a twenty-year FBI veteran who recognized a skills gap in finding qualified entry-level intelligence analysts.[78] The concentration was located within the history department and was titled the "Research/Intelligence Analyst Program." Its mission was to produce "a graduate qualified as an entry-level intelligence analyst for government and the private sector."[79] Following this, in 1996, American Military University, a university dedicated to distance education, began offering a BA in intelligence studies and offered intelligence as a concentration within their MA in military studies.

Nevertheless, despite these early offerings, most intelligence studies programs within the United States were founded after 9/11.[80] In 2002, the American Public University System, home to American Military University and American Public University, launched their MA in strategic intelligence;[81] and in 2004, Mercyhurst first offered their MS in applied intelligence.[82] Later, the American Public University System would launch its applied doctorate of strategic intelligence program in January 2018. Though now a few years old, a 2015 survey by Coulthart and Crosston found that within the United States, seventeen college-level programs were being offered, with twenty-six degrees that used "intelligence" in the degree title.[83] Building on this research, Parsons found that six years later, there were twenty-eight intelligence programs offering forty-one intelligence degrees at varying levels.[84] Since then, more programs have sprung up to include degrees at the doctoral level. In addition to the increase in degree programs, the range of program types has also increased in scope. Titles for degree programs offer more than the general "intelligence studies" degree and now include focus areas specific to cyber intelligence, geospatial intelligence, criminal intelligence, applied intelligence, and business intelligence.[85]

This is a consequence of the professionalization and skill transitions of intelligence over the past few decades. The nature of the US higher education market and the size of the governmental (including military) intelligence sector in the United States have combined to create a clear trend toward the teaching of intelligence as preprofessional preparation and professional development. Likewise, as government practitioners set their sights on retirement, many are looking to transition their skill sets to other markets. For example, private companies such as those within the entertainment, banking, insurance, oil, health care, and cyber and tech industries are looking to higher-intelligence professionals due to their diverse skill sets and analytical abilities.[86] As several contributors to this book show, this is a trend that is now international. Schools offering undergraduate and graduate degrees as well as certificates in intelligence have emerged in Australia, Belgium, Canada, France, Germany, Italy, Mexico, New Zealand, Nigeria, Poland, Russia, Spain, and the United Kingdom.[87]

THINKING ABOUT THE AIMS, OBJECTIVES, AND CONTENT OF INTELLIGENCE EDUCATION

This broad trend raises questions about the aims, objectives, and content of intelligence education. In the post-9/11 environment, selections from the two literatures outlined above—the professional literature in support of developing a profession and discipline and the academic literature produced from the outside—have been brought together to form the basis of undergraduate degree programs in the field. The development and expansion of these awards also raise questions about who should deliver them—who the providers of intelligence education should be—and the nature of the academic-practitioner divide in the field. How far can, or should, we still talk just in terms of "academics" and "practitioners" when those delivering intelligence education in the United States and beyond are often a blend of the two?

Questions over the delivery of intelligence education and collaboration between academics and practitioners are fueled by perceived differences in the goals of intelligence education for including the relevance of intelligence topics and programs in higher education. Critics argue that academic programs that provide general education on intelligence add little value to those seeking to enter the field as a practitioner.[88] This is due to the perspective that most all intelligence agencies provide specific training on how intelligence tradecraft should be carried out within that organization, so instead they seek to hire individuals with specific subject-matter expertise like foreign languages, engineering, etc. However, general intelligence programs can serve as useful tools in helping practitioners already working in the field to see how their skill sets can be used in different industries, therefore serving as a job transition tool while perhaps also captivating the interests of those considering a government intelligence career. Likewise, general intelligence studies programs also offer the public an opportunity to better understand the different dynamics occurring within intelligence communities that they might not otherwise receive. At the doctoral level, value is added as students focus their attention on growing the field through resolving problems of practice using theoretical lenses. This is also the case for faculty research and their desire to add to the current knowledge base. In particular, "academic settings offer two fundamental advantages in education when compared to closed, in-house training opportunities: their engagement in research—and thus the state of the art of the learning content—and opportunities to engage with critical and unorthodox views."[89]

The next question that must also be considered when discussing who should be providing this education to students is what should be covered within higher-education intelligence programs. For some, the key to this question hinges on how intelligence is defined; then from here, the necessary conditions for what should be taught, researched, and written on fall into place.[90] Under some early considerations, intelligence education should encompass subjects specific to the intelligence process, analysis, espionage, covert action, and other activities that are focused beyond a state's borders. However, more recently, the scope of intelligence stems beyond this externally focused definition to include activities carried out within a state's borders and activities carried out within organizations, businesses, and medicine.

Approaches to the Study of Intelligence

However, determining what should be taught in intelligence programs to some degree presents a sort of chicken versus egg conundrum when one considers how the study of intelligence can be approached in higher education. There are numerous perspectives on this ranging from three to four lines of focus. One argument states that the study of intelligence can be approached from a functional perspective, a historical or biographical perspective, a structural perspective, and also a political perspective.[91] For Len Scott and Peter Jackson, there are three distinct approaches to the study of intelligence, including a historical approach on organizational structure, policy making, and leadership decision making; an approach that seeks to assess intelligence successes and failures; and finally a political approach on state uses of intelligence for societal control.[92] In Spain, Gustavo Díaz Matey also points to four approaches with a somewhat similar military-history-based approach, along with a journalistic approach, an economic approach, and a political science/international relations approach.[93]

While organizations like the Intelligence Association for Intelligence Education have established criteria for certifying intelligence courses and programs, not all programs will have the same focus, and not all programs will be all encompassing. In most cases, programs may specialize in specific topics or niche areas of intelligence depending on the program's leadership and the faculty teaching the courses.[94] After determining the curriculum focus, next, a discussion can be had about just who should be teaching intelligence courses.

Who Should Be Teaching Intelligence Courses?

Discussions surrounding who should be teaching intelligence often focus on the stereotype-based perceptions of the different roles and cultural norms that academics and practitioners have of one another. Driving this is an unspoken assumption about the type of course or program the teaching occurs within. At one extreme, those actively working in (or retired from) an intelligence-based career position might claim that academics have no business in providing education in matters of intelligence because they lack real-world experience and fail to grasp the rigor required when assessing the problems of the intelligence community.[95] Additionally, a bias exists on the level of policy understanding held by academics.[96] In this regard, practitioners may perceive academics as lacking in their level of policy understanding, their ivory towers preventing them from seeing how actual policy comes to be created and carried out. On the academic side, perceptions of the practitioner include the stovepiping and cherry-picking of intelligence.[97] Additionally, there is a bias that practitioners are only focused on short-term, surface-level issues and are unable to drill down into the root cause of problems that emerge again and again,[98] something that becomes problematic when attempting to lead graduate-level research.

Different Goals and Cultures of Academics, Practitioners, and Practitioner-Scholars

Within the literature, there are discussions of the differences in goals and culture between academics and practitioners; these sentiments present challenges for research collaborations and send mixed messages to students. For Marrin, key distinctions exist between how both sides operate under different agendas, frame questions differently, seek different answers to similar questions, and operate under different deadlines.[99] Practitioners might be considered "action oriented," as their work carries out some specific function within the intelligence cycle.[100] Their goal is to provide a product to a specific customer to advance the customer's goal. Their formal education can be in a variety of areas, with training centered on specific tradecraft. For Marrin, "scholars are contemplative and conceptual . . . because their primary mission is to understand and explain; to maximize the growth of knowledge."[101] However, for the action-oriented intelligence practitioner, the goal is focused on "getting the job done."[102] When it comes to scholarly inquiry, the key focus of academics is to "gather data with which to test theory or build insights."[103] This is in opposition to the focus of intelligence practitioners seeking to collect information that serves to "inform decisions, better allocate resources, neutralize threats, and target enemies."[104] Due to these differences in function, practitioners typically have little time to consider theory and contemplate literature that may not totally serve their needs when looking for actionable information.

Additionally, the culture experienced by practitioners may be stifling as well. Intelligence practitioners and likewise the intelligence field are oriented with the mind-set that "the best way to learn is by doing."[105] This is something that can present challenges when it comes to the creation of course assignments solely focused on developing intelligence practitioner skill sets. The different emphases placed on time are a key cultural difference between academics and practitioners.[106] Time is scarce on the intelligence practitioner side, where emphasis is placed on short-term analytic reporting or "current intelligence."[107] Alternatively, academics have the luxury of carrying out lengthy studies and building long-term, in-depth knowledge on a specific topic or region. "Analysts only infrequently have the opportunity to think deeply and carefully about the issues they are addressing."[108]

Given these perspectives, considerations over who should be teaching intelligence results in a perception that it should only be done by practitioners, as academics studying the field of intelligence may not have the experience needed to speak to the issues occurring within the intelligence community. Academics come from largely social science backgrounds and often hold terminal degrees; their work seeks to add knowledge to the field by way of theory advancement, and in some cases by addressing problems of practice. Academics "generally do not view the degree to which their findings are adopted by practitioners as a measure of their success."[109] In this manner, the relevance of academic research and likewise the education provided by academics comes into question.

There are also discussions of "hybrid" personas that embody both the practitioner and the academic-researcher type within the literature. These personas can help serve as a bridge between two worlds where one is not considered purely academic or a practitioner but instead a combination of both. Stephan describes these hybrids as those "with a foot in both camps and have acquired the training that makes this possible."[110] While a practitioner of intelligence will be highly focused on addressing immediate threats, and an intelligence academic may be interested in addressing problems associated with the intelligence community in general, a hybrid persona would have concerns in all areas and would seek to address problems in a manner that not only adds to the body of knowledge but also helps to address immediate real-world problems.[111]

In some instances, these individuals might be referred to as "pracademics," "practitioner-scholars," or even "warrior-scholars"; to avoid confusion from here on out, we will use the term "practitioner-scholars" as an all-encompassing term that captures those individuals with practitioner experience, as well as professional research, academic faculty positions, etc. This blended persona can further help bring the academic-practitioner divide closer together by translating the needs of practitioners to academics, and likewise shape the academic research that is carried out to better address problems of practice. This is not to say that these unique individuals are the only ones capable of enhancing intelligence studies. On the contrary, academics and practitioners also play a crucial role in further closing the divide, as both groups come with their own experiences and skill sets that can help address critical problems in the field.

CONSTITUTING THE DIVIDE

Academics researching and teaching on intelligence-related subjects recognize barriers and differences between them as "outsiders" or "pracademics" and practitioners as "insiders" or former insiders that constitute a divide. One of these relates to the limits imposed by secrecy and another to the fundamentally different missions of academics and intelligence professionals. We discuss each in turn.

The Problem of Secrecy

The centrality of secrecy to the practice of intelligence means that those on the inside are privy to information that those on the outside are not. This affords those on the inside a privileged position in discussing and commenting on issues of organization and practice. Secrecy is clearly the big divider, separating those on the outside from the knowledge only available to those on the inside. Denécé and Arboit sum this up succinctly by stating that "there is nothing more difficult than an analysis of a field of activity whose main characteristic is the elimination of all trace of its existence or activity."[112] Likewise, in a 2013 survey of *Intelligence and National Security* editorial board members aimed at understanding perspectives on the state of the field, when Loch K. Johnson and Alison M. Shelton asked, "What do you see as the greatest challenge facing intelligence studies today, and how might this challenge be met?" the political scientist Richard K. Betts responded that "the greatest challenge is the same as ever: how to do systematic social science analysis when a big portion of relevant data is secret."[113]

In some respects, the challenges of information secrecy create a barrier to understanding the field of intelligence itself, its components, and different dynamics. It also presents challenges for openly teaching (and discussing) intelligence-related topics depending on the setting or country. Much like the concerns over access to information, there are also concerns regarding the accuracy of available information.[114]

While certain classified information may be of value in a very narrow setting, an academic bias emerges that perceives open-source information as having a greater degree of value than classified content.[115] Setting the value question aside, another challenge emerges over the perceived use of classified information in academia, namely the control over or restriction of its publication. In this manner, the bias that emerges is that if academics did gain access to restricted information, it could end up restricting one's academic freedom as the open sharing of findings may now become controlled given the perceived sensitivity of the information used during the assessment of a particular problem.[116] In some countries, the challenges presented by secrecy have stifled the development of intelligence studies in that area. In particular, the main reasons for the late emergence of intelligence studies in France have been linked to the secret nature of the work, and also to the work and practice of the intelligence services being widely misunderstood.[117] While there are some areas of intelligence studies that can be effectively researched without access to classified information, many believe that it is the lack of access to evidence which backs up findings that can be among the most challenging factors that scholars need to get to grips with.[118]

Such a divide is far from unique to intelligence, as we discuss below. However, there is a sense that it is particularly important for the field of intelligence because of the centrality of secrecy and, consequently, the extent to which this constitutes a barrier to understanding and openly teaching about aspects of intelligence. The secrecy divide extends to the importance of openness and exchange of ideas in generating and testing research findings in the academic social sciences.[119] Unlike the work of intelligence services, "intelligence studies scholarship benefits from openness, the encouragement of sharing methods, processes, and sources, as well as full transparency in the process of advancing knowledge, discussing results, solving relevant controversies, and transferring that knowledge and best practices to society."[120]

At the same time, just what "secrecy" involves, and just how "secret" a secret is, are complex and debated questions.[121] We can see that it becomes less essential for most secrets to remain secret over time; they degrade once exposed to the light of assessment. As some secrets become less essentially secret over time, they can be made available via national archives or shared with trusted external parties, to be communicated to the wider public in approved book or article form. This has been a pattern in the United Kingdom in recent years, with a series of authorized or official histories of the big three intelligence and security organizations—MI5, MI6, and Government Communications Headquarters.[122] In each case, some secrets are too recent or too important to current practice to allow them to be divulged, and this remains the limiting factor for outside academics. Nevertheless, albeit with gaps, in each case highly detailed organizational histories have been produced. These play a role in resetting the relationship between intelligence and the citizen in these states, and also have implications for future relations between intelligence organizations and intelligence historians. They also provide further raw material for social science approaches to the study of intelligence.

Differences in Missions

The second element is the mission. When it comes to governance and policy making, there is a long-standing suspicion that the focus of the academic at the abstract level of principles is of limited utility when applied to the harsher world of policy, and that, as a consequence, the worlds of ideas and practice are separate. There is nothing new in this. As the Empress Catherine the Great recalled telling the French philosopher Denis Diderot, during a series of conversations that took place between them in St. Petersburg during 1773–1774,

> Monsieur Diderot, I have listened with great interest to everything that your brilliant mind has inspired. But your grand principles, which I understand quite well, make for good books and bad actions. Your plans for reform neglect the difference between our two positions. You work on paper, which accepts everything. It is smooth, supple and offers no opposition to either your imagination or pen. I, a poor empress, work on human skin, which is rather irritable and sensitive.[123]

We can see something of this current thinking about the contemporary academic-practitioner relationship in the field of intelligence. For example, in the survey by Johnson and Shelton cited earlier, one question asked of *Intelligence and National Security* editorial board members was, "How would you characterize the current relationship between intelligence studies, on the one hand, and intelligence policy-making, on the other hand?"[124] The response was summarized as follows:

> Lowenthal minces no words on the relationship. "Most intelligence policy-makers are far removed from intelligence studies," he replied. "They haven't

the time, and many of them would disdain reading anything they deem as 'academic.'" Dorn agreed. "Practitioners don't have enough time (or interest) to read much of what scholars produce," he said. "Furthermore, they rarely give feedback on what they do read. However, there is mutual respect." McDermott thought, as well, that "many of the studies scholars do just simply don't seem timely or relevant to policy-makers." Just as Hans Morganthau observed about International Relations (IR) research some 60 years ago, she suggested that to-day "policy serves as fodder for scholarship, but not the reverse."[125]

Similarly, Christopher Preble has noted how "policymakers often protest that they do not have time to read journal articles, even well-written ones that are not so loaded with jargon that they seem designed to discourage prospective readers."[126] However, as he also notes, some tensions go beyond this, arising from the way academics understand their role, wherein they

> have an obligation to call attention to those policies which, on the surface, defy well-established scholarship, or that seem to be driven by a misinterpretation of the facts, or a misuse of particular historical analogies. This may offend or annoy policymakers committed to a particular course of action, but scholars should encourage deep study, not facilitate its avoidance.[127]

As this suggests, there is also some resistance from the academic side, arising from the fact that the core purpose lies in education and in enhancing under-standing. This means that those already in or seeking to enter the profession of intelligence are a vital constituency but at the same time are not the only people it seeks to address. Clearly, the question of the purpose of undergradu-ate awards in the field of intelligence (or Homeland Security) is different from the question of the purpose of intelligence modules within broader politics/ political science or international relations/strategic studies degrees. Within the former, there can be a tendency to conflate the study of intelligence with the study of intelligence analysis, so that, with preprofessional education in mind, intelligence analysis is taken to be the core focus of the study of intel-ligence. Academics housed within their own disciplinary home in a university setting are more likely to define the subject from their particular disciplinary standpoint. So, for example, for the politics/political science academic work-ing on intelligence, there could well be a focus on aspects of the impact of intelligence practice on the relationship between citizen and state, including the state's role as a security provider and its implications for what is often termed the "security-liberty trade-off." For the academic approaching intel-ligence from an international relations standpoint, one dimension of the focus could well be on the impact of intelligence activities on interstate relations: How far does it promote mutual understanding, confidence, and so aid in reducing tensions? When and under what circumstances does it contribute to these tensions? Some distance is essential to addressing these questions.

Beyond this, there is also the question of an academic's wider public education function and how far this could be compromised by working inside secrecy. As has been noted elsewhere,

> if the academic study of intelligence is viewed as being designed to complement professional practice, then it limits itself in ways that are undesirable both from the point of view of practice and, more broadly, of the academic duty to explain the role of intelligence within governance. The academic field of intelligence studies must be cultivated for a wider audience, from which effective training may well be derived, but we should not place the cart before the horse.[128]

The Academic-Practitioner Divide Elsewhere: International Relations and Security Studies

As we mentioned earlier, intelligence studies is not the only area where issues around the relationship between academics and practitioners arise. For purposes of comparison, it is worth reflecting on what is held to characterize the divide in two cognate areas, international relations and security studies. Both of these are disciplines (or subdisciplines) that, in their origins, are intimately bound with the world of government and policy making. The academic field of international relations arose in the aftermath of the First World War to facilitate the study of the conditions that gave rise to war and so help prevent a recurrence of the slaughter of 1914–1918. Its development was further shaped by the experience of the interwar period, by the rise of European dictatorships and the failure of democracies to prevent this, and by the experience of the Second World War. In its origins, then, it was very much seen as an applied social science. In many ways, one of the towering figures in the early history of academic IR personified this sense of the field as an applied social science. E. H. Carr initially worked as a diplomat in the British Foreign Office, in which capacity he was a member of the British delegation to the Paris Peace Conference at the end of the First World War. He became the fourth holder of the world's first chair in international politics in 1936 and then went on to work as assistant editor and lead writer for the *Times* during the Second World War. Hence, the British scholar William Wallace could write in the mid-1990s, a time when IR academics in the United Kingdom were reflecting on their purpose and relationship to the world of practitioners, that

> International Relations as a discipline grew out of reflections on policy, and out of the desire to influence policy, or to improve the practice of policy. The distinction between the academic theorist and the practical policy-maker was a

matter of degree: a degree of detachment from day-to-day practical concerns, but not a denial that those day-to-day concerns were relevant or real.[129]

However, as IR developed as an academic discipline, it developed its own literature that defined the discipline in terms of specific themes and different conceptual approaches to understanding them, characterized as comprising different "schools of thought." The development of theory was essential to the development of IR as an academic discipline. However, this also impacted the focus of IR, broadening its frames of reference and, at the same time, moving some of its focus and debates beyond the interests and concerns of the informed practitioner. For some, this was the inevitable consequence of the development of IR as an academic discipline. For others, it meant it was losing focus and losing its way in moving away from the world of the foreign policy practitioner. As early as 1972, in introducing a supplement of the journal *World Politics* on the theme of "Theory and Policy in International Relations," US academics Raymond Tanter and Richard H. Ullman explained that they came away from the task of editing the volume with mixed feelings:

> On the one hand, our search of the existing literature of International Relations theory has rather forcibly impressed upon us that academic theorists and working practitioners have had, and appear to continue to have, relatively little to say to one another. On the other hand, the papers we have assembled here give us at least some basis for hope. If theorists were to address their efforts to the concerns and needs of practitioners more frequently, both groups might find that the basis for a valuable exchange in fact exists.[130]

So, what was the appropriate degree of detachment or engagement that IR academics should aim for in their relations with the world of policy? What were the issues at stake in deciding this? Was it possible to have engagement while avoiding the risk of entrapment?[131]

Early answers to this question were informed by the experience of the Vietnam War and the role played by academics both in support of and in opposition to the US war effort.[132] In particular, Noam Chomsky posed the question of the "responsibility of intellectuals" ("to speak the truth and to expose lies"),[133] one which resonated with many who would go on to constitute the next generation of IR academics. It was also the backdrop to Hans J. Morgenthau's warning of the importance of a degree of separation between the academic and policy worlds, explaining that the "two worlds are separate because they are oriented towards different ultimate values . . . truth threatens power, and power threatens truth."[134] Academics, Morgenthau warned, should be wary of being drawn into the academic-political complex in which the interests of the government are inextricably intertwined with the interests of large groups of academics. These ties are both formal and informal, and the latter are the more dangerous to intellectual freedom, as they consist in the intellectuals' unconscious adaptation to imperceptible social and political pressures.[135]

This quotation was used as the departure point for a 1994 book, *Two Worlds of International Relations*, edited by Christopher Hill and Pamela Beshoff, that brought together practitioner and academic perspectives on the nature of the divide. Hill began in this book by identifying three dilemmas of IR as a social science that could be presented as questions:

- The *history question*: how far IR as an academic subject area "should be preoccupied by the contemporary world, and in particular by the current news agenda," in essence a question of how far the developing discipline should be defined by theory and how far by commentary on current events.
- The *ideology question*: "the place of normative concerns" in a subject that "deals primarily with politics and therefore finds it particularly difficult to be 'value-free.'"
- The *professional question*: "the question of academic independence, how to identify threats to it and how far to go in its defence."[136]

This final question gave rise to another, that of the appropriate distance to be maintained between academic and practitioner. "It would be tragic," Hill wrote, "if International Relations, having fought so long to establish itself as a serious, indeed indispensable, area of scholarly enquiry, should at the very point of success throw it away through an inability to resist the siren song of policy relevance."[137] But echoing Morgenthau in warning that the relationship could become too close and compromise academic independence did not of itself answer questions of "how close," how often, for how long, and on what issues or in what areas.

For William Wallace, the solution to these dilemmas lay in what he termed "semi-detachment," a prescription for the academic-practitioner relationship in IR that recognized that the

> choice is not between an uncritical commitment to power or an unvarnished commitment to truth; it would be to abandon our intellectual responsibilities either to turn our university departments into enclosed communities or to convert them into contract research consultancies for whatever government is in power. The exact point of balance chosen between detachment and engagement will necessarily depend on personal judgement, within the context of individual

assessments of the nature of the polity—its openness to outside criticism, or its resistance to (even resentment of) advice and criticism—and the importance of the issues at stake.[138]

For some, this begged as many questions as it purported to answer and did not account for the growing diversity of the field in terms of the backgrounds of academics—not just in terms of class, gender, and ethnicity, but also in terms of the type of practitioners they had engaged with and sought to engage with. Government was not the only place where practitioners whose work could be informed by IR academics could be found. They were also found in the private sector—in nongovernmental organizations (NGOs) dealing with human rights, the environment, and other policy areas.[139] In short, it was important to distinguish between academics' responsibility toward the state and civil society. Moreover, in this academic universe of increasingly diverse approaches and ideas, not all would be regarded as equally useful by practitioners, giving rise to the question of "who excludes whom?"[140] This reinforced the case for seeing the practitioner/policy world as extending beyond the narrow confines of national government. Where did the primary responsibility of academics lie? Replying to Wallace, Steve Smith argued,

> For me the purpose of a university is not primarily to train diplomats, it is to enquire into the world and try and understand it. This does not mean that academics should not give policy advice, nor that they should not be involved in training diplomats, only that these cannot be the primary goals of a university. Indeed, in many parts of the world such a prescription would be directly opposed to the interests of civil society.[141]

Security studies emerged from the broader field of IR during the Cold War, and here the issue of the relationship between academics and practitioners has been the subject of even more persistent debate, reflecting the fact that policy relevance is seen as being even more fundamental to its raison d'être than to that of IR. As Lawrence Freedman notes,

> Whereas IR is concerned with the workings of the international system as a whole, security studies tends to consider the system more from a largely national perspective with a distinct agenda derived from the most pressing contemporary challenges, such as terrorism, proliferation, and the rise of China. This is why the policy relevance issue comes up naturally. Unlike IR there is less pretence to be an academic discipline and a greater readiness to be inter-disciplinary.[142]

But here too the question of the nature of the divide is omnipresent, a consequence of US social science's engagement with US security policy in various forms during the Cold War—for example, via Project Camelot (discussed earlier) and in the respect of involvement in modeling around nuclear strategy, which included promoting the notion of limited nuclear war. Michael Desch has argued that the experience of Vietnam gave rise to an ideological backlash against policy-relevant research in the field.[143] Alongside this, what Desch sees as an increasing obsession with methodology within political science more generally, reflecting the development of the discipline and the desire for it to acquire a more "scientific" basis, impacted the policy relevance of academic research.

Clearly, here too the 9/11 attacks had a galvanizing effect on the academic-policy relationship. The post-9/11 "war on terror" generated a recognition that security studies academics could contribute to understanding and the implementation of effective policies, creating a situation in which "sustained cooperation between scholars and national security policymakers once again seemed possible and mutually beneficial."[144] However, both the rationale for and execution of the war on terror was controversial, especially outside the United States. Academic outputs focusing on it were more likely to be critical than supportive, and so not the kind of contributions that would influence policy.

Parallels and Differences for Intelligence Studies

There are several obvious parallels between issues that surface in IR and security studies and that also arise in intelligence studies. This is no surprise given that at points intelligence studies and security studies are virtually indistinguishable, having a number of core concerns in common and sharing a number of key thinkers. One parallel lies in the fact that while the academic field of intelligence studies is more circumscribed than is the case in IR or security studies, there are nevertheless more academics producing more work than is likely to be considered relevant to intelligence practice. Second, as with those other areas, intelligence studies has seen the development of "critical" approaches, which the practitioner community may view as less relevant. However, the meaning and focus of work that situates itself within a critical approach is varied and contains much of direct relevance to, for example, the issue of improving the analytical product by refining the analytical process.[145] Third, of course, is that secrecy and trust are issues in the worlds of security and foreign policy as well as intelligence. The extent of the secrecy is likely to be more variable in the wider fields of IR and security studies—for example, one would expect the degree of secrecy that attaches to engagement around migration or environmental policy and its implications to be less strict than that surrounding weapons proliferation. It is nevertheless a core fact of life in engaging with governmental practitioners.

At the same time, we can also highlight a number of key differences. First, the nature of the core practitioner consumer is different. For intelligence studies academics, the "policy maker" focus is replaced by a focus on the intelligence community and its managers. However, this is far from the entire practitioner universe. Within security studies, influencing the government policy maker is seen by some as the only, or at least the most important, path to relevance for academics. In his critique *Cult of the Irrelevant: The Waning Influence of Social Science on National Security*, Michael Desch recognizes that there are other forms of relevance but maintains that "while there is no doubt that policy influence is broader than just affecting government policy, that is ultimately the goal of the enterprise, either directly through policymakers or indirectly through the media or the public."[146]

There are other practitioners that intelligence studies academics can seek to address. In particular, legislators and intelligence overseers are a natural focus of academic-practitioner engagement in intelligence studies. Indeed, the study of oversight and accountability has developed into a core strand of intelligence studies, reflecting the origins of the academic study of intelligence in the United States in the findings of the Church and Pike Committees and their continuing relevance in thinking about the relationship between intelligence, the state, and the individual. In a sense, then, academic work on intelligence can be viewed as an essential part of the broader oversight universe, which stretches beyond formal legislative bodies to embrace the work of the media and NGOs.

Recognizing these differences and parallels is an important step in moving from identifying the nature of the academic-practitioner divide to addressing it and the questions it begs. If we accept the desirability of closing the divide—and while a majority of academics and practitioners working in the field of national security intelligence do, by no means all on both sides see this as being desirable or even necessary—this mapping helps us to articulate key questions on which we can focus in working toward this. Key to this next step are questions of "how close?" and "in what form?"

These are questions that the authors of the chapters that follow—a combination of practitioners, "pracademics," and academics from different parts of the world—address in their own ways. They offer their own experiences and insights as a basis for thinking about these questions—questions of central importance if the study of intelligence is to continue developing.

NOTE ON THE PERSPECTIVES REPRESENTED IN THIS BOOK

The most interesting feature of this collaborative work is that you will see various perspectives that do not necessarily agree with one another, but instead raise interesting positions about the nature of the academic-practitioner divide in intelligence studies across the globe, and potential ways to bridge that gap. In addition to the different professional positions represented, the authors represent a diversity of thought across different national cultures of intelligence, including the United States, the United Kingdom, Canada, Spain, Romania, Chile, Finland, France, and Australia.

Given the diversity in perspectives, a disclaimer is in order. While these chapters provide an eclectic mix of perspectives on what intelligence studies education and intelligence studies educators should look like, it is not to say that the editors of this work agree with all of the perspectives presented. Instead, our approach is such that it is the perspective itself that needs to be brought to the forefront so that a robust dialogue may emerge. Without this, a conversation on the academic-practitioner divide in intelligence studies would appear one sided and perhaps may give a false impression that no divides exist at all.

Sir David Omand's opening chapter provides his unique perspective of a thirty-five-year practitioner career and top senior management experience in the UK security and intelligence community, and a fifteen-year academic career in intelligence studies. Based on his experience, he shows ways in which practitioners and scholars can interact in a fruitful and respectful way, with a focus on the transition from government to the university. Sir David highlights the importance for the intelligence profession, as for any other profession, of having a sense of its own history as an enabler of a sense of belonging. He argues that the academic-practitioner divide in intelligence is a necessary one and contends that "what remains, and must remain, secret is which combination of techniques is being applied to which targets to acquire secret intelligence," because "that is information that would directly assist those who mean us harm," recognition of this red line constituting a moral imperative for intelligence studies scholars.

Nicholas Dujmović's chapter posits a Periclean ideal in intelligence education (both an experienced practitioner and an academic). It proposes that the intelligence community, under the leadership of the director of national intelligence, commit to a "Pericles Project." Dujmović, a CIA career intelligence officer who has crossed the bridge to the academic world, does so by discussing the why, the what, and the who of intelligence programs, which in turn becomes a discussion on who is teaching intelligence and who, ideally, should be teaching the subject. Dujmović uses in his discussion two opposing extreme stereotypes, representing the polar opposites of the divide:

> I will offer a practitioner who is a caricature of what academics might call a "Knuckle-Dragger," a lower life form pretending to walk upright and teach at the university level, while my academic caricature is what practitioners might

call a "Carpetbagger," an intelligence professor who, with no actual experience in intelligence, is an exploitative, self-promoting, shameless fraud.

Dujmović proposes a definition of intelligence studies, and from there he discusses what intelligence education should cover; that is, "collection, analysis, covert action, counterintelligence, *and* accountability."

David R. Mandel's chapter addresses the question, "How do intelligence organizations ensure that the intelligence assessments they produce are as accurate and sound as they can be?" and discusses "the absence of scientific attempts to discern what practices work from those that do not work so that intelligence organizations can effectively learn and adapt to the challenges of the modern world." Mandel proposes what he calls the "ignorance hypothesis," according to which "the absence of adequate scientific testing of analytic policies and practices is due primarily to widespread ignorance of scientific principles and values, within both intelligence and policy communities." For the same reason, intelligence communities and experts tasked by them to improve the quality of intelligence judgments should draw on science to develop effective intelligence production and test what works and what does not. This illustrates the practical consequences of the divide, enlightening at the same time the practical benefits of bridging the divide by providing scientific rigor for the benefit of intelligence production.

Genevieve Lester, James G. Breckenridge, and Thomas Spahr address the academic-practitioner relationship in professional military education by focusing on the impact of this gap and relationship in the context of teaching strategic intelligence at the US Army War College (USAWC). Their chapter contends that "at the core of the complexity of teaching intelligence at the US Army War College" stands the primary question of "what should the goal of teaching intelligence to senior military officers and their civilian counterparts be?" and that both these questions and the answers to it "engage with the confluence of institutional cultures that compose the Army War College." Lester, Breckenridge, and Spahr argue that there are several institutional cultures within the USAWC and that "the interaction of these cultures directly affects how intelligence is researched and taught at the War College, as well as how integrated it is in the common curriculum and across the enterprise." They describe the more specific goal of intelligence education within the War College as that of helping future leaders "understand capabilities and challenges within strategic intelligence." Regarding the how of intelligence education, they discuss the call for increased use of case studies grounded in history and the use of active-learning approaches like war-gaming and planning exercises in intelligence courses. The chapter highlights the importance of intelligence education within the War College, the interaction of intelligence leaders and practitioners, and the role of guest expert speakers such as former directors of strategic intelligence, journalists, and others.

José-Miguel Palacios offers his perspective as a former practitioner with top analytic responsibilities as head of the European Union Intelligence and Situation Centre (EU INTCEN) analysis division who has crossed to academia, and explores the issue of quality control of the output from intelligence organizations. He argues that "in most cases, the results would probably be better if academic knowledge were systematically used and academic researchers were involved." That is, the quality of analytic production and the systems in place to evaluate it could be improved through the use of outside academic expertise. Palacios concludes that many of the obstacles associated with measuring quality would be overcome through a fruitful interaction between intelligence practitioners and scholars, even if confidentiality remains a hurdle for that interaction, and he highlights the crucial role of both former scholars turned intelligence professionals and former practitioners moving to academia in building the bridges between the two communities.

Michael J. Ard's chapter provides the perspective of a former senior intelligence analyst developing a second career as a private-sector analyst. It offers lessons learned to aspiring analysts, and thoughts on what postgraduate programs aimed at corporate intelligence analysts might look like. Ard comparatively discusses the organizational and analytic cultures in government and the private sector and how speaking about the "politicization" of intelligence has little meaning in the corporate world. He argues that corporate intelligence practitioners can "offer invaluable insight, and it should be incumbent upon government intelligence services to break down secrecy barriers and establish better information sharing and collaboration with them."

Rasmus Hindren and Hanna Smith discuss the benefits that the collaboration of practitioners with academia and the private sector bring to the complex challenge of countering hybrid threats. Based on the multidisciplinary and multisectoral approach of the European Centre of Excellence for Countering Hybrid Threats (Hybrid CoE), Hindren and Smith's chapter discusses this comprehensive approach and how "one of the center's objectives is to provide out-of-the-box thinking and conceptual tools that help bridge the gaps between government and society and between practitioners and expert communities," being critical to the role of scholars and academia "in providing long-term context, analysis, and help in understanding the nature of the threats." Hindren and Smith argue that it is possible to identify three layers in which the contribution of academia and the private sector, under this comprehensive approach, is important when it comes to countering hybrid threats: understanding and joint situational awareness, building resilience, and effective capabilities for deterrence. The chapter constitutes an example of how a bridge between academics and practitioners can be built in the intelligence studies field.

Irena Chiru and Adrian-Liviu Ivan provide "an evaluation of the scholar-practitioner relationship grounded in almost three decades of history during which the Romanian National Intelligence Academy has experimented with multiple solutions in the attempt to bridge the gap." Their chapter develops the concept of non-dichotomic (education/training) intelligence education systems, discusses the benefits of merging education and training in intelligence schools, and extracts lessons based on their frontline experience at the "Mihai Viteazul" National Intelligence Academy (MVNIA). They argue that training programs aimed at training practitioners "how to do their job now, according to current standards, may be problematic in the long run" and might fail in offering competencies that are key in the long term, such as change adaptation. Their chapter documents the approach of MVNIA in Romania and offers a privileged view on the Romanian Intelligence Academy's strategy of integrating and balancing education, research, and practice for the benefit of the intelligence function in a particular context.

Damien Van Puyvelde's chapter offers an overview of the academic-practitioner relationship in France since the 1990s by first providing a theoretical framework based on two variables—the "extent to which academic and practitioners' interests overlap" and the "structuration of their relationship"—that result in the generation of four kinds of stereotypical relationships between academics and practitioners that are used to characterize the divide in France: strangers, acquaintances, collaborators, and partners. The chapter examines the genealogy of intelligence studies in France, arguing that its emergence can be traced back to a 1995 research seminar on "the French culture of intelligence" launched by Admiral Pierre Lacoste. Van Puyvelde highlights three outreach initiatives that, together with a public policy on intelligence, stand out in developing this relationship: the intelligence academy, the intelligence campus, and Interaxions. Further, the chapter discusses the key role of practitioners in intelligence education and finds that the relationship has evolved to one of partnership. Van Puyvelde contends that "the risk when practitioners dominate intelligence education is that teaching will be based on individual career experiences, not on research findings in the field of intelligence studies and other academic fields relevant to intelligence and security."

In their chapter, Troy Whitford and Charles Vandepeer examine and describe the landscape of intelligence studies in Australia and discuss principles to inform course design, development, and delivery by capitalizing on their experience in course design and teaching practice. They contend that "designing a course that balances academic rigor and professional experience requires close association with the intelligence community and an ability to challenge normal academic assessment and teaching practices." The chapter shows the role and importance of inputs that intelligence practitioners may provide in each stage of the course design process. Whitford and Vandepeer argue that this collaboration is essential in developing relevant course standards or students' outcomes such as "disciplinary knowledge, analysis skills, communication skills, ethics, professional practice, leadership, and research." Their chapter also discusses the challenges and opportunities associated with collaboration between the intelligence sector and higher-education institutions.

Andrés de Castro García (Spain) and Carolina Sancho Hirane (Chile) examine in their chapter the development of intelligence studies in Latin America, arguing that intelligence studies have significantly contributed to "the institutionalization of intelligence education and training in the region, the increased professionalization of this activity, and the promotion of a more transparent intelligence culture." de Castro García and Sancho Hirane use the concept of institutionalization as "the process by which intelligence agencies and their procedures acquire value, stability, and permanence over time." They contend that through education and training it is possible to increase the level of intelligence professionalization and institutionalization. To that end, they argue that the existing academic-practitioner gap in the region must be overcome to some extent. de Castro García and Sancho Hirane discuss the importance of intelligence laws and regulations as well as of the professionalization of intelligence activities in achieving the institutionalization of the intelligence function. The chapter contends that "deficits in the institutionalization of the intelligence function and professionalization of its activity" in the region are "partly related to inadequate professional profiles in charge of the leadership of academic centers, areas, and programs in intelligence" and that "in the case of intelligence services, the deficiencies are in the academic rigor necessary to lead academic training programs." They highlight issues affecting intelligence education derived from the diverse historical experiences in the regions' countries, such as how some academics in Latin America "do feel reluctant to include practitioners or former practitioners at universities due to the historical connection between the intelligence services and political police and oppression under military regimes."

Following this, Jan Goldman offers an account of the importance of teaching intelligence ethics and providing a "moral compass" to intelligence community staff, from intelligence analysts to operators. Goldman's chapter raises important questions on teaching ethics and morals in the profession and then discusses answers informed by both his practitioner and academic background. He argues that "ethics should be taught at all levels and to all members of the intelligence community, from the most senior officials to those at the entry level of apprentice in the intelligence cycle" and that "faculty teaching intelligence courses have a responsibility to discuss at the outset the moral obligations and responsibilities that individuals may be called upon to support or exercise in their potential line of work." Goldman discusses the importance of understanding the difference between law and ethics and recommends that courses focused on ethics in the context of intelligence activities provide exposure to "the philosophical tenets of Kant, consequentialism, utilitarianism, and others," so that students acquire a view of ethical discussions from different perspectives. Similarly, he discusses the importance of introducing case studies of ethical dilemmas. Finally, Goldman proposes a "National Intelligence Council on Ethics (NICE)," being staffed by "professionals and nonprofessionals seeking to balance real-world requirements in meeting threats with upholding the values we subscribe to as a nation."

Finally, the editors draw on the insights and suggestions made in these chapters to focus on approaches to bridging the academic-practitioner divide in intelligence studies and to pose the key question of "how close" the relationship can and should be.

NOTES

1. Stephen Marrin, "Intelligence Studies Centers: Making Scholarship on Intelligence Analysis Useful," *Intelligence and National Security* 27, no. 3 (2012): 398–422.

2. Liam F. Gearon and Scott Parsons, "Research Ethics in the Securitised University," *Journal of Academic Ethics* 17 (2019): 73–93.

3. For example, Robin W. Winks, *Cloak and Gown: Scholars in the Secret War, 1939–1961* (New York: William Morrow, 1989).

4. For example, Steve Hewitt, *Spying 101: The RCMP's Secret Activities at Canadian Universities, 1917–1997* (Toronto: University of Toronto Press, 2002); Robert Wright, "Spies Used Top Academic to Monitor UK Campus Radicals, Files Reveal," *Financial Times*, July 18, 2019, https://www.ft.com/content/1e1cddca-a7b2-11e9-b6ee-3cdf3174eb89.

5. For example, Suzanne Folsom and Robert Garretson, "The Continuing Danger of Academic Espionage," *Inside Higher Ed*, May 5, 2020, https://www.insidehighered.com/views/2020/05/05/threat-academic-espionage-should-not-be-overlooked-even-time-pandemic-opinion; Emily Feng, "FBI Urges Universities to Monitor Some Chinese Students and Scholars in the US," NPR, June 28, 2019, https://www.npr.org/2019/06/28/728659124/fbi-urges-universities-to-monitor-some-chinese-students-and-scholars-in-the-u-s?t=1623746295539; Kevin Powers and James Burns, "The FBI, Cybersecurity and American Campuses: Academia, Government, and Industry as Allies in Cybersecurity Effectiveness," in *The Routledge International Handbook of Universities, Security and Intelligence Studies*, ed. Liam Francis Gearon, 94–107 (Abingdon: Routledge, 2020).

6. University Foreign Interference Task Force, "Guidelines to Counter Foreign Interference in the Australian University Sector," November 2019.

7. Bowman Miller, "Soldiers, Scholars, and Spies: Combining Smarts and Secrets," *Armed Forces & Society* 36, no. 4 (2010): 704.

8. Mark Solovey, "Project Camelot and the 1960s Epistemological Revolution: Rethinking the Politics-Patronage-Social Science Nexus," *Social Studies of Science* 31, no. 2 (2001): 171–206.

9. Solovey, "Project Camelot."

10. Solovey, "Project Camelot," 175.

11. Solovey, "Project Camelot," 173.

12. Solovey, "Project Camelot," 173.

13. Matthew Crosston, "Occam's Follies: Real and Imagined Biases Facing Intelligence Studies," *Journal of Strategic Security* 6, no. 3 (2013): 40–53.

14. Crosston, "Occam's Follies."

15. Crosston, "Occam's Follies."

16. Solovey, "Project Camelot"; Miller, "Soldiers, Scholars, and Spies."

17. Solovey, "Project Camelot"; Hugh Gusterson, "Project Minerva and the Militarization of Anthropology," *Radical Teacher* 86 (2009): 4–16.

18. Miller, "Soldiers, Scholars, and Spies."

19. Solovey, "Project Camelot."

20. Solovey, "Project Camelot."

21. Solovey, "Project Camelot."

22. Gusterson, "Project Minerva."

23. Solovey, "Project Camelot."

24. Solovey, "Project Camelot," 185.

25. Allan A. Needell, "'Truth Is Our Weapon': Project TROY, Political Warfare, and Government-Academic Relations in the National Security State," *Diplomatic History* 17, no. 3 (1993): 399–420; Gusterson, "Project Minerva."

26. Peter Hinton, "The 'Thailand Controversy' Revisited," *Australian Journal of Anthropology* 13, no. 2 (2002): 155–77.

27. Hinton, "The 'Thailand Controversy' Revisited."

28. Hinton, "The 'Thailand Controversy' Revisited."

29. David S. McCarthy, "'The Sun Never Sets on the Activities of the CIA': Project Resistance at William and Mary," *Intelligence and National Security* 28, no. 5 (2013): 611–33.

30. Miller, "Soldiers, Scholars, and Spies," 704–5.

31. Miller, "Soldiers, Scholars, and Spies."

32. Crosston, "Occam's Follies," 51.

33. Charles Nemfakos et al., *Workforce Planning in the Intelligence Community: A Retrospective* (Santa Monica, CA: RAND Corporation, 2013); Damien Van Puyvelde, *Outsourcing US Intelligence: Contractors and Government Accountability* (Edinburgh: Edinburgh University Press, 2019).

34. Martin G. Clemis, "Crafting Non-kinetic Warfare: The Academic-Military Nexus in US Counterinsurgency Doctrine," *Small Wars & Insurgencies* 20, no. 1 (2009): 160–84.

35. Clemis, "Crafting Non-kinetic Warfare," 172.

36. Gusterson, "Project Minerva"; Miller, "Soldiers, Scholars, and Spies."

37. Miller, "Soldiers, Scholars, and Spies."

38. Gusterson, "Project Minerva."

39. Gusterson, "Project Minerva."

40. Harold D. Lasswell, "The Relation of Ideological Intelligence to Public Policy," *Ethics* 53, no. 1 (1942): 25.

41. Wilbur Schramm, "The Forefathers of Communication Study in America," in *The Beginnings of Communication Study in America: A Personal Memoir by Wilber Schramm*, ed. Steven H. Chaffee and Everett M. Rogers, 31 (Thousand Oaks, CA: Sage, 1997).

42. Harold D. Lasswell, "On the Policy Sciences in 1943," in "Professional Insecurities," special issue, *Policy Sciences* 36, no. 1 (March 2003): 73–75.

43. Sherman Kent, *Strategic Intelligence for American World Policy* (Princeton, NJ: Princeton University Press, 1949). See also Jack Davis, "Sherman Kent and the Profession of Intelligence Analysis" (Occasional Papers 1, no. 5, Sherman Kent Center for Intelligence Analysis, 2002), https://www.cia.gov/static/aa47b490 ac1c52c04c467a248c5cbace/Kent-Profession-Intel-Analysis.pdf.

44. Sherman Kent, "The Need for an Intelligence Literature," *Studies in Intelligence* 1, no. 1 (1955): 1–11, https://www.cia.gov/static/539a695e2365ed5a17422139 fa14e3cf/Need-for-Intelligence-Literature.pdf.

45. Kent, "The Need for an Intelligence Literature."

46. Kent, "The Need for an Intelligence Literature."

47. Kent, "The Need for an Intelligence Literature."

48. James J. Lagrone, "The Hotel in Operations," *Studies in Intelligence* 9, no. 4 (1965), https://www.cia.gov/resources/csi/studies-in-intelligence/archives/vol-9-no-4 /the-hotel-in-operations.

49. Kent, "The Need for an Intelligence Literature."

50. George S. Pettee, *The Future of American Secret Intelligence* (Washington, DC: Infantry Journal Press, 1946).

51. Willmoore Kendall, "The Function of Intelligence," *World Politics* 1, no. 4 (1949): 542–52.

52. Roger Hilsman, *Strategic Intelligence and National Decisions* (Glencoe, IL: Free Press, 1956), 123. See also his earlier article outlining his ideas: "Intelligence and Policy-Making in Foreign Affairs," *World Politics* 5, no. 1 (1952): 1–45.

53. Ralph I. Glasgow, "Planning and Intelligence," *Army Transportation Journal* 4, no. 3 (1948): 16.

54. Washington Platt, *Strategic Intelligence Production: Basic Principles* (New York: Praeger, 1957), xviii.

55. Platt, *Strategic Intelligence Production*, xviii.

56. Allen W. Dulles, *The Craft of Intelligence* (New York: Harper & Row, 1963).

57. Klaus E. Knorr, "Foreign Intelligence and the Social Sciences" (Research Monograph No. 17, Center of International Studies, Woodrow Wilson School of Public and International Affairs, Princeton University, NJ, June 1964).

58. Harold L. Wilensky, *Organizational Intelligence: Knowledge and Policy in Government and Industry* (New York: Basic Books, 1967).

59. Jan Goldman, "Foreword to Previous Edition," in *Handbook of Warning Intelligence: Complete and Declassified Edition*, ed. Cynthia Grabo with Jan Goldman, xiii (Lanham, MD: Rowman & Littlefield, 2015).

60. Cynthia Grabo, "Author's Note to the Original Edition," in *Handbook of Warning Intelligence: Complete and Declassified Edition*, ed. Cynthia Grabo with Jan Goldman, xix–xx (Lanham: Rowman & Littlefield, 2015).

61. Jerome K. Clauser and Sandra M. Weir, *Intelligence Research Methodology: An Introduction to Techniques and Procedures for Conducting Research in Defense Intelligence* (Washington, DC: Defense Intelligence School, 1976).

62. Richards J. Heuer Jr., *Psychology of Intelligence Analysis* (Washington, DC: Center for the Study of Intelligence, 1999).

63. Jack Davis, "The Kent-Kendall Debate of 1949," *Studies in Intelligence* 36, no. 5 (1992): 91–103.

64. Kendall, "The Function of Intelligence," 549.

65. Kendall, "The Function of Intelligence," 549.

66. See Loch K. Johnson, *A Season of Inquiry: The Senate Intelligence Investigation* (Lexington: University of Kentucky Press, 1985).

67. Gregory F. Treverton, *Covert Action: The Limits of Intervention in the Postwar World* (New York: Basic Books, 1987).

68. Harry Howe Ransom, "Being Intelligent about Secret Intelligence Agencies," *American Political Science Review* 74, no. 1 (March 1980): 142.

69. Kent, "The Need for an Intelligence Literature."

70. Oana Sandu, "Academia—A Strategic Resource for the Intelligence Community." In *Strategies XXI*, no. 2, supplement, 286–94 (Bucharest: Centre for Defense and Security Strategic Studies, National Defence University, 2014).

71. Stephen Marrin, "Improving Intelligence Studies as an Academic Discipline," *Intelligence and National Security* 31, no. 2 (2016): 279.

72. Kobi Michael and Aaron Kornbluth, "The Academization of Intelligence: A Comparative Overview of Intelligence Studies in the West," *Cyber, Intelligence, and Security* 3, no. 1 (2019): 117–40.

73. Eric Denécé and Gérald Arboit, "The Development of Intelligence Studies in France," *African Yearbook of Rhetoric* 3, no. 1 (2012): 23–35.

74. Alessandro Scheffler Corvaja, Brigita Jeraj, and Uwe M. Borghoff, "The Rise of Intelligence Studies: A Model for Germany," *Connections: The Quarterly Journal* 15, no. 1 (2016): 79–106.

75. Denécé and Arboit, "The Development of Intelligence Studies in France."

76. Gearon and Parsons, "Research Ethics in the Securitised University."

77. Robert J. Heibel, "Catalyst and Enabler," *Liberal Studies at Georgetown* 3, no. 2 (2005): 13–15; Stephen Coulthart and Matthew Crosston, "Terra Incognita: Mapping American Intelligence Education Curriculum," *Journal of Strategic Security* 8, no. 3 (2015): 46–68.

78. Heibel, "Catalyst and Enabler."

79. Heibel, "Catalyst and Enabler."

80. Coulthart and Crosston, "Terra Incognita."

81. American Public University System, "Catalog—2002," Richard G. Trefry Archives, accessed July 2, 2021, https://exhibit.apus.edu/items/show/1121.

82. Heibel, "Catalyst and Enabler."

83. Coulthart and Crosston, "Terra Incognita."

84. Scott Parsons, "Intelligent Studies: Degrees in Intelligence and the Intelligence Community," in *The Routledge International Handbook of Universities, Security and Intelligence Studies*, ed. Liam Francis Gearon, 272–86 (New York: Routledge, 2020).

85. Parsons, "Intelligent Studies."

86. Parsons, "Intelligent Studies."

87. Parsons, "Intelligent Studies."

88. Corvaja et al., "The Rise of Intelligence Studies."

89. Corvaja et al., "The Rise of Intelligence Studies," 83.

90. Glenn P. Hastedt, "Towards the Comparative Study of Intelligence," *Journal of Conflict Studies* 11, no. 3 (1991): 55–72; Len Scott and Peter Jackson, "The Study of Intelligence in Theory and Practice," *Intelligence and National Security* 19, no. 2 (2004): 139–69.

91. Martin Rudner, "Intelligence Studies in Higher Education: Capacity-Building to Meet Societal Demand," *International Journal of Intelligence and CounterIntelligence* 22, no. 1 (2009): 110–30; Corvaja et al., "The Rise of Intelligence Studies"; Michael and Kornbluth, "The Academization of Intelligence."

92. Scott and Jackson, "The Study of Intelligence."

93. Gustavo Díaz Matey, "The Development of Intelligence Studies in Spain," *International Journal of Intelligence and CounterIntelligence* 23, no. 4 (2010): 748–65.

94. Patrick F. Walsh, "Teaching Intelligence in the Twenty-First Century: Towards an Evidence-Based Approach for Curriculum Design," *Intelligence and National Security* 32, no. 7 (2017): 1005–21.

95. Crosston, "Occam's Follies."

96. Michael Mosser, "Puzzles versus Problems: The Alleged Disconnect between Academics and Military Practitioners," *Perspectives on Politics* 8, no. 4 (2010): 1077–86.

97. Crosston, "Occam's Follies."

98. Mosser, "Puzzles versus Problems."

99. Marrin, "Intelligence Studies Centers."

100. Walter G. Stephan, "Bridging the Research-Practitioner Divide in Intergroup Relations," *Journal of Social Issues* 62, no. 3 (2006): 597–605.

101. Marrin, "Intelligence Studies Centers," 402.

102. Marrin, "Intelligence Studies Centers," 402.

103. Miller, "Soldiers, Scholars, and Spies," 702.

104. Miller, "Soldiers, Scholars, and Spies," 702.

105. Marrin, "Intelligence Studies Centers," 402.

106. J. Ann Tickner et al., "Risks and Opportunities of Crossing the Academic/Policy Divide," *International Studies Review* 10, no. 1 (2008): 155–77.

107. Stephen Marrin, "Training and Educating U.S. Intelligence Analysts," *International Journal of Intelligence and CounterIntelligence* 22, no. 1 (2009): 131–46.

108. Marrin, "Training and Educating U.S. Intelligence Analysts," 134.

109. Stephan, "Bridging the Research-Practitioner Divide."

110. Stephan, "Bridging the Research-Practitioner Divide," 601.

111. Stephan, "Bridging the Research-Practitioner Divide."

112. Denécé and Arboit, "The Development of Intelligence Studies in France," 32.

113. Loch K. Johnson and Alison M. Shelton, "Thoughts on the State of Intelligence Studies: A Survey Report," *Intelligence and National Security* 28, no. 1 (2013): 117.

114. Matey, "The Development of Intelligence Studies in Spain."

115. Crosston, "Occam's Follies."

116. Mosser, "Puzzles versus Problems."

117. Denécé and Arboit, "The Development of Intelligence Studies in France."

118. Anthony Glees, "The Future of Intelligence Studies," Supplement, *Journal of Strategic Security* 6, no. 3 (2013): 124–27.

119. See, for example, the discussion in Mark Phythian, "Intelligence Analysis and Social Science Methods: Exploring the Potential for and Possible Limits of Mutual Learning," *Intelligence and National Security* 32, no. 5 (2017): 600–612.

120. Nicole Drumhiller, Mark Phythian, and Rubén Arcos, "IntelHub," https://www.apus.edu/academic-community/intelhub/index.

121. Didier Bigo, "Shared Secrecy in a Digital Age and a Transnational World," *Intelligence and National Security* 34, no. 3 (2019): 379–94.

122. Christopher Andrew, *The Defence of the Realm: The Authorized History of MI5* (London: Allen Lane, 2009); Keith Jeffery, *MI6: The History of the Secret Intelligence Service, 1909–1949* (London: Bloomsbury, 2010); John Ferris, *Behind the Enigma: The Authorised History of GCHQ, Britain's Secret Cyber-Intelligence Agency* (London: Bloomsbury, 2020).

123. Cited in Robert Zaretsky, *Catherine and Diderot: The Empress, the Philosopher and the Fate of the Enlightenment*, 224 (Cambridge, MA: Harvard University Press, 2019); and in Lawrence Freedman's review essay on Michael Desch's book, *Cult of the Irrelevant*, in the *Journal of Strategic Studies* 42, no. 7 (2019): 1027.

124. Johnson and Shelton, "Thoughts on the State of Intelligence Studies," 114.

125. Johnson and Shelton, "Thoughts on the State of Intelligence Studies," 114. Robert Jervis offered a different perspective: "Unlike other fields of political and policy studies," he wrote, "[intelligence] professionals are interested in what the scholars have to say, and the scholars treat the practitioners with real respect." Ibid., 115.

126. Christopher Preble, "Bridging the Gap: Managing Expectations, Improving Communications," *Journal of Strategic Studies* 40, nos. 1–2 (2017): 280. On use of specialist language as a barrier, see Tristram Riley-Smith, "Men of the 'Professor Type' Revisited: Building a Partnership between Academic Research and National Security," in *The Routledge International Handbook of Universities, Security and Intelligence Studies*, ed. Liam Francis Gearon, 368–82 (New York: Routledge, 2020).

127. Ibid. See also the points made by Jochem Wiers, "Building a Bridge or Nurturing the Gap?," *Journal of Strategic Studies* 40, nos. 1–2 (2017): 283–86.

128. Peter Gill and Mark Phythian, "What Is Intelligence Studies?," *International Journal of Intelligence, Security, and Public Affairs* 18, no. 1 (2016): 6.

129. William Wallace, "Truth and Power, Monks and Technocrats: Theory and Practice in International Relations," *Review of International Studies* 22, no. 3 (1996): 302.

130. Raymond Tanter and Richard H. Ullman, "Introduction: Theory and Policy in International Relations," in "Theory and Policy in International Relations," supplement, *World Politics* 24 (1972): 6.

131. Amitav Acharya, "Engagement or Entrapment? Scholarship and Policymaking on Asian Regionalism," *International Studies Review* 13, no. 1 (2011): 12–17.

132. Robert R. Tomes, *Apocalypse Then: American Intellectuals and the Vietnam War, 1954–1975* (New York: New York University Press, 2000); Michael C. Desch, "Strategic Modernization Theory Bogs Down in the Vietnam Quagmire," in *Cult of the Irrelevant: The Waning Influence of Social Science on National Security*, 176–204 (Princeton, NJ: Princeton University Press, 2019).

133. Noam Chomsky, "The Responsibility of the Intellectuals," *New York Review of Books*, February 23, 1967, https://chomsky.info/19670223.

134. Hans J. Morgenthau, *Truth and Power: Essays of a Decade, 1960–70* (London: Pall Mall Press, 1970), 14. Morgenthau was a notable opponent of the Vietnam War as it was being fought. See, for example, Louis B. Zimmer, *The Vietnam War Debate: Hans J. Morgenthau and the Attempt to Halt the Drift into Disaster* (Lanham, MD: Lexington Books, 2011); Lorenzo Zambernardi, "The Impotence of Power: Morgenthau's Critique of American Intervention in Vietnam," *Review of International Studies* 37, no. 3 (2011): 1335–56.

135. Ibid., 25. Cited in the preface to Christopher Hill and Pamela Beshoff, eds., *The Two Worlds of International Relations: Academics, Practitioners and the Trade in Ideas*, xii (London: Routledge, 1994).

136. Christopher Hill, "Academic International Relations: The Siren Song of Policy Relevance," in *The Two Worlds of International Relations: Academics, Practitioners and the Trade in Ideas*, ed. Christopher Hill and Pamela Beshoff, 5 (London: Routledge, 1994).

137. Hill, "Academic International Relations," 21.

138. Wallace, "Truth and Power," 318.

139. Ken Booth, "Discussion: A Reply to Wallace," *Review of International Studies* 23, no. 3 (1997): 371–77. See also Michael Nicholson, "What's the Use of International Relations?," *Review of International Studies* 26, no. 2 (2000): 183–98.

140. Booth, "Discussion: A Reply to Wallace," 372. See also Christopher Hill and Pamela Beshoff, "The Two Worlds: Natural Partnership or Necessary Distance?," in *The Two Worlds of International Relations: Academics, Practitioners and the Trade in Ideas*, 211–25 (London: Routledge, 1994).

141. Steve Smith, "Power and Truth: A Reply to William Wallace," *Review of International Studies* 23, no. 4 (1997): 510. Moreover, Smith warned, when academics did decide "to offer policy advice then they should be aware that their reception will be directly related to the degree of fit between their underlying world-view and the values and policies of the government. Their influence will therefore be determined by the closeness of the fit between their values and those held by the policy-makers, and I am not at all sure what this has to do with scholarship." Ibid., 512.

142. Lawrence Freedman, "Review Essay: Cult of the Irrelevant," *Journal of Strategic Studies* 42, no. 7 (2019): 1029.

143. Desch, *Cult of the Irrelevant*, 205–6.

144. Desch, *Cult of the Irrelevant*, 229.

145. See, for example, Peter de Werd, *US Intelligence and Al Qaeda: Analysis by Contrasting Narratives* (Edinburgh: Edinburgh University Press, 2020).

146. Desch, *Cult of the Irrelevant*, 248.

2

Being on the Outside Looking In

Reflections of a Former Practitioner Turned Academic

David Omand

I spent thirty-five years as a senior civil servant in the high-paced worlds of UK defense, security, and intelligence. I had gazed with some envy from the inside of the secret state out at the (relatively, at least) tranquil open groves of academe. For the last fifteen years since retirement, I have been based in the Department of War Studies at King's College London as a visiting professor specializing in intelligence studies. I now look from the outside back in at my former world. In this chapter I want to describe the nature of the inevitable and necessary divide there has to be between the worlds of the practitioner and of the academic studying the specialized subject of secret intelligence, and to add my own testimony on how I made that transition myself and how best to construct secure connecting bridges across that divide.

I shall confine myself to practitioner-academic interactions in policy-relevant areas where I have experience and only touch in passing on inter-face issues as they apply to the fields of science and technology where links between government departments and agencies and the universities have traditionally been very strong, especially with regard to defense research and development contracts.

FROM THE INSIDE OUT: A TRANSITION TO ACADEMIA

My last post in government service was as the UK intelligence and security coordinator, a new post created at permanent secretary level after 9/11 (now subsumed in the role of national security adviser). The homeland security part of my duties included formulating the government's counterterror-ism strategy, CONTEST, still in force today. The intelligence component involved, as the press release of my appointment put it at the time, looking after the overall health of the intelligence community. As principal accounting officer for the Single Intelligence Account that funds the three main UK agencies, MI5, MI6, and Government Communications Headquarters (GCHQ), I could nudge them to work ever more closely together. This included the creation of the Joint Terrorism Analysis Centre (JTAC) to provide all-source analysis in depth of the terrorist threat and apply that to make professional judgments on the appropriate threat levels to the United Kingdom and to UK travelers overseas. These were all areas of interest to academics working in the field of intelligence and security studies.

In my last months in post, I was visited in my grand office overlooking the garden of No. 10 Downing Street by Professor Lawry (now Sir Lawrence) Freedman who suggested that in retirement I might consider basing myself in his Department of War Studies at King's College London. An appointment as a visiting professor would provide me with the great advantage of access to the university library and to the department itself if, as he hoped, I might work with them and contribute to intelligence and defense studies research and teaching.[1] Having a university affiliation would also enable me to deliver papers at conferences and seminars and to interact with the international scholarly community. A number of senior uniformed and civilian officers and diplomats have now taken the same route of being a visiting academic in developing a formal association with a university or think tank to reflect on the nature of their profession, its past, and its future.

I would always recommend that late joiners to the academic world be assigned a specific guide and mentor to ease their passage. On arrival at King's in 2006, I was fortunate to have as a guide Michael Goodman, now professor and head of the Department of War Studies. As the historian of the Joint Intelligence Committee (JIC) (as part of the then Cabinet Office Official Histories Programme), he had embarked on the first volume that took the story from its origins in 1936 to the Suez crisis in 1956.[2] To allow him access for his research to the closed, highly classified JIC and Foreign and Commonwealth Office archives, he had been subject to a Developed Vetting, and I could therefore have conversations about the workings of the JIC (having spent seven-plus years as a member of the JIC as deputy undersecretary of state for defense policy, as director of GCHQ, and as security and intelligence coordinator) that I would otherwise have felt inhibited in conducting. I then sat as an external member of the Cabinet Office oversight committee for the history and was able to advise on some of the delicate clearance judgments that had to be made to allow the full story of the JIC, its successes and failures, to be told. That example shows one way that an academic and former practitioner can interact.

An important general lesson is the value of institutions displaying flexibility and allowing visiting scholars to explore different levels of involvement. Senior retired officials will mostly be pursuing portfolio careers after retirement, allowing incomers to sample and decide how far teaching suits them, or writing directly from their experience distilled through a scholarly lens, or perhaps embarking on primary-source archival research (there are advantages in knowing where the bodies you want to exhume from the files were buried). Academia is, from talking to other colleagues who have made the transition, usually good at accommodating a variety of models of commitment. My own personal ambition was to try to contribute to intelligence studies myself as a part-time academic, albeit recognizing the reality that I was starting late if I was to see this as a second career. I have ended up writing three books (one of them coauthored with one of the editors of this volume), together with journal articles and chapters in books edited by other academics, and with a repertoire of lectures on aspects of intelligence studies, especially those where I could bring my previous experience to bear, including counterterrorism strategy, analysis and assessment, intelligence organization, modern digital intelligence, and ethics. Eventually, finding a gap in the market, I designed my own course in modern digital intelligence and its issues, which I deliver to master's students at PSIA Sciences Po in Paris. All that has involved, for example, adjusting to the demands of the scholarly apparatus needed to guide the reader to the sources used and to carefully reference earlier writings. The civil servant has scant need of such scaffolding in their policy papers and in advice for ministers, nor would ministers welcome it. A short statement of the issue being addressed with a recommendation for action, followed by a terse statement of justification and a rather longer passage on public presentation, is as much as that market will bear these days.

Blow-ins from the intelligence community like myself can help paint a realistic picture for students coming new to the subject of what intelligence work actually consists of and, it has to be said, at times for some researchers overenthusiastic about the significance of some document turned up in the National Archives. Of course, care is needed not to be misunderstood as a spokesperson for the government point of view, and respect for academic independence of mind is important for all working within the universities.

My experience is that although most retiring practitioners from government service will have held posts with significant managerial burdens, they may well not be interested in departmental administration and all of the bureaucracy that goes with public institutions like universities. The unsalaried "visiting" scholar appellation is a useful one that is well understood in academe. For visiting academics from other universities, there are time limits on the duration of such appointments. For former practitioners, there is no need to impose such time restrictions. If they are interested in supervision of post-grads, of course then they will need the opportunity to undergo the required training in academic pedagogy. The experience of my former colleagues from the intelligence world who have made the transition is, however, that it is easy to hold the attention of a student audience, eager to be given some glimpse of the inside of the secret world. A few well-chosen anecdotes can captivate, and motivate, a student audience. Security concerns evidently cannot be ignored, a topic I consider below.

I have not been surprised to find frequent requests from students for advice on how to secure entry to careers within the government machine, with a few rather obviously hoping to catch my eye. They have read the accounts of the prewar recruitment of "professor types" to Bletchley Park by tutors such as Frank Adcock, professor of ancient history at Cambridge (although, as Christopher Andrew has pointed out, in the mid-1930s more Cambridge graduates were recruited by Soviet intelligence than by MI5 or MI6).[3] The days when academics were the principal talent scouts for the British secret world ended, however, with the public avowal of the agencies[4] and the gradual opening up of knowledge of their recruitment needs. Agencies now have websites and well-regulated impartial selection processes, as they certainly should. But I do not think it improper to encourage applications from those who have good prospects and gently to invite those who are overenthusiastic for the wrong reasons to think realistically about career choices.

Care is also needed when PhD students and postgrads seek introductions in the secret world, for example, in looking for interviewees in their research. Attitudes have changed in recent years and officials may be interested in contributing to research (within the bounds of sensitivity), the results of which could well be of professional interest to their organizations. But there is often an overoptimism that volunteers will easily be found with the help of the former practitioners prepared to unburden themselves and to provide the evidence for serious doctoral research. I have had to be rather stern in my advice to such would-be researchers that they have to be able to demonstrate at the outset of justifying their research topic just how they intend to acquire the evidence on which to test their hypotheses. Former practitioners cannot just open their address books to them.

THE PRECEDENT OF DEFENSE STUDIES

I had benefited when working in the Ministry of Defence (MOD) from contact with strategic studies scholars, along with those of military history and war studies (or peace studies, as in some universities it had been renamed).

In MOD we would, for example, invite academics from universities and think tanks to join the official pol-mil teams for defense staff talks with North Atlantic Treaty Organization (NATO) allies. The main British think tanks, the Royal United Services Institute (RUSI), the Institute for Strategic Studies (IISS), and the Royal Institute for International Affairs (RIIA—Chatham House), were familiar meeting places for discussion (including off-the-record discussion) between diplomats and defense policy officials and academics from the United Kingdom working in those fields. There were regular secondments of senior defense policy officials to think tanks, notably to IISS for the study of nuclear deterrence and to RAND.[5] There were many NATO and other international gatherings at which academics, expert commentators, policy officials, and sometimes ministers met, including those organized by the North Atlantic Association, the Munich Security Conference, Königswinter, and seminars organized by the Marshall Fund and the Stiftung of the German political parties. Unsurprisingly, there was little or no discussion of intelligence matters at such meetings.

The MOD early recognized the value of having better-informed public awareness of defense issues, the most controversial of which was and remains the future of nuclear deterrence. The MOD provided seed-corn funding to enable the Department of War Studies at King's College and its Centre for Defence Studies to flourish, and has at times commissioned specific research projects. I recall the report King's War Studies was asked to produce for the MOD at the time of the break-up of the former Yugoslavia on "How Empires End," drawing lessons from the demise of the Roman, Ottoman, Habsburg, and British Empires and the impulse toward internecine violence that follows when the center cannot hold.

The rationale for the emergence of these strong defense policy links to the universities and think tanks is not hard to see. Topics such as arms control and disarmament and NATO strategy and enlargement invited research the results of which, coupled with the teaching of military history and international affairs at the Staff Colleges, all helped to make interaction of mutual value. For the most part these were topics on which academics and visiting scholars (including many retired officers) could challenge prevailing wisdom and practitioners could join in their academic debate without being unduly constrained by the limitations of the Official Secrets Act. The Royal United Services Institute is an interesting early example, having been founded in 1831 by the Duke of Wellington to promote free speaking by young officers. It benefited from an understanding, still true today, that government accepted it as a privileged forum where military officers of whatever rank or title could speak their mind about matters military.

OUTREACH FROM THE SECRET INTELLIGENCE COMMUNITY

Within the intelligence establishment, the British tradition was that the less said outside the ring of secrecy the better. Intelligence officers on retirement were strongly discouraged from entering into academic debate, let alone writing, about their former profession. When officers had specialist expertise or language skills in particular regions of the world, then academic work was possible, but such individuals had to be meticulous in describing themselves as "former members of HM Diplomatic Service," since only the name of the chief of MI6 was to be publicly known. Such was the recognition of the fragility of cryptographic successes that the official line in GCHQ remained that all public debate about signals intelligence was discouraged, with only episodic references breaking surface (such as the 1982 blunder of the former minister Ted Rowlands in the House of Commons revealing that Argentine communication had, in his time in office, been intercepted and read,[6] and the furore that followed the 1984 banning of the trades unions from GCHQ by Prime Minister Thatcher).

That reticence was also generally the position adopted by the intelligence services of continental Europe, although less so in the United States, where the postwar intelligence community had been created with congressional approval after open debate, and where freedom of information had greater sway than in the United Kingdom. The ingrained British reluctance to promote any open discussion of secret intelligence issues changed only slowly after the avowal of the existence of MI5 in 1989 and that of MI6 and GCHQ in 1994.[7] The opening up of the history of British intelligence was certainly stimulated by well-publicized but unauthorized disclosures about Bletchley Park's wartime role and the MI5-led wartime Double-Cross strategic deception operation. The multivolume *Official History of Intelligence in the Second World War* was a milestone in openness, especially on the role played by signals intelligence.[8] The release thereafter of a limited number of official UK files and the availability of US wartime records referring to the United Kingdom gradually made substantive research into British intelligence history feasible.

It has also been the case that until recent years professional historians, political scientists, applied psychologists, lawyers, and members of other academic disciplines have tended to ignore the hidden impact of intelligence activity on their subject. In the case of the study of history, this phenomenon of disregard for the impact of secret intelligence was notably identified and publicized by Professor Christopher Andrew and David Dilks in their pathbreaking 1984 book on intelligence as "the missing dimension" of history.[9]

The value of personal contacts with known and trusted interlocutors in selected universities had in fact always been recognized by the intelligence agencies, provided they were kept discreet. A good example was the early Cold War commissioning from the Soviet expert Professor Carew Hunt of a detailed account of the theory of communism and of how the Soviet state organized and planned its economy. Originally printed "for official use only" for circulation within the intelligence community, it quickly established its status as an invaluable guide, and a version was eventually published by Penguin books as *The Theory and Practice of Communism*,[10] but without acknowledgment at the time of its origins.

University science and engineering laboratories have likewise enjoyed of necessity open links, both contractual and informal, with the Ministry of Defence and (discreetly) with the intelligence agencies. Today technical links with the universities include developments in digital communications and data science of benefit to the intelligence community, especially to GCHQ. The links between cryptography and mathematical prowess are known to go back centuries (Professor John Wallis, England's best mathematician before Newton, was both Savilian Professor of Geometry in the University of Oxford and Cryptographer Royal between 1649 and 1703). GCHQ has in modern times a tradition of recruiting Senior Wranglers from the Cambridge Mathematical Tripos, one of whom, Clifford Cocks CB, was elected in 2015 to the Royal Society to recognize his part in the discovery in 1973 of the first public key cryptography algorithm.

For the past twelve years, GCHQ has funded the Heilbronn Institute for Mathematical Research at the University of Bristol, specializing in algebra, algebraic geometry, combinatorics, data science, number theory, probability, and quantum information. The UK National Cyber Security Centre, launched in 2016 as an integral part of the modern GCHQ, has now selected a number of leading UK universities as Academic Centres of Excellence with which it can work on computer science issues relevant to cyber security.[11] Bridging the divide to academia has similarly become a priority for the other intelligence and security agencies in areas of technology of interest to them.[12] Securing the digital world we inhabit, and on which we are now dependent, demands very close collaboration between the intelligence and security community and the expertise to be found in academic institutions.

BUILDING BRIDGES ACROSS THE DIVIDE

Academic-practitioner links were boosted after the Second World War following the temporary recruitment of so many first-class academics into military intelligence and the intelligence agencies themselves and their return to the universities after the war. Bletchley Park recruited mathematicians including Alan Turing and Professor Max Newman; historians such as Professors Asa Briggs, John Plumb, Hugh Trevor-Roper, and Harry Hinsley; philosophers such as Professor Stuart Hampshire; and classicists such as Professor Vincent of my old college, Corpus Christi. An interesting historical example of the importance of these links is given by St Antony's College, Oxford. Founded in 1950, its first warden, Sir William Deakin, was a senior figure in the Secret Operations Executive during the war. It retains a habit of inviting senior Secret Intelligence Service (SIS) practitioners (including currently Sir Mark Allen, a former senior member of MI6 and a noted Arab scholar and calligraphist) to be fellows. Such was the public reputation of St. Antony's in sheltering former spies that they finally thought it best not to host the Oxford Intelligence Group (OIG) being set up by Michael Herman, a distinguished former senior officer of GCHQ and former secretary of the JIC. Michael, who sadly died as this chapter was being written,[13] became a leading scholar of secret intelligence and authored a number of classic works that helped to introduce the subject to students of intelligence studies.[14] The OIG ended up at Nuffield College, Oxford. An entertaining account of Oxford and academic spies has been published by the warden of Nuffield, Gwilym Hughes.[15] Michael Herman was also a regular contributor to the London-based Intelligence Studies Group, run out of the Department of War Studies at King's College. All Souls College, Oxford, also provided an academic home for former intelligence officers, notably Sir Maurice Oldfield, when he retired as chief of SIS (he was a distinguished medieval historian in his own right—but I am not sure from his biography that he ever completed the ambitious research program he agreed with All Souls).[16] A number of universities in the United Kingdom now offer the opportunity for serving officers to pursue full- or part-time PhDs in the field of intelligence studies (including at King's College London), and there have been a few former or seconded members of the UK intelligence community choosing to follow such study, but it would be stretching a point to describe this practice as an official scheme.

A stimulus for change in attitudes to academic outreach within the British intelligence community came with the publicizing of the role of intelligence in countering terrorism after 9/11 and the evident value of reaching out to expertise in the universities, for example, to those Arabists studying radicalization and the religious foundations of extreme Salafist thought.[17] The controversy in 2013 among scholars as well as civil society groups following publication of the material stolen by Edward Snowden from the US National Security Agency and GCHQ was less welcome. But there was evident public value in being able to have balanced views presented by intelligence studies academics, including former practitioners, alongside civil society groups exposing all sides of the arguments over privacy. An important official recognition of the value of having independent external views came with the 2015 request to RUSI from the then deputy prime minister to set up a wide-ranging Independent Surveillance Commission including academics (from the fields of war and intelligence studies, law, and moral philosophy) to provide input to the planned Regulation of Investigatory Powers Bill.[18] Such interactions on policy across the divide have grown apace over the last decade, and the model of the international Track 1/Track 2 conference has become commonplace, where the invited Track 2 academic members can debate and critique current Western strategy while the Track 1 serving officials weigh up the contributions, entering into the debate as best they can within the proper constraints of the policy of their current government. An example of a valued such trilateral gathering is the US CSIS/UK RUSI/France IFRI meetings (in the three capitals in turn) on nuclear proliferation and related issues.[19]

Today there is an expectation that when strategic reviews are commissioned by government (such as the 2020–2021 UK Integrated Review covering foreign policy, defense, and security), or major policy issues arise (such as the defense and security implications of Brexit), some form of external engagement with leading academics will be sought (as has happened with both those examples). The choice of academics to reach out to can itself be controversial,[20] but outreach work with universities now routinely goes beyond the technical into intelligence policy issues such as the application of cognitive science to intelligence analysis, ethical issues associated with persistent engagement in cyberspace, and the legal boundaries of intelligence-led counterterrorism.

Such outreach into academia appears to be valued on both sides (not least as the number of policy officials able to work on such topics shrinks due to budgetary pressures). The academic participants have to accept, however, that insofar as the official side exposes the issues on which it wants outside advice, inevitably the academics will have to respect the confidentiality of the advisory forum. This requirement for confidentiality can place the chosen academics in a difficult position in relation to their colleagues. Without such restraint, however, political sensitivities and fear of deliberate media misrepresentation will bear down on the nature of the exchanges and materially reduce their usefulness.

What is important is that the ground rules for the engagement are clear on all sides from the outset, including the confidentiality level of the work and whether permission is required to reference it, the ownership of intellectual property generated, and the ability of the researcher to publish results.

Such interactions have become more productive as the number of academics with past experience of government rises. The United States has for many years enjoyed a considerable advantage in that respect with the greater numbers of academics drawn into government on a change of administration and vice versa, including cabinet-rank positions such as the appointment of Condoleezza Rice from Stanford University to be US national security adviser and later secretary of state under George W. Bush, and Ash Carter from the Belfer Center at Harvard University to be US secretary of defense under Barack Obama. In both cases the individuals had served in more junior positions in previous administrations, in the National Security Council/State Department and in the Pentagon, respectively.

The advantages for both government and academe within the US system hardly need emphasizing. The US system of government, unlike that of the United Kingdom, involves the replacement on change of administration of the senior levels of government departments (as well as of the staff in the White House), posts that in the United Kingdom would be filled by politically un-committed civil servants. The significant downside is the churn that turnover every eight years (or even four years) represents in continuity and the prior political leanings that most academics must have shown to be appointable. A UK government seeking to inject fresh talent and expertise from academia and industry has to find ways compatible with the advantages brought by a professional career civil service. Bringing in academics as special advisers or on short-term contracts is one such route. King's College professor John Bew, an authority on Castlereagh and on "realpolitik,"[21] is at the time of writing seconded to the Policy Unit in 10 Downing Street.

At the same time, we see the move of experienced intelligence officers (especially from SIS) into the universities (Sir Richard Dearlove, former chief of SIS, was until recently master of Pembroke College, Cambridge) and into the larger think tanks like RUSI (Sir John Scarlett, former chief of SIS, is vice chair), Chatham House (Sir John Sawers, former chief of SIS, is on the Panel of Senior Advisers, while a past chair of Chatham House was former CIA analyst Dame DeAnne Julius), and IISS (director of studies is Nigel Inkster, former deputy chief of SIS and an expert on China; a senior adviser on cyber is Marcus Willett, former deputy director of GCHQ). At King's College London, apart from myself, we have other former senior intelligence and diplomatic commu-nity practitioners as visiting professors and senior research fellows, including Ciaran Martin, the former CEO of the UK National Cyber Security Centre.

EDUCATING ANALYSTS IN GOVERNMENT IN INTELLIGENCE STUDIES

When serving as the security and intelligence coordinator in the Cabinet Office, it had fallen to me in 2004 to chair the group implementing the find-ings of the independent Committee of Inquiry chaired by Sir Robin (now

Lord) Butler, the former cabinet secretary.[22] Having identified failures of intelligence in the run-up to the 2003 invasion of Iraq, Butler had called for an increase in the number of intelligence analysts and suggested forming a professional grouping on the lines of those that existed for government economists and scientists. A professional head of intelligence analysis (PHIA) was appointed and tasked with developing common analytic standards and training for young analysts and with outreach to the academic intelligence studies community. From my new perch in War Studies with Michael Goodman, we created for the PHIA the King's Intelligence Studies Programme (KISP) for young and midcareer intelligence analysts (to which were later added analysts from the law enforcement agencies that use national intelligence resources). We both felt that a young analyst whose career might to that point have been spent inside specialized domains of, say, signals intelligence or imagery analysis, or devoted to studying a specific geographical region of interest, would benefit from having a critical engagement in a university with the study of intelligence and its literature, and being encouraged to explore issues relevant to their work.

We are at the time of writing planning the thirty-fourth iteration of the basic KISP course since our start in 2006, so a significant proportion of the British analytic professional grouping has been through the experience of exposure to intelligence studies, delivered both by academic experts and by retired senior members from the intelligence agencies and from Scotland Yard's counterterrorism command. The course therefore represents the building of one type of bridge over the academic-practitioner divide. We were able to draw on the significant body of work done to construct open master's-level courses in the Department of War Studies and to obtain accreditation so that KISP students are automatically registered as master's students, and on successful completion will receive credits under the modular title "Intelligence Studies" that can subsequently be used to complete a master's degree at any British university. An account of our approach to constructing with a PHIA an appropriate syllabus can be found in the Central Intelligence Agency journal series *Studies in Intelligence.*[23]

In designing the course we were conscious that busy practitioners are unlikely to have had (I certainly had not) time to devote to keeping up with the burgeoning writing on intelligence. Even today, when I lecture to analysts from across the British intelligence community, few hands go up when I ask whether anyone reads the two main peer-reviewed journals of their subject, *Intelligence and National Security* and the *International Journal of Intelligence and CounterIntelligence.*

The KISP program has proved immensely popular with British intelligence analysts, and there is a waiting list to get on the course. The course complements the training to be given by the new UK Academy of Intelligence Assessment with their development of a New Analyst Programme and an Established Analyst Programme and associated qualification frameworks, as well as an Instructor Development Programme. The academy should be able to build links to intelligence studies programs in the universities. A steering board for the academy has been established (on which I and a number of external academics sit). KISP has also attracted considerable interest from European services. Another new initiative in which the United Kingdom is involved is the European Intelligence College, which will also facilitate outreach to intelligence studies faculties where the presence of former practitioners will be reassuring.[24]

CULTURE: PEERING INTO THE DIVIDE

I described at the outset the academic-practitioner divide in intelligence studies as a necessary one. The communities on either side of the divide have very different motivations, cultures, responsibilities, and sources of accountability. The individual academic freedom to publish openly opinions based on research that I enjoy today as a visiting professor in the Department of War Studies is rightly denied those working in the intelligence service of the state, not just for reasons of inherent secrecy, necessary as that is and which I explore later in this chapter, but also because there has to be hierarchical authority within the government system to decide what conclusions should be presented to customers from intelligence reporting.

The real debate—fierce at times—about what are the key intelligence judgments to be presented to senior customers, such as the members of the National Security Council, takes place behind closed doors within the agencies; in JTAC and in the Current Intelligence Groups drafting strategic assessments; and, finally, in the JIC itself. The outputs are sets of key judgments, explanations, and interpretations to present to key ministers and their officials. The National Security Council chaired by the prime minister could not function if every analyst in the intelligence community felt entitled to send in their own analysis and insist that it be considered. Senior officers within the intelligence community must, having weighed the arguments, decide what reporting is to be issued, and the JIC has to decide what judgments should be recorded as their view and circulated to ministers. Mechanisms exist for analysts to signal dissent to the professional head of intelligence analysis, or to the chair of the JIC, or to point out if views appear to have been overlooked.

The individual academic can and must publish and enjoy the benefits, but often rigors, of peer review. That process not only helps to keep them intellectually honest but encourages the occasional maverick opinion and revisionist interpretation, since that dialectic is how, like Kuhn's interpretation of the history of science, progress in understanding is made.[25] The closest the UK intelligence community can come to peer review is that provided when the analytic shops of the Five Eyes intelligence allies (the United States, Canada, Australia, and New Zealand) are able to examine the all-source assessments provided for the JIC. That is possible because of the unique sharing of classified raw intelligence reporting on many topics across the Five Eyes that provides a common evidence base for debate over the key judgments to be drawn. I had plenty of opportunity as a member of the JIC to study what differences in interpretation could arise even built on the same base of reporting.

I suspect that most practitioners who, as I have done, cross for the first time the divide into a university will quickly register similarities as well as differences in organizational culture. Whitehall is organized to deliver within defined functional areas, each with its own secretary of state and granted funding by Parliament. Within those mainstreams, the delivery of services can be efficiently organized. But many of the issues that most concern the citizen—such as social care, employment, or crime—cross those boundaries and are hard for the vertically organized system to cope with. We have seen this in the United Kingdom during the 2020 COVID-19 pandemic, with the tensions between NHS hospitals discharging elderly and infirm patients into care homes for which the NHS is not responsible without first testing for COVID-19. The university department or faculty also guards jealously its prerogatives based on its own definition of its traditional subject area, such as history or law. Innovation comes, as it often does in the sciences, at the intersection of disciplines, which encourages the setting up of interdisciplinary institutes to allow cross-boundary work. Over time the location of the research front line changes, leaving behind a complex organizational landscape reflecting past initiatives. For the practitioner used to the hierarchy of an intelligence agency or government department, this can be hard to navigate, since there is little sense of a single controlling mind. It is hard to identify who has authority over what or who decides on which application to submit to the small number of funders that can provide research grants. The funders' demands for evidence of relevance or policy impact are another reason for needing bridges spanning the academic-practitioner divide. The great strength of the academic system, however, is the encouragement of personal initiatives and the personal freedom to decide on one's research focus and colleagues with whom to collaborate on projects.

RESPECTING AND CHALLENGING CONFIDENTIALITY

I confess to surprise when I arrived in King's and read myself into the literature of intelligence studies at just how much detailed material had been prized from the UK archives, including much that I had previously considered was still classified or would remain sealed as official secrets. The United States has been more relaxed in recent decades about access in response to Freedom of Information requests, as the National Security Archive at George Washington University testifies, including such gems as the CIA history of Operation Ajax; the 1953 overthrow of Iranian prime minister Mohammad Mosaddeq in Iran; and Operation Gold, the 1955 digging of the Berlin Tunnel.

Academics certainly will express frustrations over continuing British restrictions on the release of intelligence archive material and reticence in helping academics wanting to get around those restrictions (which is sometimes possible on the condition that before publication there will be a security review with the last word resting with the agency). But at least in relation to modern digital intelligence, the boundary of secrecy has helpfully shifted with the 2016 Investigatory Powers Act. In previous decades, the British government would "neither confirm nor deny" the use by British agencies of techniques such as access to bulk communications data from mobile phones, equipment interference, hacking, offensive cyber, and the holding of bulk personal databases. Now these are avowed techniques open to the agencies and regulated by law and independently overseen by a former judge, president of the Queen's Bench Division and head of criminal justice Sir Brian Leveson, acting as the investigative powers commissioner, and his staff at the Investigatory Powers Commissioner's Office. Likewise, the defense secretary has announced the existence of the British program to develop offensive cyber capabilities, conducted jointly by GCHQ and the Ministry of Defence. That greater openness makes academic research easier, for example, with regard to making comparisons of legal and ethical regimes across Europe and with the United States.

Reports over the last few years by the parliamentary Intelligence and Security Committee and by the previous intelligence commissioners, together with the published judgments of the Investigatory Powers Tribunal in response to cases brought by Liberty, Big Brother Watch, and other civil society groups following the publicity given to the material stolen and released to journalists by the US National Security Agency contractor Edward Snowden, provide a depth of information about modern digital intelligence that is unprecedented. Such official material is immensely helpful to academics and former practitioners in enabling them to work together both in research and in teaching on the basis of a common understanding of the basics of how modern intelligence is conducted. That in turn helps provide an educated section of public opinion when public policy issues arise, such as the need for intelligence access to digital data in bulk and the corresponding safeguards that ought to be in place in a democracy. That has been a motivation not just in the United Kingdom but in several European nations for official encouragement for universities to set up courses in intelligence studies and to get former practitioners like myself to help deliver them.

What remains, and must remain, secret is which combination of techniques is being applied to which targets to acquire secret intelligence. That is information that would directly assist those who mean us harm, including terrorists and serious criminals seeking to evade detection, and I hope academics studying intelligence will recognize a moral obligation to understand where the boundary lies. It is possible for university agreement to be given for classified research to be undertaken in universities at the request of government, or with its consent, but this is rare in intelligence studies. The resulting security restrictions can be onerous for the researcher and department, and limiting for academic careers if a doctoral thesis, the fruits of four or more years of intensive work, is not on open-access shelves of the library or web accessible. Having colleagues who are former insiders will help educate researchers on the valid reasons for security restrictions, and, equally, passing their feedback to old colleagues on the inside may help dispel unjustified sensitivity over what academics are up to.

It is, as a former practitioner, initially daunting to take questions after delivering an intelligence studies lecture to an international group of bright, enthusiastic master's students (a few of whom you suspect may well either already be recruited by their national agencies or are hoping to be after graduation). The lecturer in those circumstances has to nurture a self-censoring angel at the back of the mind, a part of the superego, that will kick in to make an on-the-spot judgment of how far to go in answering questions on security-sensitive areas. And despite university or think tank rules, there can be no guarantee that a student, out of a deeply held belief or a sense of mischief, will not select an incautious or poorly expressed sentence or two to tweet out from the lecture hall. I have never been embarrassed in that way, either in King's College, in Sciences Po, or in the many other universities where I have delivered academic lectures, but I know those who have been.

It will help the former practitioner to acquire as quickly as possible a wide knowledge of the literature that can be drawn upon to provide examples of intelligence tradecraft or technical sources that are already in the public domain and can be used to illustrate a point or answer a question. The sensitive subject of geolocation of mobile devices can, for example, be illustrated by the direction finding of the Second World War and the search for illegal spy transmitters of the Cold War; analysis of communications data can be related back to the lessons of traffic analysis of Bletchley Park; and so on.[26] When in 2009 to show good faith I submitted to Whitehall the manuscript of my first book, *Securing the State*, although I knew it contained no previously unpublished secrets, the only comment I got back was a polite suggestion that I omit all reference to signals intelligence.[27] In response, I replaced the examples I had used with ones drawn from the history of Bletchley Park to make the same points. In the succeeding decade, much has changed, not least the commissioning of the authorized history of GCHQ.

CONCLUSION

The value of now having authorized histories published of all three of the British national intelligence agencies and of the JIC is not just to provide solid evidence for scholars of intelligence studies. Every profession needs to have a sense of its own history. That provides essential context for address-ing the issues of today. It is important to know in deciding for the future how and why the present situation arose, and what allowed major advances to be made, or not, at key moments in the past. For the member of a profession, a sense of history provides a sense of belonging, and of the breadth and height of the shoulders on which their work stands, with the spur of matching the achievements and boldness of the past to meet the challenges of today.

NOTES

1. As far as I can establish, the British practice is that visiting scholars are not salaried but can be paid the going rates for lectures and seminars or supervision.

2. Michael S. Goodman, *The Official History of the Joint Intelligence Committee*, vol. 1, *From the Approach of the Second World War to the Suez Crisis* (Abingdon: Routledge, 2014).

3. Christopher Andrew, *The Secret World: A History of Intelligence*, 593 (London: Allen Lane, 2018).

4. In the 1989 Security Service Act and the 1994 Intelligence Services Act.

5. These secondments often resulted in valuable contributions to defense policy, for example, J. Michael Legge, *Theatre Nuclear Weapons and the NATO Strategy of Flexible Response* (Santa Monica, CA: RAND Corporation, 1983).

6. *Hansard*, April 3, 1982, col. 649. The episode is recounted in John Ferris, *Behind the Enigma: The Authorised History of GCHQ, Britain's Secret Cyber-Intelligence Agency*, 631 (London: Bloomsbury, 2020).

7. David Omand, "Intelligence Secrets and Media Spotlights," in *Spinning Intel-ligence*, ed. Robert Dover and Michael S. Goodman, 37–56 (London: Hurst, 2009).

8. F. H. Hinsley et al., *British Intelligence in the Second World War*, vols. 1–5 (London: Her Majesty's Stationery Office, 1979–1990).

9. Christopher Andrew and David Dilks, eds., *The Missing Dimension: Governments and Intelligence Communities in the Twentieth Century* (London: Macmillan, 1984).

10. R. N. Carew Hunt, *The Theory and Practice of Communism* (London: Penguin, 1963). First published in 1950, revised editions appeared in 1951 and 1957 before its publication as a Pelican paperback in 1963.

11. See also the National Security Strategic Investment Fund initiative: https://www.british-business-bank.co.uk/national-security-strategic-investment-fund.

12. A list of the relevant British national security technology areas of interest can be found at https://www.british-business-bank.co.uk/wp-content/uploads/2020/05/HMG -NS-Technology-AOIs-Summary_v2.pdf.

13. An obituary of Michael Herman can be found in the *Times* of March 20, 2021, 10.

14. Essential reading for students in intelligence studies is Michael Herman, *Intelligence Power in Peace and War* (Cambridge: Cambridge University Press, 1996).

15. Gwilym Hughes, "The Oxford Intelligence Group," in *The Routledge International Handbook of Universities, Security and Intelligence Studies*, ed. Liam Francis Gearon, 231–42 (Abingdon: Routledge, 2020).

16. John N. Crossley, "Unofficial Advice and Official Policy: Sir Maurice Oldfield and All Souls College, Oxford, 1978–9," *Intelligence and National Security* 35, no. 3 (2020): 424–37.

17. An excellent current example exposes the thinking of IS terrorist Anwar al-Awlaki: Alexander Meleagrou-Hitchins, *Incitement: Anwar al-Awlaki's Western Jihad* (Cambridge, MA: Harvard University Press, 2020).

18. Independent Surveillance Review, *A Democratic Licence to Operate: Report of the Independent Surveillance Review* (London: Royal United Services Institute [RUSI], 2015), https://rusi.org/sites/default/files/20150714_whr_2-15_a_democratic _licence_to_operate.pdf.

19. See, for example, the Joint Statement, March 13, 2020, https://www.csis.org /analysis/csis-european-trilateral-track-2-nuclear-dialogues-1.

20. A recent example was the choice of academic lawyers to advise on the implications of the Internal Markets Bill for the Northern Ireland agreement. See Paul Lewis and Owen Bowcott, "Brexit Advice: Are Ministers Obliged to Comply with International Law?," *Guardian*, September 10, 2020, https://www.theguardian.com /politics/2020/sep/10/brexit-letter-are-mps-obliged-to-comply-with-international-law.

21. John Bew, *Realpolitik: A History* (Oxford: Oxford University Press, 2016).

22. Lord Butler, *Review of Intelligence on Weapons of Mass Destruction: Report of a Committee of Privy Counsellors*, HC 898 (London: Her Majesty's Stationery Office, 2004).

23. Michael S. Goodman and David Omand, "What Analysts Need to Understand," *Studies in Intelligence* 52, no. 4 (2008): 1–12.

24. I am on the advisory board for the new UK College of Intelligence Assessment, for the German government's new master's course in intelligence studies, for

the Defence University in Oslo, and for the Centre for Asymmetric Threat Studies in Stockholm.

25. Thomas S. Kuhn, *The Structure of Scientific Revolutions* (Chicago, IL: University of Chicago Press, 1962).

26. Ben Wallace, *Hansard*, July 6, 2020, col. 657.

27. David Omand, *Securing the State* (London: Hurst & Co., 2010).

3

Neither Knuckle-Draggers nor Carpetbaggers

Proposing the Periclean Ideal for Intelligence Educators

Nicholas Dujmović

The editors of this volume deserve thanks for focusing on one of the two most important issues in intelligence education. The question of the "academic-practitioner divide" in the study of intelligence at colleges and universities is really the question of "who is teaching this subject?" That question, in turn, comes with important and potentially awkward baggage—namely, whether the people teaching this stuff know what they're talking about, how well they know what they know, and how they came to know it. Moreover, the question of *who* is teaching intelligence is organically related to the other major issue of intelligence studies, namely, *what* is being taught about intelligence. The *what* or content of intelligence studies, in turn, has ramifications for where intelligence finds itself in academia—as its own discrete discipline, or as a mere variation on another field, such as law enforcement. Every question about intelligence education therefore comes back to the essential question of *who* is teaching the subject. So, the editors have chosen a vital subject.

I must also thank them for seeking to include me in the mix. As a career intelligence officer, I'm on the "practitioner" side of things and remain so at heart, even though I've followed my intelligence career with a sojourn in academia, having created an intelligence studies program at the Catholic University of America in Washington, DC. And I've noticed that we career practitioners, to no one's surprise, are decidedly in the minority in intelligence education. Of the twenty-one contributors to this volume, for example, only three (as far as I can determine) could be described as career intelligence officers, while seven-ish have biographies that mention some sort of intelligence experience.

I'm grateful to Mark Phythian for his gentle insistence that my contribution was needed, since my criticism of many established intelligence programs—

and who runs them—has annoyed some on the academic side of the debate.[1] I suppose my past use of the phrases "intelligence-academic complex" and "intelligence professoriate" didn't help relations, not to mention my suggestion that some intelligence programs seem designed to benefit only the academic institutions sponsoring them rather than the students (or their potential employers in the US intelligence community [IC]). Well, in intelligence, we ask hearers of unfavorable analysis not to shoot the messenger.

It is not true, however, that I would address the divide by trying simply to bring about some sort of 50–50 balance; that is not going to happen. I don't believe that every intelligence professor needs to be a retired intelligence officer—though having more educators with actual experience in intelligence would be a good idea. Nor do I think, far from it, that any career intelligence officer is automatically fit to serve as a teacher of intelligence—though many have potential.

My thinking is a *bit* more nuanced than that. Even so, later in this chapter, I'll sacrifice nuance by presenting two opposing stereotypes, notional professors of intelligence, that illustrate the vulgar extremes of the "divide." I will offer a practitioner who is a caricature of what academics might call a "Knuckle-Dragger," a lower life form pretending to walk upright and teach at the university level, while my academic caricature is what practitioners might call a "Carpetbagger," an intelligence professor who, with no actual experience in intelligence, is an exploitative, self-promoting, shameless fraud.

Name-calling solves nothing, so I will suggest a third way, which I call the Periclean ideal of the intelligence educator.

THE *WHY* OF ACADEMIC INTELLIGENCE PROGRAMS

Before positing the need for the Periclean ideal, we should first discuss what these programs are *for*. What is their ultimate purpose—their *telos*? To use the academic jargon I've had to learn since retiring from the Central Intelligence Agency (CIA), what are the "outcomes" of our pedagogy that we would like to see?

Let's leave the question of content to the side for now. What do university students *do* with knowledge gained from studying intelligence?

If students, having received a good grounding in intelligence, are inspired to consider careers in it, that is a good outcome, arguably the best outcome from the perspective of a retired intelligence officer who wishes to "give back" to the profession. Intelligence education should help career-minded students to become practitioners by giving them a substantive advantage in the application and hiring process and also confidence during it. Any relative edge is welcome, given that (as I tell my students) most US intelligence agencies are, roughly speaking, looking at *tens of thousands* of good applications annually for only *hundreds* of job openings. Having studied intelligence at all helps their applications stand out from the crowd's. Having studied intelligence *as it really is* gives students an advantage in interviews. I know this from the experience of my students to whom intelligence agency recruiters noted with enthusiasm that they could relate essential concepts, terminology, and insider insights.

Also important is the advantage of learning about something strange and new before going into it, and intelligence education can stave off career tragedy. I know that the CIA has suffered from the premature resignation of some promising people who found themselves unprepared for what their new profession entails. It's not just another government job—there are high expectations, stress, sacrifice, and ethical questions unique to intelligence that are absent in other lines of work. One brand new analyst at the CIA discovered in her training that the "all sources" informing her work included the fruit of spying on people, and she, upset by this revelation, was soon headed out the door.

Employment in intelligence is not, however, the only good outcome of our pedagogy. If students take their knowledge about intelligence into other parts of government—other executive agencies (especially the White House, the National Security Council, and the State Department), the military, or as staffers on Capitol Hill—it will help them in their work and will also benefit the intelligence agencies (who frequently must deal with federal job holders who are ignorant of or otherwise just don't "get" intelligence).

At the very least, even if studying intelligence doesn't lead students to a career in it or to any government service at all, even if such study merely makes them better citizens and informed voters, that is more than satisfactory as an outcome. Intelligence studies programs at a minimum must aim to speak truth to the power of an informed and responsible citizenry.

Therefore, wherever our intelligence students take the knowledge we intelligence educators provide, we should not want them to have a skewed understanding of intelligence or to persist in misperceptions foisted on them by popular culture,[2] biased media,[3] political ravings about the "Deep State,"[4] or bad scholarship.[5] Nor do we want that understanding to be incomplete. I'm actually less interested in where they go with their education than that they get there with a full range of exposure to the essential elements of intelligence.

THE *WHAT* OF ACADEMIC INTELLIGENCE PROGRAMS

Central to the question of what is taught in our programs is the definitional issue—what, in a nutshell, *is* intelligence? In my introductory course at

Catholic University, we discuss the various ways to define intelligence, such as mere information, as necessary grist for decision makers, as a product, as process, as institution, and so forth, and the shortcomings of each. Following the argument of my old friend Michael Warner,[6] I posit that an intelligence definition must include something about secrecy, is fundamentally the province of state authority for state purposes, is properly focused on foreigners, and should account for activities by which intelligence *influences* (and not merely reports and analyzes) foreign conditions. Eventually we arrive at the best, most succinct, and yet complete definition of intelligence, the "unified field theory" Warner definition, which my students are required to memorize, that

> *intelligence is secret, state activity to understand or influence foreign entities.*

Warner's insight is the basis for my own definition of what should comprise the study of intelligence:

> *Intelligence studies is the scholarly discipline that seeks to learn about the se-cret activities of the state in understanding or influencing foreign entities.* It is a specialized, multidisciplinary subdiscipline of the study of national security. It is distinct from academic programs in foreign affairs or international relations, military studies, and law enforcement or criminal justice. It encompasses the study of all essential elements of intelligence: collection, analysis, covert action, counterintelligence, *and* accountability *in a democracy.*

Academic intelligence programs ought to expose students to *all* the essential elements of intelligence as conducted by a democracy rather than simply focus on one aspect (such as analysis). Intelligence programs with this comprehensive approach ought not to be too closely associated with criminal justice or military curricula for the same reason—police intelligence is too limiting in scope, and even military intelligence often lacks a national perspective. An intelligence curriculum properly organized to cover *collection, analysis, covert action, counterintelligence* (CI), and *accountability*—and their many subtopics—will give students the best intelligence education possible, short of actually joining an intelligence agency.

The topic of *collection*, the oldest and most fundamental intelligence activity, is very broad and would encompass human intelligence (including diplomatic and attaché reporting, not just the important subcategory of espionage, with its recruiting cycle and the primacy of relationships), signals intelligence and its components communications intelligence and electronic intelligence, overhead imagery (from space satellites and atmospheric platforms, including UAVs), localized technical collection (audiovisual surveillance, weapons of mass destruction sensors), open-source collection (including social media), and cyber collection (as distinct from cyber warfare). Students have to gain an appreciation for how challenging collection is, how it cannot be taken for granted—this stuff just doesn't fall into an analyst's lap.

Analysis is key, of course, because most college graduates who do enter the intelligence profession become analysts. Students should learn about the various analytic disciplines (political, military, economic, leadership, science and technology, weapons, terrorist networks), the products (long-term forecasts versus current intelligence), the process (expertise, writing/editing, briefing, follow-up), indications and warnings (a critical specialty), and the challenges (e.g., institutional barriers, analytic standards, cognitive barriers, and policy-maker biases).

No intelligence curriculum can ignore CI as a necessary element of intelligence, for two reasons. First, it is essential for students to learn that no other intelligence element or activity will be successful without CI. CI is necessary "quality control" for collection and therefore analysis and also for covert action. Second, US intelligence increasingly has been under attack from hostile foreign services. Students must learn about personnel security (including background investigations and the polygraph), physical security, computer security, defensive operations (including mole hunts and investigations of leaks), and the potentially controversial subtopic of offensive CI operations (including the use of illegals and double agents).

It should be obvious that *covert action* is an intelligence subject that must be taught because of the controversy it has generated in US history, because of the fact that it has been used by every president since Harry Truman as a tool of the executive, and because of popular misconceptions surrounding it. Students should learn about covert influence versus paramilitary operations; the use of proxies; political activities, including election operations; economic subsidies; propaganda (black, white, and gray); assassination or "wet operations"; the issue of "blowback" on domestic audiences; and the use of the Internet and cyber operations to sway foreign audiences or create mayhem through destruction.

Finally, *accountability* is a necessary subject for intelligence students because it is a necessary condition for intelligence agencies serving a democracy. Intelligence is powerful and has great potential for misuse. Students must learn the various modes of oversight (legislative, executive, and judicial), legal authorities (e.g., Title 50 of the US Code, as well as relevant executive orders), ethics/moral dilemmas (scenarios are useful here), declassification and transparency, how intelligence agencies present themselves (public relations), and the "watchdog" role of academia and outside scholarship.

As I have argued elsewhere[7] but will reiterate here, the ideal intelligence program will cover all these subjects but *will not do so at the expense of depriving students of substantive study* and acquiring degrees in fields of interest to intelligence agencies. My view is that degree-granting intelligence programs (at least at the undergraduate level) do not prepare a student well for potential employment because the intelligence agencies are more interested in substantive specialties like Chinese studies than in intelligence studies per se. Having sat through a number of recruiting presentations and scanned most agencies' websites, I do not recall ever seeing "intelligence" as one of the majors sought after by the intelligence services.

Ashenden University's New Intelligence Major

To illustrate the problems I see in the content of the intelligence programs of many universities, let's consider the case of the new major in intelligence studies recently announced by a US institution of higher learning that I will call Ashenden University.[8] The university's intelligence program is real as described, according to the university's own website and publicity; I've obscured the university's name because I don't want my criticism to hurt feelings unnecessarily.

The bachelor of arts in intelligence studies at Ashenden University is actually quite thin on intelligence courses. The major requires a total of thirteen courses (each worth three credit hours), but there are only three actual courses in intelligence, with their content focused on analysis. The introductory course on the US IC looks adequate; students learn something about collection and analysis and write "intelligence reports." The emphasis is on the "intelligence cycle." Likewise with the intelligence "case studies" course, which covers, again, the "intelligence cycle" as students write a notional National Intelligence Estimate. The third intelligence course is a senior thesis capstone; students research and write a paper on an "aspect of security studies," which to my mind is a broader category not necessarily specific to intelligence.

Intelligence majors at Ashenden are also required to participate in an internship that involves matters concerning *security or safety* at a government agency, a government contractor, or a private company. That is to say, the "intelligence internship" need not have much at all to do with intelligence.

For most of this "intelligence major," students take courses that are mostly *not* about intelligence. Intelligence majors at Ashenden must take two courses in criminal justice, a subject that at best has a narrow overlap with intelligence. They must take one political science course about terrorism and one on methodology or statistics. After that, they must choose from a wide variety of electives dealing with history, international politics, global issues, foreign policy, or law enforcement.

The "intelligence studies major" at Ashenden University, therefore, is a good but diffuse liberal arts curriculum. I'm sorry to say, however, that to call this program of study a "major" *in intelligence* might be considered fraud, looking just at the credit hours. Of the thirty-nine credit hours required for the major, only nine hours come from the three actual courses in intelligence mentioned previously. Excuse me; that's not a major in "intelligence" or even "intelligence studies." It's about half a minor. In fact, a minor in intelligence elsewhere will probably have more intelligence content than Ashenden's "major" in intelligence.[9]

The picture at Ashenden worsens when one considers that the intelligence content is almost all about analysis. As a former intelligence analyst and manager of analysts, I will concede to no one the primacy of analysis. As former CIA director Richard Helms noted, analysis is "the absolute essence of the intelligence profession"—this from a career operations officer.[10] As much as romantic notions of secret operations and case officer work might appeal to college students, once they learn about the realities of intelligence, most of those interested in a career in intelligence decide that the analytic profession is a better fit.

Even so, a good grounding in intelligence at the college level will not neglect the other essential elements of intelligence. Ashenden University students majoring in intelligence have no opportunity to take a course in CI and consequently no deep understanding of its vital importance or what the Chinese, Russian, and other hostile foreign services are doing to thwart our intelligence efforts. What are Ashenden intelligence majors learning about covert action? The study of covert action is heavily dependent on a historical approach, since by definition ongoing and recent (and even not-so-recent) covert actions are classified. The Ashenden curriculum is silent on covert action. One can only hope that issues of intelligence accountability are included in the course material on analysis and criminal justice, because it's not evident from the curriculum or course descriptions.

The Ashenden Intelligence Professors: The Triumph of Intentions over Experience

The reason for the inadequacy of the "intelligence studies major" at Ashenden University, of course, is that this is the curriculum that the professors who created it could bring to the table by virtue of their experiences. One of the perhaps banal truths I've learned since becoming an "academic" is that academia, rather like intelligence, is highly personality dependent. The education the students receive relies on the twin pillars of what the individual professor has *studied* as well as what he or she has *experienced*. This is the "academic-practitioner" issue on a personal level. Let's look at the forgers of this major.

As with the university, I'm assigning pseudonyms to the trio of professors[11] listed for the "intelligence studies major." The senior academic, who also chairs the Department of Political Science, Dr. D. Heyer, teaches courses in government and comparative politics, focusing on Latin America and the Middle East. His professional career has been entirely in academia, with no government service, and he appears not to have published anything on any subject having to do with intelligence. Dr. Heyer's sole contribution to the intelligence program appears to consist of offering several non-intelligence electives to students in this "major."

Dr. R. Kerch is a history professor, specializing in modern European history, with his publications focused on popular cultural, gender, and ethnic issues. His CV lists only two publications that are on intelligence topics, a book chapter and an article, both of which deal with the same particular author of . . . spy fiction. Happily, Dr. Kerch is not so narrow on intelligence as his academic work suggests, for before he became a professor he served as a government intelligence analyst, in two different agencies, over a period of . . . almost four years. So, he has some intelligence experience, but not a lot of it. I cannot imagine that if I had left THE CIA after four years' work as an analyst I would consider myself enough of a "practitioner" to make an academic program out of it. (But it happens.)

In Ashenden's intelligence program, the most government experience is held by Mr. K. Jones, a criminal justice instructor. A former municipal cop, Jones served for four years in the Drug Enforcement Administration (albeit years before the DEA joined the IC) and has worked on security issues for two other federal organizations, neither of them intelligence agencies. He teaches courses on police investigations and operations, drug organizations and narco-terrorism, and the criminal justice process. All are commendable subjects, and while his government experience is laudable (I would thank him for it, given the chance, and buy him a drink), his qualifications as a professor of intelligence are not obvious either by scholarly inclination or through practical experience.

To sum up my views on Ashenden University's major in intelligence studies, I would say that this example illustrates the problems of many intelligence programs in academia. The subject, topics, and content that should be taught are not taught because the programs are skewed toward one element of intelligence (analysis, usually, or the subcategory of police intelligence), thereby shortchanging the students from a full understanding of what intelligence is. The reason for the inadequacy of the program content seems directly related to the individuals running the program, who lack relevant experience.

Newman University Does Better—with Experience

I'll impose on the reader's patience with another short example, the major in "strategic intelligence" at Newman University in Wichita, Kansas. Newman is a nominally Roman Catholic institution (and I'm using its real name here). At Newman, the intelligence program, while not ideal, is still very much an improvement over that at Ashenden University because it comes closer to providing a full grounding in all elements of intelligence. That difference appears to be the result of the intelligence and national security experience of the lead professor, Scott McIntosh (his real name, used with permission). McIntosh is a military veteran and retiree, a former military intelligence analyst, a collection manager, and a foreign area officer.

I asked McIntosh how his experience informs the structure and content of his program. He offered that "credibility is the coin of the realm" in intelligence education and that students seek to learn from professors who have "walked the walk."[12] The advantage of Newman over Ashenden only begins with this credibility.

It's no surprise, given his background, that McIntosh created an intelligence curriculum that has more content and is more comprehensive than that at Ashenden. Instead of three intelligence courses essentially about analysis, McIntosh has five with a broader scope: an introductory course; a course on analysis; a course covering counterterrorism and law enforcement intelligence; an entire course on collection (of which I am frankly envious); and a separate course dealing with legal matters, oversight, and ethics in intelligence. As a whole, these courses directly address most of the elements of intelligence, while the importance of CI is integrated into the introductory course as well as in the courses on analysis and collection. He also makes use of serving practitioners—the collection course is taught by a collection manager from the intelligence component of a local Air National Guard wing.

I am not backing down on my general opposition to undergraduate degree programs in intelligence, but if one is going to have an undergraduate major in intelligence, this is a far better way to do it: utilizing someone who has had a career in national security, with a particular emphasis on intelligence.[13] A practitioner, in other words.

Practitioners are more likely than academics to be capable of teaching the range of subjects necessary to a well-balanced, comprehensive survey of the intelligence profession, and they are more likely to understand why certain subjects are necessary. They have unique "participatory knowledge"—knowing things directly instead of merely knowing about things. Practitioners also have networks comprising other practitioners. I've done primary-source research on espionage cases but have never handled a spy. I know lots of former colleagues who have, however, and when teaching about espionage, it is really very helpful to bring in a retired case officer to tell students how potential assets are spotted, developed, pitched, and run. Or a terrorism analyst to explain how the bad guys are detected, followed, and caught. Or a former National Security Agency (NSA) senior official to discuss collection challenges and limitations. One of my best resources as a career practitioner is my Rolodex.

At the same time, I admit that academics without intelligence experience can learn and then teach useful things about intelligence. Particularly in the field of intelligence history, there are many brilliant examples of excellent scholarship that reveals a real—almost an insider's—understanding of intelligence. History, honestly studied, tends to ground one in reality. But I have seen other intelligence academics sadly unmoored from intelligence reality.[14]

Notional Extreme Cases of Intelligence Educators from Academia and Intelligence Practice

Let me illustrate potential problems with both general types of intelligence educators by presenting two caricatures, one Knuckle-Dragger and one Carpetbagger, as notional portraits of how bad it might get on the pure academic and practitioner sides alike.

From the realm of the practitioners, I offer Mr. Barry Blenkinsop,[15] a career CIA professional, specifically with a career in operations, who is nearing retirement and wants, as his final CIA assignment, to be a CIA officer-in-residence (OIR) at Vitreous State University (VSU). (The OIR program—more about which later—used to place senior CIA officers openly at willing colleges and universities to teach about intelligence, usually near the end of their careers.[16])

Blenkinsop wants this OIR position at VSU even though he has never taught at the college level, and his own academic work topped out as a mid-career CIA officer with a year at a senior military school, which was not a terribly rigorous program but got him a nominal master's degree. His idea of higher education is influenced by his experience as a guest speaker in CIA operations courses, which consisted mostly of telling stories to newly hired operations officers in training.

Blenkinsop has this idea that it would be fun, profitable, and easy to become a college professor in retirement, and he sees the OIR program as his ticket to that destination. Having served for twenty-five years mostly as a case officer and station chief predominantly in a particular geographic area, which we'll call central Laurasia, Blenkinsop lobbies hard for OIR sponsorship from his home office, the Laurasia Division of the Directorate of Operations. He is an action-oriented, capable but not stellar officer, with some personal issues in his later years involving too much drink and cohabitation with women not his wife, and has been cited for security violations and one instance of sexual harassment. His home division is happy at the prospect of his retirement and enthusiastically endorses his OIR candidacy.

Blenkinsop has a family contact with a senior administrator at VSU who persuades the dean of the college of humanities and social sciences to accept Blenkinsop as a professor of practice, even though he has neither a PhD nor college teaching experience. The chair of the international relations department, where Blenkinsop is assigned, raises objections but relents under the argument that intelligence is a hot subject that will draw students to VSU and to the department, and that in any case the CIA is footing the man's salary. On the surface, it looks like a win-win for everybody.

It ends up being lose-lose, largely because Blenkinsop's ambition exceeds his competence. At first, students flock to the two courses offered by the new CIA professor on campus—"Intelligence Basics" and a survey course on Laurasia—but find he is a terrible teacher. His lectures are stream-of-consciousness performances that betray little preparation and consist mostly of stories, during which he frequently backtracks when he thinks he has crossed the line into classified territory. When not relating his own experiences, he simply reads from textbooks and comments on them. He refuses to accept the idea that US intelligence, particularly the CIA, has ever done anything illegal or immoral. There is no meaningful discussion in class, especially on ethical matters, and Blenkinsop discourages questions, seeing them as challenges to his person. On the rare occasions he is confronted or asked a difficult question, in place of reasoned argument he just talks more loudly. He is late with his syllabi, in giving assignments, and in returning student work, and he is arbitrary and inconsistent in his grading. Word gets around, and fewer students sign up for his courses. Those who enroll end up dissing him in student evaluations.

Blenkinsop does no research, publishes nothing, and makes no contribution to the intellectual climate at VSU. After two years—and a hushed-up incident involving a female student—Blenkinsop takes full retirement from the CIA, and VSU, with a great deal of relief, declines his teaching services going forward. When the CIA ends its OIR program a few years later, the decision seems to be influenced by this unfortunate experience.

Of course I exaggerate. Blenkinsop is very much more than an amalgam of the worst characteristics of three practitioners who went into academia, including one I knew well (and was a long way from being half as bad as Blenkinsop). The point of this Knuckle-Dragger caricature is to bring together all the potential objections that academics might have to allowing a practitioner on their turf, so to speak.

On the academic side of the divide, I offer Dr. Winks Smith, who has spent his entire professional life as a professor of political science and organizational theory. He has long been interested in intelligence. Not long after the 9/11 attacks of 2001, he applied to the CIA while completing his doctorate, but he was frustrated by the polygraph and denied employment. He was also angry that the agency gave no reason why he was not hired. He seems to have channeled his anger into his intelligence scholarship, which is prodigious.

Smith becomes a well-known figure in intelligence studies, largely based on his work on institutional secrecy, about which he is highly critical, and congressional oversight, which he champions to the extreme. As an academic, he is everything poor Blenkinsop of the CIA is not: Smith is a gifted, extraordinarily talented writer; he is respected by colleagues for his expertise and well liked by students; he created and runs a very popular intelligence program that his university generously supports; he is well spoken and often lectures authoritatively on intelligence at other universities and conferences. He is not concerned in the slightest that he has absolutely no working experience in his academic specialty and does not see why anyone else should be concerned. If asked about it, Smith touts his lack of empirical knowledge as a great asset, claiming that no former intelligence employee could ever be objective about the profession.

The beauty of Smith's writing and his graceful oratory help mask the fact that he makes statements about US intelligence that are factually incorrect or that present interpretations that are skewed in terms of motivations as well as causes and effects. He is an accomplished storyteller, and his desire to craft a compelling narrative takes precedence over his scholarly duty regarding accuracy, balance, and fair play. Smith typically cites sources that are unreliable, inappropriate, unqualified, biased, or otherwise irrelevant to bolster his points, as long as they say things useful to his message. He likes to cite particular passages from spy novels, for example, to explain internal CIA processes, organizational culture, or what influences officers' psychology and decision making.

Smith's secret, however, is that, as a Carpetbagger, he really does not know what he's talking about. In his oral presentations and writings, he feeds the air of mystery about intelligence by alluding to insider sources that he, in fact, does not have. The very few former intelligence officers he talks to are disgruntled or outright renegades, yet he regards their views as gospel. Intelligence professionals who attend his conference presentations wonder what

CIA and IC he is talking about, for it bears little resemblance to the institutions they know.[17]

His book on secrecy in the US IC is lauded by academic colleagues and, predictably, journalists (and panned by former practitioners). Its thesis is that the IC is so pathologically and obsessively secretive that it literally constitutes a collective mental illness. Secrecy in the IC, he asserts, is a fundamentalist religion that is far more important to its adherents than actual intelligence activities. The usual tortured allusions to "Skull and Bones" abound. He mocks the idea that secrecy might be necessary to protect sources and methods and implies that the First Amendment should allow for the publication, without restraint, of secrets gained in intelligence service.

Smith's next book is on congressional oversight, in which he advocates his own unique theory of "intelligence paleo-originalism"—that Congress should directly run intelligence activities as the Continental Congress did in 1775–1777. Because, in his view, Congress has never erred in or abused its oversight responsibilities, he would simply hand the reins over to the legislative branch of government. He would do away with the IC as currently organized under the executive branch, making US intelligence entities exclusively creatures of Congress. Doing so, Smith asserts, would thereby efficiently combine oversight with command responsibilities and eliminate the abuses of executive branch control, not the least of which is . . . too much secrecy.

Winks Smith is admittedly too bad to be true, but I ask readers to remember he is an illustrative caricature that gathers all the objections practitioners may have to "pure academics" who teach intelligence with no empirical knowledge of it. Indeed, Winks's excesses are inspired by several career academics of my acquaintance, at least two of whom deserve the title Carpetbagger. My point here is that intelligence is one of the few present-day academic subjects that one can teach about at the college level as an expert and yet have no practical experience of. One needs never to have held a security clearance, worked overseas in an official capacity (which means living undercover), crafted a written product for policy makers based on all-source analysis, recruited or run an asset, made sense of imagery or signals intelligence, or briefed a policy maker.

In his own way, Smith is as much a piece of work as Barry Blenkinsop. Both, while working as intelligence educators, are doing great harm to students' understanding of intelligence as it really is, and by extension to the intelligence profession. The crucial difference is that the type represented by Blenkinsop must fail because of his own nature. He is an intelligence professional, a man of action, who is unsuited for the world of ideas and academic institutions and processes, and any academic system will tend to reject him as a body rejects a transplanted organ that is not a match for the host. Smith, by contrast, is a man of ideas, a natural-born citizen of academia who understands it and thrives in it, even though the substance of his scholarly work is mostly nonsense and his ideas are generally bad ones.

Clearly, what is needed is an intelligence educator who is *both* academic *and* practitioner, a man (or woman) of action *and* ideas, certainly neither a Knuckle-Dragger nor a Carpetbagger, in other words.

THE PERICLEAN IDEAL FOR INTELLIGENCE EDUCATION

Pericles, the great Athenian statesman and general of the fifth century BC, is an appropriate inspiration or icon for the ideal intelligence educator I have in mind. The quintessential man of both action and ideas, Pericles was, on the ideas or academic side, a political leader, constitutional reformer, and visionary, while remaining a practitioner as a diplomat, strategist, and military commander.[18]

"Periclean ideal" sounds nobler than "amphibian," but that works, too: a man or woman who swims in both worlds, at home in either milieu, respected by former intelligence colleagues as a professional among professionals while also excelling at meeting all the challenges posed by academia, whether they be intellectual, administrative, or personal. I envision a man or woman of action *and* thought, whose patience with students, fellow professors, and academic bureaucrats knows no bounds; whose knowledge of intelligence and eloquence in conveying its realities is unexcelled; whose conduct is unreproachable; and whose contributions to intelligence education are unquestioned.

To illustrate this Periclean ideal, I offer not a fictional creature but an actual Pericles, a real-life example: James Olson of Texas A&M University. The label "legendary" is used too much in all walks of life, especially in intelligence, but Olson is truly a legendary CIA operations officer.

During his thirty-one-year CIA career, Olson was famous for audacious operations like TAW, which involved tapping a communications cable under the streets of Moscow.[19] He had successful operational tours in several countries, including as chief of station, with proficiency in five foreign languages. He also served as the CIA's chief of CI. Many consider analysis the most cerebral of the elements of intelligence, but insiders know that CI is also highly cognitive, and perhaps outdoes analysis in its regard for history. Spies are not caught without sustained heavy thinking and close attention to the smallest detail. Olson was highly decorated for his intelligence work.

Olson is a very smart man. With degrees in mathematics, economics, and law (and a member of the Iowa Bar), and with his operational experience and leadership, Olson was an inspired choice when then CIA director George Tenet asked him to make the transition to academia as a CIA OIR in 1997. He started a highly popular intelligence program at the Bush School of Government at Texas A&M, where he became a permanent faculty member. In his twenty-three years as a successful academic, Olson has published two highly regarded books, both indispensable in the study of intelligence: *Fair Play: The Moral Dilemmas of Spying* (2006) and *To Catch a Spy: The Art of Counterintelligence* (2019). He has won awards at A&M for his teaching, and he is in high demand as a speaker at universities and at intelligence-related forums alike. I believe that no other intelligence educator is so highly regarded both by intelligence professionals and the academic world.[20]

It's obvious that intelligence education needs more Jim Olsons. Where do we find them?

The Pericles Project: A Proposal for a "Service of Common Concern"

Toward the goal of producing more intelligence educators in the Pericles line, I propose that the IC, under the leadership of the director of national intelligence, commit to a "Pericles Project," to be undertaken by the CIA's Center for the Study of Intelligence (CSI) as an IC "service of common concern." It would improve and expand upon the old OIR program and replace the ongoing Visiting Intelligence Officer Program (VIOP).

The CSI, I believe, is best positioned to identify IC officers as potential intelligence educators and to develop them. The CSI is often considered the CIA's "internal think tank," but it is more broadly a resource for the IC and for the American public at large. It is the home of the professional journal *Studies in Intelligence*, which publishes classified articles for the IC and unclassified articles for intelligence scholars and the public at large. The CSI supports several staffs, including the CIA History Staff, that research and publish on the intelligence profession. For some twenty-five years, the CSI managed the OIR program, and CIA historians (like me) helped prepare CIA officers going to universities as OIRs.

The OIR program had its flaws, some of which are illustrated in the fictional representation of Barry Blenkinsop. The CSI had responsibility for but little authority over the program, leading to the unfortunate inclusion of a few CIA officers who were unsuitable as educators. Since the officer's home component sponsored the individual and paid his or her salary while at the university, the CSI had little influence in the selection and vetting of OIR candidates. Another shortcoming was that OIRs came exclusively from the

CIA workforce. The bigger problem, to my mind, was that, while many OIRs stayed at their assigned universities as adjuncts and lecturers, very few OIRs became full-time professors and directors of intelligence studies programs, so their influence on the overall content of intelligence programs was slight.

The CIA ended the OIR program about ten years ago; among the reasons for its demise was the perceived flaw that OIRs tended to be senior officers who retired in place.[21] (The real flaw was that the program failed to have as its proper aim the placing of more practitioners in intelligence education.) In the fall of 2018, the CIA created the VIOP, which puts "resident intelligence officers" (RIOs) at certain universities, starting with the University of Texas at Austin, to teach and to provide assistance to the CIA's recruiting efforts.[22] RIOs tend to be younger than the OIRs were and are expected to return to the CIA. This program is also limited to the CIA.

The Pericles Project would scrap the CIA's VIOP and any similar individual agency program in favor of an IC-wide approach to place suitable senior intelligence professionals as resident IC officers (RICOs) at universities with the primary goal of teaching intelligence and then remaining at that university after retirement from government service. The Pericles Project would have three echelons, working on essentially parallel tracks, to ensure that officers selected as RICOs, in addition to having deep backgrounds in intelligence, will have the academic credentials and knowledge to thrive in university settings and ultimately help transform intelligence education.[23]

The first echelon would focus on career intelligence officers who already have their doctoral degrees. The CSI would work with the human resources departments of the various IC agencies to identify existing PhDs in each workforce, evaluate their suitability (based on their dissertation subjects, their career experiences, and whether they had teaching experience at the college level), and then issue invitations to selected IC officers to apply as RICO candidates for the Pericles Project. Obviously, the Director of National Intelligence (DNI) would have to grant the CSI broad authority to gather information and evaluate candidates. IC officers who accepted CSI's invitation would then spend three to six months in residence at the CSI to secure their university assignments and prepare them for deployment as RICOs.

Most of the CSI's instruction for outgoing RICOs would be conducted by the CIA History Staff, which not only taught selectees in the former OIR program but also has the highest concentration of any CIA component of officers who teach in local universities and who also lecture frequently at universities in the United States and the United Kingdom. CIA historians, perhaps augmented by detailees on rotation from other IC agency history staffs, would identify published and online resources for teaching intelligence and would help RICOs craft their courses, utilizing the History Staff's archive of intelligence course syllabi and the historians' own teaching experiences.

In the second tier of the Pericles Project, the CSI would identify promising intelligence educators among that set of IC officers who do not have PhDs but who are close (or "ABD"). Using the suitability criteria similar to those of the first echelon, the CSI could provide selected candidates in this echelon with a year to eighteen months' residency to restart PhD programs if necessary, finish dissertations, receive their doctorates, and prepare for RICO deployment. Anecdotally, over my twenty-six-year career I found within the CIA that there were about as many ABDs as PhDs, perhaps more; these officers do not complete their doctorates usually because of the press of their professional lives and family responsibilities. In the work-life balance, the PhD is often the first casualty. The Pericles Project would exploit this valuable but untapped resource.

The third echelon of the project would involve identifying high-potential intelligence educators among IC officers who have master's degrees but need assistance in doing a doctoral program at one of the many fine universities in the Washington, DC, area. The CSI would provide three years' part-time residency (perhaps as an intern for the History Staff) while doing the course work, orals, and dissertation. A precedent for this approach is the "20/20" program the CIA offered at one time: twenty hours per week in the office, twenty hours devoted to academic work. Even if some of these candidates did not achieve the PhD in the appointed time, they might still qualify as a RICO, depending on the university.

The Pericles Project should appeal to everyone who truly cares about the state of intelligence education. Thoughtful practitioners and honest academics alike should agree that this approach would help bridge the divide and, more important, improve the teaching of intelligence across the board. The Knuckle-Draggers and the Carpetbaggers won't like it, of course. Knuckle-Draggers like Barry Blenkinsop will lose their chance at end-of-career assignments that do little except make all practitioners look bad. Carpetbaggers like Winks Smith will object because practitioners eminently qualified to teach will tend to expose their fraudulence.

The Office of the DNI should persuade the House and Senate oversight committees to provide the necessary funding, and the DNI should be prepared to defend the Pericles Project from specious objections that it constitutes an unwarranted influence of the IC over the American public. The specter of "brainwashing" will be raised. The DNI and the IC should take the high road, arguing that the program will improve intelligence education at the university level, enhance the public's understanding of intelligence, boost the quality of candidates for employment in the IC, and therefore ultimately serve US national security interests.

I will close with the words of Pericles, who summarized the qualities a statesman needs to have, because these qualities are also needed in our intelligence educators: "to know what must be done and to be able to explain it; to love one's country and to be incorruptible."[24]

NOTES

1. Nicholas Dujmović, "Colleges Must Be Intelligent about Intelligence Studies," *Washington Post*, December 30, 2016, https://www.washingtonpost.com/news /grade-point/wp/2016/12/30/colleges-must-be-intelligent-about-intelligence-studies. See also my contribution to a special compendium on the teaching of intelligence, Nicholas Dujmović, "Less Is More, and More Professional: Reflections on Building an 'Ideal' Intelligence Program," *Intelligence and National Security* 32, no. 7 (2017): 935–43, and finally my "point/counterpoint" treatment, Jorhena Thomas and Nicholas Dujmović, "Educators Consider Alternative Approaches to US College Intelligence Programs," *Studies in Intelligence* 63, no. 4 (2019): 17–21.

2. Nicholas Dujmović, "Hollywood: Don't You Go Disrespectin' My Culture: The Good Shepherd versus Real CIA History," *Intelligence and National Security* 23, no. 1 (February 2008): 25–41.

3. Among countless examples is the 2006 disclosure by the *New York Times* that US intelligence monitored a financial transaction database as a counterterrorism measure. Michael Hayden has persuasively argued that the disclosure was politically motivated: Michael V. Hayden, *Playing to the Edge* (New York: Penguin, 2016), 117–18.

4. Nicholas Dujmović, "Reflections on the 'Deep State' Myth," contribution to a special compendium on US intelligence officers' involvement in politics in the Trump era, John A. Gentry, ed., "An INS Special Forum: US Intelligence Officers' Involvement in Political Activities in the Trump Era," *Intelligence and National Security* 35, no. 1 (2020): 1–19 (at 5–6).

5. Nicholas Dujmović, "Elegy of Slashes: A Review of *Legacy of Ashes: The History of the CIA*," *Studies in Intelligence* 51, no. 3 (September 2007): 33–43.

6. Michael Warner, "Wanted: A Definition of 'Intelligence,'" *Studies in Intelligence* 46, no. 3 (2002): 15–21.

7. Dujmović, "Less Is More."

8. Ashenden is the fictional British intelligence officer created by former British intelligence officer Somerset Maugham in his classic collection of spy stories; W. Somerset Maugham, *Ashenden, or The British Agent* (London: Heinemann, 1928).

9. That is the case with the intelligence certificate program (functionally a minor) I direct at Catholic University. The certificate comprises six courses overall (eighteen credits), with three required intelligence courses—the same as Ashenden's "major." A crucial difference is that Certified Usability Analyst certificate students don't settle

for the three intelligence courses to round out the certificate but typically take advantage of other intelligence-specific offerings, such as a US CI course taught by the FBI's historian, a cyber intelligence course taught by a former senior NSA official, and a forthcoming analysis course taught by a former CIA senior analyst. The fact that this is a certificate allows students interested in intelligence to avoid the opportunity costs of not majoring in substantive fields sought by the CIA and other agencies.

10. Richard Helms, with William Hood, *A Look over My Shoulder: A Life in the Central Intelligence Agency* (New York: Random House, 2003), 237.

11. Any relation between the pseudonyms I've selected and actual persons with those names is entirely accidental.

12. Telephone interview with Professor Scott McIntosh of Newman University, July 2, 2020.

13. The Newman program, to my mind, has some shortcomings beyond the fact that it is a degree-granting major, which I believe disadvantages students who apply for intelligence jobs. The operational and historical aspects of covert action are covered too briefly in the introductory course. Overall, the content is too skewed toward military applications, and the course work is 100 percent online to accommodate nontraditional and deployed students. For credibility among academics, it would help if the program director had a PhD (though, happily, he is working on it) and if the program itself were not based in the School of Business. But these are minor issues compared to the welcome range of intelligence topics covered.

14. My comparative analysis of two universities' intelligence programs is understandably inadequate, though I think it's useful to illustrate the point that experience seems to matter when it comes to content. Of course, someone ought to survey all undergraduate intelligence programs at US colleges and universities, subjecting them to the same scrutiny (and using my standards, naturally). That someone, alas, won't be me, as I am nearing the end of my career as an intelligence academic (cue the cheers from those who consider me a troublemaker), and I look forward to the life of a fully retired practitioner.

15. An intelligence officer named Blenkinsop is the main character in former British Secret Intelligence Service officer Compton Mackenzie's classic spoof on intelligence, *Water on the Brain* (London: Cassell, 1933).

16. For several years while I was on the CIA History Staff, I was actively engaged in helping prepare CIA officers selected for the OIR program, discussing with them suitable resources, making past syllabi available, and trying to convey the idea that this was going to be more work than they imagined. For an institutional perspective, see John Hedley, "Twenty Years of Officers in Residence," *Studies in Intelligence* 49, no. 4 (2005): 31–39.

17. Those of us on the practitioner side who go to academic conferences and hear presentations on intelligence from academics with little or no experience often find ourselves shaking our heads.

18. Donald Kagan, *Pericles of Athens and the Birth of Democracy: The Triumph of Vision in Leadership* (New York: Simon & Schuster, 1991), esp. 65–66. A survey of the literature on Ancient Greece indicates that the term "Periclean ideal" has dozens of different meanings, but here I use it somewhat simplistically to indicate a person

who, like Pericles, could both think and act, or, in modern jargon, "walk the talk." As John Stuart Mill observed in chapter 3 of *On Liberty* (1859), "It may be better to be a John Knox than an Alcibiades, but it is better to be a Pericles than either."

19. TAW and Olson's involvement in it are documented in various sources, including Milton Bearden and James Risen, *The Main Enemy* (New York: Random House, 2003), 28–29 passim; and Robert Wallace and Keith Melton, *Spycraft: The Secret History of the CIA's Spytechs from Communism to Al-Qaeda* (New York: Dutton/Penguin, 2009), chapter 11, "An Operation Called CKTAW," in which Jim Olsen is called "Ken."

20. Another example of a Periclean ideal for intelligence education was the late Art Hulnick, a respected CIA senior analyst who made a distinguished career in academia at Boston University. His accomplishments as a practitioner and academic can be found at https://www.bu.edu/pardeeschool/2018/04/18/rip-prof-arthur-s-hulnick.

21. An early OIR program document asserted, "The Agency benefits the most when an officer returns to work after a campus assignment," but in the life of the program the majority of OIRs were at the end of their careers. See Office of Training and Education memorandum of October 1989, at www.cia.gov/library/readingroom/docs/DOC_0000591813.pdf.

22. See, for example, the *Daily Texan* of the University of Texas at Austin, October 23, 2018, https://thedailytexan.com/2018/10/23/alan-kessler-is-uts-first-cia-resident-intelligence-officer-lbj-school-professor. I'm also indebted to Dr. Peter Usowski, current director of the CSI; telephone interview, July 15, 2020.

23. The Pericles Project would focus on equipping professionals going into intelligence education with PhDs because the doctorate, whether we like it or not, is greatly helpful where it is not essential in education. Sure, many practitioners in education, like Jim Olson (Pericles himself), do not have a PhD, but he is exceptional. Many university departments, like my own, are shortsighted in requiring even adjuncts to have doctorates. Most universities do seem to allow for "professors of practice" with lesser degrees. In all environments, however, the PhD lends both credibility and experience in academic perseverance, both of which practitioners really should have before stepping into the cruel world of academia.

24. As quoted by Thucydides, in Kagan, *Pericles of Athens*, 9.

4

Intelligence, Science, and the Ignorance Hypothesis

David R. Mandel

Intelligence organizations perform many functions. For example, they conduct covert operations that would be too politically sensitive for militaries to undertake as explicit missions. They also collect vast amounts of data that are inaccessible to others, except perhaps other intelligence organizations. However, the principal purpose of information collection is to produce substantive intelligence that can inform policy makers, commanders, and other decision makers who guard their nation's interests and security. The fundamental premise of intelligence is that it serves to improve the planning and decision making of these elite decision makers by elevating the debate about policy options.[1] If this were not so, the multibillion-dollar annual budgets would not be justified. If the premise is justified, then clearly the intellectual rigor and accuracy with which intelligence assessments are produced is of paramount importance.

How do intelligence organizations ensure that the intelligence assessments they produce are as accurate and sound as they can be? In this chapter, I will propose that the short answer is "not very well at all." Methods and policies for ensuring analytic rigor have surely been implemented over the past several decades, but what has been endemic to these efforts is a rather prescientific, if not a fully antiscientific, attitude toward their development and testing. After reviewing some examples of intelligence practices intended to ensure analytic rigor, I advance what I call the *ignorance hypothesis* to explain the absence of scientific attempts to discern what practices work from those that do not work so that intelligence organizations can effectively learn and adapt to the challenges of the modern world. At face value, the ignorance hypothesis proposes that the absence of adequate scientific testing of analytic policies and practices is due primarily to widespread ignorance of scientific principles and values, within both intelligence and policy communities. At a deeper level, however, the ignorance hypothesis posits that there is also something special about the topic of analytic rigor that makes it especially impervious to scientific thinking. Before turning to these "why" questions, I must first at least sketch what intelligence communities are aware of vis-à-vis analytic rigor and what types of institutional responses they have offered. In so doing, I will focus on the US context, although the general points also apply to other intelligence communities.

INTELLIGENCE ANALYSIS AS CORRUPTIBLE HUMAN JUDGMENT

In spite of the vast and impressive technologies brought to bear on collections challenges, intelligence organizations rely almost exclusively on human analysts to make the judgments that constitute finished intelligence. Likewise, the same analysts have considerable leeway in deciding how to express those judgments to their target audiences. As Sherman Kent aptly noted, substantive intelligence is largely human judgment made under conditions of uncertainty.[2] Among the most important assessments are those that not only concern unknowns but also potentially unknowables, such as the partially formed intentions of a leader in an adversarial state. In such cases, the primary task of the analyst is not to state what will happen but to accurately assess the probabilities of alternative possibilities as well as the degree of error in the assessments and to give clear explanations for the basis of such assessments.[3]

Intelligence communities are certainly not unaware of the problems inherent in human judgment under uncertainty. Maverick figures like Sherman Kent pioneered methods for improving the communication of uncertainty in assessments, and Richards Heuer Jr. not only summarized a great deal of relevant cognitive research for the US intelligence community in his 1999 book *Psychology of Intelligence Analysis*, but he also pioneered several of the structured analytic techniques (SATs) that are still used by intelligence communities to this day.[4] Indeed, it is common knowledge in intelligence organizations that humans are fallible and corruptible in many ways. They are often unreliable and/or systematically biased because the "fast" cognitive processes or "heuristics" they have been biologically adapted to use in prehistory are error prone under given conditions.[5] For example, when judging how frequent one event class is compared to another, humans often rely on the *availability heuristic*—namely, the ease with which instances in each event class come to mind.[6] Thus, judgments of frequency will be influenced by factors affecting mental availability, such as advertising, social media, and, yes, "fake news," which were not biasing factors in human prehistory.

In a similar vein, intelligence communities are generally aware that probability, which is so central to intelligence assessments, is often judged using the *representativeness heuristic*—namely, the process of assigning probability based on how well individuating information seems to match alternative hypotheses.[7] Thus, humans often fail to consider how influential the prior probabilities of the alternative hypotheses are on the posterior probabilities they are judging, except when the prior probabilities serve as anchors, in which case humans tend to be overly "conservative," which in the present context means they do not react fast enough to new and diagnostic information.[8] This can cause them not only to be inaccurate, but also to be incoherent, such as when they judge a representative conjunction of two events, *A* and *B*, to be more likely than one alone—namely, what is known as the *conjunction fallacy*.[9]

What is more, however, the cognitive biases to which humans (including intelligence analysts!) are susceptible are not easily self-detected. When humans are overconfident, they tend to believe that they are right, but they are unlikely to believe (accurately) that they are overconfident. Psychologists call the inaccessibility to one's own cognitive biases the *bias blind spot*.[10] This "meta-bias" does not appear to be attenuated by greater cognitive sophistication and may in fact be correlated with intelligence, or at least markers of intelligence such as academic success.[11] Moreover, any benefit of training aimed at debiasing the bias blind spot seems to decay rapidly.[12] Stated plainly, people lack self-awareness of many, and probably most, of their cognitive biases. This ignorance state would be bad enough if it were a Rumsfeldian "unknown unknown"—namely, "mere" ignorance of the nature and severity of one's cognitive biases. However, cognition (i.e., reasoning and judgment), the central tool of the analyst, remains more akin to what Rumsfeld called the "unknown known" at the beginning of his interview with Errol Morris in Morris's 2013 documentary on the former US secretary of state.[13] The unknown known refers to something one thinks one knows to be true that turns out to be false. Not only do humans fail to detect their cognitive biases, but they are quite convinced that such biases do not pose a problem for their thinking and deciding. Much as humans are adapted for cognitive bias, they are also biologically adapted for self-deception, which facilitates their ability to deceive others.[14]

The problems associated with "cold" cognitive biases are compounded by "hot" motivational biases,[15] which can corrupt the integrity of intelligence production. Intelligence analysts might find it difficult to follow the mantra of "speaking truth to power" when the views of the powerful are known in advance and the powerful themselves are not known for their open accommodation of dissenting analysis. This applies to analysts in relation to intelligence directors and to analysts and directors in relation to their intelligence clients. Accountability pressures in response to career-influencing audiences can trigger defensive bolstering of assessments or preemptive self-criticism, both of which are extra-evidentiary psychological processes aimed at minding one's reputation as an "intuitive politician" rather than focusing on achieving the most accurate, well-calibrated assessments possible under the circumstances.[16] Perhaps this is why, although overconfidence is a well-documented bias,[17] strategic intelligence forecasts systematically examined over several consecutive years have been found to be substantially *underconfident*.[18] That is, even accurate forecasts tended to be communicated as a series of watered-down, hedge-filled estimates, and this was after a considerable proportion of the forecasts were excluded because of their reliance on unverifiable weasel words. Given that there is far more to lose by overconfidently asserting claims that prove to be false than by underconfidently making claims that prove to be true, intelligence organizations are likely motivated to make timid forecasts that water down information value to decision makers—a play-it-safe strategy that anticipates unwelcome entry into the political blame games that punctuate history.[19]

Of course, the cold/hot dichotomy is closer to a rhetorical device than a scientific fact. The truth is that all products of judgment are the result of cognitive processes undergirded by biochemical mechanisms. "Hot" and "cold" are useful metaphors insofar as they help us categorize human judgment and reasoning biases into "motivated" and "unmotivated" types. The types described as motivated, however, can vary greatly in their emotional intensity and goal directedness. For example, the underconfidence caused by strategically shrouding assessments in more uncertainty than required is "lukewarm" compared to the "fiery" political biases that some former intelligence directors and senior staff members exhibit toward their political opponents. As Gentry notes, the anti-Trump diatribes of former Central Intelligence Agency director John Brennan, former Federal Bureau of Investigation director James Comey, and former Office of the Director of National Intelligence (ODNI) director James Clapper provide recent examples.[20] In such cases, the pursuit of truth and objectivity is sacrificed in favor of ends-justify-the-means tactics of "intuitive theologians," who are often firmly convinced that they are on the right side of history. If the gravitational centers of power in such organizations hold overtly biased and uncertainty-intolerant views of the world, how can the organizations they lead possibly be expected to guide decision makers to truthful, objective information about a complex world?

UNTESTED STEPS

Given that intelligence organizations principally rely on humans to produce substantive intelligence, and given the predisposition of humans to exhibit a wide range of cognitive and motivational biases, what have such organizations done to mitigate bias, and what have they done to verify whether their adopted methods are effective? In the United States, the strategy taken to deal with this immense challenge has been to issue vague process directives that aim to promote the fuzzy concept of "analytic integrity." Specifically, ODNI's Intelligence Community Directive 203 (ICD 203) admonishes all US analysts to provide assessments that are "objective," "independent of political consideration," "timely," and "based on all available sources of intelligence information," and the analyst must further ensure that he or she "implements and exhibits Analytic Tradecraft Standards," which include (1) "properly describ[ing] quality and reliability of underlying sources"; (2) "properly caveat[ing] and express[ing] uncertainties or confidence in analytic judgments"; (3) "properly distinguish[ing] between underlying intelligence and analysts' assumptions and judgments"; (4) "incorporat[ing] alternative analysis where appropriate"; (5) "demonstrat[ing] relevance to U.S. national security"; (6) "us[ing] logical argumentation"; (7) "exhibit[ing] consistency of analysis over time, or highlight[ing] changes and explain[ing] rationale"; and (8) "mak[ing] accurate judgments and assessments."[21]

On the surface, who can object to such directives? Indeed, when a sample of over one hundred Canadian intelligence professionals (who are not mandated to follow ICD 203) was asked how strongly they valued such principles, each principle was strongly endorsed. Moreover, professionals who judged their organizations to be more compliant with these principles reported being more satisfied with their jobs as well as more affectively and normatively committed to their organizations.[22] This is all well and good, but how do intelligence organizations actually promote the achievement of these aspirational principles, and how do they objectively measure how well each is met? Since the criteria are vague, it is unsurprising that individual raters' evaluations of how well an analytic product meets the ICD 203 criteria are unreliable.[23] How, for instance, does ODNI measure objectivity? Is objectivity to be measured objectively through correspondence measures such as proper scoring rules for forecasts, subjectively by analyst self-assessments or director evaluations, or intersubjectively, for example, through consensus-seeking feedback from a group of peer experts? With rare exceptions,[24] intelligence organizations do not score their assessments using objective measures such as proper scoring rules (e.g., "Brier scores"). Therefore, the directive to "be objective" is either subjectively or intersubjectively assessed, to the extent that it is assessed at all. Self-reflection and peer evaluation may each have beneficial effects on analytic practice, but neither constitutes a valid basis for gauging objectivity. One can hardly expect skeptical analysts to take objectivity seriously if the only way the requirement for objectivity is assessed is through subjective or intersubjective measures. If the intelligence community's approach to objectivity is questionable, the directive to remain independent of political consideration is laughable. How can analysts or observers of the intelligence community take such statements seriously when the political biases of former directors are put on stark display?[25] Is it likely that the overt political biases they routinely exhibit upon taking up media commentator roles after their retirements were all but absent just a short time before when they were powerful directors? Would analysts working under them fail to notice?

As noted earlier, a related strategy for promoting analytic integrity is to advise analysts to use SATs. The "philosophy" behind SATs is that analysts cannot be trusted to reason in ways that would uphold the ICD 203 criteria, and therefore they need to be aided by techniques that should debias their judgments and improve the reliability and accuracy of their assessments. Most SATs, however, lack a sound philosophical or scientific basis in development and testing. Coveted SATs such as Heuer's analysis of competing hypotheses (ACH) approach,[26] which are taught to analysts in several countries, are dubious from the start. For instance, ACH guides analysts to evaluate each piece of evidence independently of all other pieces of evidence against each hypothesis. While "independent assessment" might sound positive, it militates against reasoning about the significance of configural fact patterns that provide keys to mysteries, which a process of evaluating each fact on its own would fail to reveal. Siloing evidence into distinct pieces to be evaluated separately can also militate against proper consideration of correlational structure in evidence. Karvetski, Mandel, and Irwin found that when two perfectly correlated sources of evidence presented in a hypothesis-testing task were made highly salient, participants who used ACH were more likely to double count (rather than discount) the second, redundant source than when the redundancies were less salient.[27] Rather than correcting for redundancy, which a normative (e.g., Bayesian) approach would require, ACH amplified the mishandling of redundancy. ACH also assumes that evidence that is deemed to be consistent with a hypothesis should be given no weight in the calculation of support for alternative hypotheses. Rather, support is treated as an inverse function of the frequency of inconsistent evidence for a given hypothesis. As I have suggested elsewhere,[28] the rationale for this counter-normative information integration rule may have stemmed from Heuer's interpretation of Sir Karl Popper's theory of falsification.[29] However, Popper's theory does not apply to nonuniversal hypotheses of the sort that intelligence analysts routinely deal with. "All swans are white" exemplifies the type of hypothesis Popper was addressing. No matter how many white swans one observes, it cannot prove the universal hypothesis to be true. However, finding a single nonwhite swan is sufficient to conclusively disprove the hypothesis.

Hypotheses in intelligence are neither about universals (i.e., "All *x* are *y*"), nor is the evidence brought to bear on the evaluation of such hypotheses invariably unambiguous, such as whether a swan is white or not.

Given the conceptual failings of ACH, it is perhaps unsurprising that experiments testing its effectiveness have revealed disappointing results. Whitesmith found no evidence to suggest that ACH reduces cognitive biases or improves judgment accuracy.[30] Mandel, Karvetski, and Dhami found that intelligence analysts who were trained in and instructed to use ACH on a hypothesis-testing task were significantly less coherent in their judgments than analysts who were not trained in ACH and not asked to use any SAT in the task.[31] In follow-up analyses from the same sample, the same authors found that analysts using ACH were less likely to use relevant base-rate information than analysts who did not use ACH.[32] Karvetski et al. found that participants asked to judge the probability of alternative hypotheses being true were less accurate after using ACH than they were prior to using it.[33] Karvetski and Mandel found that participants who used ACH were, in multiple respects, less coherent in their judgments than participants who did not use the technique.

The preceding comments could easily lead one to believe that, while ACH is problematic, the overall SAT approach may be sound. Unfortunately, this is not so. Closer examination of other SATs reveals serious conceptual limitations. For instance, the SAT that Heuer and Pherson called indicators validator,[34] which is used for determining information collection priorities, has no basis in information theory and has been shown by Timms, Mandel, and Nelson to lead to collection recommendations that run counter to normative models of information utility, in part due to its neglect of relevant base-rate information.[35] More generally, the problem is that the intelligence community does not appear to have sufficiently drawn on relevant areas of science or philosophy in the idea-generation phases of SAT development, nor has it utilized scientific methods to test whether the SATs they recommend that analysts use actually improve intelligence analysis one iota. This lack of scientific rigor persists despite many calls over the years for proper scientific attention to the development of methods for intelligence analysis.[36]

To be fair, over the last decade, the US intelligence community, through ODNI's Intelligence Advanced Research Programs Activity (IARPA), has invested vast sums of money into programs aimed at improving intelligence analysis through funded research conducted by academic institutions and industries. This is a positive development and, in some sense, a valid response to calls for better scientific engagement. On smaller scales, some other intelligence communities are probably doing likewise. However, what remains unclear is how the new research is influencing intelligence training, current on-the-job practices, and executive-level plans to address the yawning gap between the status quo and optimal intelligence practice. From extensive discussions with tradecraft experts in several countries over more than a decade now, I have never gotten a sense that the status quo is being fundamentally transformed. Nor, as I have argued elsewhere, has the IARPA model proven to be a good model for the intelligence community's challenges.[37] While it beneficially shifts focus from overreliance on "occasional mavericks" like Kent and Heuer to programmatic applied research, it is also limited by its high-risk/high-reward mandate and a contractual process that locks funded research teams into the equivalent of scientific straitjackets. In this sense, IARPA has not fulfilled Rieber and Thomason's call for a "National Institute for Analytic Methods"[38] because it does not routinely empirically test in randomly controlled trials the methods that analysts in the intelligence community are instructed to use. Yet that is precisely what is needed to separate the wheat from the chaff—namely, to know what works and what doesn't. Intelligence organizations should be routinely performing such tests of their methods and adapting their analytic practices in response to the evidence they collect. They should also be tracking scientific research that directly tests the effectiveness of their methods, such as the several studies cited earlier, and they should be tracking developments in research fields, such as the cognitive and decision sciences, which have good prospects for informing the development of new analytic methods.[39]

IARPA programs are also often launched as tournaments between competing "performer" teams that are scored roughly annually for the purpose of winnowing the performers. The tournament ends with a single winner, while the rest are presumably "losers." This process distorts the value of the funded research by making the winner's contributions appear more important than they actually are and the losers' contributions correspondingly less important. In reality, most teams will conduct research of value, and the differences in practical value to the intelligence community may be marginal, just as the difference between Olympic gold and silver medalists in a race can be a fraction of a second. Uncertainty is a key facet of all scientific research, and scientists should highlight the limitations of their research, which might cast doubt on the reliability and validity of their findings. However, "performing" for funders incentivizes masking uncertainties and instead telling the most compelling narrative possible about the findings. Science aims to disentangle multiple causes of focal effects, yet it is in the interest of performers to bundle as many possibly effective tactics into a brand in the hope that some subset of these tactics will eke out a victory. One could hardly blame the victors for this. It would be naive to think that scientists do not act as intuitive politicians too.[40]

THE IGNORANCE HYPOTHESIS REVISITED

The intelligence community is aware that human judgment is central to intelligence production and that judgment is highly susceptible to cognitive and motivational biases, unreliability, imprecision, and ultimately error. Furthermore, it has taken steps to improve analytic rigor in day-to-day practices by implementing community-wide directives on analytic integrity and by training analysts to use SATs and then encouraging them to use them on the job. However, most of these endeavors are of questionable value because they have not been tested to verify if they work as intended. The same can be said of the intelligence community's methods for communicating uncertainty to end users, which are based on the untenable assumption that the meaning of vague verbal probability terms can simply be stipulated by organizational fiat.[41] Ample research,[42] including on uncertainty communication methods used in intelligence production,[43] have shown that such attempts at establishing meaning by decree are ineffective, yet intelligence communities have doubled down on these methods in many cases, such as in the United States and United Kingdom, turning them into community-wide reporting requirements.[44]

Why have intelligence communities not done a better job of drawing on science to develop methods for effective intelligence production, and why have they not also drawn on well-established research methods for testing their best ideas in order to determine what works and what doesn't? As noted earlier, the ignorance hypothesis posits that the "experts" tasked with improving the quality of judgment in intelligence are not steeped deeply enough in scientific culture. They are unfamiliar with basic scientific concepts and lack sufficient knowledge about substantive areas of scientific research that are pertinent to improving judgment quality. They do not have the scientific tools at their disposal to approach the challenges they face with the requisite degree of skepticism. The experts tasked with making methodological improvements to intelligence practice typically don't want to get "down in the weeds" about research aimed at testing their preferred solutions. In all likelihood, their organizations provide them with no formal support mechanisms for such research even if they wanted it, and some may very well want it.

However, I doubt that most do. The likelier scenario is that most do not approach the task from a scientific frame of reference at all. Rather, they are likely to perceive their task as deciding what to borrow from existing methods and then deciding whether they want to adapt the methods in some number of ways to make it more sensible, useful, or facile. In this process, they rely primarily, if not exclusively, on their "best judgment," which in practice means what they believe to be true or at least what they judge to be plausible. They may synthesize elaborate explanations of why a particular SAT is useful in training or why another isn't, but these explanations are meant to stand on their own; they are not treated as working hypotheses that give rise to necessary experimental tests of their validity. If challenged on the effectiveness of the methods they propose, they might cite anecdotal evidence to support their decisions, not realizing that such evidence is of low reliability, validity, and demonstrable generalizability.

Scientists also have beliefs about what is right and wrong. They formulate theories and hypotheses, but these must then be tested under controlled procedures that enable valid inference to be drawn from the test data. Moreover, if a test is designed in such a way that is biased in favor of the hypothesis, peer reviewers may challenge it. If the researchers nevertheless manage to publish it without correcting the flaws, other researchers may challenge it by designing better experiments and publishing their results, and these may cast doubt on the validity of the original research and its findings. Certainly, in practice, the system is not optimally self-correcting. However, it is the best system for knowledge generation that has ever been invented by our species.[45]

The flaws in virtually all of the organizational interventions I have mentioned remain undetected by the intelligence community precisely because they do not apply a scientific lens to the problem or to their proposed solutions. For scientists, the reliability and validity of tests and measures is of paramount importance. Thus, it is natural for scientists such as Marcoci et al. to ask how reliable the scoring of analytic products is on ICD 203—can it be done?[46] It is not merely that asking such questions is important. One must know how to translate those questions into experimental tests that are likely to yield test data from which one can draw valid inferences. Doing so requires considerable knowledge of research methodology, which most tradecraft experts I have encountered do not possess.

If those in charge of minding the system of intelligence production are not scientifically minded, as the ignorance hypothesis posits, then the current state of affairs could have been anticipated. Why have those higher up the management and oversight chain not seen this coming? Is it because most directors, policy makers, and other elite decision makers are also insufficiently steeped in scientific culture to have seen the problem? If so, then why does the intelligence community draw heavily on science in other areas of interest, such as advancing collections technology? The discrepancy seems to be related to the topic. Where intelligence methods concern human affairs such as judgment and decision making and person-to-person communication, intelligence professionals seem to trust their intuitions about which methods will be beneficial and which won't. In other words, they lack skeptical prior probabilities about their skill in picking winners and avoiding dud methodologies. They will be the first to acknowledge that their solutions aren't perfect, but most I have spoken with accept the general premise that whatever they are doing is at least making the situation better. However, as noted earlier, this belief is contradicted by mounting research evidence that SATs can impede the quality of judgment.[47]

Why don't analytic tradecraft methodologists assign nonzero probabilities to the possibilities that a proposed method has no appreciable benefit or a negative benefit? If, for instance, an analyst with an educational background in Russian studies were asked to design the next-generation technology for encryption, he would probably refuse the task. If given no choice, he would surely be aware that his best efforts would probably fail. However, if the same analyst moved into a tradecraft development position, it is likely that he would believe that he could think his way through the problem space and make valuable contributions. After all, he was an analyst, and that would seem to confer a nontrivial degree of expertise. I propose that this fictional analyst's relatively optimistic attitude in the second case owes greatly to the bias blind spot discussed earlier: the analyst overestimates the degree to which his prior experience prepares him for the task of developing and testing analytic methods, and, additionally, he fails to detect that he is overestimating his pertinent knowledge.

Most people are not cryptographers and know their limits if asked to make contributions in that area. In contrast, everyone has experience in thinking and reasoning, judging, and deciding—and analysts have done so for a living, serving powerful clients. Accordingly, it may be extremely difficult for them to detect the limits of their knowledge. Those promoted to positions requiring oversight of analytic methods are likely to fall prey to what I have called the *goodness heuristic*, which specifies the following conditional rule: *If, upon mental inspection, an idea seems good, then act on it as if it were good because it probably is good.*[48] The goodness heuristic is a logical extension of Kahneman's WYSIATI principle (WYSIATI—pronounced *whiz-E-at-E*—stands for "what you see is all there is").[49] When tradecraft developers try to think of what would help analysts, they are likely to use a "positive-test strategy,"[50] recruiting ideas that form a positive match to the query, "What helps?" In WYSIATI terms, the positive attributes associated with one's idea will be "seen clearly," but the drawbacks may remain imperceptible. The goodness heuristic takes this one step further by supporting the inference that if an idea "looks" or "sounds" good, then it probably *is* good, and one should act upon it as if it is good.

However, for better or worse, reality does not bend to our misperceptions. When it comes to the promotion of analytic integrity, intelligence communities remain mired in Rumsfeldian unknown knowns, believing to be true that which is not true. Unfortunately, this had led to overly optimistic assessments of methodological success within intelligence communities and the misperception that they have ensured analytic rigor through their prescientific efforts.

NOTES

This work was supported by Canadian Safety and Security Program project CSSP-2018-TI-2394. The views expressed in this chapter are solely those of the author and do not represent the official position of Defence Research and Development Canada or other parts of the government of Canada.

1. Sherman Kent, "The Need for an Intelligence Literature," *Studies in Intelligence* 1, no. 1 (1955): 1–11.

2. Sherman Kent, "Words of Estimative Probability," *Studies in Intelligence* 8, no. 4 (1964): 49–65.

3. Jeffrey A. Friedman and Richard Zeckhauser, "Assessing Uncertainty in Intelligence," *Intelligence and National Security* 27, no. 6 (2012): 824–47; David R. Mandel and Daniel Irwin, "Uncertainty, Intelligence, and National Security Decisionmaking," *International Journal of Intelligence and CounterIntelligence* 34, no. 3 (2020): 558–82.

4. Richards J. Heuer Jr., *Psychology of Intelligence Analysis* (Washington, DC: Center for the Study of Intelligence, 1999).

5. Daniel Kahneman, *Thinking, Fast and Slow* (New York: Farrar, Straus and Giroux, 2011).

6. Amos Tversky and Daniel Kahneman, "Judgment under Uncertainty: Heuristics and Biases," *Science* 185 (1974): 1124–31.

7. Tversky and Kahneman, "Judgment under Uncertainty."

8. Ward Edwards, "Conservatism in Human Information Processing," in *Formal Representation of Human Judgment*, ed. Benjamin Kleinmuntz, 17–52 (New York: Wiley, 1968).

9. Amos Tversky and Daniel Kahneman, "Extensional versus Intuitive Reasoning: The Conjunction Fallacy in Probability Judgment," *Psychological Review* 90, no. 4 (1983): 293–315.

10. Emily Pronin, Daniel Y. Lin, and Lee Ross, "The Bias Blind Spot: Perceptions of Bias in Self versus Others," *Personality and Social Psychology Bulletin* 28, no. 3 (2002): 369–81; Irene Scopelliti et al., "Bias Blind Spot: Structure, Measurement, and Consequences," *Management Science* 61, no. 10 (2015): 2468–86.

11. Richard F. West, Russell J. Meserve, and Keith E. Stanovich, "Cognitive Sophistication Does Not Attenuate the Bias Blind Spot," *Journal of Personality and Social Psychology* 103, no. 3 (2012): 506–19.

12. Elena Bessarabova et al., "Mitigating Bias Blind Spot via a Serious Video Game," *Computers in Human Behavior* 62 (2016): 452–66.

13. Errol Morris, dir., *The Unknown Known* (2013).

14. William von Hippel and Robert Trivers, "The Evolution and Psychology of Self-Deception," *Behavioral and Brain Sciences* 34, no. 1 (2011): 1–16.

15. Ziva Kunda, "The Case for Motivated Reasoning," *Psychological Bulletin* 108, no. 3 (1990): 480–98.

16. Philip E. Tetlock, "Social Functionalist Frameworks for Judgment and Choice: Intuitive Politicians, Theologians, and Prosecutors," *Psychological Review* 109, no. 3 (2002): 451–71.

17. Sarah Lichtenstein, Baruch Fischhoff, and Lawrence D. Phillips, "Calibration of Probabilities: The State of the Art to 1980," in *Judgment under Uncertainty: Heuristics and Biases*, ed. Daniel Kahneman, Paul Slovic, and Amos Tversky, 306–34 (Cambridge: Cambridge University Press, 1982); Don A. Moore and Paul J. Healy, "The Trouble with Overconfidence," *Psychological Review* 115, no. 2 (2008): 502–17.

18. David R. Mandel and Alan Barnes, "Accuracy of Forecasts in Strategic Intelligence," *Proceedings of the National Academy of Sciences* 111, no. 30 (2014): 10984–89; David R. Mandel and Alan Barnes, "Geopolitical Forecasting Skill in Strategic Intelligence," *Journal of Behavioral Decision Making* 31, no. 1 (2018): 127–37.

19. Christopher Hood, *The Blame Game: Spin, Bureaucracy, and Self-Preservation in Government* (Princeton, NJ: Princeton University Press, 2011); Philip E. Tetlock and Barbara A. Mellers, "Intelligent Management of Intelligence Agencies: Beyond Accountability Ping-Pong," *American Psychologist* 66 (2011): 542–54.

20. John A. Gentry, "'Truth' as a Tool of the Politicization of Intelligence," *International Journal of Intelligence and CounterIntelligence* 32, no. 2 (2019): 217–47.

21. Office of the Director of National Intelligence, *Intelligence Community Directive 203: Analytic Standards*, 3–4 (Washington, DC: DNI, 2015) https://fas.org/irp /dni/icd/icd-203.pdf.

22. David R. Mandel, Tonya L. Hendriks, and Daniel Irwin, "Policy for Promoting Analytic Rigor in Intelligence: Professionals' Views and Their Psychological Correlates," *Intelligence and National Security*, October 2021, https://www.tandfonline .com/doi/full/10.1080/02684527.2021.1999621.

23. Alexandru Marcoci et al., "Better Together: Reliable Application of the Post-9/11 and Post-Iraq US Intelligence Tradecraft Standards Requires Collective Analysis," *Frontiers in Psychology* 9, article 2634 (2019): 1–9.

24. Mandel and Barnes, "Accuracy of Forecasts"; Mandel and Barnes, "Geopolitical Forecasting Skill."

25. Gentry, "'Truth' as a Tool."

26. Heuer, *Psychology of Intelligence Analysis.*

27. Christopher W. Karvetski, David R. Mandel, and Daniel Irwin, "Improving Probability Judgment in Intelligence Analysis: From Structured Analysis to Statistical Aggregation," *Risk Analysis* 40, no. 5 (2020): 1040–57.

28. David R. Mandel, "Can Decision Science Improve Intelligence Analysis?," in *Researching National Security Intelligence: Multidisciplinary Approaches*, ed. Stephen M. Coulthart, Michael Landon-Murray, and Damien Van Puyvelde, 117–40 (Washington, DC: Georgetown University Press, 2019).

29. Karl Popper, *The Logic of Scientific Discovery* (originally published in 1935 as *Logik der Forschung Verlag* by Julius Springer, Vienna, Austria; New York: Routledge, 2002).

30. Martha Whitesmith, "The Efficacy of ACH in Mitigating Serial Position Effects and Confirmation Bias in an Intelligence Analysis Scenario," *Intelligence and National Security* 34, no. 2 (2019): 225–42.

31. David R. Mandel, Christopher W. Karvetski, and Mandeep K. Dhami, "Boosting Intelligence Analysts' Judgment Accuracy: What Works, What Fails?," *Judgment and Decision Making* 13, no. 6 (2018): 607–21.

32. Mandeep K. Dhami, Ian K. Belton, and David R. Mandel, "The 'Analysis of Competing Hypotheses' in Intelligence Analysis," *Applied Cognitive Psychology* 33, no. 6 (2019): 1080–90.

33. Karvetski et al., "Improving Probability Judgment."

34. Richards J. Heuer Jr. and Randolph H. Pherson, *Structured Analytic Techniques for Intelligence Analysis* (Washington, DC: CQ Press, 2014).

35. Mark A. C. Timms, David R. Mandel, and Jonathan D. Nelson, "Applying Information Theory to Validate Commanders' Critical Information Requirements," in *Handbook of Military and Defence Operation Research*, ed. Natalie M. Scala and James P. Howard, 331–44 (Boca Raton, FL: CRC Press, 2020).

36. For example, Welton Chang, Elissabeth Berdini, David R. Mandel, and Philip E. Tetlock, "Restructuring Structured Analytic Techniques in Intelligence," *Intelligence and National Security* 33, no. 3 (2018): 337–56; Mandeep K. Dhami et al., "Improving Intelligence Analysis with Decision Science," *Perspectives on Psychological Science* 106, no. 6 (2015): 753–57; David R. Mandel and Philip E. Tetlock, "Correcting Judgment Correctives in National Security Intelligence," *Frontiers in Psychology* 9, article 2640 (2018): 1–5; Stephen Marrin, "Intelligence Analysis: Structured Methods or Intuition?," *American Intelligence Journal* 25, no. 1 (2007): 7–16; Stephen Marrin, "Training and Educating U.S. Intelligence Analysts," *International Journal of Intelligence and CounterIntelligence* 22, no. 1 (2009): 131–46; Robert Pool, *Field Evaluation in the Intelligence and Counterintelligence Context: Workshop Summary* (Washington, DC: National Academies Press, 2010).

37. David R. Mandel, "The Occasional Maverick of Analytic Tradecraft," *Intelligence and National Security* 35, no. 3 (2020): 438–43.

38. Steven Rieber and Neil Thomason, "Creation of a National Institute for Analytic Methods," *Studies in Intelligence* 49, no. 4 (2005): 71–77.

39. Mandel, "Can Decision Science Improve Intelligence Analysis?"

40. David R. Mandel and Philip E. Tetlock, "Debunking the Myth of Value-Neutral Virginity: Toward Truth in Scientific Advertising," *Frontiers in Psychology* 7, article 451 (2016): 1–5.

41. Mandeep K. Dhami and David R. Mandel, "Words or Numbers? Communicating Probability in Intelligence Analysis," *American Psychologist* 76, no. 3 (2020): 549–60; Jeffrey A. Friedman, *War and Chance: Assessing Uncertainty in International Politics* (New York: Oxford University Press, 2019).

42. David V. Budescu et al., "The Interpretation of IPCC Probabilistic Statements around the World," *Nature Climate Change* 4 (2014): 508–12.

43. Emily Ho et al., "Improving the Communication of Uncertainty in Climate Science and Intelligence Analysis," *Behavioral Science & Policy* 1, no. 2 (2015): 43–55; David R. Mandel and Daniel Irwin, "Facilitating Sender-Receiver Agreement

in Communicated Probabilities: Is It Best to Use Words, Numbers or Both?," *Judgment and Decision Making* 16, no. 2 (2021): 363–93; David R. Mandel and Daniel Irwin, "On Measuring Agreement with Numerically Bounded Linguistic Probability Schemes: A Re-analysis of Data from Wintle, Fraser, Wills, Nicholson, and Fidler (2019)," *PLoS ONE* 16, no. 3 (2021): e0248424; Bonnie C. Wintle et al., "Verbal Probabilities: *Very Likely* to Be *Somewhat* More Confusing Than Numbers," *PLoS ONE* 14, no. 4 (2019): e0213522.

44. Mandel and Irwin, "Uncertainty, Intelligence, and National Security."

45. Yuval Noah Harari, *Sapiens: A Brief History of Humankind* (New York: Harper, 2014).

46. Marcoci et al., "Better Together."

47. For example, Mandel et al., "Boosting Intelligence Analysts' Judgment"; Karvetski et al., "Improving Probability Judgment"; Christopher W. Karvetski and David R. Mandel, "Coherence of Probability Judgments from Uncertain Evidence: Does ACH Help?," *Judgment and Decision Making* 15, no. 6 (2020): 939–58; Timms et al., "Applying Information Theory."

48. Mandel, "Can Decision Science Improve Intelligence Analysis?"

49. Kahneman, *Thinking, Fast and Slow.*

50. Joshua Klayman and Young-won Ha, "Hypothesis Testing in Rule Discovery: Strategy, Structure, and Content," *Journal of Experimental Psychology: Learning, Memory, and Cognition* 15, no. 4 (1989): 596–604.

5

Intelligence and the US Army War College

The Academic-Practitioner Relationship in Professional Military Education

Genevieve Lester, James G. Breckenridge, and Thomas Spahr

The gap between theory and practice is often discussed—and bemoaned—among scholars who perceive that their contributions to the policy world are being discounted, dismissed, or deemed irrelevant. Legions of academics have discussed the growing gap between the "ivory tower" and the applied world, where important decisions are made. Some look askance at brand new political appointees tackling the problems to which scholars have dedicated their entire careers. Policy makers, on the other hand, with very little time, fear being thrust into the weeds of complicated academic arguments presented to them in arcane verbiage.

The gap varies based on the discipline and the open-mindedness of both sides of the relationship. In an ideal world, academics are pressed to do more relevant and accessible work—and learn how to communicate it to government officials—while policy makers are guided to provide access to these scholarly inputs while dealing with quick turnaround times and packed schedules.[1]

The problem—or the gap between the worlds—still has not been solved. There are a range of explanations for why this gap exists; this chapter focuses on culture and communities to frame the relationship between the academic and practitioner and the impact of this relationship on teaching strategic intelligence at the US Army War College.

This chapter explores the challenges and incentives of intelligence education and analyzes how students of professional military education (PME) can benefit from learning about this art and science. At the core of the complexity of teaching intelligence at the US Army War College is a primary question: What should the goal of teaching intelligence to senior military officers and their civilian counterparts be? This question and the answers described below engage with the confluence of institutional cultures that compose the Army War College.

Academia and the policy world each have their own cultures, hierarchies, bureaucratic processes, and incentive structures.[2] In the words of intelligence scholar Stephen Coulthart, "The differences in culture stem in part from institutional incentive systems. While academics' focus is on making contributions to the scholarly literature and knowledge, practitioners need to solve specific 'real-world' problems."[3] The Army War College has several institutional cultures operating side by side within the organization. These individual cultures share a mission, but they all possess their own career paths, incentive structures, perceptions of value and worth, and goals. The concept of cultures at variance with one another is common; the dynamics of the cultural relationship present at the Army War College are somewhat unique, perhaps because they remain unresolved. While the discussion above focuses on the academic and the policy maker, this chapter turns to a slightly different relationship: that between academics and military practitioners. The interaction of these cultures directly affects how intelligence is researched and taught at the War College, as well as how integrated it is in the common curriculum and across the enterprise. The individual dynamics are discussed in more detail below.

US ARMY WAR COLLEGE: MISSION AND COMPOSITION

The overall mission of the college is to educate senior military officers and their civilian counterparts to serve and lead at the strategic-enterprise level. Put more formally, the learning outcomes of the college are as follows:

- Think strategically and skillfully develop strategies to achieve national security objectives.
- Provide strategic context and perspective to inform and advise national-level leaders, providing sound, nuanced, and thoughtful military advice.
- Apply intellectual rigor and adaptive problem solving to multidomain, joint war fighting and enterprise-level challenges.
- Lead teams with expert knowledge and collaborate with others to provide innovative solutions to complex, unstructured problems.
- Exercise moral judgment and promote the values and ethics of the profession of arms.
- Convey complex information and communicate effectively and persuasively to any audience.

The core of the institution is the School of Strategic Landpower, which offers two graduate degree–granting programs, one in residence and one via blended learning that integrates distance/online education with residential instruction. Initially designed as an army school for senior leader development, the college began offering an accredited graduate degree in 2000 and senior-level joint military education in 2006. The size of graduation classes has grown from nine students in 1904 (six army and three US Marine Corps officers) to around 1,400 students annually across all academic and professional development programs. In addition to the School of Strategic Landpower, the college consists of two educational centers, two professional institutes, and one program office offering research and professional development programs. The centers and institutes develop curricula, conduct research related to national security affairs, and educate students.

War College students are on the cusp of high operational or strategic-level leadership assignments and have already been on their career tracks for longer than two decades when they arrive at the college. In order to be chosen for the Army War College, students have attained a high level of technical mastery at the tactical level. The objective of senior PME is to introduce them to a wider range of issues than they have been exposed to up to this point in their careers. The curriculum is intended to provide the building blocks for a broadening experience; students at this level—in a PME distinction—are "educated," not "trained." Senior service school will prepare them for their next assignments, which will be at the high operational or strategic levels. They may go on to become strategic leaders or to advise those who are charged with strategic-level responsibilities. War College marks an inflection point in the careers of students; it orients them toward future leadership opportunities and differentiates their trajectories from those who did not make the meritocratic cut.

The core curriculum offerings are wide, while not perhaps as deep as a strictly academic program would offer. Students at this level engage with a blended curriculum that is intended to broaden their awareness of major issues in history, international relations, security policy, strategy, leadership, operations, and defense management. They also choose a regional focus and are permitted to select from a range of elective courses, which complement the core curriculum. The curriculum is intended to expand students' exposure to academic literature and also to require them to improve their academic writing and presentation abilities, skills that many have not used for a decade or more, but it is also intended to prepare students for their next operational assignments. Students cap their experience with a research thesis on a topic of their choosing, but one that preferably aligns with the army's research priorities.

A relatively recent addition to the final stages of the ten-month program is an oral comprehensive exam conducted by three faculty members.

Overall, the academic platform is condensed, multidisciplinary, and confronted with the age-old problem of balance—how much theory and how much practice to include? As stated by Marrin and Cienski, "Tensions arise because there are many ways to combine different kinds of knowledge and skills, and there are likely to be disagreements over the dominant emphasis and values."[4] Further, as Stanford education professor Lewis Mayhew articulated the issue,

> [A] particularly vexing problem for professional education is the play of theory and skill. Professional service requires mastery of a body of knowledge as well as professional craftsmanship. But the question as to which a professional school should emphasize has had almost a pendulum-like quality, swinging between too much emphasis on theory and too much emphasis on practice.[5]

This comment leads us to a consideration of the internal culture of the US Army War College and how this frames the relationship between academics and practitioners, and between theory and practice, and finally how all of this is relevant to intelligence. One can view the Army War College as disparate *epistemic communities* as defined by Haas:

> They have (1) a shared set of normative and principled beliefs, which provide a value-based rationale for the social action of community members; (2) shared causal beliefs, which are derived from their analysis of practices leading or contributing to a central set of problems in their domain and which then serve as the basis for elucidating the multiple linkages between possible policy actions and desired outcomes; (3) shared notions of validity—that is, intersubjective, internally defined criteria for weighing and validating knowledge in the domain of their expertise; and (4) a common policy enterprise—that is, a set of common practices associated with a set of problems to which their professional competence is directed, presumably out of the conviction that human welfare will be enhanced as a consequence.[6]

While the concept of epistemic community tends to be used regarding the relationship between the academic technical community and the policy maker, the concept also has relevance for the military within an academic setting. It may also be used for the counterpart academic community. The coexistence of two epistemic communities with relatively high bars of entry raises a series of questions: How is information exchanged between the internal communities? Who decides which knowledge has the most bearing on a particular issue? How can ideas be integrated and validated?

Community in a military environment is deep, and this chapter can only brush the surface in order to demonstrate the strength of the ties uniting one of the cultures that constitute the Army War College. The college is a military organization imprinted with a core military culture, but it is also an academic institution with an educational mission that employs civilian academics as well as military officers. The question of which culture is and *should be* dominant has been an open one for many years and touches upon how the practitioner and academic share the same institutional space. One practical aspect of the culture question concerns the composition of the Army War College faculty. The War College tends heavily toward the military, both active and retired. As of fall 2021, those numbers stand at 68 military and 77 civilian faculty, with retired military counted among the civilians. All but two leadership positions at the college are also held by either active-duty military officers or those with prior military careers. This includes "academic" positions such as dean, deputy dean, provost, deputy provost, associate provost, and department chairs. Significantly, only three leadership positions are held by female civilians. In the words of historian Jennifer Mittelstadt, who was a visiting fellow at the Army War College, there is quite a lot more "war" than "college" at the War College.[7] What this means in reality is that the institution is heavily imbued with the expectations of the military, which can inhibit successful achievement of the academic objectives of the college. The problems range from overuse of jargon and the "othering" of civilian students and faculty to the challenges many military officers have when faced with analytical problems characterized by uncertainty and ambiguity.

The 2018 US National Defense Strategy delivered a rebuke to the institutions that deliver PME by stating that PME has "stagnated, focused more on the accomplishment of mandatory credit at the expense of lethality and ingenuity."[8] The criticism aroused consternation among PME practitioners and graduates, engendering a wide range of responses, notable for their concentration on creative fixes. The discussion of the direction of PME is an important one. PME has been criticized for a lack of rigor and lack of creativity and, as mentioned above, as a checkbox requirement to be met by officers on their way somewhere else.[9] But PME, while criticized from many directions, is considered crucially important to the development, adaptability, and resilience of the military force. The next section discusses how the study of intelligence can perhaps uniquely fill this gap.

STRATEGIC INTELLIGENCE AND LEADERSHIP

In the politico-military world of competition and conflict, uncertainty plagues decision makers more than any other element. Nevertheless, it is not without remedy. The proper use of accurate, timely intelligence can significantly reduce uncertainty, thereby enabling political and military leaders to improve the quality of their decisions, develop more effective strategies, and conduct more successful military operations. The information provided by intelligence is thus only a means to an end—an instrument essential for the attainment of a leader's goals in the most efficient way.[10]

An objective of intelligence for Army War College students is similar to its universal goal within the framework of decision making: improved decision-making ability under uncertainty. War College students are studying at this level in order to become strategic leaders and critical thinkers; thus, intelligence has a multifaceted role. In order to acquire the necessary tools and perspective, both sides of the theory-practice divide must be engaged as robustly as possible.

The more specific goal of the Army War College intelligence education is to help future leaders understand capabilities and challenges within strategic intelligence. This helps students to ask the right questions of analysts, enable their subordinate intelligence professionals, and make good decisions. In a recent directive, the Joint Chiefs of Staff, anticipating future wars against a technological equal, emphasized building leaders who can outthink their enemy.[11] To do so, military leaders must understand strategic intelligence capabilities and limitations to discover and exploit adversaries' vulnerabilities in both competition and combat. In this context, it is important for students to receive as complete an understanding of intelligence as possible. They must become good "consumers" of intelligence in order to become competent strategic decision makers and leaders.

Intelligence in military operations has always suffered from a rather ambiguous role. Whether from perceived historical critiques delivered by Clausewitz—that intelligence had minimal impact on the outcomes of battles—or the disdain of its importance in relation to firepower or manpower, intelligence has been sidelined in many discussions of military practice, particularly in conventional warfare. For others, intelligence plays a singular role and can be a definitive asset in providing contextual support for the military, for example, in counterinsurgency and nonstate warfare.

Producers provide intelligence information in reaction to the priorities of the decision maker, honing arguments and material to provide context for decision and responding to advancing needs and questions of the consumer as they emerge. This is part of the intelligence cycle that roughly guides the production of intelligence work products. Producers are taught to research and analyze, anticipate and support, but never to provide policy advice to the decision maker. This approach focuses on the nexus between consumer and producer of intelligence from the perspective of the military consumer. An understanding of this relationship complements the wealth of case studies on intelligence and war that provide the backbone of studies on the topic of intelligence and military operations.[12]

The problem of cultural differences, a theme throughout this chapter, arises here again. Producers and consumers operate in "different worlds" and possess inherent personal biases—not to mention the consequences of deception, which can be levied against both analysts and decision makers.[13] Decision-making heuristics—"rules of thumb"—facilitate the speed of decisions by leaders with very little time and large numbers of difficult decisions to make. These can improve the efficiency of the process but can also skew decisions in the direction that unconscious bias may lead them. Finally, ideology and a political agenda affect decision making, either from an inherent inclination or from a prescribed policy approach to an issue. The lessons to be drawn from historical case studies must be chosen carefully and articulated well. Approaches to case studies will be discussed in the closing sections of this chapter.

Bad experiences with intelligence can affect intelligence consumers' trust in and reliance on intelligence. For example, President Kennedy began to distrust intelligence after the Bay of Pigs disaster.[14] A crucial factor on this nexus between the consumer and producer is that it is relational—the personal relationship between these two actors impacts deeply how intelligence is received and how credible it is perceived to be. Finally, technology is changing rapidly, forcing faster reactions and more sophisticated analyses to counteract the activities of a wider range of adversaries. Conventional ways of viewing the connection between intelligence and operations are evolving under the pressure of technological change.[15] Traditional frameworks, such as the DIME model—which describes the use of the diplomatic, informational, military, and economic instruments of power—no longer have the traction on analytic debates that they once did.[16] The overall purpose of this education is to provide a progressive map toward an attainment of intelligence consumption skills as part of the senior officer's fundamental tool kit. It aims to help facilitate active engagement with intelligence on the part of the military decision maker. It does not intend to create intelligence analysts out of the senior officer corps, simply to improve their skills so that all are better prepared to use intelligence to better support their own needs. Finally, intelligence, particularly strategic intelligence, can seem abstract and not relevant to officers, who up to this point have professionally focused on immediate, tactical problems. The point of introducing this field of study at the War College is that it naturally includes a range of skills useful to students at this level: critical thinking, appropriate use of evidence, and accounting for uncertainty and ambiguity in decision making—all skills students will need as they progress to more senior and strategic assignments. Further, while students may not have engaged actively with intelligence earlier in their careers, they will as their assignments approach the strategic level, particularly if they are deployed to war.

A PRACTICAL APPROACH

One product of military training is a relatively narrow expertise based on technical competency. War College education is intended to broaden this foundation and, within the realm of intelligence education, this means expanding and redefining the concept of intelligence for students. For example, if an operational commander feels that a strategic analyst is misreading a situation, his understanding of intelligence processes can help him comprehend different perspectives and perhaps his own prejudices. A more universal understanding of strategic intelligence will produce a better-aligned assessment for policy makers and military commanders. The Army War College approach has evolved through a partnership between an academic and a practitioner, who each contribute materials and topics from their respective areas of expertise. The academic contributes theoretical literature and analytical frameworks to the discussion of strategic intelligence, while the practitioner engages with topics such as how to transform intelligence into operations, and how to address specific intelligence-related problems from combat.

Because Army War College students have spent most of their careers in tactical formations, instructors often struggle to orient students on intelligence to support strategic objectives versus short-term tactical targeting. This tactical focus extends beyond just the Senior Service College population and is typical across a US military that, since World War II, has struggled to translate its tactical victories into strategic gains. This force-wide tactical focus makes inculcating an understanding of strategic intelligence in senior leaders of all occupational specialties even more important.

Intelligence instructors at the Army War College aim to fill their classrooms with diverse leaders from operational and intelligence backgrounds. Historically, intelligence courses have attracted intelligence leaders or special operations officers, the latter generally seeking to expand their tactical intelligence knowledge. These students add value, but the goal is to also draw civilian leaders and military commanders who will formulate strategy and translate strategy into operations. The ideal class is a blend of future military commanders, senior-leader advisers, and intelligence professionals. The range of backgrounds allows students to educate each other on their individual specialties and experiences.

In terms of considering how to deliver intelligence education, the Joint Chiefs have also called for greater use of "case studies grounded in history to help students develop judgment, analysis, and problem-solving skills."[17] Faculty include intelligence case studies in each lesson to expose students to past challenges and help them anticipate the results of future decisions. Cases also illustrate analogues to potential scenarios that students will face. Examples of cases used in courses include North Korea and negotiations regarding nuclear weapons, the intelligence failure of 9/11, and the escalation of bombing in Vietnam during the war, to name a few. The study of intelligence history can also help students understand the complex organization and procedures across the eighteen organizations that compose the US intelligence community.

The Army War College is also taking an active-learning approach by incorporating planning exercises and war games into its intelligence courses. While still nascent, the intelligence faculty are working with the army wargaming team at Carlisle Barracks to develop a capstone exercise. Through an online war game, students allocate resources globally and decide how to collect against strategic threats to the United States and its allies. Faculty do not intend to make students masters of collection planning or analysis, but rather to have them work through the challenges, limitations, and risks associated with allocating collection assets and analytical capability. Gaming feeds into the overarching goal of teaching students how to be good consumers of intelligence.

Interaction with intelligence leaders and practitioners is also part of nearly every class on strategic intelligence. Discussions with practitioners reinforce what students read and help them appreciate the human factors involved in intelligence production. Analysts and intelligence leaders experience pressures from politics, deadlines, health, and family that require skilled leaders to manage. Guest speakers include former directors of strategic intelligence agencies, military intelligence leaders who translate the strategic to the operational (and vice versa), and practitioners engaged in collection and analysis. The Army War College has also extended the concept of intelligence expertise by inviting journalists and others to speak, who are tangentially but crucially related to the intelligence enterprise. In addition to senior leaders, students are exposed to collectors and analysts. All of the guest speakers serve to broaden and deepen students' perceptions of the meaning and utility of intelligence. When discussing the interface between strategic and operational intelligence, the speaker could be an acting Army Theater Intelligence Brigade commander or an Army Component Command J2, typically a colonel, who would likely be accompanied by one or several analysts. During the lesson on intelligence capabilities, the faculty might invite the open-source intelligence team from a combatant command and a technician working on artificial intelligence capabilities.

The course starts with a brief overview of the intelligence community and collection capabilities. However, it quickly transitions to challenges strategic leaders face and how intelligence can (and cannot) help. Class topics include the following:

- Informing senior decision makers (the producer-consumer relationship)
- Intelligence at echelon: headquarters analysis versus in-theater analysis
- Building an intelligence enterprise to translate the strategic vision into operations: World War II, counterinsurgency, great powers competition
- Modern espionage and the cyber domain
- Recognizing and managing tactical intelligence with strategic effects

A typical class consists of reading one or more vignettes, discussing the trends, and then engaging with a speaker who has experience with the topic or was directly involved in a particular activity or mission, if applicable. For example, in preparation for the lesson on informing decision makers, students might read about the following incidents:

- General Douglas MacArthur missing indicators of the Chinese invasion during the Korean War
- American leaders' belief that Iraq had weapons of mass destruction (WMD), prompting the 2003 US invasion
- CENTCOM analysts' 2015 accusations that superiors suppressed their assessments because of political pressure for results against the Islamic State

The Officer Professional Military Education Policy (OPMEP) states that officers should be educated to "demonstrate critical and creative thinking skills, interpersonal skills, and effective written, verbal, and visual communications skills to support the development and implementation of strategies and complex operations."[18] Writing and briefing reinforce learning and serve as accountability mechanisms and reinforce learning. Students conduct oral presentations on one of the class topics or their analysis of a case study. Students can write a research paper on an issue of interest or submit a weekly journal reflecting on each lesson's relevance to their future position as strategic leaders or advisers. The journaling helps students link education to future assignments and provides feedback to the instructors on the course's relevance.

The intelligence faculty's efforts to employ a more active-learning model, including an intelligence war game, reflect a trend across the War College and a partial response to guidance from the Joint Chiefs. The chiefs recently directed that PME institutions prioritize "wargames and exercises involving multiple sets and repetitions to develop deeper insight and ingenuity."[19] War Colleges incorporating war games into their curriculum is nothing new. After leading the victory against the Japanese during World War II, Admiral Ernest King said that nothing surprised him because he had fought the Pacific campaign over three hundred times in simulations run by the Navy War College. Likewise, the Army War College acted as a virtual extension of the War Department during the interwar period, planning and iteratively conducting map exercises on anticipated future campaigns. In 1923, the Army and Navy War Colleges began joint war games—the first year's exercise focused on the defense of the Philippines in case of a Japanese attack.[20]

The war colleges never stopped war-gaming but have increased both the quantity and quality in recent years. The Department of Military Strategy, Plans, and Operations (DMSPO) leads the core curriculum that teaches translating strategic objectives into campaign plans. For academic year 2021, DMSPO dedicated the last ten lessons of its thirty-two-lesson course to planning a campaign in Eastern Europe (three lessons) and then executing that campaign (seven lessons) so that nearly every student experiences multiple turns of this advanced simulation. The War College also has several programs that enable students to specialize in campaign planning and war-gaming for scenarios highlighted in the National Defense Strategy, notably the Joint Land, Air, and Sea Strategic Exercise (JLASS) and the Joint Warfighting Advanced Studies Program (JWASP).

The Joint Land, Air, and Sea Strategic Exercise

JLASS is a War College program that allows students to practice designing and implementing campaign plans for crisis resolution at the high operational and strategic levels. It is designed as experiential learning intended to support the lessons learned in the core courses of the War College curriculum, and helps students prepare for assignments on the Joint Staff and geographic combatant commands. Students role-play the various members of a strategic staff who would be involved in planning for a future crisis, set in 2030–2031. This includes, for example, the Office of the Secretary of Defense, the Joint Chiefs of Staff, and the NORTHCOM, CENTCOM, and AFRICOM geographic combatant commands. Students begin by conducting a theater assessment of the scenario and then draft and refine a campaign plan. The final step is a five-day war game executed in conjunction with three other Senior Service Colleges and an international partner.

Joint Warfighting Advanced Studies Program

While JLASS focuses on the strategic-level campaign and alliances (particularly NATO) in a futuristic (2030–2031) scenario, the Army War College offers the JWASP, which educates and trains students on building an operational-level, multinational campaign plan and then fighting the plan in a war game. Students act as part of a Combined Joint Task Force command in a scenario focused on one of the National Defense Strategy's primary threats. Instructors introduce game-changing technologies (artificial intelligence, robotics, quantum computing, hypervelocity, directed energy) that will affect the future war-fighting environment. JWASP is popular with the War College's international fellows, many of whom came to War College to learn to plan and fight at war's operational level.

JWASP occupies all of the students' elective credits and focuses on planning and then decision making and assessment in a simulated combat scenario. The course incorporates senior mentors who are former Joint Task Force commanders or senior staff officers from multiple services and allied nations. Early on in the course, students study historical campaigns and emerging technologies that will change the conduct of future wars. Students visit combatant commands and functional component commands throughout the academic year to discuss ongoing planning and operations. Finally, joint planning groups analyze a regional scenario and use the United States' joint planning process to develop a concept of operations. Using war-gaming and simulation, the students then execute their plan and assess the results. Assessment of campaigns in terms of achieving strategic goals is a learning objective for War College students and is treated with equal importance to the other parts of the JWASP course.

AN ALTERNATIVE VIEW: CURRICULAR THREAD

An alternative approach to the one described above, which places intelligence in the elective section of the curriculum, is to integrate intelligence throughout the entire core curriculum by complementing the learning objectives that already exist, while providing space to develop new ones as threat and technology change. The argument in support of this approach is that the strategy development process should incorporate intelligence as a core component as students progress, not as an afterthought or isolated area of interest. This requires deliberate consideration, which can only come with some minimum level of understanding about the tool, which functions in a range of different ways and contexts. Absent at least a basic understanding of the multifaceted nature and character of intelligence, strategists risk overlooking critical vulnerabilities and opportunities. As has been reiterated throughout this chapter, the point of developing an intelligence program at the Army War College is clearly not to create analysts, but rather to build in a natural proclivity to assess intelligence critically and use it as well as possible in strategic decision making. This is not about knowing about every intelligence capability; rather it is about recognizing what knowledge, information, and context are critical to a strategy. This affects how we think about a problem, understanding what we need to know, and how we can know it better. A "thread" of intelligence also cuts across the cultural divide at the Army War College, and through issue areas and topics. Academics can discuss ethics and intelligence, decision analysis, or Thucydides and intelligence, while practitioners can focus on the role of intelligence in the "joint preparation of the operational environment" or how intelligence can serve as a force multiplier. Approaching intelligence in this way can demonstrate that academics and practitioners are actually not that far apart, although their approaches can vary quite significantly.

The conceptual framework guiding integration of intelligence into the curriculum consists of two parts: complementarity and consumption. Complementarity means building into the curriculum as it currently exists and supporting it with intelligence themes and examples. Intelligence education will fall short if it is relegated to the fringes and only taught in optional elective courses but not included in the core. One part of this approach will be explicit—talking about intelligence disciplines, covert action, and interagency organization—while another will be less obvious, drawing from the history of intelligence through case studies, or exploring the critical thinking that supports intelligence analysis. Consumption here reiterates the goal of creating students who are good consumers of intelligence. Its role changes based on the needs of the particular course.

This approach requires that a through-line run throughout the curriculum and reinforce students' skills in terms of understanding how to lead and direct intelligence officers in order to support their decision making, how to develop the right questions to ask, how to understand what the limits of intelligence are, and how to handle the disparate intelligence disciplines and information flows. Further, they must learn how to bound the demands they make of the intelligence services as well as how to think critically about intelligence products, challenging reports and querying the validity of assumptions, data, and outcomes. In order to accomplish all of this, the War College must also surmount its own cultural hindrances that inhibit choice. Many students at this level view intelligence from the operational and tactical perspective. They must therefore be continually exposed to the distinction between strategic and operational methodologies but also to the high degree of uncertainty that characterizes strategic intelligence. This approach demonstrates to students how relevant and useful intelligence can be as they apply it to a wide range of scenarios. Some hurdles to achieving this strategic intelligence curricular thread include the reluctance of academic departments to trade current course content for new additions. Curriculum space and time is also very limited, as students are expected to complete a master of arts degree within ten months. In some cases, it is not only students who have not yet discovered the relevance of strategic intelligence, but also faculty, which leads to an unwillingness to learn how to teach it.

Intelligence scholar Stephen Marrin has sought to evaluate the effects of analyst–decision maker proximity in two case studies: pre-9/11 intelligence analysis regarding the terrorist threat, and pre–Iraq War intelligence analysis regarding Iraq's links to terrorism and possession of WMD.[21] He raises interesting questions with regard to the relative proximity of intelligence analysts and decision makers. The implications for strategic leader education are clear. Both sides—the producer and the consumer, the analyst and the decisionmaker or leader—must learn more about each other. Singular electives devoted to intelligence in senior PME are inadequate in preparing future strategic leaders. Instead, intelligence, both its theory and practice, should be addressed throughout the curriculum. The adoption and integration of a theme or thread stressing strategic intelligence and its role in decision making is a good place to start.

CONCLUSION

The academic-practitioner relationship at the US Army War College is complex—both divisive and complementary. The very strong military culture that governs the organization permeates the institution. It must, however, share space with the academic culture and incentive structure. This relationship may never be entirely resolved, as both sides maintain a somewhat cooperative rivalry. The study of intelligence has begun to bridge this gap as course offerings blend the complementary expertise of academics and practitioners. Further, traditional military education tools, such as war-gaming, can be used to simulate and develop intelligence-based decision making, while teaching field-grade officers about strategic national-level intelligence can help them as they move into assignments where they will be interacting with civilians and the interagency process with much more frequency. A final approach, threading intelligence throughout the curriculum, integrates military and national-level intelligence, practitioners and academics, and their respective cultures, in the most thorough way. While this approach is currently nascent at the Army War College, it is a marker for the way forward in best practices for educating the student body. The objective of intelligence education at the War College is to create skilled consumers of intelligence who can use their skills to support decision making at the strategic level, one that is often imbued with uncertainty. The above discussion considers possible ways forward to achieve this goal, as well as some of the hurdles that must be overcome in order to do so.

NOTES

The views expressed in this chapter are those of the authors and do not necessarily reflect those of the US Army War College, the US Army, or the US Department of Defense.

1. Stephen Coulthart, "From Laboratory to the WMD Commission," *Intelligence and National Security* 34, no. 6 (2019): 818.

2. Bruce W. Jentleson and Ely Ratner, "Bridging the Beltway–Ivory Tower Gap," *International Studies Review* 13, no. 1 (2011): 7.

3. Coulthart, "From Laboratory," 820.

4. Stephen Marrin and Sophie Cienski, "Experimenting with Intelligence Education: Overcoming Design Challenges in Multidisciplinary Intelligence Analysis Programmes," in *The Routledge International Handbook of Universities, Security and Intelligence Studies*, ed. Liam Francis Gearon (Abingdon: Routledge, 2020), 294.

5. Lewis Mayhew (1971), quoted in Marrin and Cienski, "Experimenting," 294.

6. Peter M. Haas, "Introduction: Epistemic Communities and International Policy Coordination," *International Organization* 46, no. 1 (1992): 3.

7. Jennifer Mittelstadt, "Too Much War, Not Enough College," *War Room*, June 20, 2018, https://warroom.armywarcollege.edu/articles/too-much-war-not-enough -college.

8. US Department of Defense, *Summary of the 2018 National Defense Strategy of the United States of America: Sharpening the American Military's Competitive Edge* (Washington, DC: Department of Defense, 2018), 8.

9. James Joyner, "Soldier-Scholar [Pick One]: Anti-Intellectualism in the American Military," *War on the Rocks*, August 25, 2020, https://warontherocks. com/2020/08/soldier-scholar-pick-one-anti-intellectualism-in-the-american-military.

10. Michael I. Handel, "Leaders and Intelligence," *Intelligence and National Security* 3, no. 3 (1988): 3.

11. Joint Chiefs of Staff, *Developing Today's Joint Officers for Tomorrow's Ways of War: The Joint Chiefs of Staff Vision and Guidance for Professional Military Education & Talent Management* (Washington, DC: Joint Chiefs of Staff, 2020).

12. For a seminal source using this approach, see Michael I. Handel, ed., *Intelligence and Military Operations* (Portland, OR: Frank Cass, 1990).

13. John A. Gentry and Joseph S. Gordon, *Strategic Warning Intelligence: History, Challenges, and Prospects* (Washington, DC: Georgetown University Press, 2019), 202.

14. Gentry and Gordon, *Strategic Warning Intelligence*, 206.

15. John A. Gentry, "Intelligence in War: How Important Is It and How Do We Know?," *Intelligence and National Security* 34, no. 6 (2019): 833.

16. Joint Chiefs of Staff, Joint Doctrine Note 1-18, *Strategy* (Washington, DC: Joint Chiefs of Staff, 2018), https://www.jcs.mil/Portals/36/Documents/Doctrine/jdn_jg/jdn1_18.pdf.

17. Joint Chiefs of Staff, *Developing Today's Joint Officers*.

18. The Officer Professional Military Education Policy (OPMEP).

19. Joint Chiefs of Staff, *Developing Today's Joint Officers*.

20. Peter Perla, *The Art of Wargaming: A Guide for Professionals and Hobbyists* (Annapolis, MD: United States Naval Institute, 2011), 6; Michael R. Matheny, *Carrying the War to the Enemy: American Operational Art to 1945* (Norman: University of Oklahoma Press, 2011), 58–59.

21. Stephen Marrin, "Training and Educating U.S. Intelligence Analysts," *International Journal of Intelligence and CounterIntelligence* 22, no. 1 (2009): 131–46.

6

Assessing the Quality of Strategic Intelligence Products

Cooperation and Competition between Scholars and Practitioners

José-Miguel Palacios

A Spanish intelligence scholar wrote in 2006 that (at least in his country) "one of the main problems we have detected is the lack of evaluation of intelligence products. We find a mostly unidirectional system in which what arrives is consumed, without any systematic evaluation of its quality, its usefulness, or its effectiveness."[1]

According to Robert Behn, public managers need to measure the performance of their organizations for eight different reasons: "to (1) evaluate; (2) control; (3) budget; (4) motivate; (5) promote; (6) celebrate; (7) learn; and (8) improve."[2] Three of the eight reasons (to evaluate, learn, and improve) are oriented explicitly to organizational development and for intelligence organizations may help them to decide which analytical techniques and specific intelligence practices are worth introducing, modifying, or maintaining, based on the advantage that can be obtained with their use.

On the other hand, as the clients of the intelligence organizations, governments also need to assess the quality of the service they receive. Rather than organizational improvement, their focus is on control: "to evaluate, control, budget, or punish."[3] Other intelligence stakeholders, such as academics, the media, or the population at large, also have a legitimate interest in ensuring that "intelligence agencies . . . address their mission competently and most of the time efficiently,"[4] something that cannot be verified without an effective and transparent system for evaluating intelligence products and processes.

For different reasons, as we have just seen, intelligence managers, governments, and other stakeholders need to assess the performance of intelligence organizations, but unfortunately they cannot rely on "broadly applicable and widely acceptable . . . measures."[5] Mainly for practical reasons, practitioners, both in the intelligence community and the government, have traditionally used three different strategies:

1. to observe whether the products follow the rules of tradecraft accepted within the organization;
2. to verify whether the judgments and predictions included in intelligence products turn out to be accurate; and
3. to assess the impact of intelligence on policy making or, what is very similar, the clients' appreciation of the intelligence support they receive.[6]

Other stakeholders have not contributed significantly to the identification of alternative evaluation strategies.

Considerations of secrecy make it advisable for intelligence organizations to develop in-house procedures for measuring their production quality, in most cases following any of the three strategies mentioned above. However, such an approach's main shortcoming is that it does not allow intelligence to take full advantage of the methodological and subject-related knowledge and understanding generated by outside specialists, particularly in academia. As Irwin and Mandel have observed, "The [intelligence community] IC all too often tasks intelligence personnel with 'thinking up' something better than the status quo," but "does not routinely put what it regards as good ideas for intelligence production methods to well-conceived scientific tests."[7]

This chapter aims to examine the quality control strategies most frequently used by intelligence organizations. It is argued that, in most cases, the results would probably be better if academic knowledge were systematically used and academic researchers were involved. Attention is placed on strategic intelligence, as most publicly available information on intelligence work relates to the strategic level. Finally, it is assumed that the findings and proposals may also be valid, at least in part, for the operational and tactical levels.

The intelligence literature that has been developed to date is based largely on the study of the United States and, to a much lesser extent, the British experience. However, given that, as Davies and Gustafson have observed, "there are profound, even fundamental differences between the political and therefore intelligence values, norms and conduct within the 'Anglo-sphere' liberal tradition and the Continental European notions of governance,"[8] this chapter attempts to expand the body of knowledge by using examples from the European Union (EU) common intelligence bodies and the intelligence communities of some EU member states.

For instance, at the EU level, the question of the quality of intelligence products was raised in the first European External Action Service (EEAS) discharge review in 2011.[9] The answer given by the then high representative, Catherine Ashton, suggests that quality control was carried out employing in-house reviews and periodic feedback exercises: "Internally, . . . by EUMS INT and INTCEN[10] management: respect of the rules of intelligence analysis tradecraft. Externally, measuring the satisfaction level of intelligence customers using the feedback mechanism. . . . EUMS INT and INTCEN periodically carry out a feedback exercise among users of their information products."[11] Although postmortems (the second strategy identified earlier) were not explicitly mentioned, they have also been occasionally used, as we will see later in this chapter.

FOLLOWING THE RULES OF TRADECRAFT

A first criterion for assessing whether an intelligence document has the minimum level of quality required by the organization is to verify that, in its preparation and final form, it complies with the standards that the organization itself has defined. This is done during the so-called review process, performed by the different management levels. As Rob Johnston explains, "These reviews should derive lessons for individuals and for teams and should look at roots of errors and failures."[12]

Most intelligence organizations have established procedures and routines to perform their work,[13] and managers presume that the outcome is of quality if the procedural rules have been scrupulously followed. It is also relatively frequent for the analytical units to compile some formal rules for their output. From this point of view, a good report must necessarily respect such formal rules.[14] Finally, some intelligence organizations may create more sophisticated standards for defining what a good intelligence product is. That is, for instance, what the US intelligence community did in 2007 when it issued a directive on analytic standards (ICD 203, superseded by a new edition in 2015).

Martin Petersen, a former Central Intelligence Agency (CIA) manager, has explained that a sophisticated review process may include several review levels and cover three different areas: the style (formal issues); the clarity of the message delivered to decision makers; and, finally, the observance of the rules of tradecraft.[15] In small intelligence organizations, collection-oriented intelligence agencies, and intelligence systems with a traditional understanding of "tradecraft," the third area may be ignored entirely. In UK military intelligence, for instance, quality control before dissemination is based on the assessment of every product's "a. Clarity . . . b. Relevance . . . c. Brevity . . . d. Security . . . e. Ease of Assimilation."[16]

EU INTCEN uses a two-level review process in which particular attention is paid to the products' timeliness, pertinence, consistency, and political sensitivity.[17] The first review level (head of section, deputy head of analysis) checks the following aspects:

1. Readability and intelligibility of the product
2. Quality and multiplicity of the sources
3. Fair use of infographics and maps
4. Acceptance of the member states directly concerned by the topic, if any
5. Civil-military coordination

At the second review level (head of analysis division, director), the leading causes of rejection were, in descending order, (1) lack of political sense, (2) untimeliness, and (3) lack of consistency with the center's previous production. Suppose one compares this system with the one described by Martin Petersen in his article "Making the Analytic Review Process Work."[18] In that case, we could say that in the EU INTCEN, the first-level reviewer covers two of the three review areas (style and clarity of the message), while the second-level reviewer focuses on the second one. The tradecraft quality is not assessed during the review process, at least in an explicit form.

Spain's central intelligence service CESID (Centro Nacional de Información para la Defensa), renamed Centro Nacional de Inteligencia (CNI) in 2002, used a somewhat different approach during the 1990s and 2000s. A first-level review was conducted inside the analytical divisions and mostly dealt with factual accuracy and observance of the basic style rules. In the second review, performed by the service's central coordination bodies, attention was focused on the following:

1. Consistency with the service's previous production
2. Internal coherence (i.e., between the reporting and analytical lines of the different analytical divisions)
3. Timeliness
4. Clarity of expression and respect of the style conventions
5. Adaptation to the particular needs of the intended recipients[19]

Again, we have an example of focus on the first and second areas (formal issues and adaptation to the client's needs), with almost complete disregard of the third one (tradecraft).

A similar approach is followed in other European national intelligence services. For example, Ivars Indāns, a Latvian intelligence analyst and manager, explains how the review process is conducted in his country in the following way:

Regarding the internal control of analysis. When we do the review of analysts' work, we have internal guidelines like we had the SIAC[20] style handbook in Brussels. This helps to organize the products (style, executive summary, chapters, outlook). We also make a reference to the previous reports on a particular issue. This helps to check the consistency of the work with previous analytical products. We pay attention to the formal issues but we make exceptions quite often. Analysts enjoy a lot of freedom during the writing process. When it comes to presentation we have collective brainstorming in order to make products easier for customers.[21]

As we see from the examples above, in European intelligence organizations, the review process is mostly focused on the first two areas of Petersen's model (style guide and clarity of the message). Simultaneously, the third one, concerning observance of the rules of tradecraft, is mostly ignored. We have previously argued that in Europe, at least until now, "the knowledge of structured analytical techniques is . . . something that experienced intelligence officers are supposed to have heard about, not necessarily a set of tools they should have been using since they joined the service."[22] The limited empirical evidence available to us suggests that even if they have received training on structured analytic techniques European analysts use them very little. For them, such techniques are mostly an "important element of the intelligence culture,"[23] something they are supposed to have heard about, but do not necessarily use in their daily work.

The review process controls whether products meet the formal and informal standards that the intelligence organization has created over the years and are part of its institutional tradition. As Rob Johnston has observed, "An organization's culture shapes individual behavior by establishing norms and taboos and, ultimately, determines the quality and character of an organization's products. Culture and product are inseparable, and one cannot be changed without affecting the other."[24] However, culture is not immutable, as inherited standards continuously evolve under the influence of common sense, lessons learned, international trends in professional practice, and, in some cases, political pressure.

Scholars have often played a significant role in fostering this evolution. As Pauletta Otis has pointed out, "Academics can make significant contributions in creative thinking, the rigor of analysis, and professional presentation of products."[25] Academics' influence may be beneficial in areas where their standards of rigor can improve the intelligence community's practice (analytic techniques or reviewing procedures, e.g.). On the other hand, they can contribute very little to clients' relations, a key challenge for intelligence organizations that plays only a marginal role in scholars' experience.

The US intelligence community has always shown a refreshing curiosity for new developments in the social sciences and has tried to use them to improve intelligence analysis. As Richards Heuer recalled many years later, when he joined the CIA's new Analytic Methodology Division in 1975, the division's task was "to examine quantitative methods that were developed in the 1960s during what was called the behavioral revolution in academic political science, and to test how these methods could be applied to intelligence analysis."[26] As is well known, the ultimate fruit of Heuer's interest for contemporary social sciences (in particular, the psychology of judgment and decision making) is the analysis of competing hypotheses (ACH) approach, which remains the best known of the structured analytic techniques.

In a report commissioned by the US Office of the Director of National Intelligence (DNI) and produced in 2011 by a committee of the US National Academy of Sciences, we can read that one of the key recommendations was that the DNI should "ensure that the IC adopts scientifically validated analytical methods and subjects its methods to performance evaluation."[27] Moreover, some of the most fruitful research lines developed by academia over the last few years can help improve intelligence practice. Academic research can be useful, for instance, in providing empirical evidence of the benefits that can be obtained from the use of specific techniques. Despite the difficulties posed by the fact that intelligence work is generally classified, in recent years various researchers have been trying to verify the scientific validity of different analytical practices accepted within the intelligence community.

Philip Tetlock, for instance, discovered by researching into experts' predictions that "experts were only slightly more accurate than one would expect from chance."[28] On the other hand, Mandel, Karvetski, and Dhami found in 2018 that ACH and other structured analytic techniques failed to improve the accuracy of analytic judgments.[29] Furthermore, "a Canadian assessment unit has demonstrated that numeric probabilities can be used effectively in the preparation of intelligence reports. . . . However, implementing the methodology requires overcoming a widely shared aversion among analysts and intelligence managers to thinking in numeric terms."[30]

Some European (continental) scholars have also contributed to this mostly Anglophone research effort. For instance, Tore Pedersen and Pia Therese Jansen (Norway) have recently studied how intelligence analysts process classified and open-source information and the credibility they attach to information from each of these categories. Their findings clarify some of the heuristics used in intelligence analysis and should be taken into account both for training purposes and in the review process. As they have written, "We found that intelligence analysts assign significantly more credibility to secret intelligence than to identical open-source intelligence. However, this was true only when the intelligence estimate concerned a 'complex' problem characterized by a high degree of uncertainty and not when it related to a 'simple' problem characterized by a low degree of uncertainty."[31] Furthermore, between 2012 and 2015, the European Commission funded the RECOBIA project, meant to "improve the quality of intelligence by reducing the impact of cognitive biases through the development of mitigation strategies."[32] In this project, it was implicitly assumed that better tradecraft would necessarily improve the professional level of the overall production, and no specific metric was envisioned to verify whether it was so. The RECOBIA project consortium included universities (University of Konstanz, Graz University of Technology), research centers (France's Commissariat à l'Energie Atomique et aux Energies Alternatives), as well as individual psychologists who specialize in cognitive biases.

Summarizing some of the main findings of this section, the following could be said:

- In most intelligence organizations, the review process is conducted in-house, following procedures designed and controlled by the organization's hierarchy and by intelligence officials under its command. It reflects the organization's official views on how analytical work should be ideally performed.
- In continental Europe, the review process is less sophisticated than it is in the United States. Usually, it does not include any check on whether the tradecraft rules approved by the organization have been correctly followed.
- So far, there is no European school of intelligence analysis. The growing volume of work done by European (continental) scholars follows lines previously defined by Anglophone researchers.

POSTMORTEM EXERCISES

One of the most popular criteria used to evaluate intelligence production quality is assessing (post factum) its explanatory and predictive accuracy. In principle, good intelligence is supposed to describe the current situation and its possible evolution correctly. Whenever something unexpected happens (or whenever expected problems fail to materialize), we face an "intelligence failure."[33] At least this is a prevalent perception, particularly among politicians and opinion makers. Although it is doubtful that intelligence (agencies, communities) could ever constitute a high-reliability organization,[34] conventional wisdom suggests that by systematically investigating their failures, intelligence bodies can find ways to improve performance and reduce the probability of repeating the same mistakes in the future. Of course, it is possible to learn both from success and failure, but postmortems are carried out only in the latter case.

We can distinguish two different kinds of postmortem. On the one hand, we have those that could be called "external postmortems" and are commissioned by the clients to attribute responsibility for a severe political or security failure. Implicitly, it is understood that the primary responsibility has to be found precisely within the intelligence system. On the other hand, we can also have postmortems commanded by an intelligence organization wishing to improve its internal processes and overall performance (internal postmortems).

A well-known example of an external postmortem is the Butler review that examined in 2004 the work of British intelligence on weapons of mass destruction (WMD) in the lead-up to the 2003 invasion of Iraq.[35] The commission was composed of peers, MPs, and a top-level civil servant. Among the witnesses who testified before the commission, there were politicians, officials, and former officials, some of them having moved in the meantime to academia. Scholars had no role in the review's conduct, although it could be argued that the vivid scholarly debate triggered by the final report can be seen as a sort of unofficial academic postmortem.

Something similar could be said about the National Commission on Terrorist Attacks upon the United States (the 9/11 Commission), created by the president and Congress and conducted by a commission staffed by independent experts. Like its British counterpart, the commission had access to relevant intelligence information and could interrogate officials and former officials. A small number of academics could be counted among the supporting staff and witnesses.[36] During the Bush presidency, another postmortem was conducted by the Commission on the Intelligence Capabilities of the United States Regarding Weapons of Mass Destruction, established by the US president in 2004 and which concluded its work in 2005. The commission was composed of experts of different profiles, mostly with executive experience. The staff consisted mostly of intelligence professionals. Scholars had no significant role in the work of this second commission.

In continental Europe, we can find a few examples of external postmortems, similar to those mentioned from within the Anglosphere. In Belgium, for instance, the Permanent Committee R, in charge of supervising the work of the intelligence services, conducted a postmortem immediately after the terrorist attacks on March 23, 2016.[37] The committee identified structural problems in sharing information between the two Belgian intelligence services, the VSSE (civilian security service) and SGRS (military service).[38] Although the committee maintains excellent cooperation with the academic community,[39] the report, like the American and British postmortems just mentioned, was made based almost exclusively on official information.[40] This is probably the case because of the very limited access that academics, with few exceptions, have to really sensitive intelligence material.

Usually, "internal" postmortems, that is, those commissioned by intelligence organizations themselves, are conducted "in-house," and we know very little about them. In the United States, for instance, the CIA began in the early 1950s to systematically review its National Intelligence Estimates and Special National Intelligence Estimates in a series of "validity studies."[41] In 1968–69, the then director of the State Department's Bureau of Intelligence and Research (INR) commissioned an internal postmortem on the bureau's analytical production on the war in Vietnam. Usually the existence of reports of this kind only becomes known decades after the event, but not in this case, thanks to partial leaks to the press. As *Time* magazine reported in 1971, "The study compared the Kennedy and Johnson Administrations' key Vietnam decisions with the Bureau's own major judgments during the same period. In almost every case, the intelligence reports called the shots perfectly about such matters as the ineffectiveness of the bombing campaign, Vietnamese political upheavals and North Vietnamese troop buildups."[42]

In the EU SITCEN,[43] a postmortem was conducted a few weeks after the Russo-Georgian War of August 2008. The purpose was to assess whether SITCEN had been able to issue a precise warning about the imminence of armed conflict in time for it to be useful to policy makers and then check whether the reaction mechanisms had worked appropriately. Given that SITCEN did not have any collection capabilities of its own and received from the member states' intelligence organizations (civilian and military) almost all the sensitive information the center processed, the fundamental problem was to analyze whether the national contributions arrived in a timely manner and were accurate. According to a former head of unit in SITCEN, "The 'quality control' for intelligence support could be measured postmortem by assessing timeliness, accuracy, and impact on behavior/action."[44]

The primary working method in this postmortem exercise consisted of reviewing the analytical production before the beginning of the fighting and seeing whether the possibilities of a Georgian offensive operation and a Russian strong-handed response had ever been mentioned in SITCEN's analytic products and, if so, what probability had been attached to it. Furthermore, contributions received from member states' intelligence organizations were reexamined to check whether elements of alert were present and had been given sufficient weight. Finally, the rapidity of the reaction, once the fighting started, was also considered and measured. This postmortem report is still classified, and no references to its contents have ever been published.

Scholars are naturally interested in using the results of postmortems or, better still, participating in the examination. As Klaus Knorr wrote in 1964, "The most productive method of empirical research is sure to be carefully conducted postmortems of past intelligence performances."[45] The problem, however, is that such "studies could be undertaken only with the cooperation, if not under the direction, of the intelligence authorities and would no doubt necessitate special conditions in view of the classified nature of the material."[46] That requires a high level of trust on the part of the intelligence organization in the scholar and an excellent reputation of the scholar in the academic community, which must believe that the results are objective and not dictated by the necessities of serving intelligence. If this is difficult to achieve in a particular country, it is even more so at the level of the EU because of the significant differences existing in national interests and sensitivities.

However, despite this academic interest, scholars' participation in the design and conduct of internal postmortems seems to be almost exceptional. Of course, the problem is the necessary trust that must exist between the intelligence organization and the given scholar. The well-known example of Robert Jervis's postmortem on the CIA's performance during the crisis leading to the Iranian Revolution of 1979 was only possible because Jervis had already been working some time for the CIA as a consultant.[47]

Some conclusions can be drawn based on the discussion in this section:

- Postmortems are only conducted in cases of failure. That is a problem, as we can also learn from success. As Rob Johnston has observed, "By focusing only on failure, one risks sampling bias by only choosing cases in which there was error."[48]
- The participation of scholars in the design and conduct of postmortems (both "external" and "internal") is exceptional. The main problem is the lack of sufficient mutual trust.
- The examples found in continental Europe are very similar to those known in the practice of the Anglosphere.

THE CLIENTS' SATISFACTION: FEEDBACK MECHANISMS AND EXERCISES

Feedback exercises are common ways of investigating the level of clients' satisfaction. If intelligence is a service provided to clients, the latter's satisfaction is, in principle, a good measure of quality. As Rubén Arcos has observed,

"Understanding well an intelligence consumer's requirements and obtaining feedback from policymakers on the usefulness of its products and on any changes in their agenda priorities is of much importance for the successful achievement of the intelligence service's mission."[49] Or, in Stephen Marrin's words, "If decision-makers find the analysis informative, insightful, relevant or useful, then the intelligence analysis has succeeded whereas if the decision-makers are left unsatisfied then the analysis has failed."[50] For many authors, feedback is even an integral part of the intelligence cycle, given that "without orderly feedback, a common outcome is overconfidence, with experts and laypeople expressing greater confidence than their knowledge warrants."[51]

Feedback mechanisms (such as appending feedback questionnaires to intelligence products) and periodic or episodic feedback exercises are commonly used to explore the clients' satisfaction with the intelligence support they are receiving. Such mechanisms and exercises are commonly developed and conducted in-house, due mostly to confidentiality considerations. They are useful, although they may suffer from methodological inadequacies and, on some occasions, from the "live and let live" rule that often governs bureaucratic interactions. In exceptional cases, researchers and auditors have been able to conduct external feedback exercises, particularly within the framework of more comprehensive studies of intelligence failure.

In Europe, some intelligence services have tried to improve their understanding of their clients' and customers' needs and reactions by appending feedback forms to the products they disseminate. In Romania, for instance, "a few years ago, a feedback sheet to assess the level of satisfaction with the intelligence products was attached to documents transmitted to decisionmakers. Their responses were used in improving the SRI's[52] analytical and operational work, with hopes that, in the future, more dedicated procedures will be used to enhance the utility of such feedback into the system."[53] Practitioners, however, have frequently found that such a mechanism is less than optimal. Customers do not always respond to routine requests for feedback, and when they do so, their comments may be only polite or stereotypical. After all, as Kerbel and Olcott have rightly asked, "What policymaker would ever take the time after an event to, in effect, 'grade' the analysis he or she had received?"[54]

EU INTCEN and EUMS INT (its military counterpart) conducted regular feedback exercises after 2013.[55] The member states' ambassadors to the Political and Security Committee, the EEAS top management (managing directors and above), and some of their closest collaborators were targeted for personal interviews. Simultaneously, many lower-level officials received an email questionnaire and were invited to fill it in (around 40 percent of them did so).[56] Most respondents said that they appreciated INTCEN's and EUMS INT's production, although "there were also some more critical comments, depending on the customer's personal level of knowledge/experience (the usual problem of bias) and sometimes on their perceptions on what intelligence was and should do (facts/assessments/advise; time span)."[57]

The feedback exercises were mainly oriented toward improving the relationship between the two EU analytical bodies and their customers and had only a limited impact on the internal procedures of EU INTCEN and EUMS INT.[58] As one of the officials in charge of the exercises remembers,

> The results of the feedback exercises were mainly used for addressing the gaps, which included lack of awareness of the capabilities and the tasking mechanism (on this basis, we, for example, created a short training for intelligence customers, and enhanced our interactions with customers on all levels). And certainly the result that of our respondents more than 70 percent found the products to be of high quality and that they added value to their work was encouraging feedback not only internally, but also vis-à-vis the providers. . . . The question of tasking was identified as one of the areas where the customers still needed to be educated. . . . The dissemination challenges are inherent in the environment in which we worked, so there was not much we could do about it—other than make our products so attractive that people would go through the bureaucratic hurdles to read them.[59]

There are also informal ways of requesting and receiving feedback, and in some environments, such ways are frequently used. For instance, Tom Fingar has written that "in my experience, customers are more likely to show their appreciation for analytic assistance by asking more questions and granting greater access to deliberative meetings than they are to give analysts credit for providing an insight that triggered or facilitated new policy recommendations."[60] Otherwise, he has argued that "informal feedback is critical, such as emails from consumers as well as the notes of senior officials in the margins of INR products." In a similar vein, Antonio Díaz Fernández has explained how the Spanish intelligence service CNI receives feedback from policy makers in a mostly informal way:

> Only in an intuitive way can CNI analysts deduce that the product they generate is useful for the political decision-maker. This estimate is made based on whether there are: 1) positive comments or absence of negative ones; 2) evidence of the use of intelligence by consumers (sometimes provided by the media and sometimes by their superiors); 3) evidence of ability enhancement by previously supplied intelligence; or 4) estimates of the number of attacks averted, operations closed.[61]

Obviously, when intelligence is embedded in decision making, the contact with clients is close and permanent, which means that very often the feedback received through informal channels may be highly valuable. This is the case of INR in the US State Department, or with EU INTCEN and EUMS INT in the EEAS.[62]

One of the main problems with using the clients' feedback as a metric for assessing intelligence production quality is that clients often show higher appreciation for the work of intelligence when this is perceived as supportive of their political objectives, independently of its intrinsic value, objectivity, or accuracy. As Stephen Marrin has explained, "Decision-makers may not be satisfied with intelligence analysis if it conflicts with their own biases, assumptions, policy preferences, or conveys information that indicates a policy may be failing. . . . Therefore, the use of consumer satisfaction as a proxy metric for the value of intelligence analysis can lead to confusion between analytic quality and its confluence with policy agendas."[63]

Scholars' involvement in the design and/or conduct of feedback systems and exercises could make them more rigorous and helpful, and more valuable as a measurement of the intelligence production quality. Social scientists have extensive experience in collecting and analyzing customers' opinions, which is not substantially different from obtaining intelligence feedback. If feedback mechanisms are usually developed and implemented in-house, it is mostly for confidentiality reasons and the absence of trusted scholars who can be granted access to sensitive intelligence information and procedures.

Summarizing the main findings of this section:

- Feedback from clients and customers is irreplaceable for assessing an intelligence product's usefulness, one characteristic of their intrinsic quality.
- Feedback is a metric that is difficult to handle, as clients tend to better rate intelligence products supporting their views and projects, irrespective of their quality.
- Scholars' involvement in the design and development of intelligence feedback mechanisms and exercises would probably improve the quality of the results such measures may offer. Nevertheless, confidentiality considerations hinder closer cooperation between intelligence services and academia.

CONCLUSION

Measuring quality is challenging. On the one hand, there are methodological problems that are difficult to solve. As a CIA analyst, quoted by Johnston, says, "People talk about quality, but, in the end, the only measurable thing is quantity."[65] On the other hand, quality by itself does not guarantee bureaucratic success for intelligence organizations. Politically useful intelligence, even if factually wrong, may prove to be highly appreciated by policy-making clients.

Part of the problem lies in the difficulties of defining "quality" in intelligence. Different definitions would guide us in different directions while trying to find workable methods to measure quality. However, also, the intelligence community's limited expertise with advanced techniques of measurement and control represents a severe obstacle to the development of more efficient procedures. A fruitful interaction between intelligence professionals and scholars would help to overcome many of the difficulties associated with measuring quality, as in-house schemes are not reliable enough: "A considerable body of evidence from a wide range of fields indicates that the opinions of experts regarding which methods work may be misleading or seriously wrong. Better analysis requires independent scientific research."[66] Unfortunately, confidentiality rules prevent the access of most scholars to intelligence materials.

Scholars turned intelligence professionals and intelligence practitioners moving into academia after retirement can help to build the necessary bridges between both communities. The adoption of an enlarged concept of "intelligence community," able to integrate all the relevant stakeholders, including policy makers, civil society representatives, and interested scholars, could also help to put at the disposal of the intelligence organizations crucial expertise that they do not easily generate for themselves.[67] The new realities of the post-COVID-19 world, reflected in different priorities for decision makers and a new style of relationship between intelligence and its clients, can help accelerate this transition to "enlarged intelligence communities."

NOTES

1. Antonio Díaz Fernández, "El Papel de la Comunidad de Inteligencia en la Toma de Decisiones de la Política Exterior y de Seguridad de España" (Working Paper 3, Fundación Alternativas, Opex, 2006), 49.

2. Robert D. Behn, "Why Measure Performance? Different Purposes Require Different Measures," *Public Administration Review* 63, no. 5 (2003): 588.

3. Behn, "Why Measure Performance?," 599.

4. Rubén Arcos, "Academics as Strategic Stakeholders of Intelligence Organizations: A View from Spain," *International Journal of Intelligence and CounterIntelligence* 26, no. 2 (2013): 334.

5. Behn, "Why Measure Performance?," 599.

6. In their research on Fusion Centers, Fussell, Hough, and Pedersen found that most practitioners measure effectiveness by using (1) internal metrics and criteria, (2) objective indicators of performance, and (3) clients' satisfaction, three directions that are very similar to those explained in this chapter. Christopher Fussell, Trevor Hough, and Matthew Pedersen, "What Makes Fusion Cells Effective?" (MSc thesis, Naval Postgraduate School, Monterey, CA, 2009), 55. On the other hand, Stephen Marrin has proposed a slightly different list of evaluation strategies: "All three criteria—accuracy, preventing surprise, and influence on policy—are employed in retrospective evaluations of intelligence agency performance even though each has significant limitations and problems." Stephen Marrin, "Evaluating the Quality of Intelligence Analysis: By What (Mis) Measure?," *Intelligence and National Security* 27, no. 6 (2012): 897.

7. Daniel Irwin and David R. Mandel, "Improving Information Evaluation for Intelligence Production," *Intelligence and National Security* 34, no. 4 (2019): 511.

8. Philip H. J. Davies and Kristian C. Gustafson, eds., *Intelligence Elsewhere: Spies and Espionage Outside the Anglosphere* (Washington, DC: Georgetown University Press, 2013), 293.

9. European External Action Service (EEAS), "2011 Discharge to the EEAS" (answers by the High Representative/Vice President Catherine Ashton to the Written Questions of the Committee on Budgetary Control, January 1, 2013).

10. EUMS INT is the EU Military Staff's Intelligence Directorate, while INTCEN was in 2012–2015 the EEAS Intelligence Analysis Centre. EUMS INT and INTCEN are the only all-sources intelligence bodies in the EU institutions. For an overview of the EU-level intelligence community, see José-Miguel Palacios, "EU Intelligence: On the Road to a European Intelligence Agency?," in *Intelligence Law and Policies in Europe*, ed. Jan-Hendrik Dietrich and Satish Sule, 201–34 (Munich: C. H. Beck, 2019).

11. EEAS, "2011 Discharge to the EEAS," 9.

12. Rob Johnston, *Analytic Culture in the US Intelligence Community: An Ethnographic Study* (Washington, DC: Center for the Study of Intelligence, 2005), 18.

13. "To produce finished intelligence analysis, CIA analysts use a particular writing style designed for communicating judgments with precision and clarity while removing idiosyncratic phrases and the personality of the writer so that it becomes a 'corporate' product." Stephen Marrin, *Improving Intelligence Analysis: Bridging the Gap between Scholarship and Practice* (Abingdon: Routledge, 2012), 16.

14. The CIA Office of Strategic Research developed in the early 1970s a guide to intelligence analysis meant to assist analysts in the production process. See Raymond B. Firehock et al., "Negotiating the Review Process: A CIA Guide to Intelligence Analysis, 1970," *Intelligence and National Security* 33, no. 5 (2018): 774–83. Similarly, the EEAS intelligence organizations have used a "style guide" since 2013.

15. Martin Petersen, "Making the Analytic Review Process Work," *Studies in Intelligence* 49, no. 1 (2005): 55–61.

16. UK Chiefs of Staff, *Joint Doctrine Publication 2-00: Understanding and Intelligence Support to Joint Operations*, 3rd ed. (London: Ministry of Defence, 2011), 3–28.

17. Head of the Analysis Division, EU INTCEN, personal message to the author, May 14, 2019.

18. Petersen, "Making the Analytic Review Process Work."

19. Colonel Rafael Jiménez Villalonga, a former senior manager in CESID and CNI, private email to the author, May 14, 2019.

20. The Single Intelligence Analysis Capacity (SIAC) is a functional structure set up to coordinate the analytical production of INTCEN and EUMS INT.

21. Ivars Indāns, private email to the author, May 13, 2019.

22. José-Miguel Palacios, "Intelligence Analysis Training: A European Perspective," *International Journal of Intelligence, Security, and Public Affairs* 18, no. 1 (2016): 44.

23. Rubén Arcos and José-Miguel Palacios, "EU INTCEN: A Transnational European Culture of Intelligence Analysis?," *Intelligence and National Security* 35, no. 1 (2020): 85.

24. Johnston, *Analytic Culture*, 116.

25. Pauletta Otis, "The Intelligence Pro and the Professor: Toward an Alchemy of Applied Arts and Sciences," in *Bringing Intelligence About: Practitioners Reflect on Best Practices*, ed. Russell G. Swenson, 14 (Washington, DC: Joint Military Intelligence College, 2003).

26. Richards J. Heuer Jr., "The Evolution of Structured Analytic Techniques" (presentation to the National Academy of Sciences, Washington, DC, December 8, 2009).

27. National Research Council, *Intelligence Analysis for Tomorrow: Advances from the Behavioral and Social Sciences* (Washington, DC: National Academies Press, 2011), 3.

28. Philip E. Tetlock, "Theory-Driven Reasoning about Plausible Pasts and Probable Futures in World Politics: Are We Prisoners of Our Preconceptions?," *American Journal of Political Science* 43, no. 2 (1999): 335–66.

29. David R. Mandel, Christopher W. Karvetski, and Mandeep K. Dhami, "Boosting Intelligence Analysts' Judgment Accuracy: What Works, What Fails?," *Judgment and Decision Making* 13, no. 6 (2018): 607.

30. Alan Barnes, "Making Intelligence Analysis More Intelligent: Using Numeric Probabilities," *Intelligence and National Security* 31, no. 3 (2016): 327.

31. Tore Pedersen and Pia Therese Jansen, "Seduced by Secrecy—Perplexed by Complexity: Effects of Secret vs Open-Source on Intelligence Credibility and Analytic Confidence," *Intelligence and National Security* 34, no. 6 (2019): 881.

32. See CORDIS, "Final Report Summary—RECOBIA (REduction of COgnitive BIAses in Intelligence Analysis)," November 26, 2015, https://cordis.europa.eu /project/id/285010/reporting/es.

33. According to Robert Jervis, intelligence failure "is a mismatch between the estimates and what later information reveals." Robert Jervis, *Why Intelligence Fails: Lessons from the Iranian Revolution and the Iraq War* (Ithaca, NY: Cornell University Press, 2010), 1.

34. "High-reliability organizations" are hazardous organizations that "have operated nearly error free for very long periods of time." See Karlene H. Roberts, "Manag-

ing high-reliability organizations," *California Management Review* 32, no. 4 (1990): 101–13. Scholars and practitioners, such as Greg Treverton, Jeffrey Cooper, and William Shapcott, have argued that practices drawn from High Reliability Organizations theory can be used to improve the work of intelligence.

35. The Butler Review is the best known of the four inquiries conducted in Britain between 2003 and 2004 on the performance of the intelligence system in matters related to Iraq, WMD and counterterrorism. For an overview, see Richard J. Aldrich, "Whitehall and the Iraq War: The UK's Four Intelligence Enquiries," *Irish Studies in International Affairs* 16 (2005): 73–88.

36. See https://govinfo.library.unt.edu/911/about/bio_thompson.htm, 2003–2004.

37. Kenneth L. Lasoen, "For Belgian Eyes Only: Intelligence Cooperation in Belgium," *International Journal of Intelligence and CounterIntelligence* 30, no. 3 (2017): 481.

38. VSSE: Veiligheid van de Staat/Sûreté de l'État. SGRS: Service Général du Renseignement et de la Sécurité.

39. Guy Rapaille, the head of the Comité R between 2006 and 2018, is also the chairman of the Belgian Intelligence Studies Centre, comprising intelligence practitioners and scholars.

40. Robin Libert, former director of analysis in the Belgian civilian service VSSE, personal email to the author, October 19, 2020.

41. Jim Marchio, "'How Good Is Your Batting Average?' Early IC Efforts to Assess the Accuracy of Estimates," *Studies in Intelligence (Extracts)* 60, no. 4 (2016): 3–4.

42. *Time*, August 9, 1971; as quoted by Catherine A. Beck, "Bureau of Intelligence and Research and Washington Politics" (MA thesis, University of Georgia, 2005), 19.

43. At the time, the EU Situation Centre (SITCEN) was the EU civilian intelligence analysis body and reported to Secretary General Javier Solana. SITCEN was transferred to the newly formed EEAS in January 2011 and renamed EU INTCEN in March 2012.

44. Personal email to the author, May 19, 2019.

45. Klaus Knorr, "Failures in National Intelligence Estimates: The Case of the Cuban Missiles," *World Politics* 16, no. 3 (1964): 466–67.

46. Knorr, "Failures," 466–67.

47. Jervis, *Why Intelligence Fails*, 15.

48. Johnston, *Analytic Culture*, 81.

49. Arcos, "Academics as Strategic Stakeholders," 335.

50. Marrin, "Evaluating the Quality," 908.

51. National Research Council, *Intelligence Analysis*.

52. The SRI (Serviciul Român de Informaţii) is the main domestic intelligence service in Romania.

53. Mihaela Matei and Ionel Niţu, "Intelligence Analysis in Romania's SRI: The Critical 'Ps'—People, Processes, Products," *International Journal of Intelligence and CounterIntelligence* 25, no. 4 (2012): 721.

54. Josh Kerbel and Anthony Olcott, "Synthesizing with Clients, Not Analyzing for Customers," *Studies in Intelligence* 54, no. 4 (2010): 17.

55. The methodology described in this chapter is the one used between 2013 and 2015. Regular feedback exercises are still conducted by EU INTCEN and EUMS INT using a slightly modified methodology.

56. Colonel Józef Kozłowski, a former head of division in the EUMS Intelligence Directorate, personal email to the author, August 31, 2019. Kozłowski was one of the officials in charge of designing and conducting the feedback exercises.

57. A former INTCEN official, who was responsible for several feedback exercises during the directorship of Ilkka Salmi, personal email to the author, June 20, 2019.

58. Colonel Kozłowski, personal email to the author, August 31, 2019.

59. A former INTCEN official, personal email to the author, June 20, 2019.

60. Thomas Fingar, *Reducing Uncertainty: Intelligence Analysis and National Security* (Palo Alto, CA: Stanford University Press, 2011), 5.

61. Díaz Fernández, "El Papel de la Comunidad de Inteligencia," 49.

62. Björn Fägersten has argued that "proximity to power" is one of the main characteristics of the EU intelligence system. Björn Fägersten, "Intelligence and Decision-Making within the Common Foreign and Security Policy," Swedish Institute for European Policy Studies, *European Policy Analysis* 22 (2015): 5.

63. Marrin, "Evaluating the Quality," 910.

64. Johnston, *Analytic Culture*, 16.

65. Steven Rieber and Neil Thomason, "Creation of a National Institute for Analytic Methods," *Studies in Intelligence* 49, no. 4 (2005): 71.

66. Rubén Arcos and Joan Antón, "Reservas de Inteligencia: Hacia una Comunidad Ampliada de Inteligencia," *Inteligencia y Seguridad: Revista de Análisis y Prospectiva* 8 (2010): 34.

7

Lessons Learned for the Private-Sector Intelligence Analyst

Michael J. Ard

Private-sector intelligence analysis[1] has become an established career path as many corporations see the need for developing an intelligence analytic capacity to anticipate political and security risk. According to Recruiter.com, since 2004 in the United States, the broadly defined intelligence analyst field experienced around 5 percent annual growth, and in 2018, demand for private-sector analysts was estimated to be more than twenty thousand jobs.[2] The private-sector intelligence analyst, a "nice-to-have" position in past years, now often plays an important role in corporate security programs, especially for industries with a large overseas presence.

In 2012 the Marathon Oil Company hired me, a senior Central Intelligence Agency (CIA) intelligence analyst, to develop a strategic intelligence program from scratch to forecast risks for its people, assets, and operations overseas. I seized this great opportunity to apply the knowledge and skills of a government intelligence analyst to the problems of the private sector. The company was big enough to provide great scope for intelligence work, but scaled so that intelligence analysis could make a positive contribution to individual business units.

This second career as a private-sector analyst exposed me to a host of exciting issues and greatly expanded my repertoire as an analyst, collector, and manager of intelligence. I found the freedom provided to private-sector intelligence and the variety of the problems rewarding. However, the experience also highlighted the cultural differences between the government and corporate intelligence worlds and the challenges in making corporate intelligence programs sustainable and effective. This chapter offers my perspective on lessons learned from private-sector intelligence that might be useful to current and aspiring analysts. To prepare aspirants for this field, I will give my thoughts on what a postgraduate education for private-sector intelligence analysts might look like.

COMPARING THE ANALYTIC WORLDS

Different Organizational Cultures

Understanding the difference between these two "analytic worlds" of CIA and corporate intelligence requires a broad comparison of the differences in their organizational objectives and cultural norms. Organizational "culture" is an elusive concept, but a 2018 article in the *Harvard Business Review* defines it as "the tacit social order of an organization: It shapes attitudes and behaviors in wide-ranging and durable ways. Cultural norms define what is encouraged, discouraged, accepted, or rejected within a group."[3] Some of the "cultural norms" of the CIA are readily identifiable to its practitioners: (1) adherence to sound "tradecraft"; (2) a deep respect for expertise in a given area; (3) a collaborative mind-set; (4) a detachment from the policy debate and, related to this, (5) a strong aversion to "politicizing" analysis to suit customers' policy needs; and, finally, (6) respect for the integrity of classified information and the secrecy of the process. Analysts' performances are reviewed on the basis of how well they adhere to these norms, which are constantly reinforced by organizational culture.

These cultural norms fit the CIA's organizational needs. Naturally, government and private-sector analysts share many of these same cultural traits, such as the commitment to tradecraft and respect for expertise, but the analyst

Table 7.1. Government and Private-Sector Analysts Compared on Key Characteristics

Characteristics	CIA analyst	Private-sector analyst
Organization	Public financed; nonprofit; bureaucratic; hierarchical	For-profit enterprise; working in a "cost center"; often a flatter hierarchy
Duties	Well defined; predictable; based on career service	Defined but more flexible
Client base	Established communication to policy makers	Area for development in many firms; not necessarily well established
Information sources	Classified and open sources	Mainly open sources
Work environment	Collaborative internally and more limited externally	Independent internally and more collaborative externally
Job security	Stable	Contingent on the business cycle and evolving needs

in the corporate sector has to adapt to different expectations and occasionally pressures. For example, "politicization"—intentional slanting of analysis to fit a policy objective—might be a near taboo in the CIA because of the effort to keep analysis independent from policy concerns. However, politicization has little meaning in the corporate context, in which the analysis is more closely tied to corporate policy objectives.

Besides cultural adaptation, private-sector intelligence analysts have a challenging task, in some ways more challenging than that of their government counterparts. In an era of specialization, they have to be agile generalists. They often must be well informed on both the international scene and the domestic and must pivot adroitly as new needs arise. They must be comfortable performing the full range of analytic tasks and, in many cases, executing nearly all the steps in the intelligence cycle themselves.[4] Moreover, they operate in a corporate environment that differs from government intelligence in some important ways, as set out below.

Suiting the Needs of the Corporation

Most government analysts work in an environment in which the intelligence analysis either is "the main mission" or closely supports the organization's main mission. Their work represents an important component of mission success. The government analyst also has a well-defined, specialized role. The analyst in the US government is not subjected to the normal business cycle and other rules for determining future staffing. The analyst will be managed by his or her peers in the profession and will aspire to higher positions in a contained and predictable organizational environment. Often analysts are warehoused by the organization for future use in crises.

Unlike the government analyst, the private-sector analyst is likely to be located in a "cost center"—a business department that does not add directly to profits but draws on organizational funds to operate. Intelligence analysis ideally can save the enterprise money and, in theory, improve the organization's return on investment, but it cannot directly earn money, and its support usually subtracts from the bottom line.[5] The corporate analyst must constantly be seeking ways to prove their value-added worth to the enterprise. The contribution to the mission, therefore, must be clear cut and continuing. Economic downturns might tempt many businesses to cut the intelligence function entirely.

To minimize costs, the private-sector analyst must be efficient and adopt a wider skill set. In many ways, the analyst will need to define the position in ways his government counterpart does not need to. The private-sector analyst must be able to move to nearly any topic and get "up to speed" very quickly.

Intelligence More Broadly Defined

The CIA analyst typically is well resourced and works in a proprietary intelligence medium involving clandestinely obtained information and performed in a secretive and contained process with restrictive rules.[6] Although open-source intelligence is used frequently, especially to help frame a problem, CIA analysts prioritize the use of expensive, hard-to-attain, and sensitive intelligence, such as human intelligence and signals intelligence for priority targets.[7] The CIA communicates in classified language and forms an insulated community. It sometimes discourages analysts from reaching outside that community for fear of compromising classified information.[8]

On the other hand, the private-sector analyst culture is quite different. First, for this analyst, the broadest definition of intelligence best applies in this setting: intelligence is knowledge and foreknowledge about the world that assists the policy debate.[9] Even if the corporate security intelligence analyst has a security clearance, little if any of the information they process will be subject to the same restrictions as government-produced intelligence. This gives one a great deal of latitude in deciding what information can be used. However, there are natural pitfalls to this: one does not benefit as at the CIA from a system run by professional collectors in which raw information is culled for accuracy and relevance.

Limited Internal Collaboration

The government analyst is likely to be working in a team of fellow analysts. Although they may be considered an expert in a particular area, the analyst will engage with many colleagues who also share similar knowledge and act as a check on bad ideas. Therefore, collaboration in governmental intelligence analysis is the norm, and especially so in the broader intelligence community since the reforms of 2004.[10] In contrast, the private-sector analyst might be the only person in the organization working on their issue and have few peers to engage on analytic topics or even to judge their work. Therefore, private-sector analysts must seek opportunities to collaborate with other analysts outside the company to vet information and ideas.

Developing a Client Base

The CIA analyst typically has an established client base. Although analysts have to develop some demand for their work, in general, contacts with policy makers are well established and enduring. The analyst in the corporate environment, however, might have a greater challenge in developing their client base. The private-sector analyst, unlike their government counterpart, must work diligently to find their audience. In the corporate environment, it is not always understood what their role is and how they can support the business. The analyst must discover and define their niche, working directly for corporate security but enterprising enough to connect with and assist other business elements.

LESSONS LEARNED FROM THE CORPORATE WORLD

With a clearer view of how corporate organizational needs and culture differ for intelligence analysis, I will suggest some ways to achieve success in this environment. What is the value the private-sector analyst brings to the company? The key is to look for ways in which intelligence analysis helps it secure its people, assets, operations, and even its reputation and, by anticipating risk, spare the company from great expense.

Understand the Corporate "Risk Appetite"

One issue to consider is why businesses are eager to establish intelligence analytic units in the first place. The right reason would be ensuring that well-rounded intelligence on the business risks in the operational environment is integrated as part of the security assessments. A wrong reason might be simply to satisfy the corporate board by hiring an outside expert from a three-letter agency. In such a case, analysis may become window dressing with no impact on actual decision making. How committed the enterprise is to the intelligence analysis might depend on how much exposure the analyst's intelligence products get to senior leadership in the "C suite."

Acclimate to the Corporate Culture

When entering into the private sector, prospective analysts have to ask themselves, "What are the corporation's values and culture?" Many of these values will be shaped by the dominant profession in the building. For example, in an oil company like Marathon, engineers probably are the main decision makers, and their values predominate. Understanding how the corporate audience prefers to receive and process information is a key to success. As such, the analyst needs to tailor each presentation to the intended audience to ensure it appeals to how they absorb information. Engineers tend to like to see how you arrived at your answers; they appreciate seeing the thinking behind the work. One might need to create dense, detail-rich PowerPoints instead of the terse and succinct versions usually favored by intelligence analysts.

Incorporating structured analytic techniques into the intelligence, where appropriate, can demonstrate intellectual rigor. The use of these techniques can assist with the analyst's organizational socialization.[11]

Set Realistic Expectations for Intelligence Analysis

Analysts should educate their audience on knowledge gaps and offer reasonable estimates on prediction. Consider that few members of the corporation, if any, will have direct experience with the world of intelligence and may not understand its strengths and limitations. Government analysts often have good insight, impressive connections, and strong forecasting skills, but future predictions still involve guesswork. This reality of intelligence work is not always understood and consequently fails to meet expectations. For example, after we in corporate security produced a high-quality analytic report that predicted more instability in northern Iraq, when an invasion by the Islamic State insurgency forced an evacuation of our personnel near the city of Mosul, our CEO still asked us, "Why didn't we see this coming?"

Adapt to the "Risk-Based" Culture

Private-sector analytic work needs to integrate itself into the decision-making process. The intelligence unit should be part of the process in deciding on new business ventures and resolving problems in the operating environment. One will likely be taking a "risk-based" approach to security management in the corporate sector.[12]

Corporations have shifted to "risk-based" security plans and require intelligence analysts to help them calculate the risk. Part of the formula for determining risk is the probability of the threat being realized and the likely amount of damage done, as expressed in this simple formula: risk = threat × vulnerability × consequence, or $r = f(c, v, t)$.[13] Intelligence is a vital part of the process in determining the likelihood of threats to the business. Integrating intelligence analysis into the company's enterprise risk-management process must be a fundamental goal.[14]

The analyst's task is to put these risks in proper perspective so that business opportunities can be evaluated objectively. I once briefed an asset manager on risk management in Mexico and cautioned that an employee still might be kidnapped in Mexico, despite our ability to mitigate this risk.[15] The manager commented that even if there were *any* kidnapping possibility, he would reject the business opportunity. This appeared to be an unusually low risk tolerance threshold for an experienced professional working in the oil and gas industry, which must pursue opportunities in some of the world's most dangerous regions. However, it represented a common reaction to certain dramatic security threats.

Develop Unique Contacts

One of the most rewarding aspects of private-sector intelligence, and the best means to improve one's analytic repertoire, is to engage with outside experts. In government, many analysts seldom need to reach outside the building's confines for information; it was all provided on the computer screen. Moving to the private sector reinforced the need to cultivate a broad network of contacts to do my job properly. The company had assets in Africa and the Middle East and, of course, was searching for new opportunities throughout the globe. As a corporate security analyst, I became both a collection manager and an evaluator of expertise. This wide circle of contacts included fellow analysts in other firms, think tank experts, federal and local law enforcement, and so forth. It was imperative to have at one's call regional experts who could give expert commentary on emerging problems.

Cultivating strong ties with other members of the enterprise must also be emphasized and encouraged. The analyst should take advantage of his position in the organization chart to forge new links. Good collection can come from a variety of nontraditional sources. As in many large organizations, different parties talk to each other about specific issues, but they do not know what they have to offer. Information flows vertically but not necessarily horizontally. The intelligence analyst in a security department, by virtue of this unique role, is uniquely positioned to penetrate information silos and communicate with different departments to determine what they know.

At our Equatorial Guinea asset, one of my best company contacts headed the corporate social responsibility project. Because of his specialized role, his information was stovepiped within his department. However, his unique position allowed him to operate outside the normal chain of command, and he had leave to "go outside the main gate" into the community and meet with state officials. Therefore, as part of his duties, he obtained unmatched information about the political class of the country and the local security environment that few of our colleagues could match. He provided us with an excellent perspective on our intelligence analysis on the country, especially with regard to sensitive issues like presidential succession.

In one case, having extensive outside contacts helped elevate the internal debate on a new opportunity in Lebanon, a country with little history in oil exploration. The discussion deadlocked because the head of corporate insurance still imagined Beirut circa 1982, with images of rockets hitting our future offshore platform and militias kidnapping company employees dominating the discussion. We hired a former CIA senior case officer to provide a detailed assessment of the business and security risks in a conference call with the principals. I asked him not to downplay the risk but to focus on how companies mitigate risks there. The presentation enabled the principals to overcome their forebodings of Hezbollah kidnappings and regional insecurity and to concentrate on the business opportunity, which is where we needed to focus.

Some vendors responsible for traditional overseas services, like "journey management" firms who arrange secure travel for business executives, can also be fertile sources of intelligence. In the course of their duties, they often collected valuable local security information. One such company also published a valuable and affordable monthly intelligence report on the turmoil in Libya. Building a relationship with the company's vendors allowed me to gain insight into on-the-ground security issues in other countries. Their on-the-ground reporting filled the gap when our travel was restricted for security reasons.

Promote Strategic Intelligence

Establishing a strategic intelligence program and making it a success was the key objective for our corporate security department at Marathon. As a more sophisticated product than short-term tactical intelligence, we regarded our "strategic assessments" as the signature product to help the enterprise in its longer-term planning.[16] This program opened many roles for us, including projecting our security measures and contributing to the company's ability to plan for disaster and protect its employees. It also, importantly, was designed to establish an analytic baseline for how the company's units perceived the challenges in its overseas operations.

One immediate challenge was to develop an audience for strategic intelligence. What would be the security and stability challenges over the next year? This product would be coordinated with the major enterprise units associated with the asset and, we hoped, would be shared with our most senior executives.

Our corporate colleagues had little familiarity with this type of product. Likewise, it was difficult to avoid encroaching on the terrain of asset managers and business units like public affairs. In this case, the analyst's role required some diplomatic skill. We argued that these products would play a major role in determining security resources for the coming year. We incorporated the intelligence from these products into our risk analysis on security. In time, senior decision makers grew to appreciate a product used with the board to help their yearly projections.

However, arriving at an analytic line that everyone could endorse proved difficult. Asset managers, by virtue of their position, demand to be the main conduit of information to senior leadership. Corporate security taking the lead was unfamiliar terrain. To please everyone, we had to relent and agree to give the asset managers some editorial license over it. A key lesson learned here was developing a solid relationship with the asset managers. The products would never have had any bureaucratic credibility without their input. It circumscribed our analytic independence, but the cost of not doing so was institutional irrelevance.

Our strategic intelligence product endured its "trial by fire" when trying to forecast Libya's outlook in 2012. We relied on various local contacts and experts, many of whom knew the country well but were perhaps unduly optimistic of its prospects for democratic governance. It was an unstable environment, and some analytic caution was warranted. My philosophy of identifying the key trends and taking a strong analytic line probably should have been tempered by this uncertainty. Intelligence professor Richard Betts speaks about "normal theory" in intelligence analysis; that is, what has been happening will likely continue to happen.[17] Unfortunately, after rosily predicting that the Libyans would muddle through, the country's parliament split, and a civil war broke out between the rival militia factions. In retrospect, perhaps a practical methodology such as scenario quadrants might have had better success covering Libya's turbulent politics.

Fortunately for our program, other products delivered more impact. In 2014 we presented timely warning on instability issues in Iraqi Kurdistan due to the ongoing war in Syria. Our analysis drew from a commissioned report by a former CIA senior case officer who visited the region and provided great insight on Kurdish politics and long-term political risk. The indications and warning system that we provided in our document enabled us to make timely recommendations on when to evacuate personnel, which were used effectively by our asset in-country. It should count as a success any time intelligence can play an important role in corporate decision making.

Developing a strategic assessment on Equatorial Guinea's internal and external security represented perhaps the biggest challenge due to the issue's sensitivity with senior management. We focused on security threats from outside the country, especially local piracy that might seriously impact personnel and operations. Nevertheless, many in the organization were reticent to discuss issues such as reputational risk in aligning with the authoritarian regime and the controversy of these presidential succession issues. Some denied the need to collect better intelligence on internal politics, believing the company's close contacts with the presidential family were sufficient!

Drafting a product that touched on these issues, however tentatively, counted as a step forward for the conservative, risk-averse organization.

Seize the Moment to Add Value

Marathon's CEO announced one day to his senior executives that, according to his contacts in Washington, DC, the Israelis were planning an imminent air attack to destroy Iran's nuclear enrichment facilities. How would such a dramatic move disrupt or endanger our operations and safety in the region? We saw this as an opportunity to place a unique product in front of the CEO that would provide various possibilities. Drawing from the scenario-building concepts discussed in Peter Schwartz's *The Art of the Long View*,[18] we created a series of scenarios explaining the potential range of options and their likely effect, helping us to engage in "a strategic conversation" with senior leadership.[19] Our primary argument—that Israel was unlikely to take such a bold move without full US backing and without the Israeli security establishment's support—proved to be persuasive to our CEO, and this analysis placed our analytic unit squarely on his radar.

"Scenario building" is a great example of government intelligence borrowing from a corporate best practice. According to Schwartz, scenario building gained attention with analysts at Royal Dutch Shell predicting the 1970s' oil shocks, and the techniques are taught at the CIA's Sherman Kent School for Intelligence Analysis as a creative means to not necessarily predict but to "re-perceive" the future.[20] In my former position on the National Intelligence Council, I had received training in these scenario-building techniques, and in this case it paid dividends in my new position at Marathon.

Assist Other Business Units

The intelligence analyst can play a role in the enterprise's cyber security preparedness by raising awareness of the geopolitical drivers behind many advanced persistent threats. Russia might have tried to attack Ukraine with the 2017 NotPetya malware attack, but it affected companies like FedEx, Maersk, and Merck, costing billions of dollars.[21] Corporations are collateral damage when it comes to geopolitical cyber attacks. Our cyber analysts highlighted how many probes there were against the business's industrial control systems on a routine basis.

Intelligence should also be aware of the growing risk of industrial espionage. With notable incidents of intellectual property loss, the insider threat has emerged as a new area of emphasis in corporate security.[22] Companies are becoming aware that employing foreign nationals might open the door to exploitation by foreign powers. If companies want to protect their intellectual property, they need to be aware of these inherent vulnerabilities.[23]

One area where we gained traction was providing analysis to the company's new ventures unit. We contributed weekly to the discussion on the security cost of doing business in far-flung locations, and our analysis became a regular feature of the business unit's opportunity analysis. This relationship turned into a surprising growth area for our intelligence unit and provided consistent value-added to corporate decision making.

Likewise, it is useful for the intelligence analyst to join committees or working groups on special issues. Serving on a workplace violence working group was a valuable experience to get more exposure to everyday security issues and participate in decision making. Having a seat on the company's insider threat working groups offered insight into personnel issues, including potential workplace violence. Our contacts with federal law enforcement gave us access to experts experienced in managing these threats.[24]

Participate in Intelligence Exchanges

Government and private-sector analysts can learn much from one another. Interaction and sharing, if not open collaboration, is important because today's threat environment does not distinguish between national and private-sector targets. Twenty-first-century security requires perspectives both broad and deep, and no single institution has a monopoly on insight.

Government managers need to see the value in more outside, nontraditional connections. Government analysts need more exposure to the kinds of sources private-sector analysts use. Government analysts know that the private sector has a lot of insight and contextualized information to give, and it is perhaps more important now that threat vectors have become more diffuse.

Corporate intelligence analysts should engage with their government peers, but they should also keep in mind that the exchange is bound to be slanted to one side. Government analysts have little incentive to "let their hair down" to outside analysts, even if they both hold secret clearances. Why risk uncomfortable polygraph sessions for information exchange with private-sector intelligence? Government analysts are initiates to an exclusive club and want to keep that status.

Despite the one-sided nature of it, liaising with government counterparts can be an essential source of information on some issues, and it has credibility with senior management. Organizations such as the Domestic Security Alliance Council and Overseas Security Advisory Council offer beneficial exchange opportunities.[25] However, on issues such as projecting instability, government analysts often have no greater special insight than private-sector ones.[26] Nevertheless, helping them builds institutional goodwill and also helps burnish your credentials within your company as being "in the know." In some cases, it is beneficial to say back at corporate that at least the government does not seem to have any better insight than you do!

EDUCATIONAL PRIORITIES

The educational needs of the intelligence analyst of the future differ significantly from the past generation's. The private-sector analyst plays a unique role in both domestic and overseas issues. My experiences and lessons learned from being a private-sector intelligence analyst convinced me that a broader education for the position is required. A master's program focused on intelligence for the private sector, with hands-on applications, would incorporate areas of study missing from traditional programs. The private sector handles a host of issues for which most government analysts have little experience. Analysts today will be expected to be conversant in a wide range of subjects related to potential threats and have experience with basic technology and databases available in corporate America, such as search engines like Lexis and TLOxp.

The traditional liberal arts education in area studies, modern languages, and writing that most analysts receive is a necessary but insufficient precondition for success in this profession. A master's program focused on intelligence for the private sector would incorporate areas of study missing from traditional programs.

Here are some ideas on what such a program might look like:

To begin, any program should emphasize the cognitive science and tools of intelligence analysis. Especially in an environment where you are trying to persuade senior managers with engineering backgrounds, the organizational methods of these techniques can help bridge the credibility gap. Besides their obvious benefit to the analyst in organizing, collating, and prioritizing information, these techniques are instrumental in displaying information for a diverse set of customers.[27] Learning the elements of forecasting also helps with respect to strategic forecasting. For example, work done by psychologist Philip Tetlock and his team with the "Good Judgment Project" offers important findings on how analytic teams can improve their forecasting by eliminating cognitive biases.[28]

An essential course for the analyst should cover the fundamentals of corporate security for business, which would provide both business and security basics. Most government analysts have little background in this area. The course should see security within the enterprise as a complex system that, as security expert Bruce Schneier puts it, "interacts with itself, the assets to be protected, and the surrounding environment."[29] Having a holistic view of security will enhance collection efforts, inform analysis, and direct recommendations. Additional certification from the American Society of Industrial Security can improve the analyst's credentials and credibility with other members of the security team.[30]

Such a course would offer the basics of physical security and travel security. The latter, although seemingly mundane, can pay great dividends for the analyst because it is the area where they have the greatest routine contact with the company's workforce. Many companies offer expensive travel tracking systems for their travelers, which probably help give some peace of mind and cover the company on "duty of care" issues. Intelligence can brief senior travelers on the risk of intellectual property theft in visiting certain countries. Part of the plan should be to advise travelers on the risk to their personal information and raise awareness.[31] Analysts can also assist in determining hotel security and the best journey management plans.

Another important course of study, and one in which all analysts can benefit, is the study of risk management and such systems as developed in the widely used ISO 31000 series of standards. The corporate world places greater emphasis on estimating risk than government. It is a crucial skill, especially for the business's security component. However, understanding the limitations of the corporate emergency risk-management process and especially the subjectivity of its input should not be overlooked.[32]

To contribute to the risk assessment process, the analyst must be the organization's political risk expert. This is vital both for entering new markets and for surviving and thriving in existing ones. Somehow the analyst must step outside corporate thinking in looking at risk objectively. Credibly assessing instability in a country, its political dynamics and its particular security risks, and the nature of its corrupt practices is a vital skill for the analyst. The analyst's job is also to help identify and diminish blind spots.[33] External risks to the corporation include global, political, and societal trends, as well as hazards from natural disasters, terrorism, and malicious activity in cyberspace, pandemics, transnational crime, and human-made accidents.[34] A model for such a course can be found in the book by former US secretary of state Condoleezza Rice and Stanford University professor Amy Zegart, *Political Risk: How Businesses and Organizations Can Anticipate Global Insecurity.*

Emergency management is another vital area for education. Analysts can play essential roles in emergency response, especially in the company's incident command system (ICS).[35] All companies with an industrial focus will have an ICS, and it pays to understand when an emergency response might be necessary. The analyst should be familiar with plans for employee evacuation and advise when to implement these plans.[36] Some familiarity with this process can go far for the analyst's overall contribution to the enterprise.[37]

Such a course might feature the 2013 terrorist attack on the In Amenas, Algeria, gas plant and other large-scale attacks that have direct pertinence to corporate intelligence analysts. The Norwegian state oil company Statoil produced a seminal after-action report on the attack and the corporate response that should be part of any class on emergency management.[38] This document provides a helpful guide on how a company can instill a more profound security culture among its employees and be intimately familiar to any private-sector intelligence analyst.

Finally, I would recommend a strong background in open-source analysis. Using tools that have become available to cull social media has become an essential part of the analysts' warning function. For companies with far-flung assets and in controversial industries, having some capacity to monitor social media is essential. The use of social media analysis sites like Flashpoint and Bellingcat has broken ground in understanding protester "ecosystems." Numerous companies can give a profile of a company's social media exposure. Social media has been used to understand and respond to intended protests. The analyst might be able to do this themselves but likely would be managing a contract with an outside firm. These tools can be used to red team the C suite's exposure online and help protect senior executives. The private-sector intelligence analyst's mastery of open-source and social media tools might have the greatest value-added for the intelligence program's contribution to the enterprise.

CONCLUSION

Private-sector intelligence analysis is a profession that is coming of age. Although in many ways similar to its government counterpart, private-sector intelligence analysis has its own set of unique challenges and requires an education in security issues and modern open-source collection technique to be effective and versatile in a competitive marketplace. Given that they often work in business environments unaccustomed to using their form of intelligence production to full advantage, analysts must be alert to opportunities to "add value" and bring their unique skills to bear on emerging security problems.

How these private-sector analysts use information today compels us to think more expansively about "intelligence" in general. No longer should "intelligence" be considered an exclusive government preserve. As private-sector analysts are demonstrating, intelligence must be less reliant on "secrets" and more dependent on a wide variety of open sources. Given their need to innovate and their unique perspective on security issues, these private-sector intelligence practitioners offer invaluable insight, and it should be incumbent upon government intelligence services to break down secrecy barriers and establish better information sharing and collaboration with them.

NOTES

1. Private-sector intelligence analysis focuses mainly on security risks to a company's personnel, assets, operations, and reputation. This is distinct from competitive, or corporate, intelligence analysts, who collect information on customers, competitors, and markets, and cyber intelligence analysts, who monitor threats to the company's information security.

2. Employment data searched at Recruiter.com, https://www.recruiter.com /careers/intelligence-analysts/outlook. Intelligence here can refer to a range of like positions, including business intelligence and cyber intelligence.

3. Boris Groysberg et al., "The Leader's Guide to Corporate Culture," *Harvard Business Review* (January–February 2018), https://hbr.org/2018/01/the-leaders -guide-to-corporate-culture.

4. The traditional intelligence cycle is (1) planning requirements, (2) collection, (3) processing and exploitation, (4) analysis, and (5) dissemination. A private-sector intelligence analyst can at times be involved in all five. See Roger Z. George, *Intelligence in the National Security Enterprise* (Washington, DC: Georgetown University Press, 2020), 85–87.

5. Daniil Davydoff, "How Intelligence Analysis Can Drive Corporate ROI," *Security Magazine*, July 1, 2018, https://www.securitymagazine.com/articles/89193 -how-intelligence-analysis-can-drive-corporate-roi.

6. Michael Warner, "Wanted: A Definition of 'Intelligence,'" *Studies in Intelligence* 46, no. 3 (2002): 18.

7. George, *Intelligence in the National Security Enterprise*, 199.

8. Some parts of the intelligence community are more receptive to outside contact. The author spent three years on the National Intelligence Council, where connections with think tanks and academics were more the norm.

9. Warner, "Wanted: A Definition of 'Intelligence,'" 16.

10. The Intelligence Reform and Terrorism Prevention Act legislation. See Rob Johnston, *Analytic Culture in the US Intelligence Community: An Ethnographic Study* (Washington, DC: Center for the Study of Intelligence, 2006), 5.

11. Johnston, *Analytic Culture in the US Intelligence Community*, 98.

12. Robert J. Fischer, Edward Halibozek, and Gion Green, *Introduction to Security*, 8th ed. (Burlington, MA: Elsevier, 2008), 147.

13. John Mueller and Mark G. Stewart, *Terror, Security and Money: Balancing the Risks, Benefits, and Costs of Homeland Security* (New York: Oxford University Press, 2011), 24.

14. William G. Parrett, *The Sentinel CEO: Perspectives on Security, Risk, and Leadership in the Post-9/11 World* (Hoboken, NJ: Wiley, 2007), 43–44.

15. For information on Mexico's kidnapping problem, see Charles E. Goslin, *Understanding Personal Security and Risk: A Guide for Business Travelers* (Boca Raton, FL: CRC Press, 2017), 72–74.

16. For a brief discussion, see Robert M. Clark, *Intelligence Analysis: A Target-Centric Approach* (Washington, DC: CQ Press, 2010), 50–51.

17. Richard K. Betts, *The Enemies of Intelligence: Knowledge and Power in American National Security* (New York: Columbia University Press, 2007), 53–54. "Normal theory is indispensable because it usually produces the right conclusion."

18. Peter Schwartz, *The Art of the Long View: Planning for the Future in an Uncertain World* (New York: Crown Business, 1996).

19. Schwartz, *The Art of the Long View*, 219–21.

20. Schwartz, *The Art of the Long View*, 7–9.

21. Andy Greenberg, "The Untold Story of NotPetya, the Most Devastating Cyberattack in History," *Wired*, August 22, 2018, https://www.wired.com/story /notpetya-cyberattack-ukraine-russia-code-crashed-the-world.

22. Ponemon Institute, *2020 Cost of Global Threats Insider Report*, 19, https:// www.observeit.com/2020costofinsiderthreat.

23. Matt Bromiley, "Effectively Addressing Advanced Threats," SANS, July 2019, 2.

24. Excellent guidance is available from the Cybersecurity and Infrastructure Security Agency of the US Department of Homeland Security, https://www.cisa.gov /insider-threat-mitigation.

25. For access to both DSAC and OSAC, see https://www.dsac.gov.

26. In the oil and gas industry, many were disappointed by the State Department's poor grasp of the unraveling situation in Libya in 2011, which caused a chaotic scramble to evacuate. If you are working overseas, it pays to keep in mind that in an evacuation situation the US embassy will focus on its own personnel first.

27. In a RAND study, the authors argue that the intelligence community has never troubled to assess whether analysis improves in effectiveness with SATs. See Stephen Artner, Richard S. Girven, and James B. Bruce, "Assessing the Value of Structured Analytic Techniques in the U.S. Intelligence Community," RAND Corporation, 2016, 1.

28. Paul J. H. Schoemaker and Philip E. Tetlock, "Superforecasting: How to Upgrade Your Company's Judgment," *Harvard Business Review*, May 2016, https://hbr .org/2016/05/superforecasting-how-to-upgrade-your-companys-judgment.

29. Bruce Schneier, *Beyond Fear: Thinking Sensibly about Security in an Uncertain World* (New York: Copernicus Books, 2003), loc. 563, Kindle.

30. For information, see https://www.asisonline.org.

31. See Goslin, *Understanding Personal Security and Risk*.

32. See, for example, Douglas W. Hubbard, *The Failure of Risk Management: Why It's Broken and How to Fix It* (Hoboken, NJ: Wiley, 2009).

33. Condoleezza Rice and Amy B. Zegart, *Political Risk: How Businesses and Organizations Can Anticipate Global Insecurity* (New York: Hachette, 2018), 129.

34. US Department of Homeland Security, *Risk Management Fundamentals*, April 2011, 13.

35. Access to be found at https://training.fema.gov/emiweb/is/icsresource/assets/ics%20review%20document.pdf.

36. Donald P. Moynihan, "The Network Governance of Crisis Response: Case Studies of Incident Command Systems," *Journal of Public Administration Research and Theory* 19 (2009): 895–915.

37. Federal Emergency Management Agency, National Incident Management System, 2017, 24–34.

38. In January 2013, thirty-two terrorists linked to Al-Qaeda attacked a major gas plant in the Sahara Desert and held numerous hostages for three days before being suppressed by the Algerian military. The plant, jointly run by the Algerian state company Sonatrach, BP, and the Norwegian state oil company Statoil (now Equinor), suffered forty employees killed and major damage. Statoil conducted an important analysis of the attack, which can be found at https://www.equinor.com/en/news/archive/2013/09/12/12SepInAmenasreport.html.

8

Understanding and Countering Hybrid Threats through a Comprehensive and Multinational Approach

The Role of Intelligence

Rasmus Hindrén and Hanna Smith

This chapter is based on the work completed by the European Centre of Excellence for Countering Hybrid Threats[1] (henceforward, Hybrid CoE) and may be utilized as an example of how a bridge can be constructed between academics and practitioners in the intelligence studies field. The Helsinki-based Hybrid CoE was established in 2017 to complement and assist its participating states, the European Union (EU) and North Atlantic Treaty Organization (NATO), to counter hybrid threats. According to its foundational memorandum of understanding, the center is expected to serve as a hub of expertise supporting participants' individual and collective efforts to enhance their civil-military capabilities, resilience, and preparedness in countering hybrid threats. A special focus is on European security from "a comprehensive, multinational, multidisciplinary and academic-based approach."[2]

Research and analysis, training, and engagement between government practitioners and outside experts from different government sectors, industries, and scholars from diverse disciplines are part of the center's mandate to accomplish its mission. The relationships with academic experts include the publication of open-source strategic analysis papers and other flagship publications like trend reports.[3]

The center's approach to countering hybrid threats is multidisciplinary and multisectoral. One of the center's objectives is to provide out-of-the-box thinking and conceptual tools that help bridge the gaps between government and society and between practitioners and expert communities. Under this comprehensive approach, the role of academia and researchers is critical in providing long-term context, analysis, and help in understanding the nature of the threats. To support this endeavor, the center has set up pools of experts that tap into expertise from academia, think tanks, and other stakeholders that can complement the assessments from practitioners, provide new insights, and identify synergies from different analyses. The center also engages with the private sector to complement knowledge from academics and practitioners. Bringing together different perspectives and assessments helps to build more comprehensive situational awareness among Hybrid CoE–participating states, the EU, and NATO, as well as to find new capabilities and use existing capabilities more efficiently in facing and countering hybrid threats.

In the hybrid threat environment, it is increasingly difficult to detect and analyze the threat. Hybrid activities might be misinterpreted as an accident or an isolated incident, and, conversely, something that looks like a threat may be the result of an accident or isolated incident. The deliberate nature of hybrid threat activity only manifests itself when repeated over time, in another sector of society, in another country, or when the actor behind the action makes a mistake. In such an environment, intelligence analysis faces new pressures. Attribution has always been notoriously difficult and correct situational awareness challenging. Today, however, this might be even more the case. In such an environment, the need for cooperation between practitioners, academics, and businesses has increased.

The information the different actors utilize in their daily working environment has different functions. Practitioners have nearly real-time information and activity reporting. The environment they work in is full of information flows and many simultaneously occurring events. Often a response is needed when only very few facts are known. This means that long research reports are of very little use to practitioners, even if they contain relevant and important information. Academics work in a very different working environment. They have time to explore, build a context, apply theories, and seek alternative explanations. The information that the private sector requires consists of statistics, risk analyses, and technical data. This serves the purpose for the private sector to execute its functions. Naturally, this distinction between practitioners, academics, and the private sector represents a simplification; however, it does highlight how the same information can be used differently. In today's increasingly complex security environment, all of these different ways to collect and use information have their place when facing the challenge of hybrid threats. Confronting this challenge requires a wide range of information and all the different perspectives that information can provide for better situational awareness; connecting the synergies between different events; identifying malign tactics, activities, and strategies; and mapping different vulnerabilities.

Responding to hybrid threats, as described above, has to start with ideas connected to resilience, both material and societal, with a comprehensive view beginning with understanding the threat and how to best counter it. As the threats are cross-societal, cross-governmental, and multinational, there is a requirement for comprehensive situational awareness. The stovepiped nature of governmental work must give way to broader information sharing and, when formulating responses, broader decision making. In short, the responses should be based on an integrated strategy where there is a vital role for the information and analysis that comes from the academic security community and the private sector.

The role of information is central to a complete situational picture. All decision making depends on information, data, expertise, and in some cases algorithmic calculations. Today, when information flows fast and the amount of information is more extensive than ever, the importance of making decisions also grows quickly. In this situation, content confusion is a reality for all, meaning that "sharing, commenting and liking often happen without knowing the original production context and based on recommendations by friends in the social networks, who might also be recommending without any knowledge of the original purpose of the content."[4] This means that when decisions need to be made quickly, there is a risk that correct information is not trusted or considered. Case studies show that in a time of crisis, early decisions are based on advice that can turn out to be faulty or inaccurate due to either a deficit in knowledge or dubious information sources, and therefore lead to nonoptimal decision making.[5] Other studies underline the fact that long-term disinformation activity reinforces existing divisions in society and plays these divisions against each other to activate individual-level decisions, resulting in unhealthy polarization.[6]

The decision-making environment is not likely to get any easier. Misleading and inaccurate information remains a risk, and decisions will need to be taken in the context of unverified data or incomplete analysis. At the same time, the ability of governmental structures to combine the signals emanating from different directions remains a serious challenge. This exacerbates the challenges posed by an insufficient situational picture. Therefore, from the perspective of the hybrid threat environment, information gathering and analysis should be informed by at least three key objectives. The first is to provide timely information and analysis. Next is to combine various signals from different sectors of society and analyze their interaction to extract the potential strategic intent behind those signals. The final objective is to allow decision makers to weigh the risks associated with any given course of action.

Meanwhile, the changes in the information environment have also affected intelligence gathering. The roles of OSINT (open-source intelligence) and PROTINT (protected information) have been growing. Still, in societies, information based on professional intelligence gathering, let alone on secret intelligence, is only available to a small number of those who need to make significant decisions.[7] Secret information is the information our adversaries want to keep away from us, while we want to keep our secrets away from them. A piece of information that has been obtained through covert intelligence can make all the difference from a national security perspective, either confirming OSINT or bringing new insights that will affect decision making. The role of professionally collected and analyzed information continues to be crucial, but there is an emerging set of new requirements for it in the world of hybrid threats. Building and sustaining resilience takes on new meaning and new importance. The same is true for deterrence.

In this chapter, the nature of hybrid threats will be first examined. This provides a basis for understanding the challenges facing intelligence gathering and intelligence-based decision making today. Then the role of intelligence and the comprehensive approach for countering hybrid threats is examined against the backdrop of the nature of the hybrid threats by concentrating on three layers: understanding, resilience building, and deterrence. Finally, the role of intelligence will be explored in all three of these layers, including how closer cooperation between the practitioner community, private sector, and academics is needed to enhance situational awareness and capability building to counter hybrid threats.

THE NATURE OF "THREAT" IN HYBRID THREATS

The concept of hybrid threats has entered the broader lexicon in the last ten years. The concept has been accompanied by a wide-ranging and persistent debate, focusing on its analytical utility, historical roots, and the perceived tendency to overuse it.[8] One of the arguments within the debate is that the concept is so broad that it is effectively rendered devoid of meaning.

From a policy perspective, the breadth of the concept led to specific challenges in defining the problem and finding effective methods to counter it. There is agreement that EU and NATO countries today face a threat that has been absent for some time and now has reoccurred, and with new tools—the battle between democracy and authoritarian state systems. Although this common understanding exists, there continue to be different understandings of the concept of hybrid threats and their usage. The EU definition covers nearly a full spectrum of threats.[9] In the United States, hybrid threats are most often understood as threats below the threshold of kinetic activities, sometimes referred to as the "gray zone" or asymmetric threats. Within NATO, the discussion circulates around a combination of military and nonmilitary means, the hybrid methods of warfare. All ultimately talk about a similar type of threat. The report *The Landscape of Hybrid Threats: A Conceptual*

Model by the EU's Joint Research Centre (JRC) and Hybrid CoE identifies five critical characteristics of the challenge hybrid threats pose to decision making and, through that, also for intelligence analysis:

- Use of multiple synchronized tools to create linear and nonlinear effects
- Ability to create ambiguity with plausible or implausible deniability and to hide true intent
- Deliberate threshold manipulation when it comes to detection and response
- Exploitation of the seams of democratic societies and the different jurisdictions (individual, local, state, international)
- Use of decoys, meaning to include a distraction element, such as action in one place and a target somewhere else[10]

However, the concept is comprehensive in nature, which should be seen as a feature, not a challenge, of defining the threat. In fact, this approach of characterizing the phenomenon instead of aiming to define it allows for better preparedness and considers today's constantly changing security environment and provides better ways to counter the existing challenge. The "hybrid" in hybrid threats refers to various tools that the malign actor has at its disposal. The tools target various domains like information, social and culture, space, cyber, and military. In the report by the JRC and Hybrid CoE, thirteen different domains, including intelligence and information as domains, are identified as areas where hybrid threat action has been and can be happening. As the combinations of these tools are endless, the preparedness for hybrid threats should not exclude any of them. Furthermore, technological trends suggest that the portfolio of hybrid threat tools will expand.[11]

On top of hybrid threat characteristics, the following needs to be considered: there is always an actor behind the action. Actions are based on an aim or strategic goal and often involve "priming," which refers to preparatory activities, usually undertaken covertly and often over a long duration. The adversary can exploit these actions if an opportunity arises.

Hybrid activities, up to the level of hybrid warfare, sometimes constitute a strategy on their own. However, they often support an existing strategy or policy in the eventuality that the strategy or policy is viewed as unsuccessful or failing. This means that traditional tools of international influence like diplomacy, economic deals, and legal agreements alone do not allow the actor to achieve its strategic goals. Also, the military-centric approach is excluded or may not apply, and there is still interest in minimizing the risk of open escalation or conflict. Since this type of action is connected to authoritarian strategic culture, it tries to be two steps ahead and undertake priming on the ground even before it is necessary. This means a whole new type of challenge for threat assessments and preparedness, both at the national and international levels. In this kind of security environment, exchange of information between practitioners, academics, and the private sector increases in importance.

THE ROLE OF INTELLIGENCE AND THE COMPREHENSIVE APPROACH IN COUNTERING HYBRID THREATS

The use of intelligence when it comes to the landscape of hybrid threats can be described in the following manner. From the perspective of the hybrid aggressor, intelligence is used in two principal ways. They will usually employ their intelligence capabilities to support planned or ongoing hybrid threat activities, or they may attempt to affect the target state's intelligence operations. In both cases, "the actor seeks to undermine the target state's capability to develop and maintain situational awareness."[12] This means that intelligence can be used as one tool in different types of activities like interference, influence, and operations in or across many different domains—cyber, information, society, diplomacy, political, military, etc.—to advance the hostile actors' interests. It also means that intelligence as a domain can be used as a target. If intelligence is one of the target domains, the main aim is to reduce the quality of decision making in the target countries. This is done by trying to interrupt, infiltrate, and confuse the intelligence cycle in different ways. In today's information environment, speed, volume, artificial intelligence, and degrading expert and official voices are challenges that can affect intelligence gathering.[13] All this becomes even more complex and important when considering the comprehensive need to counter hybrid threats. Bringing together the information and analytic expertise from practitioners, academics, and the private sector can give a competitive edge against hostile actors.

When it comes to countering hybrid threats, three layers can be identified: understanding, building resilience, and effective capabilities for deterrence. Understanding forms the base layer. This means that there has to be a whole-of-society and whole-of-government joint situational awareness of the nature of hybrid threats. The picture of hostile actors, their strategic aims, and their capabilities needs to be more or less understood and updated regularly. This is true not only in the national context but also in the international context. When the base layer is in place, building resilience against hybrid threats becomes clearer. In the understanding layer, the role of intelligence is vital. At the same time, it can become one of the main targets and a tool of the hostile actor, especially in the priming phase of the hybrid activity. The activity manifests itself primarily through cyber and information spaces by infiltrating and intercepting the OSINT environment and gathering as much information as possible in the PROTINT sphere. While the hostile actors seek ways to exploit and explore the possibilities to interfere with the target's situational awareness, what the target can do is comprehensively gather information on different activities and seek to connect this to the strategic aims of the hostile actor. In this work, close cooperation between practitioners, academics, and the private sector is vital for disrupting the intelligence activities of threat actors, including those of hostile intelligence services. Understanding different perspectives and their role in one's own work can deepen the understanding of the situation and mitigate the possible impact of manipulative interference that aims to blur understanding, create ambiguity, and deceive. If this layer has weaknesses, it can weaken the ability to build resilience and develop efficient deterrence policies. The contribution of academic experts in providing further context and new ideas and deepening understanding on hybrid threat–related issues is critical.

The second layer is building resilience, where a comprehensive approach also needs to be taken. Traditionally, resilience refers to sectoral resilience—resilience of systems, resilience of institutions, resilience of nations (resilience of individuals/societies), etc. It involves the ability to resist disturbance by absorbing a negative impact entirely, or at least partially (*robustness*); the ability to restore capabilities after the damage (*recovery*); the ability to conduct subtle changes in order to adapt to a new operational environment (*adaptation*); and the ability to enact more extensive reforms of the system in order to meet new resilience requirements (*transformation*).[14] When it comes to countering hybrid threats, the resilience of different sectors of society needs to be assessed simultaneously. In addition, the interconnected and interdependent nature of the sectors must be understood.

Effective resilience building is therefore comprehensive and integrated. It is comprehensive because we must be ready to mobilize efforts in various government sectors. Resilience building is also integrated because those sectors must respond and operate together. In the hybrid threat security environment, there are multiple vectors the adversary is using, often across different sectors of government or society. If we focus too much on any one sector, the adversary will look for other avenues, weaknesses, and vulnerabilities elsewhere. Here the international level is critical. It is questionable whether effective resilience can be built only in a national context in today's interconnected world.

For the intelligence enterprise, the work of intelligence needs to be connected to other government sectors and other governments. Nationally, this implies that requests for intelligence-based information should come from a broader actor base within the government in the sense of both strategic guidance and specific RFIs. Similarly, the distribution of intelligence products needs to be expanded from the current narrow basis.

Another element that speaks to the need to emphasize comprehensive and asymmetric responses is that while the hostile actor is external, the effects of its activities are usually felt in the domestic sphere in the context of internal security. It is also in the internal security sphere where a broad range of possible countermeasures can be activated. Unfortunately, in practice, states' political culture and bureaucratic structures are not necessarily conducive to bridging the gap between what traditionally have been construed as "internal" and "external" security challenges. The conventional lines dividing the foreign and security policy community and the internal security community are still too infrequently crossed. The same could be said, to an extent, for academics, the private sector, and practitioner communities' interaction. The need for increased cooperation and information exchange between academics, the private sector, and practitioners has been acknowledged, but in practice there is still further to go before full use of this can be made in policy making. The new hybrid threat environment means that the concept of security policy should be widened and at least partially redefined.[15] While the community of intelligence analysts has taken steps to integrate the various policy perspectives (see, e.g., the role of the Office of the Director of National Intelligence in the United States or SIAC in the EU), the challenge also applies to intelligence as a target domain for hostile activity. This means that different policy perspectives are important to integrate and should include academic and private-sector perspectives as well. If one argues that a resilient state can be robust, recover from shocks fast, adapt to new situations, and transform when needed, conventional lines need to be broken.

The final layer in countering hybrid threats is deterrence. In the context of conventional deterrence theories, this forms the pillar based on a country's ability to withstand attacks and recover from their impact. In this way, deterrence can be seen as a concept that comes close to resilience. The difference is that resilience deals with internal capabilities to resist and recover as well as adapt and transform practices to new situations regarding external shocks, whether manufactured challenges, major accidents, or natural disasters. At the same time, deterrence incorporates several elements of resilience in the form of deterrence by denial.[16] However, it also deals with external capabilities, involving countermeasures beyond one's borders, instead of merely trying to prevent hostile actors from challenging us in our own space. Thus, deterrence in the hybrid threat context is broadening and transforming conventional deterrence thinking.

Multinational cooperation also plays a crucial role in deterrence. As in resilience building, it is good to note that effective deterrence against hybrid threats might not be possible on a national basis only. For example, counter-measures might involve the use of economic sanctions, which are amplified when agreed upon and carried out jointly in an international framework. However, the need for international coordination in countermeasures sets additional requirements for transparency. This is sometimes difficult due to national sensitivities involved in sharing information about vulnerabilities in a given country or, perhaps just as often, about sensitivities in talking about one's capabilities.

Academia and the security and intelligence studies communities, in particular, can play an essential role in educating broader sectors in society on these issues. Effective deterrence is an integral part of countering hybrid threats. However, deterrence is also a subject that divides. It is already difficult to have a comprehensive approach when it comes to situational awareness and resilience building. Active deterrence requires joint international action and requires more attribution and detection than the two previous layers in countering hybrid threats. This also means that to bring together different policy perspectives, the academic approach can assist in giving context to deterrence perspectives and find new creative ways to develop deterrence studies. In contrast, the private sector can develop risk analysis relating to deterrence and provide new tools. There is still a place for conventional deterrence in international politics, but deterrence needs to be viewed in a new, comprehensive way in the landscape of hybrid threats.

CASE STUDY OF THE SOLARWINDS HACK

Hybrid threats include so-called below-the-threshold threats, against which conventional theories of deterrence are of limited use. A good example is cyberspace. Cyberspace is more or less immune to conventional deterrence theories. As Mariarosaria Taddeo has observed, "Conventional deterrence theory does not work in cyberspace, as it does not address the global reach, anonymity, distributed and interconnected nature of this domain."[17] The three core elements of conventional deterrence theory—the attribution of attacks, defense, and retaliation as types of deterring strategies and the defender's capability to signal credible threats—therefore are not attainable in cyberspace. As Taddeo suggests, cyber deterrence could instead include identification instead of attribution, demonstration instead of signaling, and retaliation as the focus instead of denial. This would mean an entirely new kind of thinking and capability building. Nevertheless, as Taddeo argues, "Deterrence in cyberspace is possible. But it requires an effort to develop a new domain-specific, conceptual, normative, and strategic framework."[18] For this kind of work, a joint effort between practitioners, academics, and the private sector would be well placed.

However, deterring hybrid threats cannot be only domain based, albeit each domain has an important role. It requires a more holistic ecosystem approach. In the more comprehensive and integrated picture, the role of intelligence in identification would be central. Also, the role of intelligence in demonstration action as part of deterrence activity should be developed. This means that we need a more active posture, including preemptive activities on several levels, ranging from diplomatic tools to more kinetic methods. At the same time, we need to think about our own internal space and ensure that there are as few vulnerabilities to be exploited as possible. For this type of work, closer cooperation between the policy community and academics from different countries would be very beneficial.

An initial assessment of how the three layers of countering hybrid threat activities manifest themselves can be done by looking at the recent SolarWinds hack. In that hack, at least one group of hackers inserted malware into network software supplied by SolarWinds, a maker of information technology infrastructure software.[19] The decision to target SolarWinds is likely to have been deliberate and strategic, considering the company's vast clientele in the public, private, and nonprofit sectors in the United States and globally.[20]

The effects of the hack are not yet known but likely extend far beyond the target company and the national borders of the United States. What is also unknown is whether the main objectives were related to espionage or something even more sinister. As the nature of the threat becomes more challenging to define, the more difficult it becomes to formulate a proportionate response. The lines between elements of power, in this case, espionage and warfare, are effectively blurred. Adding to this, even if the objectives of the attack can be ascertained, the attribution of responsibility remains difficult. Even when there are technical means to attribute the attack, political and other considerations might lead a country not to attribute. This means that the baseline of understanding needs to be there and shared comprehensively before an effective response can be created. It also becomes a matter of calculating the likelihood of plausible alternative explanations of what happened, who was behind it, how much damage occurred, and what might be the intent behind such an act. The last part is notoriously difficult. It is not self-evident that even closer cooperation between practitioners, academics, and the private sector would bring clear solutions to this problem. However, it might bring better preparedness for "surprises" like the annexation of Crimea.

These elements should then feed into the decision-making system and guide the assessment of the risks associated with different courses of action. They will need to set up a basic understanding of what kind of response would be proportionate in that situation. They would also need to lay out the risks of escalation. Here, we are talking about both vertical and horizontal escalation. The hybrid threat environment and its activities tend to cross sectoral boundaries and, almost by definition, have a substantial asymmetric escalation potential. Asymmetry is, therefore, part of the equation, regardless of whether the responses are in the end asymmetric. In the same vein, preparing for the decision making and potential countermeasures requires both a comprehensive view of the horizontal escalation potential of the situation and a comprehensive view of all the (symmetrical and asymmetrical) tools the country has at its disposal. Intelligence plays a role in combining the various elements to form the escalation risk model. In this, insights from the private sector would be helpful, and from academics, some different perspectives and out-of-the-box thinking could give new angles to the problems and analysis.

Taking a step back and looking at how this situation might have been averted or mitigated, we must look at how to build effective resilience against cyber attacks and similar hybrid threats. More effective vulnerability assessments, not only risk assessments, need to be done and compared to threat assessments. Again, cooperation between practitioners, academics, and the private sector (comprehensive approach), not only between intelligence and other agencies, is crucial. The SolarWinds case is one of the best examples of how new interdependencies have been created between the public and private sectors. Only by working together can these types of threats be countered effectively. This also implies that the intelligence world will benefit from cooperation with the private sector and different sectors on the public side. In the end, it is also a matter of assigning responsibilities and making sure that legislation is up to date. The academic community's value here is that it can assess and express different possible vulnerabilities more easily than practitioners and even the private sector. In particular, the vulnerability assessment approach benefits from academic research. In the vulnerability assessment, not only are the target's vulnerabilities examined, but also the hostile actor's capabilities, strategic aims, and exploitation possibilities.

The same logic applies when we extend this to the realm of deterrence. There has to be a tighter interaction and even integration across the various communities, especially those dealing with new threats on the landscape, like cyber threats. The communities—including those concerned with the internal market, law enforcement, diplomacy, and defense—need to work more closely toward a shared awareness of threats. In this work, both the private sector and academics can provide beneficial information to all. They can connect different activities in different domains under one strategy and aim by a particular hostile actor.

The different policy communities and states should be ready to respond, sometimes individually and sometimes collectively, when an attack materializes.[21] Moreover, as underlined in the previous paragraphs, sometimes a cyber attack must not be met with cyber means but by other means—here, new deterrence thinking is needed. It entails a horizontal assessment of the most effective responses and an integrated strategy for utilizing the government toolbox and, sometimes, for optimal effectiveness, the private-sector and society toolboxes. In democratic states, the government's toolbox usually consists of diplomatic, political, and legal tools, as well as military if the situation so requires. In some cases, like those relating to sanctions, economic tools are applied. The private sector has many more economic tools at its disposal and often ownership of infrastructure. What comes from the societal toolbox is often more to do with resilience building. Aspects like culture, education, and the social fabric become very important. If all of these toolboxes are combined, the situational awareness, resilience building, and deterrence capabilities required are in place to counter hybrid threats.

CONCLUSION

This chapter has looked at the intelligence domain in the landscape of hybrid threats. Hybrid threats are a present and future security challenge for all democratic states and states trying to undergo democratization. The role of intelligence is essential in this context and needs to be framed and understood in a slightly revised manner. More holistic intelligence collection methods, analytical tools, and mechanisms for intelligence sharing are needed for comprehensive situational awareness and effective decision making. This means that closer cooperation between practitioners, academics, and the private sector should be embraced.

The base layer of countering hybrid threats—understanding the threat—requires good and comprehensive information to build accurate situational awareness. Moreover, the understanding needs to cross sectoral, governmental, societal, and multinational environments to be effective. Here, the combination of different perspectives will help to withstand attempts to blur the facts with disinformation, create ambiguity, and use deception to bring about harmful decision making.

The intelligence studies community, aware of covert activities and strategic thinking of authoritarian states' intelligence services and nonstate actors, can provide valuable insights on these issues for government and private-sector practitioners. Similarly, since public opinions of foreign countries are often the targets of disinformation as part of hybrid threat activity, academia can play an essential role in informing public debates on security issues and education, both being key for resilience building.

The second layer—building resilience—needs to be characterized by jointness, which refers to jointness in the military sense, thinking and acting in a connected manner, having good situational awareness, and making sure that all the components are interoperable. Nationally and between allies and partners, jointness also refers to interagency cooperation and a whole-of-government and whole-of-society approach. The intelligence community must situate itself in this interagency cooperation as an enabler of that cooperation and strengthen its resilience against external threats.

Finally, in the third layer of countering hybrid threats—deterrence— comprehensiveness is also an enabler for asymmetric responses. A direct tit-for-tat response might be impossible or ill advised for technical or political reasons. Therefore, it becomes imperative to look for responses on a broader scale. In essence, the situation and its escalation potential need to be managed horizontally. Horizontal escalation management is possible only when broad situational awareness; clear delineation of responsibilities; and a comprehensive, integrated strategy emerge. To deter and counter hybrid threats, new capabilities and new operating models need to be created. Capabilities are required in several domains, including the military, police, communications, cyber, and intelligence. As the example in this chapter showed, cyber is a domain where the line between a defensive and offensive capability becomes blurred and where many domains become intermeshed. Intelligence is another example in that it can act as a strategic enabler of comprehensive and integrated responses.

As the analysis in the previous sections makes clear, the new hybrid threat environment raises questions about the way we collect and analyze information, the way we share it, and how it informs decision making. When considering the nature of the threats in our current security environment, their interconnectedness, and the risks of escalation inherent in them, governments would benefit from broader cooperation with academia, think tanks, and the private sector. The threats themselves are elusive, and the longer-term trends are hard to ascertain. As a result, new conceptual tools and new methods of working are sometimes needed. This will help to enhance the anticipation capabilities, which are needed for effectively countering hybrid threats. The Hybrid CoE has tried to facilitate this process by doing conceptual work and organizing exercises to test those concepts. While the main stakeholders are governments, it has been clear that a complete picture and a comprehensive analysis can and should use outside views, including those in the private sector and academia.

NOTES

1. European Centre of Excellence for Countering Hybrid Threats, "Hybrid CoE," https://www.hybridcoe.fi.

2. Memorandum of Understanding on the European Centre of Excellence for Countering Hybrid Threats, 2017, 2, https://www.hybridcoe.fi/wp-content/uploads /2017/08/Hybrid-CoE-final-Mou-110417-1.pdf.

3. Rubén Arcos, "Understanding the Relationships between Academia and National Security Intelligence in the European Context," in *The Routledge International Handbook of Universities, Security and Intelligence Studies*, ed. Liam Francis Gearon, 156–67, 160 (Abingdon: Routledge, 2019). Examples of trend reports include "Hybrid CoE Trend Report 7: Trends in MENA; New Dynamics of Authority and Power" (2021) and "Hybrid CoE Trend Report 4: Trends in the Contemporary Information Environment" (2020). Other examples of research products are "Hybrid CoE Working Paper 2: From Nudge to Novichok: The Response to the Skripal Nerve Agent Attack Holds Lessons for Countering Hybrid Threats" (2018), by Sir David Omand; and "Addressing Hybrid Threats" (2018), produced by a team led by Greg Treverton and published by CATS (Swedish Defence University) in cooperation with Hybrid CoE.

4. Katja Valaskivi, "Beyond Fake News: Content Confusion and Understanding the Dynamics of the Contemporary Media Environment," Hybrid CoE Strategic Analysis 5, February 2018, https://www.hybridcoe.fi/wp-content/uploads/2020/07 /Strategic-Analysis-5-Valaskivi.pdf.

5. Thonos Dokos, "The Ukraine Crisis: A Story of Misperceptions, Miscalculations & Mismanagement; Is There Still Time to Avoid Permanent Damage to the European Security Order?," *Eliamep Thesis*, December 2014, https://www.files.ethz .ch/isn/186245/ELIAMEP-Thesis-1-2014_Th.Dokos-1.pdf.

6. Kathleen Hall Jamieson, *Cyberwar: How Russian Hackers and Trolls Helped Elect a President* (New York: Oxford University Press, 2018); Thomas Kent, *Striking Back: Overt and Covert Options to Combat Russian Disinformation* (Washington, DC: Jamestown Foundation, 2020).

7. David Omand, interview by Hanna Smith, November 2020.

8. Bettina Renz and Hanna Smith, "Russia and Hybrid Warfare—Going beyond the Label," *Aleksanteri Papers*, 2016, https://helda.helsinki.fi//bitstream /handle/10138/175291/renz_smith_russia_and_hybrid_warfare.pdf; Bettina Renz, "Russia and 'Hybrid Warfare,'" *Contemporary Politics* 22, no. 3 (2016): 283–300; Jyri Raitasalo, "Hybrid Warfare: Where's the Beef?," *War on the Rocks*, April 23, 2015, https://warontherocks.com/2015/04/hybrid-warfare-wheres-the-beef; Mikael Wigell, "Hybrid Interference as a Wedge Strategy: A Theory of External Interference in Liberal Democracy," *International Affairs* 95, no. 2 (2019): 255–75.

9. European Commission, "Joint Framework on Countering Hybrid Threats: A European Response," Joint Communication to the European Parliament and the Council, April 6, 2016, https://eur-lex.europa.eu/legal-content/EN/TXT/?uri =CELEX%3A52016JC0018.

10. Georgios Giannopoulos, Hanna Smith, and Marianthi Theocharidou, eds., *The Landscape of Hybrid Threats: A Conceptual Model*, EUR 30585 EN (Luxembourg: Publications Office of the European Union, 2021), 11.

11. Ralph Thiele, "Hybrid Warfare: Future & Technologies" (Inspiration Paper No. 2, Helsinki, May 14, 2019), s. 5.

12. Giannopoulos et al., *The Landscape of Hybrid Threats*, 31.

13. Hanna Smith, "Hybrid Threats to Allied Decision-Making," in *NATO Decision-Making in the Age of Big Data and Artificial Intelligence*, ed. Sonia Lucarelli, Alessandro Marrone, and Francesco N. Moro, 44–56 (Brussels: NATO HQ, 2021), https://www.iai.it/sites/default/files/978195445000.pdf.

14. Ari-Elmeri Hyvönen et al., *Kokonaisresilienssi ja turvallisuus: Tasot, prosessit ja arviointi* (Finland: Prime Minister's Office, 2019), https://julkaisut.valtio neuvosto.fi/bitstream/handle/10024/161358/17-2019-Kokonaisresilienssi%20ja%20 turvallisuus.pdf.

15. Fredrik Löjdquist, "An Ambassador for Countering Hybrid Threats," Royal United Services Institute (RUSI), September 6, 2019, https://www.rusi.org/explore -our-research/publications/commentary/ambassador-countering-hybrid-threats.

16. Vytautas Keršanskas, "Deterrence: Proposing a More Strategic Approach to Countering Hybrid Threats," Hybrid CoE Paper 2, March 2020, https://www.hybrid coe.fi/wp-content/uploads/2020/07/Deterrence_public.pdf.

17. Mariarosario Taddeo, "How to Deter in Cyberspace," Hybrid CoE Strategic Analysis 9, June–July 2018, https://www.hybridcoe.fi/wp-content/uploads/2020/07 /Strategic-Analysis-9-Taddeo.pdf.

18. Taddeo, "How to Deter in Cyberspace."

19. Isabella Jibilian and Katie Canales, "The US Is Readying Sanctions against Russia over the SolarWinds Cyber Attack: Here's a Simple Explanation of How the Massive Hack Happened and Why It's Such a Big Deal," *Insider*, April 15, 2021, https://www.businessinsider.com/solarwinds-hack-explained-government-agencies -cyber-security-2020-12; Alexandra Villarreal, "Russian SolarWinds Hackers Launch Email Attack on Government Agencies," *Guardian*, May 28, 2021, https:// www.theguardian.com/technology/2021/may/28/russian-solarwinds-hackers-launch -assault-government-agencies.

20. Robert Muggah, "Why the Latest Cyberattack Was Different," *Foreign Policy*, January 11, 2021, https://foreignpolicy.com/2021/01/11/cyberattack-hackers-russia -svr-gru-solarwinds-virus-internet.

21. European Commission, "The EU's Cybersecurity Strategy for the Digital Decade," Joint Communication to the European Parliament and the Council, December 16, 2020, https://eur-lex.europa.eu/legal-content/EN/TXT/PDF/?uri=CELEX:52020J C0018&from=EN.

9

Building Ecosystems of Intelligence Education
"The Good, the Bad, and the Ugly"

Irena Chiru and Adrian-Liviu Ivan

> Beyond this separation of academia and intelligence, another and perhaps
> far more problematic divide becomes increasingly visible, a divide caused
> by over-stated certainty and loss of trust.[1]

The views and opinions expressed in this chapter are those of the authors and
do not necessarily reflect the views or positions of any entities they represent.

OVERVIEW

Since the very beginning of professionalizing intelligence, the "ménage"
between academia and practitioners in the field of intelligence studies and
practices has been a bone of contention. Despite significant attempts to reconcile these "two worlds," finding the right ways to create a synergy between
them is still an open topic that continues to require careful consideration.
This chapter provides an evaluation of the scholar-practitioner relationship
grounded in almost three decades of history during which the Romanian National Intelligence Academy has experimented with multiple solutions in the
attempt to bridge the gap. The whole case is analyzed against the background
of a conceptual framework provided by the training-education nexus for intelligence. In addition, the chapter develops the concept of a non-dichotomic
intelligence education system that uses the "ecosystem" as a theoretical and
practical foundation. Hence, this chapter's overarching goal is to frame the
process of preparing future intelligence experts not as a specific activity performed by a separate entity but, rather is in the broad context of knowledge
ecosystems.

EDUCATION AND TRAINING: KEY CONCEPTS IN SHAPING THE LANDSCAPE OF INTELLIGENCE PROGRAMS

Comprehending the intelligence education landscape and the particularities of intelligence programs is highly relevant in analyzing the nature of the "divide" between academia and practitioners in intelligence. In shaping and deciphering the features of this landscape, a significant role is played by two constitutive and correlated elements: *education* and *training*. Not only are these two representative of how academics, on the one hand, and practitioners, on the other, have contributed to the development of intelligence programs over the last decades, but they can also be used as analytic lenses to look at the dichotomic discourses coming from outside or from within the intelligence communities about what constitutes a successful intelligence program.

Several definitions of these two key concepts have been offered to understand the differences and similarities between intelligence programs. Generally, the term "training" implies the act of conveying special skills and behaviors; hence, it is a process of skills acquisition. "Education" is understood as a process of systematic learning leading to the development of judgment and reasoning; hence, it is a process of knowledge acquisition (for a comparison, see table 9.1).

Table 9.1. Understanding the Differences between Training and Education

Area	Training	Education
Focus	Skills	Knowledge
Orientation	Practical	Theoretical
Perspective	Narrow	Wide
Duration	Short	Long
Final purpose	Improving performance and productivity (how to do a specific task)	Developing a sense of reasoning and judgment (how to think and address future challenges)

Depending on the overall architecture of an education system, training and education can be regarded as subsystems, principles, teaching techniques, or a permanent source of debate and controversy, as has been the case in intelligence. From the beginning of intelligence studies, several authors have expressed more or less polarized opinions of the need, progress, and utility of education as an accompaniment to the training traditionally used to develop future intelligence experts' competencies. The debate started with explicit arguments favoring intelligence professionalization by developing an intelligence literature and an academic foundation.[2] It has continued with the practical illustrations[3] of how the success of an intelligence mission is shaped by the academic background.[4] More recent and pessimistic opinions about the "anti-intellectualism" of intelligence communities have emphasized a so-called predisposition on the part of intelligence practitioners to undervalue knowledge and neglect developing it.[5] In our view, it is the practitioners who own the data and the academics who have the mind map to understand the bigger picture. In a similar vein, Sageman argues that "we have a system of terrorism research in which intelligence analysts know everything but understand nothing, while academics understand everything but know nothing."[6] The distance between theorists and practitioners translates into a lack of data for research and, implicitly, into a slow and unequal development of global intelligence studies, both geographically and thematically. To a certain extent, the debate has overshadowed the vocational programs in an attempt to demonstrate the benefits that a solid academic foundation may bring to intelligence professionals. As such, the comparison between education and training has become emblematic for the "divide" between intelligence scholars and practitioners. Moreover, it illustrates the "deep political, cultural, and epistemological" separation[7] between science in general, intelligence theory, and intelligence practice in particular. Despite their similarities, these are regarded as remarkably interlinked domains of knowledge production.

In an attempt to go beyond this inherent separation, other contributions have analyzed the nexus, concluding that it is important to acknowledge both the differences and the similarities. This particular perspective was advanced by Frerichs and Di Rienzo almost a decade ago. According to them, "Training and education are different concepts, and while these differences should be celebrated for what they are and what they do, an understanding of the minute details that make them unique offers a way of not confusing the strengths that make each of them mandatory for the IC mission."[8] In other words, training and education are complementary and often overlap. Although they have different goals, they are equally necessary to a comprehensive and balanced intelligence education project. Training involves applicable knowledge and focuses on detailing routinized activities to develop specific skills (e.g., learning how to utilize technology or how to write an analytical product). It is developed based on existing tradecraft, which absorbs the practices and the lessons learned from the field and provides instructions for a particular situation and the steps to apply them effectively and efficiently. In a nutshell, learning how to perform certain tasks in certain circumstances is at the heart of the training process. To this, intelligence education adds a new dimension that brings it close to metacognition. This enhances students' capacity to explore and explain by integrating a wide assortment of knowledge sources;

exposing them to various epistemologies; and developing the critical thinking necessary to understand, integrate, and share knowledge.

The international landscape of intelligence programs reflects the dichotomy between training and education. There are two major types of intelligence programs that have been developed over the last decades: (1) academic programs organized and/or hosted by universities and (2) training programs provided by intelligence services.[9] A brief introduction to each of these is needed.

The academic programs dedicated to intelligence have a relatively recent history going back six decades but experiencing a significant upward trend in the last three decades, especially after 9/11. The current portfolio includes academic programs mostly developed in the United States and the United Kingdom, with a more recent expansion in the Netherlands,[10] Spain,[11] Romania,[12] and France.[13] In general terms, these academic programs display a series of shared features: (1) they seek to advance the analysis of intelligence as a social and political phenomenon through the lenses provided by social science; (2) they usually combine intelligence studies with security studies or integrate intelligence as a topic in broader security-focused programs; (3) they have had a systematic evolution in recent years that has run parallel with the acknowledgment of intelligence studies as a growing area of activity of high relevance to contemporary security and governance; (4) despite their significant upward trend, they remain rather unbalanced, with few programs organized beyond the Anglosphere; and (5) where they come from outside the intelligence community, they are predominantly focused on education and, consequently, on specific skills necessary to achieve educational goals. In a nutshell, they are focused on developing the students' competency in acquiring and processing information in the search for understanding.

If the winding and progressive evolutionary trends of these programs are extensively illustrated in the literature through the cogent contributions of several authors,[14] the same cannot be said about the intelligence training courses. Little has been written about the training or vocational courses designed by practitioners for practitioners. The specificity of these programs, which are developed as part of the human resources development strategy within the closed environment of intelligence organizations, can explain the lack of dialogue and debate. While directly targeting those who are looking for a career or already working in intelligence, training courses are based on the idea that intelligence is a profession that requires less the exercise of academic knowledge and more practice-oriented programs, tailor-made to meet the cultural, technological, and normative variables of an intelligence organization.

Several observations can be made—useful in understanding the specificity of these training courses, which are usually put in place by intelligence schools as part of one or more national intelligence organizations. If academic intelligence programs are designed in line with higher-education accreditation quality standards, which determine certain auditable commonalities in their format and content, vocational programs are more diverse, their configuration being fully impacted by the different cultural and historical values that usually shape a strategic national culture. They provide a type of training directly bounded by the national security policy and the national intelligence doctrine. Their primary focus is on testing skills and developing abilities rather than challenging and questioning established beliefs, personal mindsets, and perspectives. Without being a substitute for academic education, training dwells on the bachelor's or master's level studies that intelligence trainees previously completed. This makes the competencies acquired by the experts/students at the end of the vocational program highly dependent on their prior educational background.

A certain imbalance between skills and knowledge seems to characterize these programs. This has been pointed out in the more recent contributions, which may be considered the promoters of an antipositivist intelligence critical theory. One may notice observations regarding such vocational programs (the CIA's Career Analyst Program) in the sense that they are focusing on analytical assumptions and biases but do not appear "to engage the implications of the intersubjective nature of language at a theoretical level."[15] Moreover, the progress from the history and literature of intelligence to specific analytical skills (e.g., analytical thinking, writing and self-editing, briefing, data analysis, teamwork) is made without providing the necessary conceptual and theoretical framework (i.e., by introducing analysts to contemporary theories of language) that might help students to critically assess and interpret implications.[16] Hence, this predominant focus on developing the skills required for intelligence collection and analysis to the detriment of research and theoretical frameworks has served as the premise for the critique directed at the schools of intelligence and their "ongoing legacy of positivism"[17] that generally characterizes intelligence studies theorizing.

It can be inferred that intelligence training schools provide short- to medium-term programs that reflect both the existing knowledge in the intelligence service where the curriculum is generated and taught and its historically contextualized practices. A training program fails to offer the development of key competencies necessary in the long term, such as changing and adapting to change. As organizations, intelligence services inevitably experience change and need to adapt their operations to address emerging threats. Hence, training intelligence practitioners on how to do their job now, according to current standards, may be problematic in the long run since they are not equally trained to explore how to adapt; modify; and, most of all, optimize their endeavors. Building competencies for change in an organization is not just a strategic management job. Intelligence practitioners work in a change-competent organization and need to define their job in relation to change; they need to understand and expect that change will happen and value the ability to change as one of their primary responsibilities. On the other hand, intelligence training focuses on specific collection and analysis skills based on practices already proven to be successful and applicable only for routinized activities. Is this sufficient if we are to consider the attitude and approach individuals need to display to be change competent?

While many skills that lead to intelligence operational success can be taught and learned, other competencies such as adaptation to change require a fundamental shift in culture and values, which cannot be simply developed and tested via training or on-the-job instructional activity. Moreover, if one considers that the training is being overseen and conducted by frontline employees (which is regularly the case), it is fair to say that the learners are trained to match the trainer's level of performance and experience. However, to build the competencies needed beyond the requirements dictated by the current orientations of an intelligence organization and put things into perspective, trainees must be provided with the mind-set, tools, and techniques to optimize and implement change in their professional lives successfully. That may require leaving behind routinized practices and identifying the need for new systems, processes, or approaches. To legitimately build optimization into an organization, intelligence tailor-made training may not be enough. If vocational training programs are present oriented, academic education programs develop competencies to learn, learn to learn, and learn how to learn, thus providing an impact beyond the needs and requirements of the present.

Finally, the approach intelligence schools take in their relationship with academia is highly relevant for understanding the relationship between academia and intelligence professionals and the related nexus between education and training. Given their scope, mission, and affiliation, intelligence schools may encounter difficulties initiating and maintaining functional and bidirectional cooperation with academia. From this perspective, an existing relationship between intelligence training schools and academia, which may take the form of joint events, invited lectures, or joint research projects, mirrors a certain degree of maturity in the evolution and development of intelligence studies. Be it either strong or weak, continuous or discontinuous, strategy or contingency driven, this relationship can also serve as an indicator of the degree of openness and dialogue an intelligence organization embraces outside its secret frontiers.

Merging Education and Training: Lessons Learned from the Front Line

This section will discuss the experience of an intelligence school in developing intelligence programs by integrating both education and training. As will be illustrated, the case was selected given the school's systematic endeavor to harmonize its intelligence program's academic and training dimensions. It has done so while evolving from a small institute preparing future intelligence officers for a counterintelligence service to a full-fledged university. The analysis will apply process tracing as a criterion useful in illustrating progress, gaps, challenges, and historical circumstances. However, limited attention will be given to precise historical events that could only add unnecessary contextual knowledge. The privileged gaze of the authors, who have been an integral part of the process from the beginning of the academy's development, allows for a truthful testimonial and an in-depth perspective. At the same time, we must also acknowledge the inevitable limitations in any subjective and personal account. Hence, in building the narrative, we shall try to avoid a direct and descriptive account of facts but rather look at the organizational processes set in motion and how they aggregated knowledge and distribution in intelligence education.

The history of Romanian intelligence programs spans a relatively short period, about three decades. What the National Intelligence Academy is today, with its successive institutional forms, dates back to 1992 when the training unit dedicated to future intelligence operatives was split from the Police Academy, where training took place traditionally (before the Romanian Revolution in 1989 as well). It was then located independently on a new campus. In 1992, the idea of an academic foundation for future intelligence officers' training was seriously raised. This translated into the reorganization of the training unit under a university formula as an academic entity regulated by the Ministry of Education. The new entity, called the Higher Institute of Information at that time, was led from the start by an academic personality—the rector. The rector developed a university structure so that the activity could be carried out through a faculty with departments, according to a higher-education institution structure. Since then, the departments have been reuniting full-fledged academics, practitioners turned into trainers, and current practitioners invited for special lectures and workshops.

One of the strategic decisions of this new start was establishing two bachelor's degree programs with a double status. Thus, the first program was both academic, involving a bachelor's degree in psychology, a field considered to be the most relevant for the training of intelligence officers, and professional, developing and assessing practical skills in information collection. This was soon followed by a program in communications and public relations in the second faculty, a field of study that is rather unique by comparison to other intelligence programs. The project also involved bringing in academics who could develop academic content and who could teach, but also who would continue the process of recruiting and mentoring future faculty members who were selected from among the undergraduate program graduates. The latter started to build an academic background by enrolling in the PhD programs of civil universities, mainly in sociology and psychology. Consequently, the faculty teams brought together both academics, former practitioners turned trainers, and young graduates who, as a profile, were both academics and trainers from among the intelligence practitioners. However, the publication of academic writing at that time, for example, in books and articles, was the exclusive prerogative of the academics, with no content generated jointly with the practitioners.

The initial option for psychology as a field in which the undergraduate programs were developed, followed by communication and the academic training of the graduates who in turn became academics in the fields of psychology, sociology, social psychology, and communication, is indicative of how intelligence studies started in Romania. This construction once again reflects their multidisciplinary nature. It is worth highlighting that in the case of Romania, the foundation for the academic development in intelligence was not set by political sciences or international relations—much more vocal disciplines in the emergence of intelligence studies globally—but by psychology, sociology, and communication sciences; in other words, the study of the behavior of the individual and social groups, as well as the development of communication skills and decoding communication.

The first students of the new intelligence school could study the history of psychology, deviant psychology theory, cognitive development theory, statistics, logics and sociology, research methods, media studies, public relations, and investigative journalism, in addition to other "nonacademic" disciplines meant to train students in "how to become a good intelligence officer." At that time, education and training were two paths contributing to the knowledge, skills, and abilities of the future intelligence expert, but the way and the extent to which education content, on the one hand, and training content, on the other, intertwined was highly dependent on both the capacity of the student to mix them and the opportunities and challenges he or she faced in the first years after graduation. Most probably the only exception was the History of Intelligence Studies course that was academic, while directly focusing on intelligence practices at the same time.

Progressively, combining the two dimensions of education and training beyond their simple juxtaposition has become increasingly real, so that the two ingredients should steer toward a unified vision, for example, psychology disciplines running along specialized intelligence disciplines. The attempt to perfectly harmonize them continues to be an aspiration—as the later historical stages can prove.

The next important step was to initiate a master's degree program beyond the orientation toward traditional fields of study (e.g., psychology and communication sciences) that focused on intelligence as the object of study. The new program curriculum was multidisciplinary, focused on the principle that "one needs to select all content that can contribute to the competencies needed in intelligence collection and analysis." In addition, what had only slightly been touched upon on the "to-do list," namely merging academic-driven and training-based content, was finally assumed as a strategic orientation in a formalized manner. Accordingly, the curriculum has integrated four major pillars: psychology, communication sciences, international relations, and intelligence training. However, what is important to mention is that the way the curriculum was built was specifically dictated by the targeted competencies of the future intelligence practitioners and not by the already existing development of intelligence studies at the international level. In other words, the construction was deeply rooted in the national experience. This construction was also due to circumstances that governed the first decade of the twenty-first century, when the academy had not yet gained access to the already advanced and consistent intelligence studies literature. In addition to the scarcity of international literature available at the national level, the intelligence school lacked a Romanian intelligence literature and doctrine, its major reference points coming from historical documents. In fact, access to the intelligence studies literature has been a key element in developing the academy as a university center with a unique profile in Europe: a university entity that combines academic training and vocational training of future (military and civilian) intelligence experts. The development of the Internet offered the unprecedented opportunity to apprehend and connect to the existing literature and gradually integrate knowledge content.

Currently, although part of an intelligence service, the academy offers both bachelor's and master's programs that bring together both fundamental disciplines and provide a theoretical framework for a broad understanding of security issues. It also includes disciplines with more specialized content to teach how to utilize technology, handle human intellligence, and write an analytical product. To these dimensions, a new one was added during the last decade—the research dimension. Several research units and laboratories under the academy's umbrella were gradually created to meet the need for innovation. These are oriented toward core research (e.g., the National Institute for Intelligence Studies, the National Center for Simulation and Modeling) or applied research, bringing together researchers and practitioners who can orient research to operational needs (e.g., the Behavioral Sciences Laboratory).

Research results can lead to new teaching techniques and can create interdisciplinary connections that may influence curriculum change while avoiding the risk of limiting intelligence teaching to the current norms and practices of the intelligence organization. Moreover, perhaps the best illustration of merging education and training is the opening of a doctoral school in intelligence and national security.

Its primary mission is to improve intelligence research using rigorous scientific methods and interconnect it with similar sciences. The research topics are advanced and approached by considering intelligence missions and values and the national security and defense strategy. At the same time, the relevant results are being tested and disseminated within the national intelligence community. The mechanisms connecting knowledge production to knowledge use bring the doctoral school research strategy close to the conceptual framework of "user-inspired research," intertwining pure academic research with practitioners' grassroots perspective. This model promotes research combining scientific knowledge with an applied orientation while engaging external reviewers and users from the practical realm. Therefore, although research projects are primarily concerned with basic science, in line with scientific research principles and practices, they might help resolve practical problems or issues.

Although a unit of an intelligence service, the academy, via the Doctoral School in Intelligence and National Security, embraces academic cooperation within university networks and prioritizes closer links between the "business" in intelligence and national security and academia. One of the recent and challenging experiences the academy has had is illustrative of how practice and research about intelligence and security can merge. The ESSENTIAL project[18] is promoted by an international consortium formed of academic institutions, governmental organizations, and private companies. In the last four years, ESSENTIAL has provided the framework for fifteen security and intelligence–related research topics developed by a multicultural team of early-stage researchers through joint multi- and interdisciplinary contributions.

ESSENTIAL was designed to comprise interdisciplinary research in the area of security science, spanning four established fields of study: the socioeconomic sciences, humanities, and sociology; legal science, which includes law; the media and knowledge sciences, which include information policy and governance and cognitive science; and computer science, which includes information security, digital forensics, and cyber security. By creatively undertaking a holistic design for research, ESSENTIAL has integrated the various PhD programs of the partner universities and created interdisciplinary learning experiences for researchers. It has exposed doctoral students to different learning environments (governmental and private research institutions, commercial research and development units, and university-based research) but also to heterogeneous supervision—that is, combining supervisors and mentors from academic and nonacademic partners coming from different economic and industrial sectors (e.g., intelligence, law enforcement, digital forensic) and multiple countries (e.g., the Netherlands, Romania, Malta), including non-EU member states (e.g., Norway and Australia).

By bringing the "industry" of intelligence and security into the process of training and research, a hands-on experience was provided, helping doctoral candidates convert knowledge and ideas into security and social benefits. The experience of fusing education and research with professional requirements and standards enables both ESSENTIAL doctoral students and supervisors to address security issues while creatively and progressively exploring and exploiting the complementarity between the various elements of the network. In doing so, the program stands as an example of how multiple actors representing specialized fields of study and practice can create learning ecosystems through exchanging and sharing knowledge on security and intelligence in an international context.

This project is just an example of how research can be combined with education to benefit the intelligence profession while creating networks in intelligence and security. In MVNIA's case, involvement in international research projects has contributed significantly to a paradigm shift, in the sense that intelligence practices solely aimed at incessantly uncovering more secrets were gradually replaced by accessing multiple-source knowledge. Therefore, research can provide a solution to the enduring problem that most intelligence services face—not knowing enough, with enough certainty, and early enough. By tailoring projects to meet the practitioners' needs and providing conceptual grounding, research has worked as a catalyst for education programs. It has allowed for the production of "academic intelligence" that can be used in addition to other traditional INTs, and opens new communities of practice by integrating different governmental and nongovernmental institutions.

Today, the academy's educational programs are concerned with knowledge building, whereas vocational programs at the same university will apply existing and emerging knowledge to address specific technical problems. At the heart of the intelligence programs that prepare future intelligence practitioners remains learning how to be a "good" operative or analyst. However, this final destination is reached via a combination of highly theoretical research-driven content with vocational training activities. The Romanian Intelligence Academy's road map demonstrates that a trinomial strategy equally integrating and balancing education, research, and practice can be implemented. Such a strategy, fusing all three components, allows for the creation of internal mechanisms that connect training activities with recent developments in the field. It creates the premises to enhance educational content standards via academic accreditation. Nevertheless, although academic, the educational process remains inherently linked to the intelligence organization and hence maintains the necessary level of trust both in the process and in the result of education.

This gradual development allowed for a shift in goals as well. The first goal was to train individuals who could understand the instructions and effectively, efficiently, and repeatedly implement them, thereby producing highly skilled and competent professionals. However, it should be noted that to achieve this fusing formula, based on progressive development, multiple obstacles had to be overcome, and challenges had to be addressed. The profoundly ingrained predisposition toward secrecy and reticence in uncovering and sharing practices embedded in the internal intelligence culture is to be taken and understood as a general premise in any attempt at opening the training activities toward the "outside world" of education and research.

Step-by-step, mechanisms for cooperation and accountability must be created to achieve the necessary level of inclusiveness, participation, and, most of all, trust, which are essential preconditions in developing an intelligence education ecosystem. A certain obstinacy and resistance are also needed in looking for solutions that may counter the enduring perception of academia as living in an ivory tower away from the mundane and pressing tasks pertaining to national security missions. The words of Roger Hilsman describing practitioners distrusting the researcher, as they see him as "a long-haired academic poring over musty books in dusty libraries far from the realities of practical life," are still true and illustrative of the prejudices intelligence practitioners and academia have of each other.[19] Further reflection is still needed on how academics can promote their work and engage with intelligence practitioners and trainers without jeopardizing the value of the theoretical knowledge, technical vocabulary, and expertise academia produces. Also under consideration must be the permanent quest for creating joint educational projects that reunite practitioners and academics, demonstrating their results' practical utility in terms of conceptual grounding ("research for the sake of research") and solving real-life problems.

Last but not least, what can be taken as a lesson learned from this particular experience is that creating ecosystems to the benefit of intelligence education does not come as a moment in time but is a long-term process. In addition, no matter the willingness and perseverance that academics and practitioners may display (together or separately), a robust endeavor requires strategic vision and determination in creating the necessary frameworks for academics and practitioners to meet and work together.

Further Arguments for Fusing Education and Training in Intelligence

In the last decades, we have witnessed an unprecedented growth of intelligence programs outside the secretive frontiers of an intelligence organization. Hence, the discussion so far in this chapter is primarily applicable to intelligence (training) schools that may want to go beyond the long-standing and core truth of intelligence organizations: "the secret of my success is the very secret of my success." Intelligence collection, analysis, and production have long ago ceased to exist as mere tradecraft learned from and taught by experienced professionals. Accordingly, the debate in intelligence studies depends upon creating inclusive frameworks for dialogue and teamwork along with the involvement of all actors that are part of the intelligence education ecosystem. The extent to which this debate will remain fractured, placing intelligence training on one end and intelligence education on the other, represents a predictor of the intelligence services' capacity to adapt and jointly rethink their mission and interventions.

A blended intelligence program delivers multiple complementary benefits: it produces a convergence of visions and interests between intelligence practitioners and academics, it develops a unified culture of cooperation and coordination, it fosters mutual awareness and understanding, and it relies on and contributes to a collaborative learning community. The case study provided by the Romanian intelligence school embedded in an intelligence university can be discussed in terms of its relative strengths and limitations. It seeks to describe a particular experience that is culturally, geographically, and historically driven. It also shows that, despite profound affinities toward one side or another, academics' and practitioners' expertise can empower each other.

There is no doubt that the success of intelligence communities in preserving a nation's security depends on the human resources involved. The intelligence professionals are critical to the mission, and intelligence communities must certify that the very best education is provided. To this end, in addition to a systematic discussion about the need to bridge the gap between practitioners and academia, mostly initiated and conducted by academics, intelligence education requires very concrete, action-oriented patterns of interaction between intelligence partners. Above all, it needs a solution-orientated mind-set reducing one's cognitive and emotional affiliation to one side against the other.

Last but not least, by debating the challenges of intelligence education interoperability and bringing together the various perspectives of its peer actors, what we aim to do is discuss the foundation of an integrated approach, able to build on the different solutions generated by experts from different countries. The interrelated process generated will help investigate insufficiently explored instruments that facilitate better educational ecosystems.

Otherwise, although vital for many reasons, education will remain an Achilles' heel of intelligence.

NOTES

1. Wilhelm Agrell and Gregory F. Treverton, *National Intelligence and Science: Beyond the Great Divide in Analysis and Policy* (New York: Oxford University Press, 2014).

2. Sherman Kent, "The Need for an Intelligence Literature," *Studies in Intelligence* 1, no. 1 (1955): 1–11.

3. Dating back to World War II, the observation made by Calvin B. Hoover (as noted by Wilhelm Agrell and Gregory Treverton), head of the OSS North Central European Division, is illustrative: "Intelligence officers who lacked a university or college background did not perform well out on mission, since these operators often were left to solve or even formulate tasks on their own, without any detailed guidance from remote headquarters and over unreliable and slow communications. These field officers needed the perspective gained by a theoretical education to grasp the complexity of the conditions under which they had to operate and the kind of information they needed, not to mention assessing the crucial distinction between gossip and hearsay, on the one hand, and information that could be verified and documented on the other." *National Intelligence and Science: Beyond the Great Divide in Analysis and Policy* (New York: Oxford University Press, 2014), 18.

4. Agrell and Treverton, *National Intelligence and Science*, 18.

5. Mark M. Lowenthal, "Is the US Intelligence Community Anti-Intellectual?," in *The Future of Intelligence: Challenges in the 21st Century*, ed. Isabelle Duyvesteyn, Ben de Jong, and Joop van Reijn, 39–47 (New York: Routledge, 2014).

6. Marc Sageman, "The Stagnation in Terrorism Research," *Terrorism and Political Violence* 26 (2014): 576.

7. Agrell and Treverton, *National Intelligence and Science*, 3.

8. Rebecca L. Frerichs and Stephen R. Di Rienzo, "Establishing a Framework for Intelligence Education and Training," *Joint Force Quarterly* 62 (2011): 71.

9. Another category of training course is represented by those organized by private training providers. However, given the scope of this chapter, such courses will not be included in our analysis.

10. See, for example, the intelligence studies discipline developed by the University of Leiden, available at https://studiegids.universiteitleiden.nl/en/studies/7295/intelligence-studies#tab-1.

11. Master's studies program in intelligence analysis, https://www.uc3m.es/ss/Satellite/Postgrado/en/Detalle/Estudio_C/1371284311065/1371219633369/Master_Interuniversitario_en_Analista_de_Inteligencia.

12. Bachelor's studies program developed by Babeş Bolyai University on security, intelligence, and competitiveness in organizations, available at https://www.ubbcluj.ro/en/programe_academice/masterat/#istorie.

13. Master's program developed by Notre Dame College on national security and intelligence studies, available at https://www.notredamecollege.edu/admissions/graduate/masters-security.

14. Martin Rudner, "Intelligence Studies in Higher Education: Capacity Building to Meet Societal Demand," *International Journal of Intelligence and CounterIntelligence* 22, no. 1 (2009): 110–30; Peter Gill and Mark Phythian, "What Is Intelligence Studies?," *International Journal of Intelligence, Security, and Public Affairs* 18, no. 1 (2016): 5–19; Liam Francis Gearon, ed., *Routledge International Handbook of Universities, Security and Intelligence Studies* (New York: Routledge, 2020).

15. Stephen Coulthart, "Why Do Analysts Use Structured Analytic Techniques? An In-Depth Study of an American Intelligence Agency," *Intelligence and National Security* 31, no. 7 (2016): 933–48.

16. Hamilton Bean, "Intelligence Theory from the Margins: Questions Ignored and Debates Not Had," *Intelligence and National Security* 33, no. 4 (2018): 531.

17. Nate Kreuter, "The US Intelligence Community's Mathematical Ideology of Technical Communication," *Technical Communication Quarterly* 24, no. 3 (April 2015): 218.

18. ESSENTIAL—Evolving Security SciencE through Networked Technologies, Information Policy and Law, financed by Marie Sklodowska—Curie Actions (MSCA), 2014–2020, implemented by an international consortium formed of Rijksuniversiteit Groningen—the Netherlands; Norges Teknisknaturvitenskapelige, Universitet—Norway; Universita Ta Malta—Malta; Consiglio Nazionale Delle Ricerche—Italy; Academia Nationala de Informatii Mihai Viteazul—Romania; Edith Cowan University—Australia; and Netherlands Forensic Institute—the Netherlands.

19. Roger Hilsman Jr., "Intelligence and Policy-Making in Foreign Affairs," *World Politics* 5, no. 1 (October 1952): 9.

10

The Academic-Practitioner Relationship in France

From Strangers to Partners

Damien Van Puyvelde

This chapter provides an overview of the evolving relationship between academics and intelligence practitioners in France from the establishment of the "French school" of intelligence studies in the 1990s to today. The first section develops a theoretical framework that presents the relationship between academics and intelligence practitioners according to two variables: the extent to which academics' and practitioners' interests overlap and the structuration of their relationship. These two variables generate four stereotypical relationships—strangers, acquaintances, collaborators, and partners—that are used throughout the chapter to characterize the academic-practitioner "divide" in France. The second section examines the emergence of intelligence studies in France in the 1990s and emphasizes the key role played by the former director general for external security Admiral Pierre Lacoste in establishing an initial platform to explore shared interests and structure the relationship between scholars and practitioners. This initial effort helped two communities that were largely strangers to collaborate and become more acquainted. The third section presents the multiplication of government outreach programs in the mid-2000s. The establishment of intelligence as a public policy has been accompanied by a structuration of the exchanges between academics and practitioners. Three government initiatives that have sought to bridge the gap between academics and intelligence practitioners stand out: the intelligence academy, the intelligence campus, and Interaxions. Together these projects have expanded the basis of collaboration between the two communities. The fourth section focuses on the role practitioners have played in intelligence education in France. The recent establishment of a series of intelligence studies diplomas that seek to bridge the academic-practitioner divide in higher education suggests that the relationship is now moving closer to a partnership. The chapter concludes that practitioners have played a key role in establishing and structuring their relationship with the academic community. Their prominent role raises unanswered questions about the sources of legitimate expertise in the development of intelligence studies.

FRAMING THE ACADEMIC-PRACTITIONER RELATIONSHIP

The theoretical framework driving the analysis developed in this chapter hypothesizes that two key factors shape the academic-practitioner relationship: the extent to which respective interests overlap and the structuration of this relationship. For the two communities to cross the "divide" that separates them, they first need to identify an interest in bridging the gap. For scholars, this might include better access to sources and practices that will inform their research, and different forms of rewards (self-reward, esteem, and career progression) associated with exchanging knowledge with government officials. From the perspective of practitioners, academics can provide access to specialized knowledge relevant to the missions and activities of their service. They also provide a separate channel to communicate about their role publicly. While both sides might have an interest in liaising with each other, they do not necessarily do so for the same reasons, and the extent to which their interests overlap varies.

When they share an interest in bridging the gap, academics and practitioners can liaise in an ad hoc manner or in more institutionalized ways. The different means available to cross this divide can be represented as a spectrum ranging from low to high institutionalization or structure. For example, ad hoc engagement could include an intelligence service inviting a scholar to deliver a talk to its staff on a topic of interest. More structured forms of partnership involve contracts granting specific rights and duties to academics who might, exceptionally, be allowed to access intelligence agencies' records and settings. Similarly, practitioners might be invited to deliver a talk or teach a course at an academic institution. Besides these individual forms of cooperation, intelligence agencies in a number of countries have set up dedicated training and outreach units that tap into academic expertise to support their needs.

Figure 10.1 presents academic-practitioner relationships along two axes showing variations in interest and structure, from low to high. The resulting quadrants represent four stereotypical relationships. This theoretical framework simplifies reality to build and later test expectations of what different academic-practitioner relationships look like. In any given context, the four stereotypes are not mutually exclusive. Some academics and practitioners are likely to remain perfect strangers, while others might collaborate and develop a more formal partnership. While a majority of intelligence scholars seem to have an interest in engaging with practitioners, not all scholars welcome such a partnership. Some might prefer a clear divide and very little to no engagement with practitioners. From this detached perspective, there is no ideal relationship, just multiple possibilities.

In the bottom left quadrant, academics and practitioners have little to no overlapping interests, and their relationship is not structured. They are *strangers* separated by a clear divide. Here, academics do not really engage with practitioners or, when they do so, it is to publicly condemn intelligence practices. Practitioners deem academia irrelevant.

In the bottom right quadrant, academics' and practitioners' interests overlap significantly, but their relationships remain unstructured; they are *collaborators* that long for more engagement. Here, academics develop intelligence-relevant research and actively seek to reach out to practitioners in the hope of triggering their interest and being invited to present their research

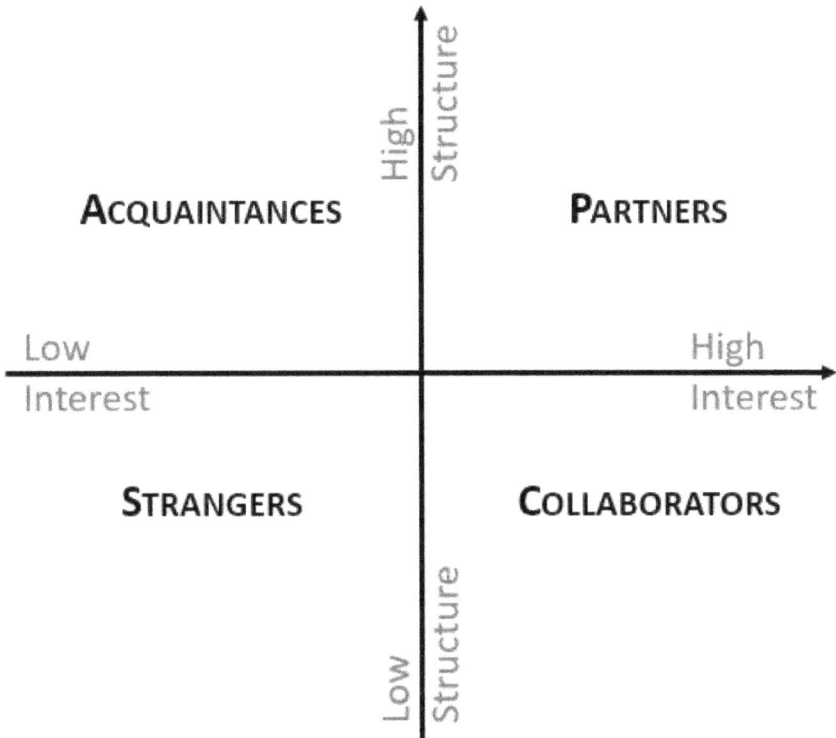

ACQUAINTANCES | High Structure | **PARTNERS**

Low Interest | High Interest

STRANGERS | Low Structure | **COLLABORATORS**

Figure 10.1.   Interest and Structure in the Academic-Practitioner Relationship.

at guest talks. Practitioners systematically survey academic research, and some of them attend academic events. They occasionally invite researchers to present their research, and they give talks at academic institutions. Mutual interests establish a collaboration, but this relationship lacks an institutional structure that would stabilize the relationship and make it more permanent.

The upper quadrants present more highly structured relationships. At the top left, academics and practitioners are *acquaintances*. Here, structures require them to engage with each other, but their relationship is limited because their respective interests do not overlap significantly. Academics develop seminar series and conferences on topics linked to intelligence and security practices such as "mass surveillance" but do not invite or include practitioners. Occasionally, structures might require some interaction, for example, when university management arranges for a senior intelligence official to speak on campus. Similarly, practitioners engage in outreach because their institution mandates it, mostly for public relations and communications reasons. They have an interest in using academia to frame the public debate on intelligence and show that their service is "transparent," but they do not care much about academic research and teaching.

The top right quadrant presents a situation in which both communities have a strong interest in each other's work and the relationship is highly structured. Here, academics and intelligence practitioners are *partners*. Academics systematically invite and engage with practitioners during seminars and conferences and include them in the leadership of their organizations. Universities invite and hire serving and retired practitioners to teach and speak to students regularly. Practitioners systematically tap into academic expertise through outreach programs that organize joint events and sometimes contract out specific tasks to academics, such as the writing of an internal or official history or the drafting of external audit reports. The two communities are significantly intertwined.

THE EMERGENCE OF INTELLIGENCE STUDIES IN FRANCE

The French conception of the role of the state and its intelligence services has had a significant effect on the study of intelligence in France. Due to its strong position as secret keeper, regulator, and subject of study, the state and its bureaucracy have logically been the most central factor influencing the nature of the relationship between academics and practitioners. France has traditionally conceived of intelligence as an attribute "at the disposal of the political power without any form of oversight,"[1] and the attitude of French politicians toward intelligence has long oscillated between disregard and mistrust.[2] This experience contrasts with more liberal models where governments have sought to strike a balance between secrecy and openness. Public access to information on intelligence, and by extension the place of intelligence in academic and public debates, has historically been more limited in France than in the United Kingdom and the United States.[3]

The genealogy of intelligence studies in France can be traced back to an initiative to bridge the academic-practitioner divide. In 1995, Admiral Lacoste, who served as director of the French foreign intelligence agency (Direction Générale de la Sécurité Extérieure, or DGSE) from 1982 to 1985, launched a research seminar on the French culture of intelligence at the University of Marne-la-Vallée. Though intelligence research had been published before, Lacoste's seminar was the first attempt to establish a structure to foster a dialogue between practitioners and intelligence researchers.[4] The establishment of this seminar can be linked to Lacoste's career as a defense and intelligence leader, but also to broader developments in the history of French intelligence, such as the creation of the Directorate of Military Intelligence (Direction du Renseignement Militaire, or DRM) in 1992 and the emphasis the 1994 Defense White Paper placed on intelligence in a post–Cold War context marked by uncertainty.[5]

Comparing France to the Anglophone world, Lacoste lamented the fact that intelligence remained a "taboo" in French academia and public debate. He thought secrecy had become a pretext to "oppose a fundamental reflection on the role and place of intelligence in modern society."[6] The paucity of academic research on intelligence meant that, more often than not, journalists and former officers filled key information gaps.[7] But interviews and memoirs provide, at best, personal representations of historical facts and, as historian Jeffreys-Jones notes, former practitioners "can be expected to put the best possible spin" on their period in office.[8] To fill this gap in public understanding and knowledge about intelligence, Lacoste proposed adopting a multidisciplinary approach drawing on history, political science, economics, law, sociology, and information sciences.[9] Conscious of some of the difficulties confronting intelligence scholarship, he pointed out that researchers would need to get "greater access to sources of information that have too long remained inaccessible."[10] The seminar he coordinated thus provided the first platform bringing together a variety of scholars and practitioners to engage in dialogue and reflect on how sociocultural norms and political institutions affected decision makers' use of intelligence. This initiative was successful in inspiring a generation of intelligence researchers and fostering the emergence of foundational texts.[11]

The seminar series at Marne-la-Vallée took place at a time when French historians were conducting pioneering research that helped to establish the field of intelligence studies in academia. Alain Dewerpe's historical anthropology of state secrecy remains, to this day, a pioneering work on intelligence as a profession, a set of practices and organizations that reflect broader societal trends.[12] Historians like Sébastien Laurent were able to corroborate multiple sources of information to produce rigorous research on French intelligence.[13] Historical research and archival releases progressively facilitated access to information, establishing a basis for further research, for example, through the conduct of oral history interviews made available at government archives.[14]

By the mid-2000s, the editor of *Intelligence and National Security* could point to the emergence of a "French school" of intelligence studies.[15] In March 2008, several years after the end of Lacoste's initial seminar series, two historians (Sébastien Laurent and Olivier Forcade) and a civil servant (Philippe Hayez) established a new seminar series titled "Metis: Intelligence in Liberal Democracies,"[16] hosted by the Center for History at Sciences Po Paris. Following the British model, Metis used the Chatham House rule to facilitate engagement between the two communities and bridge the gap.[17] In 2018, the seminar celebrated its tenth anniversary by organizing the first public event bringing together the national coordinator for intelligence and counterterrorism (CNRLT) and the directors of the six leading intelligence agencies (the so-called first circle of the French intelligence community): the DGSE, the Direction du Renseignement et de la Sécurité de Défense, the DRM, the Direction Générale de la Sécurité Intérieure (DGSI), the Direction Nationale du Renseignement et des Enquêtes Douanières, and Tracfin (a financial intelligence unit). The panelists agreed on the need to strengthen their relations with higher-education institutions.[18] This event signaled practitioners' willingness to liaise with academics and identify ways to structure their relationship.

The structuration of intelligence studies in France has benefited from government research funding. From 2015 to 2019, the National Research Agency funded a social science project on the use of communications intelligence technologies.[19] Funding from the Ministry of Armed Forces and its Direction Générale des Relations Internationales et de la Stratégie further contributed, together with private support, to the establishment of an Association for War and Strategic Studies in 2015 that includes a "working group on intelligence." This working group, led by university researchers, organizes research seminars and public events on intelligence.[20] Other scholarly associations, such as the French association for security and defense law have organized events to support the academic debate on intelligence from a legal perspective.[21] A recent study on the state of intelligence research in France finds that historical work continues to dominate the field, but a number of PhD research projects focusing on public law and intelligence, as well as information and communication sciences, literary studies, and linguistics, suggest the field is diversifying.[22] In sum, the seminar organized by Admiral Lacoste can be considered a turning point, when academics and practitioners moved from being "strangers" to becoming "acquaintances." More than a decade later, the establishment of Metis and other scholarly seminars, as well as government funding, have helped to structure this relationship closer to the ideal type of collaboration.

INTELLIGENCE OUTREACH

In the last decade, a series of events have contributed to bringing intelligence to the fore of the public debate. Political scientists Jean-Vincent Holeindre and Benjamin Oudet correlate the legitimation of intelligence to three key developments: the contemporary threat environment, changes in public perception following terror attacks, and the development of a new public policy on intelligence.[23] The 2008 White Paper on Defense and National Security formally introduced the notion of a French intelligence community, presenting the services of the first circle as a pillar of French foreign, military, and security policies, and introduced "knowledge and anticipation" as a strategic function of the French defense and national security apparatus.[24] According to Chopin, government white papers and the subsequent 2015 law on intelligence have helped to "normalize" intelligence as a public policy.[25] In turn, the normalization of intelligence has legitimized intelligence as a research subject.

Public institutions have played an important role in this legitimization effort and have actively sought to build bridges with academia. Three initiatives stand out in this context: the intelligence academy, the intelligence campus, and Interaxions. Together these projects show the active role that the government and some intelligence agencies have played in developing more robust collaborations between academics and practitioners. For more critical observers, however, these efforts raise questions about the appropriate distance between the study and practice of intelligence, between "the scientific purpose of explanation and understanding" and "policy-oriented research supporting the actions of intelligence services."[26]

Intelligence Academy

The French Intelligence Academy (Académie du Renseignement) was established in 2010. Its creation was recommended by the 2008 White Paper on

Defense and National Security and enacted by decree of the prime minister two years later as part of a broader wave of intelligence reform.[27] Directly attached to the prime minister (the head of government but not the head of state in the French political system), one of the main roles of the academy is to provide training and courses for practitioners belonging to the first circle of the intelligence community. These training courses seek to foster greater mutual understanding of each service's role and organization, build interpersonal relationships to develop stronger cooperation, and foster a common intelligence culture. The academy also seeks to develop a public "culture" of intelligence in the sense of greater public understanding. Its efforts in this domain include actions that seek to bridge the gap between academics and practitioners of intelligence. These activities have intensified since 2015 and include two main types of initiative: institutional initiatives that directly stem from the academy's organization and mandate within the French intelligence community, and outreach initiatives that specifically target intelligence researchers and related productions.

The academy's institutional initiatives include training and courses that are only accessible to intelligence practitioners and that engage with a broad array of issues that include and go beyond the study of intelligence. The academy provides the practice-oriented initial training designed to present the specificities of the first circle services to new senior intelligence officials. It is also responsible for developing and managing an academic program that reflects the variety of topical issues and world areas covered by these six services.[28] As a part of these activities, academics and experts working in a wide range of disciplines are frequently invited to give talks and contribute to roundtables tailored for an audience of practitioners. These initiatives, often structured around one or a few experts or academics, provide fresh insights into international issues and the latest academic debates to practitioners. By engaging outside specialists in the education and initial formation of intelligence officers, these events contribute to the development of a public culture of intelligence.

The academy's outreach initiatives focus more specifically on intelligence studies and related outputs. First, the academy established two public prizes in 2018. The first prize rewards a French PhD thesis (the project needs to be written in French and the degree awarded at a French university) that provides a significant contribution to the development of intelligence studies. The second rewards a fictional creation that raises awareness about the nature of intelligence work and activities. Both prizes come with a €4,000 reward, and the selection committee includes the national intelligence coordinator as well as the heads of the six services of the first circle. Since 2020, the academy has added a third award for an "essay," defined as a creative work inspired from reality. This category includes academic research monographs and textbooks but also memoirs, biographies, and documentary movies.[29] This initiative demonstrates a willingness at the highest level of the French intelligence community to engage with academic research and fictional work on intelligence. Second, the academy organizes an annual colloquium that brings together scholars and practitioners to discuss intelligence issues. In 2016, this event focused on "Intelligence in the Early Cold War." The 2019 colloquium focused on legal issues in intelligence and provided important contributions to the public debate at a time when the 2015 law that established a firm legal grounding for the French intelligence community was due to be revised. These colloquia proceedings have been published and edited by leading scholars (who also contributed to the seminar organized by Admiral Lacoste two decades earlier).[30] Third, the academy established a historical committee in 2019 to facilitate dialogue between historians and the French Intelligence Services.[31]

Intelligence Campus

The DRM is the only French intelligence service dedicated to military and defense intelligence. It is a key component of the French intelligence community and an active member of the first circle. Like many other defense intelligence agencies around the world, the DRM has been concerned with the development of new security and military technologies. The changing character of war and the fast pace of technological progress in the digital era require significant efforts to understand, anticipate, and adapt to the latest trends. To meet these challenges, then defense minister Jean-Yves Le Drian created the Intelligence Campus in 2015. This initiative seeks to foster academic outreach and crosscutting exchanges between the ministry and outside expertise in technological matters such as artificial and signals intelligence, automatic image recognition, and data analysis. The director of the DRM explains that "putting personnel and competencies in direct relation will enable us to improve the acquisition cycle of these tools, which tend to evolve really quickly in the civilian world. We need to adapt permanently. This initiative will be based on the following triptych: academic world, research, and acquisition."[32]

The second type of action undertaken by the DRM seeks to leverage academic expertise in the social sciences and related disciplines. As a military intelligence service, the DRM is interested in all the regions and areas where French troops deploy. Since intelligence analysts often face time and production constraints, reaching out to academic institutions and universities can provide important insights that contribute to the analytical process. In 2018, the DRM and the National Center for Scientific Research (CNRS)—the biggest French public research institution—signed an agreement that institutionalized their cooperation and sought to facilitate exchanges between practitioners and academics in three different ways.[33] First, this agreement establishes a platform to organize workshops and seminars that bring together analysts and CNRS researchers working on issues or regions of common interest. These events provide a safe space for fruitful exchanges between academics and practitioners. Second, this agreement provides select researchers with access to sensitive DRM data and creates a legal framework for their exploitation in research projects. Third, select CNRS researchers are now invited to take the training offered to junior DRM analysts. This agreement represents an important step in bridging the academic-practitioner divide in France and brought about fierce debates in the academic community between those in favor of a closer relationship between the intelligence community and the academic world and those who think the two communities should remain clearly separated. Critics argue that close relationships between academics and practitioners threaten the independence of academic research, put researchers at risk when conducting field research in some countries, and may prevent them from getting access to research fields.[34] More recently, the DRM has launched new initiatives and organized a series of conferences and symposia on issues of interest such as "hybrid warfare."[35] Although these initiatives do not necessarily focus on intelligence scholars, they seek to bridge the divide between intelligence practitioners and academics working in a variety of cognate fields in the social sciences and beyond.

Interaxions

Interaxions, sometimes considered the think tank of the DGSE, was established in 2017 by then director general Bernard Bajolet as part of a broader effort to foster foresight and anticipation in the French Defense Ministry.[36] Interaxions leverages academic outreach to contribute to strategic analysis. This platform, inspired from the academic outreach program of the Canadian Security Intelligence Service (CSIS), is the only structure of its kind in the French intelligence community and contributes to bridging the academic-practitioner divide in many different ways. Directly attached to the Directorate for Strategy of the DGSE, Interaxions seeks to understand current and emerging security trends to contribute to the anticipation efforts of the Ministry of the Armed Forces.[37] The unit seeks to develop long-term views, horizon scanning, and foresight assessment of the changing international landscape. It develops strategic intelligence and analysis while also acting as a red cell in charge of challenging commonly held views, cultural biases, and assumptions. Although most of its publications are classified, select public communications indicate an interest in topics ranging from "Islam after Daech,"[38] to the rise of radical Islam in West Africa, to the future security role of the western Balkans.[39]

To make its analyses and assessments possible, Interaxions—as its very name suggests—heavily relies on the exchange of views and perspectives with other organizations, experts, and academics. In this regard, its methods can be compared to those of the US National Intelligence Council.[40] Interaxions taps into networks of experts in various disciplines and sectors, including government, think tanks, research institutes, and universities, in France and abroad. Exchanges take multiple forms ranging from conferences to seminars, to presentations and roundtable discussions. The unit also organizes annual symposia dedicated to emerging issues and trends, which provide another opportunity to facilitate exchanges between academics and practitioners. These events are open to other members of the French intelligence community, institutional partners, and a broader ecosystem of strategic thinkers in France. The organization of symposia with foreign intelligence services also contributes to the international cooperation policies of the DGSE. For instance, its first event was jointly organized with the academic outreach program of CSIS.[41]

Through its outreach function, Interaxions has sought to stimulate the academic study of intelligence and security issues in France. In November 2018, its annual symposium, organized with the French Institute for Strategic Research (IRSEM, a public institution often presented as the think tank of the French Ministry of the Armed Forces) and inaugurated by the director general of the DGSE, Bernard Émié, focused on the development of intelligence studies in France.[42] This event gathered over a hundred professionals and academics and provided an opportunity for them to think about possible improvements on both sides of the divide. The proceedings of this symposium will appear in a new handbook to be published at a leading academic press in France and edited by researchers working at the French Institute for Strategic Research.[43] This publication follows the establishment of a new unit focused on "intelligence, anticipation and hybrid threats" at the institute, which seeks to bring together researchers and practitioners in an effort to develop policy-relevant research on intelligence and security.[44]

The national intelligence coordinator has also supported and emphasized the importance of academic outreach. The first (publicly available) national intelligence strategy recognizes the importance of "communication and openness" to explain "the challenges and risks confronting French society and foster the emergence of an intelligence culture." This strategy emphasizes that academic research, universities, and think tanks constitute an essential resource to understand crises and key issues confronting the services.[45] Yet an overview of the latest initiatives shows that efforts to bridge the gap are unequal across the French intelligence community. The Ministry of Armed Forces (which hosts the DGSE and the DRM), the CNRLT, and the intelligence academy, which represents the entire community, have played more active and visible roles. While other services such as the DGSI reach out to research institutions to warn them about threats to intellectual property, their academic outreach efforts are more limited and much less visible.[46]

INTELLIGENCE EDUCATION

Capitalizing on growing public interest in intelligence and a demand from the CNRLT to become more involved in intelligence education to foster a French "culture" of intelligence, a handful of French higher-education institutions have recently developed intelligence curricula.[47] These courses have provided another opportunity to bridge the gap and develop partnerships between universities and practitioners. Sciences Po Paris (the leading public affairs school in France) has long offered courses on intelligence taught by former practitioners. For example, figures such as Mark Lowenthal (a former senior CIA analyst), Sir David Omand (former director of Government Communications Headquarters), French civil servants including a former director of the French Intelligence Academy, and senior military officers taught several courses on intelligence in 2019–2020.[48] The same year, Sciences Po Saint-Germain-en-Laye launched a postgraduate diploma in "intelligence and global threats" in partnership with the French Intelligence Academy. This diploma targets both traditional students and professionals seeking to develop and expand their skill set. The curriculum offers a mix of academic-oriented courses such as History and Sociology of Intelligence and more applied modules such as Practices of Operational Intelligence, which includes contributions from senior practitioners.[49]

In 2020, Sciences Po Aix, another public affairs school, established an "academic chair" dedicated to the study of intelligence. This chair will be held by General Cholley (Ret.), who served as deputy director for operations at the DRM and defense adviser to the prime minister. The initiative will benefit from the support of the intelligence academy. The teaching team—which at the moment is largely composed of professionals—will initially offer a certificate before moving on to a master's degree in 2021, offered in partnership with the Ecole de l'Air (French Air Force School). The involvement of a professor (Walter Bruyère-Ostells) as a scientific director suggests that an effort will be made to strike a balance between professional and academic perspectives.[50] Another recent initiative brings together Sorbonne University and the DRM to offer a specialization on geopolitics and geospatial intelligence (GEOINT) to its master's students starting in 2020. The specialization, available as a Master 2, aims to form GEOINT analysts to work in government or the private sector.[51] The new degree will benefit from the support of the DRM, whose director officially launched the program in September 2020. Some of the courses will reportedly be taught in the headquarters of the DRM.[52]

The proliferation of professionalizing courses, diplomas, and degrees taught in partnership with former and serving practitioners raises a series of questions that have not been clearly addressed in the French public debate. Public affairs schools are now well aware of the opportunities that intelligence education can bring them, not least in terms of recruitment and publicity. Sciences Po Paris and its school of public and international affairs has long adopted a teaching strategy that puts an emphasis on senior practitioners, including senior civil servants and policy makers, in addition to more traditional academic courses. New programs at Sciences Po Saint-German-en-Laye and Sciences Po Aix-en-Provence emphasize the experience and publicity that come with hiring senior practitioners. The extent to which these programs manage to maintain a balance between intelligence training and academic education remains to be seen. The involvement of practitioners in academic education begs the question of who should teach intelligence in higher-education settings and how they should do so. While this debate is well established in the United States,[53] it has barely started in France and deserves further attention.

Who teaches and, by extension, is recognized as an expert on intelligence inevitably affects the state of intelligence studies. One of the defining features of higher education is that teaching is inherently linked to research findings.[54] The risk when practitioners dominate intelligence education is that teaching will be based on individual career experiences, not on research findings in the field of intelligence studies and other academic fields relevant to intelligence and security. While intelligence education should not overlook the views and experiences of professionals, it should engage students in the broader pursuit of scientific knowledge on intelligence and security and strike a balance between the leading role of academics in education and the essential role practitioners' expertise plays in professionalizing master's programs. The responsibility for striking this balance lies firmly on the academic side of the divide. Higher-education institutions should not only launch new degrees but also foster and eventually hire a generation of researchers who can teach and develop scientific knowledge on intelligence and security affairs. To this day, only a handful of tenured university lecturers and professors in France research and teach on intelligence. This suggests that, despite the establishment of new programs, French academia remains somewhat resistant to the notion that intelligence is a legitimate field of academic enquiry.

CONCLUSION

The relationship between academics and practitioners has evolved significantly since the establishment of intelligence studies in France in the mid-1990s. Practitioners and government institutions have played a central role in supporting the emergence of intelligence studies and the broader development of a public debate on—or as French commentators often say, a culture of—intelligence. Academics have established a number of associations running research seminars on intelligence, and a handful of higher-education institutions have recently launched diplomas in intelligence studies. While some academics would prefer the two communities remain strangers, collaborations and partnerships have emerged in the last two decades. This rapprochement raises important questions that remain largely unanswered about who has a legitimate voice to produce public knowledge on intelligence.

NOTES

1. Olivier Chopin, "Intelligence Reform and the Transformation of the State: The End of a French Exception," *Journal of Strategic Studies* 40, no. 4 (2017): 537.

2. Jean Guisnel, Roger Faligot, and Rémi Kauffer, *Histoire politique des services secrets français: De la Seconde Guerre mondiale à nos jours* (Paris: La Découverte, 2013).

3. Jean-Vincent Holeindre and Benjamin Oudet, "Intelligence Studies in France: History, Structure and Proposals" (IRSEM Research Note 67, November 27, 2018), 4–5.

4. See, for example, Jean-Pierre Alem, *L'Espionnage et le Contre-Espionnage* (Paris: Presses Universitaires de France, 1980); Alain Dewerpe, *Espion: Une anthropologie historique du secret d'Etat contemporain* (Paris: Gallimard, 1994).

5. Ministère de la Défense, *Livre Blanc sur la Défense* (Paris, 1994), 52, 78–80.

6. Chopin, "Intelligence Reform," 2.

7. See Roget Faligot and Pascal Krop, *La Piscine* (Paris: Seuil, 1985); Jean Guisnel and Bernard Violet, *Services secrets: Les services de renseignement sous François Mitterrand* (Paris: La Découverte, 1988). For some memoirs see Colonel Passy, *Souvenirs I. 2e Bureau Londres* (Monte-Carlo: Raoul Solar, 1947); Pau Paiolle, *Services spéciaux (1935–1945)* (Paris: Robert Laffont, 1975); Jean Deuve, *La Guerre secrète au Laos contre les communistes* (Paris: L'Harmattan, 1995); Constantin Melnik, *1000 Jours à Matignon* (Paris: Grasset, 1988); Pierre Marion, *La mission impossible: À la tête des Services Secrets* (Paris: Calman-Lévy, 1991); Jacques Foccart, *Journal de l'Elysée. Tome 1. Tous les soirs avec de Gaulle (1965–1967)* (Paris: Fayard, 1995);

Claude Silberzahn with Jean Guisnel, *Au cœur du secret: 1500 jours aux commandes de la DGSE* (Paris: Fayard, 1995); Constantin Melnik, *La mort était leur mission: Le service Action pendant la guerre d'Algérie* (Paris: Plon, 1996). Examples of interviews include Alexandre de Marenches and Christine Ockrent, *Dans le secret des princes* (Paris: Stock, 1986); Philippe Gaillard, *Foccart Parle* (Paris: Fayard, 1995).

8. Rhodri Jeffreys-Jones, "Commentary: Loch Johnson's Oral History Interview with William Colby, and Johnson's Introduction to That Interview," in *Exploring Intelligence Archives: Enquiries into the Secret State*, ed. R. Gerald Hughes, Peter Jackson, and Len Scott (London: Routledge, 2008), 271.

9. Pierre Lacoste, "Trois ans de séminaire sur la culture française du renseignement," in *Le Renseignement à la française*, ed. Pierre Lacoste (Paris: Economica, 1998), 1.

10. Lacoste, "Trois ans de séminaire sur la culture française," 3.

11. Some of the scholars who contributed to this seminar became leading intelligence scholars in France. See, for example, Olivier Forcade, *La République Secrète: Histoire des Services Spéciaux français de 1918 à 1939* (Paris: Nouveau Monde, 2008); Sébastien Laurent, *Politiques de l'Ombre* (Paris: Fayard, 2009); Bertrand Warusfel, *Le renseignement français contemporain: Aspects politiques et juridiques* (Paris: L'Harmattan, 2003).

12. Dewerpe, *Espion*, passim. For a recent review, see Pascal Engel, "Alain Dewerpe et l'histoire dormante du secret," *L'Atelier du Centre de Recherches Historiques* 17 (2017), https://doi.org/10.4000/acrh.7996.

13. See, for example, Sébastien Laurent, "Renseignement militaire et action politique, le BCRA et les services spéciaux de l'armée d'armistice," in *Le Renseignement à la française*, ed. Pierre Lacoste, 79–100 (Paris: Economica, 1998).

14. See, for example, Service Historique de la Défense (SHD), Vincennes: 3K66, "Témoignage oral de Raymond Muelle," February 8, 2000; 3K71, "Témoignage oral de Robert Maloubier," October 19, 2000; 3K60, "Témoignage oral du général Paul Aussaresses," July 24, 2000.

15. Peter Jackson, "Intelligence and the State: An Emerging 'French School' of Intelligence Studies," *Intelligence and National Security* 21, no. 6 (2006): 1061–65. See also David Kahn, "Intelligence Studies on the Continent," *Intelligence and National Security* 23, no. 2 (2008): 249–62.

16. "Metis" is an ancient Greek word for craft or wisdom.

17. Sciences Po Centre d'Histoire, "Le renseignement: Planification, stratégie et prospective—Séminaire METIS—Programme saison 17—séance 5," 2015, http://www.sciencespo.fr/newsletter/archive-e52eb0eeb8b076757c624e6c40edf033.html.

18. Holeindre and Oudet, "Intelligence Studies in France," 13.

19. Sciences Po, "Uses of Technologies for the Surveillance of Communications (UTIC)," https://www.sciencespo.fr/ceri/en/content/uses-technologies-surveillance-communications-utic#equipe-tab.

20. Association Pour les Études Sur la Guerre et la Stratégie, "Renseignement," http://www.aeges.fr/groupes-travail/gt-renseignement.

21. Association Française de Droit de la Sécurité et de la Défense, "Actualités," http://www.afdsd.fr.

22. Holeindre and Oudet, "Intelligence Studies in France," 9–10.

23. Holeindre and Oudet, "Intelligence Studies in France," 2.

24. Chopin, "Intelligence Reform," 543–44.

25. Chopin, "Intelligence Reform," 547.

26. Chopin, "Intelligence Reform."

27. Philippe Hayez, "'*Renseignement*': The New French Intelligence Policy," *International Journal of Intelligence and CounterIntelligence* 23, no. 3 (2010): 474–86.

28. Académie du renseignement, "L'académie du renseignement," http://www .academie-renseignement.gouv.fr/academie.html.

29. For more details about these awards, see French government, "Création du grand prix de l'académie du renseignement," undated, https://www.gouvernement.fr /creation-du-grand-prix-de-l-academie-du-renseignement.

30. Olivier Forcade and Maurice Vaïsse, eds., *Le Renseignement au début de la Guerre Froide, 1945–1955* (Paris: La Documentation Française, 2016); Olivier Forcade and Bertrand Warusfel, ed., *Le droit du renseignement* (Paris: La Documentation Française, 2020).

31. Académie du renseignement, "L'académie du renseignement."

32. Laurent Lagneau, "La Direction du renseignement militaire a signé une convention de partenariat avec le CNRS," *OPEX 360*, June 10, 2018, http://www .opex360.com/2018/06/10/direction-renseignement-militaire-a-signe-convention-de -partenariat-cnrs.

33. Lagneau, "La Direction du renseignement militaire."

34. Gilles Dorronsoro, "Quand le CNRS met en danger les chercheurs," *AOC*, June 21, 2018, https://aoc.media/opinion/2018/06/21/cnrs-met-danger-chercheurs; Syndicat National des Travailleurs de la Recherche Scientifique, "En Bref No. 476: Communique Presse SNTRS CGT: 'La Convention CNRS-Direction du Renseignement Militaire Nuit à l'Indépendance de la Recherche,'" July 5, 2018, https://sntrscgt .vjf.cnrs.fr/spip.php?article2537.

35. Guerric Poncet and Emmanuel Durget, "La guerre hybride expliquée par le renseignement militaire," *Le Point*, November 25, 2019, https://www.lepoint.fr/societe /la-guerre-hybride-expliquee-par-le-renseignement-militaire-25-11-2019-2349437 _23.php#.

36. Ministère des Armées, "Interaxions," September 24, 2018, https://www.defense .gouv.fr/dgse/tout-le-site/interaxions.

37. Jean Guisnel, *Histoire secrète de la DGSE: Au cœur du véritable bureau des légendes* (Paris: Robert Laffont, 2019), 302.

38. Ministère des Armées, "Interaxions."

39. Guisnel, *Histoire secrète de la DGSE*, 305.

40. Christopher A. Kojm, "Change and Continuity: The National Intelligence Council, 2009–2014," *Studies in Intelligence* 59, no. 2 (2015): 7.

41. See report of the symposium Islam after Daech, available at Ministère des Armées, "Interaxions."

42. Damien Van Puyvelde et al., "Comparing National Approaches to the Study of Intelligence," *International Studies Perspectives* 21, no. 3 (2020): 298–337.

43. Jean-Baptiste Jeangène Vilmer, Jean-Vincent Holeindre, and Paul Charon, eds., *Le Renseignement: Approches, acteurs et enjeux* (Paris: Presses Universit-

aires de France, forthcoming). See also Van Puyvelde et al., "Comparing National Approaches," 98–337.

44. Institut de Recherche Stratégique de l'Ecole Militaire, "La Lettre de l'IRSEM," July–September 2020, 1, https://www.irsem.fr/media/5-publications/la-lettre/lettre -irsem-07-08-09-2020.pdf.

45. Coordination Nationale du Renseignement et de la Lutte contre le Terrorisme, *La Stratégie Nationale du renseignement*, July 2019, 12.

46. Intelligence Online, "La DGSI revoit son lien avec l'université," July 22, 2020, https://www.intelligenceonline.fr/renseignement-d-etat/2020/07/22/la-dgsi -revoit-son-lien-avec-l-universite,109596173-bre; Intelligence Online, "La DGSI met les bouchées doubles sur les universités," September 9, 2020, https://www.intelligence online.fr/renseignement-d-etat/2020/09/09/la-dgsi-met-les-bouchees-doubles-sur-les -universites,109604975-bre.

47. "Sciences Po Aix: Création de la première chaire académique sur le renseigne-ment en France," *L'Express*, July 16, 2020, https://www.lexpress.fr/actualite/societe /sciences-po-aix-creation-de-la-premiere-chaire-academique-sur-le-renseignement -en-france_2131084.html.

48. Sciences Po, "PSIA Curriculum 2019–20," 2019, 58.

49. Sciences Po Saint-Germain-en-Laye, "Synopsis-DiReM 2019–2020, Module technique," May 2020, https://www.sciencespo-saintgermainenlaye.fr/wp-content /uploads/2020/05/Les-pratiques-du-renseignement-op%C3%A9rationnel.pdf; Sci-ences Po, "Le DiReM—Diplôme d'établissement sur le Renseignement et les Menaces globales," March 2019, https://www.sciencespo-saintgermainenlaye.fr/wp-content /uploads/2019/03/DiReMVF.pdf.

50. Antoine Izambard, "Sciences Po Aix va créer la première chaire française 100% dédiée au renseignement," *Challenges*, July 3, 2020, https://www.challenges .fr/education/sciences-po-aix-va-creer-la-premiere-chaire-francaise-100-dediee-au -renseignement_717661; "Sciences Po Aix," *L'Express*.

51. Philippe Chapleau, "Un Master Géopolitique-Geoint, à la rentrée, à Sor-bonne Université," *Lignes de défense* (blog), June 5, 2020, http://lignesdedefense .blogs.ouest-france.fr/archive/2020/06/04/master-geopolitique-geoint-a-la-rentree-a -sorbonne-universit-21217.html.

52. Intelligence Online, "La bataille des master 'renseignement' est lancée," Sep-tember 14, 2020, https://www.intelligenceonline.fr/renseignement-d-etat/2020/09/14 /la-bataille-des-masters-renseignement-est-lancee,109606432-art.

53. See, for example, Stephen Marrin, "Training and Educating U.S. Intelligence Analysts," *International Journal of Intelligence and CounterIntelligence* 22, no. 1 (2009): 131–46; William C. Spracher, "Teaching Intelligence in the United States, the United Kingdom, and Canada," *Oxford Research Encyclopedia of International Studies*, March 2010, https://oxfordre.com/internationalstudies/view/10.1093/acre fore/9780190846626.001.0001/acrefore-9780190846626-e-308?rskey=ZyzDHZ.

54. Jan Schapper and Susan E. Mayson, "Research-Led Teaching: Moving from a Fracture Engagement to a Marriage of Convenience," *Higher Education Research & Development* 29, no. 6 (2010): 641–51.

11

Playing to Our Strengths

Combining Academic Rigor and Practitioner Experience in Delivering Intelligence Education in Australia

Troy Whitford and Charles Vandepeer

THE CHALLENGE

Combining academic rigor and practitioner experience in delivering intelligence education is a multidimensional practice. It involves deliberate curriculum design that engages academic content experts and stakeholders in the intelligence community and educational specialists in assessment and pedagogical design. This chapter outlines some of the broad features of intelligence studies in Australia, then takes a more detailed approach to course design, development, and delivery through the lens of Charles Sturt University's intelligence and security discipline at the Australian Graduate School of Policing and Security. The chapter is designed to inform the course development process and provide a contextualized example of the relationship between academic rigor and professional practice. It is an overview of the key principles underlying intelligence curriculum development. Charles Sturt University's master's of intelligence analysis is one of Australia's oldest intelligence studies postgraduate degrees, commencing in the 1990s. In addition to an overview of intelligence studies course design principles, other less tangible aspects of intelligence education are identified, specifically the challenges of teaching decision making, working within ambiguity, asking questions, and understanding the question. The chapter is a survey of some issues surrounding intelligence education from a teaching practitioner perspective. It reflects some of the challenges and opportunities for collaborations between the intelligence sector and educational institutions based on the authors' teaching practice and course development experience.

AUSTRALIAN INTELLIGENCE STUDIES

Australia has a small intelligence academic community, reflecting the size of the nation and the limited number of formal intelligence degrees offered across the university sector. As a smaller community than, say, those in the United States and the United Kingdom, the divide between intelligence agencies and academia in Australia appears smaller in terms of the number of intelligence academics within Australia. Where intelligence agencies are looking toward academic qualifications for their staff or engagement of academics in delivering teaching and training, there is a clear field of academic options, probably helping to avoid the worst excesses of a major divide. The relationships appear to be more between individual policing, defense and national security agencies, and specific academic institutions rather than anything like the broader, formally established Intelligence Community Centers for Academic Excellence as in the United States. However, following the 2017 Independent Intelligence Review, the broadening of the Australian National Intelligence Community from six to ten agencies reflects a growing recognition of the interconnectedness of threats and the broader intelligence role in addressing these across agencies. This recognition of the transnational nature of threats to Australia's national security and the increasingly interconnected aspects of problems facing the nation has coalesced as an increased emphasis on intelligence within the public and private sector. Prior to the challenges brought on by COVID-19, intelligence analysis was seen as a strong employment growth area,[1] further highlighting increased interest in intelligence and intelligence education. Up until COVID-19, the trend in focus for Australian intelligence agencies, under the lead of the Australian Cyber Security Centre within the Australian Signals Directorate, has seen a heavy focus on the country's growing cyber threats. In June 2019, the Australian prime minister very publicly announced that "Australian organisations are currently being targeted by a sophisticated state-based cyber actor."[2] Recent trade challenges with China have also brought into focus the idea of economic security. Questions on the intelligence implications of COVID-19 and health intelligence have now come to the fore and indicate that health intelligence is likely to become a future academic and intelligence focus.[3] Consequently, intelligence education in Australia is diverse. It traverses practical skills such as human intelligence collection, geospatial intelligence, intelligence analytics, strategic studies, and international diplomacy.

Currently, there are forty-two universities in Australia, with approximately eight teaching intelligence studies in one form or another. At a tertiary level, the study of intelligence is featured at an undergraduate and postgraduate level. It is difficult to obtain national data on the number of students undertaking intelligence studies courses or subjects. Anecdotally, the background of students undertaking intelligence studies at least at a postgraduate level is predominately intelligence practitioners seeking formal qualification beyond in-house training. The balance are students seeking a career in law enforcement, military, or national security intelligence. It is also challenging to identify what courses or subjects can be realistically termed intelligence studies subjects. Some housed under the title of intelligence studies are in some cases more akin to politics, history, or international affairs. However, some impressionistic findings can be made. At the undergraduate level, intelligence studies is offered as an elective subject. This means students undertaking undergraduate degrees in criminology, the arts (history or politics, etc.), or justice studies/law may choose intelligence studies as a subject to complement their degree. The undergraduate student may choose intelligence as a subject outside of their core subject requirements. Intelligence studies subjects also feature in professionally targeted degrees such as bachelor's degrees in security studies or terrorism. While there are a number of single intelligence subjects offered, there are actually only a few complete degrees specializing in intelligence studies at the undergraduate level. Edith Cowan University is one example of a university that offers an undergraduate degree in counterterrorism and intelligence, highlighting the availability of a major in intelligence studies. Intelligence studies subjects offered at an undergraduate level are a blend of practice and theory. Some are historical or political, perhaps more akin to strategic studies in nature, while others, such as intelligence analysis subjects, are true practitioner skills-based learning. Intelligence analysis as a subject appears a staple in the Australian intelligence studies landscape as it is featured in most undergraduate or postgraduate studies.

The interdisciplinary nature of intelligence studies has been identified as a problem for the field.[4] However, as intelligence draws on such a large number of academic and research areas, there is plenty of scope for academics and practitioners in a complementary approach. It appears that such a broad field reflects a diversity of academics with practitioner experience as well as those from academic fields directly related to intelligence. Charles Sturt University's intelligence program appears to be indicative of the wider Australian academic community in Australian universities. A review of university programs and associated teaching staff teaching intelligence includes a mixture of teaching by former practitioners and academics without practitioner experience. We cannot speak for the relationship at other institutions, but this combination has been a productive one, drawing upon former practitioners' experience, insights from academics in related fields, and active engagement with the broader intelligence community.

Most intelligence studies specializations at a tertiary level are offered through postgraduate studies. Graduate courses are offered at the graduate certificate, graduate diploma, and master's degree levels. Of the eight identified universities offering courses or subjects in intelligence studies, it appears four offer postgraduate qualifications or training in the field. The Australian National University, Macquarie University, Curtin University, and Charles Sturt University appear the most active in postgraduate intelligence studies. At the postgraduate level, subjects and courses are again a blend of theory and practice—but on the whole, there is a greater emphasis on skills-based learning, particularly in technological fields such as data mining and geospatial intelligence. There is also greater emphasis on the application of intelligence in an operational and strategic setting. In the higher research degree stratosphere, there are two forms of postgraduate study that dominate the Australian intelligence studies landscape. The doctor of philosophy is naturally a part of further research into intelligence studies, but also a feature in the professional doctorate and workplace research subjects embedded in master's-level courses. Within Australian intelligence higher research degrees, the doctorate of philosophy provides a vehicle for students to develop or test theories pertaining to intelligence studies. However, further interesting developments in higher-degree research in intelligence studies are apparent in professional doctorates and workplace research projects. Professional doctorates allow the professional intelligence practitioner the opportunity to research and respond to emerging issues in their area of expertise. Undertaking a shorter dissertation of approximately sixty thousand words, professional doctorate students address an issue or idea that will better improve intelligence practice. Workplace research projects are developed for postgraduate students in conjunction with their employers. The aim of the workplace research project is to identify and make recommendations to address problems of intelligence collection, analysis, and management.

COURSE DESIGN RATIONALE:
ACADEMIC RIGOR AND PROFESSIONAL PRACTICE

Teaching academic rigor and professional practice is a challenge faced by most professional-based tertiary courses such as nursing, law, and accounting. Courses in intelligence analysis are certainly no different. Without the correct balance of academic rigor, students may not be exposed to theoretical and intellectual ideas underpinning intelligence collection and analysis. Alternatively, without exposure to industry standards, students may not be exposed to elements of professional practice and may subsequently lack the skills and knowledge required to accomplish at an agency, military, or law enforcement level. Naturally, agency, military, and law enforcement sectors conduct extensive training for their personnel. Yet "in-house" training can be limited in scope and is often solely directed at equipping personnel to undertake their appointed duties within a specific and often tightly defined context. Alone, in-house training does not fully address the requirement for theoretical understanding or intellectual rigor and is therefore likely to limit the ability for critical and creative thought. It is critical thought[5] and creative problem solving that are vital to effective intelligence collection and analysis.

Designing a course that balances academic rigor and professional experience requires close association with the intelligence community and an ability to challenge normal academic assessment and teaching practices. In addition to ongoing engagement with the intelligence community, as discussed below, Charles Sturt University lecturers are themselves a mixture of academics and intelligence-practitioners-turned-academics, providing a useful balance between research and practice that can be applied to course design, development, and delivery.

At the center of any course design is knowing the expectations of students. Based on feedback from students, we would argue that students of intelligence usually undertake the course for three specific reasons: formalization of their education and training, promotion or transfer within their intelligence roles, or ambition to gain employment in the intelligence sector. Each rationale for undertaking study is accompanied by a variety of backgrounds and experiences of the student. A further challenge in course design is providing learning experiences that meet the various levels of existing skills and knowledge. What is increasingly evident in student backgrounds is that those with experience in intelligence collection or analysis generally lack academic skills in writing and reasoning arguments. Students new to intelligence analysis and collection tend to be overwhelmed by analyzing data and producing intelligence products such as target profiles or operational assessments. A critical response to students' mixed abilities is assessments that allow each student to play to their individual strengths.

COURSE DESIGN PROCESS

Effective course design for intelligence studies starts with what is termed "backward design." The backward design process maps a pathway to specific learning goals (outcomes) and requires clear evidence that students have reached those outcomes. Evidence that students have achieved those goals is often the assessment provided to students. Backward design reflects an appreciation of external-based standards and responsibility to ensure students reach those standards. It is a departure from traditional approaches that place teaching as the central focus of learning. By mapping clear paths to meeting standards, students can see their progress through a course and understand relationships between assessment items, standards, and subjects.[6]

The process to backward design begins with the formation of course advisers. These advisers comprise intelligence community members, intelligence studies academic staff, educational designers, and assessment specialists. An analysis of the intelligence course is conducted to determine the drivers, strengths, needs, and risks (DSNR) of the course. Undertaking a DSNR analytical process is similar to conducting a SWOT analysis. Intelligence-sector standards are also identified along with nationally recognized higher-education standards. It is at this point that the blending of academic rigor and professional practice commences. Outcomes are drafted from intelligence industry and academic standards to define the knowledge and skills required to meet those standards. Assessments are then created and linked to subjects. The assessments allow students to clearly demonstrate their ability to meet the standards-based outcomes. Within the subjects, modules are created to support learning and teaching strategies that help students meet the learning outcomes. On completion of the "backward-mapping" process, the course outline and mapped content is presented, and feedback is gained from the intelligence community, university education designers, and assessment specialists. This feedback then leads to further refinement and modification of the course.

COURSE STANDARDS

The foundation of course design is developing and integrating standards. Standards are similar to outcomes—areas where students should be able to demonstrate proficiency. Integration of standards is twofold: First, it is integrating academic standards with industry standards—developing a continuum of learning with the intelligence community's in-house training. Second, it is ensuring that the standards are integrated with course content and assessments.

Collaboration with the intelligence community is essential in developing relevant standards. Consultation with the intelligence community and developing standards is a baseline approach. More extensive shifts toward greater links between tertiary institutions and the intelligence sector are emerging within the Australian intelligence community. In Australia, a Criminal Intelligence Training and Development Continuum is being developed by the Australian Criminal Intelligence Commission and Australian Federal Police to provide a professional development framework for criminal intelligence analysts and field intelligence officers.[7] The continuum has been designed at a postgraduate level and articulates into Charles Sturt University's master's of intelligence analysis course.[8] Further, this is not just a once-off development but a reflection of an enduring relationship between Charles Sturt University and these agencies, reflected in the recently signed memorandum of understanding between Charles Sturt University and the Defence Force School of Intelligence and the Australian Criminal Intelligence Commission, reflecting the evaluation of courses across institutions and recognition of prior learning toward CSU qualifications.

Matching industry standards with tertiary education standards is essential in ensuring that intelligence courses are at the expected educational level. In the Australian context, university courses are linked to the Australian Qualifications Framework (AQF). The AQF governs a national qualifications framework ensuring that each higher-education and vocational education qualification meets standards. The AQF provides broad criteria in knowledge and skills reflecting different education levels. For example, at a master's level, AQF requires graduates to demonstrate expert specialized cognitive and technical skills in a body of knowledge or practice to independently

- analyze critically, reflect on, and synthesize complex information, problems, concepts, and theories;
- research and apply established theories to a body of knowledge or practice; and
- interpret and transmit knowledge, skills, and ideas to specialist and nonspecialist audiences.[9]

When combined, the intelligence sector and tertiary institution standards form the basis of an intelligence course design. The design has standards that include disciplinary knowledge, analytical skills, communication skills, ethics, professional practice, leadership, and research.

Disciplinary Knowledge

Intelligence as an academic discipline is relatively new and borrows from other disciplines, including the social sciences.[10] As part of this disciplinary knowledge, students are required to demonstrate an understanding of the methodological origins of intelligence. In addition, students must demonstrate an understanding of key intelligence principles—notably that intelligence results in the production of value-added information available for use by decision makers—and the role of intelligence in supporting strategic, operational, and tactical objectives. Disciplinary knowledge also includes the ability to explain trends and provide insights into the field of intelligence studies.

Analytical Skills

Analytical skills are essential. The ability to use technical and creative skills to investigate, analyze, and synthesize complex information and problems is indispensable in intelligence and must be reinforced throughout intelligence courses. Evaluating complex ideas, concepts, and problems at an abstract level is a skill that academic rigor is able to teach and foster. Such academic skills are compatible with professional practice.

Communication Skills

Communication skills that a student can develop to share results, information, and insights are an important standard. The ability to communicate to a broad audience of both specialists and nonspecialists using a range of modes—written, oral, and visual—should be developed and taught throughout the life of an intelligence course.

Ethics

Standing apart from legal dimensions, ethics is a facet of the intelligence discipline that requires significant attention. Demonstrating an understanding of ethical issues in the intelligence community is required so that effective judgments and reasoning can be made. Students need to be made aware that there is a role for ethics in intelligence collection and analysis.

Professional Practice

Professional practice does not have to be reserved for working in the intelligence sector. A professional practice standard encourages "lifelong learning." An important part of professional development, lifelong learning recognizes that education does not have to begin and end with formal study or training,[11] but rather students of intelligence should be encouraged to be creative and take initiative in developing their professional practice. The adoption of reflective practice into their learning makes students engage more in the process. Developing a reflective practice involves the student thinking about what they have learned and what further knowledge and skills they may wish to develop in the future. This approach is particularly articulated in CSU's capstone subjects.

Leadership

Including leadership as a course standard is designed to develop critical thinking and judgment that will influence change and challenge ideas and practices. It also provides scope to encourage students to learn to evaluate and reflect on leadership management and theory within the intelligence context.

Research

The ability to research using academic methods in a professional intelligence setting is an important standard, as it is a bridge between academic rigor and professional practice. Specifically, teaching the knowledge and skills associated with planning and executing a research project (workplace or more academically) provides benefits for the intelligence community and strengthens intelligence studies as a discipline within its own right.

All of these standards are applied to course standards with the recognition that the field of intelligence continues to develop as our understanding of the field continues to grow. As knowledge and insight into the practice and underpinning research of intelligence develops, these insights need to be incorporated into the teaching of the field.

OUTCOMES

As highlighted earlier in the course design process, course standards are expanded upon and drafted into clear outcomes. Outcomes in an educational sense are articulated expectations of student knowledge, skills, and values. Standards are broken down into outcomes that can be assessed. Below are some examples of learning outcomes developed from standards in Charles Sturt University's master's of intelligence analysis course:

- synthesize and apply advanced knowledge of intelligence theory, principles, and recent developments to communicate and explain trends and threats in order to provide options and insights for actions and intelligence products in a range of intelligence contexts;
- apply technical, critical-thinking skills to evaluate complex ideas, concepts, and problems at an abstract level using alternative perspectives related to a range of intelligence contexts to provide decision-making support and insights;
- explain and apply contemporary legal frameworks and ethical practices to make judgments that reflect the application of ethical decision making in the intelligence context;

- synthesize and articulate information pertaining to current intelligence and emerging threats, as a result of gathering and interpreting data to construct knowledge in order to influence stakeholder groups in multiple domains;
- provide expertise and leadership in a range of intelligence and cultural contexts;
- exercise self-reflection, critical thinking, and sound judgment in order to influence change and challenge existing views or practices;
- apply cross-cultural competency in the intelligence profession; and
- use specialized technical and creative skills to plan and execute a substantial workplace research-based as and practices.

The outcomes are matched to relevant existing subjects, or where there is clear evidence of a gap in knowledge and skills, new subjects are created. The outcomes are then mapped to the course structure and sequenced to develop knowledge and skills through to advanced mastery of such knowledge and skills. The subjects allow for the opportunity to teach to those outcomes at a more detailed level.

ASSESSMENT

The standards and outcomes highlighted above are critical aspects of developing a basis for academic rigor and professional practice. However, demonstrating that students have attained those outcomes originates through rigorous assessment. Assessment items need to develop academic skills while also equipping students for practice. In addition to the traditional essays and exams as a means to communicate academic ideas, intelligence products are also a cornerstone of assessment. Learning to draft tactical and strategic assessments and analytical and collection plans are important parts of assessment. Analytical methods such as predictive mapping, SWOT, PEST, and indicators and warnings are also part of the assessment landscape. Assessments of intelligence products and academic essays and exams are criteria based and marked against the outcomes.

SUBJECTS

Within the tertiary-education sector, subjects are often seen as the driving factor of a course. In a traditional university setting, subjects are often designed to reflect the expertise of teaching staff or particular research interests. Further, in a traditional university setting, students undertake subjects that then form the body of a degree. Within a backward-mapping approach, subjects are articulated and driven by course expectations and standards. Essentially, the subjects serve the courses rather than the other way around. Decisions to develop subjects or redesign existing subjects are informed by meeting intelligence community standards rather than academic interests. Consultation with the intelligence sector assists in the identification of gaps in knowledge, skills, and values. It ensures subjects remain relevant to professional practice. Simultaneously, subjects must be robust enough to encompass a changing emphasis in intelligence collection and analysis. Subjects should not be based on responding to specific trends in the intelligence community but rather provide fundamental knowledge and skills that can be applied to new trends and emerging intelligence issues.

MODULES

Modules are the topics within a subject that teach to the outcomes. Designing modules and learning experiences (activities) should, for the most part, be contextualized into professional practice. The use of scenarios, guest speakers from the intelligence community, and teaching practical analytical tradecraft are some ways professional practice can be better integrated into learning. To cater to students with limited academic backgrounds, modules that provide study and research skills are necessary for the student learning experience. The balance of academic rigor and professional practice has to be evident at the module level so students can appreciate the necessity for both approaches. To this end, a mixture of learning experiences (activities) is included that caters to academic and professional learning. Learning experiences should also allow students to work collaboratively where possible. The adoption of online communications between students and teacher as well as student to student not only fosters collegial learning but also sets the basis for future networking within the intelligence community.

CHALLENGES TO THE CURRICULUM

Despite the best curriculum, teaching intelligence presents challenges that cannot always be addressed through course design. There are inherent aptitudes and outlooks possessed by intelligence professionals that cannot easily be taught through formal educational avenues. Specifically, abilities to think laterally, act on intuition, and make choices are some of the anecdotal challenges to intelligence students and teachers. Some professional observations have shown increasingly that students can deal less and less with ambiguities and lack confidence in decision making. The rise in artificial intelligence (AI) and machine learning has only exacerbated the problem. Relying on AI to make assumptions or decisions is allowing analysts to avoid making judgments. Students need to be exposed to decision making and working within ambiguity. Research conducted by Queensland University of Technology in 2017 found that tolerance of ambiguity was also related to an individual's ability to think critically, make decisions, accept risk, and be creative.[12] However, increasingly, in structured education we are encouraged to remove ambiguity from the teaching practice. Detailing steps in completing assessments, study schedules, and orientation to learning materials all eliminate ambiguity. The challenge is how to expose intelligence studies students to ambiguity in an authentic educational and assessment setting. It remains an area of intelligence pedagogy that requires further research.

Decision making is another aspect of the more intangible skills that need to be taught in intelligence education. The rise of AI, while providing benefits to intelligence collection and analysis, can impact an individual's ability to make sound decisions. Experts in the field of AI suggest that computers and algorithms are likely to take away key aspects of the human ability to be independent and make choices.[13] The challenge in teaching intelligence is to accept the role of technology but balance the students' dependence on it. Indeed, recent research within Australia, sponsored by the Office of National Intelligence, specifically highlighted the enduring importance of the human aspect of intelligence in the face of increased use of AI. Emphasizing the importance of social science research for the National Intelligence Community (NIC), *Social Science Research and Intelligence in Australia* highlighted some of the opportunities and challenges for social sciences as well as intelligence analysts, noting:

> Social science research can assist in shaping how AI is used—automation will involve confirmation bias and risks will remain throughout AI's evolution. High-level skills will need to be cultivated within the NIC, and the role of the intelligence analyst will continue to be an essential component of analysis. Such high-level skills are reserved only to humans and will remain as such. AI may further assist with pattern recognition, but social science expertise can be tapped by the NIC to help inform context and more rigorous analysis. The more AI accounts for intelligence gathering and the easier tasks made possible by big data, the higher the level of human ability will be required. This education and upskilling of the intelligence analyst can be achieved through engagement with social science research.[14]

Traditional forms of collection and analytical tradecraft have to be featured in a curriculum. Analytical tradecraft such as decision trees, scenario planning, and operational design need to be demonstrated by students independent from AI and computer software. Collection tradecraft is more problematic given the sensitive nature of the content. It is in this realm that the continuum of learning between the intelligence sector and education institutions is required. From the education institution perspective, the theory of human intelligence and counterintelligence can be taught with confidence along with ethical considerations.

TEACHING AND LEARNING THROUGH
QUESTION ASKING AND DEEP QUESTIONS

Questions form the basis of any analytic technique. Understanding the questions to ask is a crucial aspect of intelligence, and the use of questions as a means of engaging students is fundamental to teaching and learning throughout the program. The education sector has clearly established through empirical research the strong benefits of having students engage with deep questions.[15] The use of deep questions in teaching (i.e., why, how, and what-if questions) assists students by encouraging reflection and a deeper level of thinking, going further than simple answers and moving into providing explanations and justifications. Given that many students have experience in intelligence or related fields, the deliberate employment of deep questions throughout the course has been used as a means of consolidating course content and enabling students to draw on their own insights and experiences, as well as a means of engaging with their fellow students. Indeed, in a number of courses, a series of *why* and *how* questions as well as *yes/no* questions *that also require justification* were developed and trailed through online blogs as a method for students to reflect on course content and engage with their peers, a crucial aspect of master's-level study.[16]

As part of the Introduction to Intelligence course, the importance and centrality of questions to intelligence is deliberately emphasized, with students consistently presented with deep questions to reflect on the nature of intelligence and intelligence practice. As one example, students are asked to reflect on and respond to the questions "Why do questions matter to intelligence analysts?" and "What are the questions intelligence analysts should be asking?" This approach is reflected across courses, with a similar approach used in the course Intelligence Management; noting questions also provides the means to obtain information relevant to the development, delivery, and evaluation of intelligence products. Some good questions for intelligence managers to ask themselves and their teams include:

- Is the intelligence being produced actually useful? How do we know?
- If it is useful, who is using it? How are they using it? How can it be improved?
- If it is not useful, why not? What needs to be done to make it useful?

These questions reflect the importance of encouraging intelligence practitioners to seek answers that they might not want to hear and, based on the professional intelligence experience of one of the authors, reflect a series of questions too often ignored by practitioners, namely asking, "Is what we are producing of any value?"

It is not simply utilizing questions as part of teaching and learning, but deliberately emphasizing to students the fundamental importance of questions to intelligence as a knowledge development field. Questions are not just important; they are foundational to understanding, research, problem formulation, and any analytic approach or technique. The ongoing importance of teaching question asking as a skill is reflected even in the technology sector. As noted in IBM's paper "Computing, Cognition and the Future of Knowing," "In the 21st century, knowing all the answers won't distinguish someone's intelligence—rather, the ability to ask better questions will be the mark of true genius."[17] What this means for teaching in the CSU course is reflected in one of the author's joint papers presented at the Annual Intelligence Association for Intelligence Education Conference:

> As educators, we do not know with certainty what future problems, challenges or opportunities each of our students will face. Instead, intelligence educators can best assist intelligence practitioners by helping them to develop deep-question asking and answering skills that allow them to adapt to future situations and challenges, whatever they might be. It is this question-asking and answering skill that best prepares intelligence practitioners with the ability to adapt and innovate in a complex and changing environment.[18]

LEARNING THE TOOLS AND THE LIMITATIONS

Part of teaching in any field of study is ensuring that students develop an understanding of the fundamentals of the field in terms of key concepts, terms, and ideas. Critical too is developing in students an appreciation of both the strengths of these fundamentals as well as their limitations.

One example is the concept of the *intelligence cycle*. As a method for describing and understanding the process of intelligence, the intelligence cycle remains a frequently referenced and employed concept within the intelligence community. Consequently, the approach adopted in the program is to have students reflect on what for many is an already well-known concept and then deliberately provide an opportunity to critically consider the intelligence cycle as a model. Following a deliberate critique of the intelligence cycle as a concept, including identification of limitations and alternative models, students are challenged to consider whether they are to employ the model, then identify what version of the model they would employ and how they would apply it in practice. To ignore or simply reject the concept of the intelligence cycle would be seen as disconnected from the wider intelligence community, which uses variations of the cycle as a foundational element of their own internal training. Consequently, by using the intelligence cycle as a recognized concept, the teaching of the approach from a critical and considered perspective is used as a means of reinforcing critical thinking and highlighting how ingrained such models become, as well as the need to consider both strengths and limitations of *any* concepts or models students (and the wider intelligence community) employ. In this way, the course recognizes the benefits of adopting a questioning approach to the tools (including ideas and concepts) that intelligence adopts, in line with George Box's observation that "all models are wrong, but some are useful."[19]

The teaching of formal analytic techniques provides another useful approach for capturing *current practice* within many parts of the intelligence community, as well as highlighting the limitations of what we know about the application and benefits of such techniques to problems. The awareness and use of analytic techniques (or structured methods) within intelligence analysis have increased in recent years. These structured techniques include approaches such as analysis of competing hypotheses, key assumptions checklists, indicators and warnings, and network analysis.[20] Such analytic techniques are popular and provide analysts with a structure to follow and allow for the formal capture of the underpinning basis for answers. Intelligence managers should familiarize themselves with existing techniques and approaches used by their intelligence units or being used more widely. Familiarity with the process (formally structured or otherwise) that their intelligence analysts use, and their unit follows, is critical in both understanding what is done (and also what is not done) as well as improving the process. However, analytic techniques are still in their relative infancy in terms of evidence-based conclusions about their value or suitability. Indeed, recent and ongoing research suggests that some techniques used by intelligence analysts do not match the positive claims or remain untested.[21]

Knowledge of intelligence keeps developing, but much of the empirical research required for understanding how intelligence practitioners remains far into the future. What is required then is a recognition of what we know and just how much remains to be known. Roger George and James Bruce provide useful insight into how much remains to be learned when they argue that analysis is greater than printed or electronic information and includes what they refer to as "analytic transactions." These analytic transactions are also part of the intelligence analysis process and include various interactions: discussions, emails, meetings, and phone calls with peers, commanders, and executives. George and Bruce argue that these analytic transactions, where information, questions, and ideas are exchanged and accepted or rejected, are "possibly where the most insightful cognition is occurring, rather than on the page of a finished assessment or a PowerPoint slide."[22] A true understanding of the nature, influence, impact, and outcomes of these variables might not ever be achievable, and yet it is logical to understand that intelligence analysis consists of all of these. There is still much to learn as practitioners and educators, but there will always be limits to our knowledge.

Perhaps one way of illuminating this is the idea of an ever-developing concept of *leading practice*, namely what practitioners and academics consider to be the leading knowledge, practices, and concepts, recognizing that these are currently *leading* but are in no way fixed. This contrasts with the idea of *best practice* and the risk of thinking that what is "best" is final and fixed. As noted elsewhere and captured in the intelligence program, the limits to our understanding of the intelligence analysis process, particularly the absence of empirical research into the questions that intelligence analysts ask, remain an ongoing focus of attention. This requires that students understand that limits in our current understanding of the intelligence process remain, as well as questions for addressing these gaps in our knowledge.

CONSIDERING FUNDAMENTAL SKILLS

Essentially, concentration on core knowledge and skills that can be applied to emerging issues and trends is more favorable. One aspect of intelligence practitioners undertaking CSU's master's course is that many commence at the graduate certificate level, reflecting that this may in some cases be the first university study that they have been exposed to. This provides an opportunity to develop and establish what academics might consider basic skills in terms of writing communication, identifying and drawing on peer-reviewed publications, weighing up differing perspectives, and arriving at justified and logically traceable judgments. However, while often overlooked, it is evident that such seemingly "basic" or "fundamental" skills are not simply a given, meaning that academics have much to offer in terms of building and expanding these "meta-skills." Indeed, a foundational requirement for intelligence professionals—even in highly technical fields—is the ability to articulate (whether verbally or in writing) arguments and the basis for these. As one of the authors noted elsewhere, "Intelligence analysis is not simply a set of conclusions or assessments. For credibility, there must be some understanding of how and why an analyst reached one set of conclusions and not others."[23] As we teach, "it is not enough for analysts to say 'the answer is X!'; the analyst, analytic team, and, ultimately, the intelligence manager need to be confident in the process used to arrive at this final answer."

These skills have clear and direct relevance to intelligence analysis but might often go unconsidered by practitioners, not because they do not engage in them, but because these are not necessarily their primary focus. The development and delivery of timely, tailored, and insightful intelligence products to a particular audience (often action focused in terms of police or military personnel) require the ability to "get the job done." Through academic study, students have the opportunity to reflect on some key and fundamental aspects of developing and articulating arguments. The opportunity is provided for students from these backgrounds to further develop their written communication skills; consider how to build and develop arguments; recognize credible resources and sources (and the basis for this credibility); reconcile (or simply acknowledge) disagreements within the information; and produce a well-reasoned, evidence-based, and justifiable argument in response to a defined problem. Simple, but not simplistic.

INTELLIGENCE SCHOLARSHIP IN AUSTRALIA

Intelligence scholarship in Australia is a growing field, building on earlier developments. In a recent review of publications by Australian academics in Australia and overseas from 2007 to 2017, Rhys Crawley and Shannon Brandt Ford found a problem in "the lack of much at all in the areas that traditionally dominate Intelligence Studies literature and educational programs. On the positive side, nothing is yet overdone."[24] That might be changing, along with recognition of the importance of intelligence scholarship and its relevance to intelligence agencies. In 2018, the director general of Australia's most secretive intelligence agency, the Australian Secret Intelligence Service, chose the launch of the book *Intelligence and the Function of Government*, an edited work of Australian researchers and academics, as his first public speech as leader of the agency. Intelligence agencies' engagement with academia is also evident in the publication of an Office of National Intelligence–sponsored report. The report actively engages the Academy of the Social Sciences in Australia to review the social science academic community in order to assess what it could offer the national intelligence community in Australia.[25]

There are a number of Australian peer-reviewed journals directly related to intelligence, usually under a broader framework of security, policing, and counterterrorism. Three journals are worth considering here, all of which are peer-reviewed journals and accredited by the Australian Research Council as an Excellence in Research for Australia. In terms of a singular focus on intelligence, the Australian Institute of Professional Intelligence Officers publishes a formal, peer-reviewed journal, established in 1992, with an academic and practitioner focus on intelligence articles from across the breadth of the field.[26] Macquarie University established the *Journal of Policing, Intelligence and Counterterrorism* as a peer-reviewed journal, representing an Australian-based international journal published by Taylor & Francis. The journal has been a particular success in terms of the publication of research from Australian and international authors since its launch in 2006, in the three overlapping areas of policing, intelligence, and counterterrorism, with a focus on theory and practice.[27] Charles Sturt University's Australian Graduate School of Policing and Security established the *Salus Journal* in 2013 as a peer-reviewed, open-access journal addressing law enforcement, national security, and emergency management, which has included the publication of numerous intelligence and intelligence-related journal articles.[28] In recent years, Australian academics have also published in the intelligence studies fields in numerous overseas intelligence journals, most notably the journal *Intelligence and National Security*. Further, recent years have seen the consistent publication of intelligence books by Australian authors through both Australian and international publishers on topics including intelligence analysis, counterintelligence, and a historical series on the Australian Security Intelligence Organisation. Overall, this appears to reflect a maturing and growing field of intelligence scholarship in Australia.

CONCLUDING REFLECTIONS

There is still much for both practitioners and educators to learn about the field of intelligence. The most effective approach to understanding the practice and discipline of intelligence is maintaining close intellectual and organizational ties. At the center of academic rigor and professional practice is the necessity for consultation and awareness of developments in teaching pedagogy and professional practice. Neither can effectively work in a vacuum when they share the same objectives—intelligence practitioners that are skilled and working at their peak performance. We want intelligence professionals to be equipped with knowledge, skills, and ethical values that allow an individual to think critically and solve problems. We want practitioners who can assist decision makers and, where necessary, lead complex intelligence operations.

The challenge for curriculum development is maintaining the balance between exposing students to practical learning experiences and academic rigor. The two are not mutually exclusive and in many ways are complementary. An intelligence course needs to start from the premise of what kind of professional it wants to produce and what the intelligence community needs. It requires learning opportunities that are industry relevant. It must recognize and respond to the diverse backgrounds and experiences of its students. Finally, an intelligence course should be recognized as belonging to the broader intelligence community. It needs to be accepted as part of its overall training continuum.

NOTES

1. Anna Patty and Nigel Gladstone, "Spooks and Psychologists: Jobs of the Future," *Sydney Morning Herald*, August 12, 2019, https://www.smh.com.au/business /workplace/spooks-and-psychologists-jobs-of-the-future-20190802-p52dae.html.

2. Department of Prime Minister and Cabinet, "Statement on Malicious Cyber Activity against Australian Networks," June 19, 2020, https://www.pm.gov.au/media /statement-malicious-cyber-activity-against-australian-networks.

3. Patrick F. Walsh, "Improving 'Five Eyes' Health Security Intelligence Capabilities: Leadership and Governance Challenges," *Intelligence and National Security* 35, no. 4 (2020): 586–602.

4. Rhys Crawley and Shannon Brandt Ford, "The Current State of Intelligence Studies," in *Intelligence and the Function of Government*, ed. Daniel Baldino and Rhys Crawley (Melbourne: Melbourne University Press, 2018).

5. Noel Hendrickson, "Critical Thinking in Intelligence Analysis," *International Journal of Intelligence and CounterIntelligence* 21, no. 4 (2008): 1.

6. Elizabeth A. Thomson et al., "Course Design as a Collaborative Enterprise: Incorporating Interdisciplinarity into a Backward Mapping Systems Approach to Course Design in Higher Education," in *Research and Development in Higher Education: Curriculum Transformation*, ed. R. G. Walker and S. B. Bedford, 356–67 (Sydney, Australia: Higher Education Research and Development Society of Australasia Inc., 2017).

7. Mark Harrison et al., "Tradecraft to Standards: Moving Criminal Intelligence Practice to a Profession through the Development of a Criminal Intelligence Training and Development Continuum," *Policing* 14, no. 2 (June 2020): 312.

8. Harrison et al., "Tradecraft to Standards," 312.

9. Australian Qualifications Framework, "What Is the AQF?," accessed 2020, https://www.aqf.edu.au/what-is-the-aqf.

10. Marjan Laal, "Benefits of Lifelong Learning," *Procedia—Social and Behavioral Sciences* 46 (2012): 4268–72.

11. Laal, "Benefits of Lifelong Learning," 4268.

12. Kerryn Fewster and Peter O'Connor, "Embracing Ambiguity in the Workplace," Queensland University of Technology, May 2017, 1, https://eprints.qut.edu.au/108255/1/Industry%20Report%20TOA.pdf.

13. Janna Anderson and Lee Rainie, "Artificial Intelligence and the Future of Humans," Pew Research Center, December 10, 2018, https://www.pewresearch.org/internet/2018/12/10/artificial-intelligence-and-the-future-of-humans.

14. Academy of the Social Sciences in Australia Inc., *Social Science Research and Intelligence in Australia*, September 2019, https://socialsciences.org.au/publications/social-science-research-intelligence-in-australia.

15. Harold Pashler et al., *Organizing Instruction and Study to Improve Student Learning* (IES Practice Guide, National Center for Education Research, September 2007), 29, https://files.eric.ed.gov/fulltext/ED498555.pdf.

16. For a discussion of this approach and the results, refer to Charles Vandepeer, "Increasing Student-to-Student (Peer) Learning through Deep Questions and Online Blogs," *iTeach* (blog), Charles Sturt University, July 15, 2019, https://iteach.csu.edu.au/2019/07/15/increasing-student-to-student-peer-learning-through-deep-questions-and-online-blogs.

17. John E. Kelly, "Computing, Cognition and the Future of Knowing: How Humans and Machines Are Forging a New Age of Understanding," IBM Research, 2015, 2, http://publicservicesalliance.org/wp-content/uploads/2015/10/Computing_Cognition_WhitePaper.pdf.

18. Charles Vandepeer and James L. Regens, "Teaching and Mentoring in Intelligence Education: Preparing Intelligence Professionals for Asking Better Questions" (paper presented at the Fourteenth Annual Intelligence Association for Intelligence Education Conference, Sydney, Australia, July 2018).

19. G. E. P. Box, "Robustness in the Strategy of Scientific Model Building," in *Robustness in Statistics*, ed. Robert L. Launer and Graham N. Wilkinson (New York: Academic Press, 1979).

20. Mandeep K. Dhami, Ian K. Belton, and David R. Mandel, "The 'Analysis of Competing Hypotheses' in Intelligence Analysis," *Applied Cognitive Psychology* 33, no. 6 (2019): 1080–90.

21. David R. Mandel and Philip E. Tetlock, "Correcting Judgment Correctives in National Security Intelligence," *Frontiers in Psychology* 9, article 2640 (2018): 1–5, https://www.frontiersin.org/articles/10.3389/fpsyg.2018.02640/full; Dhami et al., "The 'Analysis of Competing Hypotheses,'" 2019.

22. Roger Z. George and James B. Bruce, eds., *Analyzing Intelligence: National Security Practitioners' Perspectives* (Washington, DC: Georgetown University Press, 2014).

23. Vandepeer and Regens, "Teaching and Mentoring in Intelligence Education."

24. Crawley and Ford, "The Current State of Intelligence Studies."

25. Academy of the Social Sciences in Australia Inc., *Social Science Research*.

26. Australian Institute of Professional Intelligence Offices, *AIPIO Journal*, accessed January 11, 2021, https://www.aipio.asn.au/aipio-journal.

27. Macquarie University, *Journal of Policing, Intelligence and Counter Terrorism*, accessed January 11, 2021, https://www.mq.edu.au/faculty-of-arts/departments -and-schools/department-of-security-studies-and-criminology/our-research/journal -of-policing,-intelligence-and-counter-terrorism.

28. *Salus Journal: A Journal of Law Enforcement, National Security, and Emergency Management*, accessed January 11, 2021, https://salusjournal.com.

The Academic-Practitioner Divide in Intelligence

A Latin American Perspective

Andrés de Castro García and Carolina Sancho Hirane

This chapter examines the development of intelligence studies in Latin American countries, which has been significant in contributing to the institutionalization of intelligence education and training in the region,[1] the increased professionalization of this activity, and the promotion of a more transparent intelligence culture. In this chapter, the term "institutionalization" refers to the process by which intelligence agencies and their procedures[2] acquire value, stability, and permanence over time. We propose that through intelligence education and training, we can see an increase in the levels of professionalization and in the development of intelligence activities that can favor its institutionalization. However, a gap in the outdated training provided in intelligence agencies, compared to new training needs, must be overcome to achieve this. To address this, we have structured our chapter around a four-axis approach. The first axis explains the institutionalization of intelligence specific to states in Latin America. The second axis explains the nature of the academic-practitioner divide in the region. The third axis analyzes how universities can contribute to reducing or overcoming this gap. Finally, the fourth axis considers the globalization of the profession and its study and the lessons that can be drawn from this and applied to the region.

AXIS 1: INSTITUTIONALIZATION OF INTELLIGENCE WITHIN LATIN AMERICA

Institutionalization through State Regulations

Within Latin America, challenges persist in the institutionalization of intelligence agencies. The institutionalization of intelligence is closely related to the development of professionalization and is generally held to contribute to helping government organizations avoid scandals and enhance operational effectiveness. While there are no studies that establish a direct relationship between practitioner training levels and the reduction of negative intelligence practices,[3] we believe it is possible to infer a directly proportional relationship between intelligence institutions, professionalization of intelligence practitioners, and their level of training.

One way of understanding the level of institutionalization of state intelligence is through studying state regulations. Regulations can take the form of a decree issued by the government or laws approved by the legislature. For example, in Chile, after the return to democracy, between 1991 and 1993, the Public Security Coordinating Council was regulated first by Supreme Decree 363/1991[4] and later by Supreme Decree 4/1992.[5] However, since 1993, entities that carry out intelligence have been regulated by a law, which, in the sense of Kelsen's pyramid, is a much higher form of regulation.[6] Kelsen insisted on the need for a legal system with the Constitution at the top, followed by laws and then by decrees, creating a normative hierarchy. In this regard, in 1993 through Law 19212/1993, the Directorate of Public Security and Information, and later its successor, the ANI, with Law 19974/2004, created the Intelligence System of the State and the National Intelligence Agency.[7] In Kelsenian terms, we see an evolution in the regulation of state intelligence activities based on developments in state legal systems. The cases of Paraguay and Uruguay also illustrate a growing institutionalization of intelligence via legal regulation. In the case of Paraguay, this occurred in 2014, with Law 5241/2016, which created the National Intelligence System, and in the case of Uruguay, it occurred in 2018, with Law 19,696, called the State Intelligence System.

Good practices that contribute to the institutionalization of the intelligence function correspond to the formulation of specific laws that regulate the state's intelligence function, which are approved in the legislature. These laws also create regulations surrounding the appointment of intelligence agency leadership; the matters it must address; the identification of the entities that can carry out this activity; their attributions and competencies; internal and external control mechanisms; admission and promotion requirements in various performance categories; and separation mechanisms, as well as capacities and means for the development of their function.

Institutionalization through Professionalization of Intelligence Activities

Together with enhanced accountability, professionalizing intelligence activities is one of the best safeguards in terms of avoiding their politicization.[8] For this reason, the characteristics that distinguish a profession such as vocation, responsibility, corporatism,[9] and ethical sense are desirable for officers of an intelligence service. The search for a high level of professionalism in the intelligence services should be seen as a permanent, continuous task. The orientation of it depends on factors such as preparation and specialization of its officials, a civil service career in which public-sector workers are aware of promotion requirements, and the amelioration of certain working conditions such as salaries throughout public administration ranks.[10] Additional factors include the potential for training and continuing education and the existence and validity of a professional code of ethics that allows for reporting any undue pressure. Finally, the capacity to register those who access information managed by the intelligence services[11] is another important component related to the development of a profession.

We observe throughout Latin America certain practices that can weaken intelligence institutions. These often stem from hiring and layoff processes based on elements related to partisan political preferences rather than professional performance. For example, in Argentina, during the last two presidential periods where government coalition changes occurred, significant layoffs of intelligence officials from the Federal Intelligence Agency took place at the beginning of each term. This occurred during a transition between Cristina Fernández and Mauricio Macri (2015) and, later, between Mauricio Macri and Alberto Fernández (2019).[12] In the Chilean case, with Sebastián Piñera's presidencies in 2010 and 2018, significant layoffs occurred in the National Intelligence Agency.[13] In both Argentina and Chile, a new government resulted in a change of a significant percentage of officers.[14]

Likewise, when a change in state leadership occurs in other Latin American countries, personnel changes within intelligence organizations often follow suit. In the case of Ecuador, in 2017, when Lenín Moreno replaced Rafael Correa as president, not only were there important dismissals in the intelligence service, but an important institutional change occurred as well. Following the shift in presidential leadership, in 2018, the National Intelligence Secretariat was replaced by the Strategic Intelligence Center.[15] Similarly, in Colombia, after Juan Manuel Santos replaced Álvaro Uribe as president in 2010, an important change occurred in the institutional framework in the main intelligence service as important dismissals were carried out. Following the election of the new president in 2011, the Administrative Department of Security was replaced by the National Intelligence Directorate.[16] In the case of Peru, the dismissal of civil servants has been more associated with political scandals than with changes of governments, which have implied modifications in the institutional framework of the service. These occurred on several occasions, such as in 2000 during the presidency of Alberto Fujimori and in 2015 under Ollanta Humala.[17]

Brazil is one Latin American country that differs from the others mentioned above regarding practices relating to personnel changes. The Brazilian Intelligence Agency (Agência Brasileira de Inteligência; ABIN) guarantees better continuity of its officials due to the avoidance of massive politically based layoffs during government changes. A possible explanation for this may be found in its open recruitment system and the existence of an official agency career path that promotes training and merit and offers a good retirement provision. While ABIN is not totally free of problems, massive dismissals of officials have not occurred so far.[18]

Two key challenges emerge as a result of these administrative practices. The first challenge is that since politicians can determine who remains in the service, they might use it as a secret police to spy on their political opponents. The second is that training cannot be properly carried out with officers who are not serving continuously in the institution. These administrative issues are important to consider when mapping out the nature of the academic-practitioner divide in Latin America.

AXIS 2: THE NATURE OF THE ACADEMIC-PRACTITIONER DIVIDE IN LATIN AMERICA

Discussion of the divide between theory and practice is not a new one but continues to be a topic among practitioners in the region. This discussion can be shaped by considering the kind of education and training required by intelligence practitioners. Doing this can then help determine how academics and practitioners can come together to develop education and training programs that meet the needs of today's intelligence practitioners. The thoughts developed in this chapter are mainly applicable to intelligence education provided in higher-education settings, where various academic courses and programs in intelligence are taught. Universities work to address different topics for various audiences. Among those served include students who want to become more aware of the intelligence field, working professionals interested in specializing in intelligence topics, and intelligence officers pursuing continuing education.

Within Latin America, there are a few countries that offer intelligence studies courses in university settings. In Chile, intelligence analysis has been taught as an undergraduate course since the late 1990s at the Universidad de Chile. Following this, institutions such as the National Academy of Political and Strategic Studies offered postgraduate courses, including a course in a master's program both alone and also together with the Universidad de Concepción. The Universidad Bernardo O'Higgins later followed that effort with a module on economic intelligence at the bachelor's level. In addition, Universidad Mayor has a full program on intelligence and communication at the postgraduate level. Brazil has also developed programs within the Escola Superior de Guerra framework, which belongs to the Brazilian Ministry of Defense and conducts high-level training for officers and research in security and defense issues. Of particular note is the high course on strategic intelligence open to civilians and military officers.[19]

Other Latin American countries that also offer intelligence education include Peru, Ecuador, Argentina, Mexico, and Colombia. Peru provides intelligence education in the Centro de Altos Estudios Nacionales framework, a postgraduate school of the Peruvian government that offers high-level training and research to government officials. They have developed intelligence education at the postgraduate level in the form of a master's degree in strategic intelligence.[20] Ecuador has developed courses in Facultad Latinoamericana de Ciencias Sociales (FLACSO) at the master's degree level in international relations, security, and conflict.[21] The Universidad de la Plata in Argentina offers a postgraduate degree in national strategic intelligence,[22] while the National Technological University also offers a degree in the same subject.[23] Mexico offers intelligence degrees at the undergraduate and graduate levels. A bachelor's degree in strategic intelligence is offered at Anáhuac University,[24] while a master's degree in intelligence for national security is offered at the National Institute for Public Administration by the National School of Governmental Professionalization. Though the program is open to the general public, greater focus is placed on the recruitment of government employees.[25] Finally, Colombia offers a master's-level course in strategic intelligence at the Intelligence and Counter Intelligence School.[26]

Latin America is, of course, a diverse region composed of countries that are often difficult to compare. However, we can see efforts being made to enhance the development of intelligence training and education and draw out some general observations. While we can see an increase in new course and program offerings, a trend has emerged that indicates a lack of diversity among university intelligence studies faculty. This comes as a result of the similarities in the professional backgrounds of the faculty themselves. In particular, intelligence studies faculty in Latin America tend to have similar training, expertise, and approaches to what an intelligence agency does. This lack of diverse perspectives limits the education that students and trainees can acquire and thus their ability to fully understand the complexity of the intelligence studies field.

To better understand the challenge this presents, we first identify the different profiles of students who typically study intelligence and its related fields in Latin America. Figure 12.1 illustrates the diversity of student profiles, which justifies the need for recruiting equally diverse intelligence studies faculty.

Who / Where	Intelligence practitioners	Non-Intelligence practitioners	
Exclusive for intelligence services.	Initial training and continuing training in intelligence.	Clearance that would allow participation in certain issues.	
Academic or equivalent of the intelligence services.	Exclusive training related to intelligence studies or university education required by the services.	University degrees in the different social sciences and engineering	

Figure 12.1.   Student Profiles in Intelligence Studies.

This student segmentation helps justify the need for faculty selection to occur within the framework of an intelligence field that is professionalized and institutionalized.[27] Such a model requires a shift in hiring practices, where faculty are hired based on their subject-matter expertise specific to the field of intelligence. This would be in contrast to the current model, where faculty may know something about the subject but lack specializations in the different components that make up the intelligence studies discipline. This would be a fundamental step in enhancing intelligence studies education in Latin America.

Heads of academic programs and academic leaders may be unaware of the importance of having an intelligence studies department made up of faculty from a wide variety of backgrounds. This is one of the frequent reasons that help to explain this gap between intelligence studies education and its practice. Having faculty with diverse backgrounds helps to strengthen university intelligence studies programs. Faculty teaching within intelligence should come from a variety of professional backgrounds with varying areas of expertise. The following faculty profiles should be considered when hiring faculty to teach intelligence studies: The *intelligence professional*, an expert in intelligence issues specific to an intelligence service (e.g., institutional doctrine), in active duty or retired. The *academic who specializes in intelligence studies*, an expert in intelligence services and issues related to them, integrating different approaches and disciplines around this topic. The *academic who does not specialize in intelligence studies*; these faculty members are from outside the intelligence studies field. They know a particular topic necessary and relevant for a professional who is trained or provides training in intelligence, for example, discourse analysis, social networks, etc. Finally, there is the *nonacademic professional not directly involved with an intelligence service*; these are experts based on their professional experience, who may or may not have had professional experience in the intelligence services, such as an ambassador, among other professional groups, who deal with serious crises for the country where intelligence can play a key role. From this perspective, it is possible to distinguish different types of faculty members whose expertise is key for educating students on intelligence courses. The courses and subjects taught in academic programs should determine the type of faculty needed within the program.

AXIS 3: HOW UNIVERSITIES CAN HELP ADDRESS THE ACADEMIC-PRACTITIONER DIVIDE

The third axis focuses on the prevalence of the academic-practitioner divide both globally and more specifically in a Latin American context. Addressing this gap requires identifying the type of institution where intelligence education is carried out. We can distinguish two types of entities: intelligence schools (ISS) within the intelligence services and intelligence centers in universities.

To help provide guidance on how these different profiles can be integrated into intelligence studies programs in academia, it is recommended that an academic consultant be utilized who is able to interact with and speak to the different academic and practitioner-based faculty profiles. When it comes to intelligence training within an intelligence service or community, it would be advisable that guidance be provided by an intelligence practitioner who has received training in the same service and holds a doctoral degree. This type of individual would be able to speak to the need for the generation of knowledge according to scientific standards, which is a key issue in the leadership of academic entities even when they are from intelligence services.

For both cases, the existence of two different profiles is considered. One profile corresponds to that of the academic doctoral degree holder who specializes in intelligence, and the other is the intelligence professional with an academic education who also holds a doctoral degree. Both profiles have a valid interaction resulting from the intersection of their shared knowledge, as indicated in figure 12.2.

PROFILE A   PROFILE B

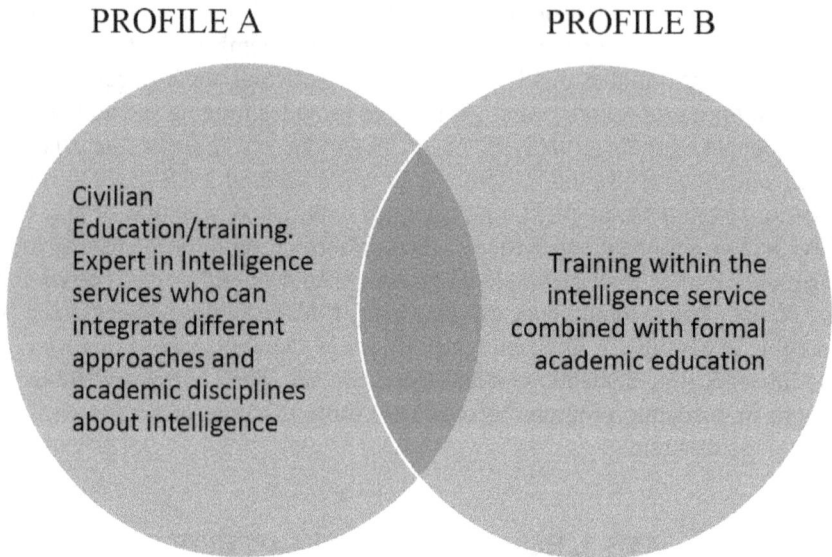

Civilian
Education/training.
Expert in Intelligence
services who can   Training within the
integrate different   intelligence service
approaches and   combined with formal
academic disciplines   academic education
about intelligence

Figure 12.2. Profiles of Intelligence Practitioners and Non–Intelligence Practitioners.

To help transform academic departments and training within intelligence services, these two profiles can help guide an organization's personnel requirements. In the case of a university, guidance should be provided by an academic with a specialization in intelligence and recognized experience and trajectory. In the case of an intelligence service, guidance should be provided by an intelligence professional, as they will be knowledgeable about that institution's needs. However, a different profile might also be considered in exceptional situations. Alternatively, it may be that the academic or educational center of an intelligence service chooses a professional who is external to the service but has an academic trajectory with specialized knowledge on the subject. Such an individual could be suitable to lead a transformation in the way it is approached in the service.

The profiles proposed as the most convenient for leading instances of intelligence studies and academic programs correspond to hybrid profiles. In fact, these are intelligence professionals with high-level academic education or academics with a specialization in intelligence that can be assessed through their research, publications, teaching, and conference contributions. In other words, for the universities, it is a question of "intelligencizing" academics and for intelligence services "academicizing" intelligence professionals. This must be understood in terms that each professional profile internalizes the logic and good practices in their area of expertise to enrich their work. In this manner, none of them loses the essence of the profession in which they were educated/trained. In this regard, an analogy may be helpful to look for solutions in different situations, as, for example, in the case of intelligence service leaders in crisis situations encountering the dilemma of choosing either civilians with security or defense training or military officers with civilian education (i.e., practitioners versus academics).

In the description of profiles that we have been able to study, we see how there are certain common characteristics that can be observed regarding the institution and place where each of the profiles comes from in terms of theoretical versus practical knowledge, the divide between creativity and the tendency to follow orders, and expertise in institution and team building. In this regard, we have observed how faculty coming from a pure university experience have stronger theoretical knowledge and more experience in formulating research questions and in the areas of critical thinking and creativity. However, academics are not a homogeneous group. There are academics who work in the field of intelligence studies who have an intelligence background, but not necessarily in all the topics involved. Conversations with experts show that people from that background could have less knowledge of other academic disciplines. What is clear is that intelligence studies is an interdisciplinary area of study. There needs to be a synergy of academics coming from different fields and practitioners that makes this group more heterogeneous. This helps to ensure that the group benefits from different experiences. Those with theoretical knowledge can make discussions more academic, and those who come from intelligence backgrounds can ground or focus debates and add a certain degree of realism to the formula. We advocate a synergy between the intelligence services and academics who study intelligence to contribute to the national interest, maintain the democratic system in the national context, and contribute to international security.

Frequently, though, we find a common mistrust between practitioners or intelligence professionals and academics in the region. Among the academics who do not specialize in intelligence, there is a lack of knowledge of what it means to serve as an intelligence officer and the work they carry out. There is also a certain suspicion among intelligence officers that academics do not understand specific intelligence matters. This stems from the perception that they are trapped in a theoretical world and fail to understand the essential aspects of this function, such as the necessity of secrecy and the special procedures for information gathering, to name just two. In this way, the former feel that they are facing professionals whose profession is a mystery and whose practices might sometimes be on the edge of violating certain democratic principles. The latter feel misunderstood in the essence of their profession and the contribution of their work. There cannot be a bridge between these two worlds if they cannot understand each other. For this reason, we propose that overcoming this divide can only be achieved by focusing on the area of intersection illustrated in figure 12.2.

AXIS 4: PROFESSIONALIZATION AND INSTITUTIONALIZATION AS A CHALLENGE

Since we have addressed globalization and the transnational nature of intelligence studies, we want to draw on this to point out differences and propose certain paths to be followed in intelligence professionalization and institutionalization. Peter Gill and Mark Phythian made explicit mention of intelligence after democratization in Latin America since the late 1970s, and this prompted reflection about the best way forward.[28] In this sense, we have identified steps for forming and consolidating an IS in countries with a low level of professionalization and institutionalization.

In democratic systems, an IS within the intelligence service(s) can decisively support the development of the state intelligence function[29] from a public policy perspective. In this manner, an IS can contribute to creating or strengthening the intelligence profession's institutional framework, professionalization, cooperation, accountability, and intelligence culture.[30] The existence of an IS is based on the assumption of an explicit recognition of the need for intelligence professionals to receive education on the main intelligence disciplines and theoretical frameworks necessary for them to perform their roles adequately. Additionally, within an IS, practitioners have the capacity to practice the roles that need to be performed and adjust to a constantly changing context that can sometimes be fast and even disruptive. This proposal for modernization in the twenty-first century, in countries with little tradition in the professionalization and institutionalization of the subject, is organized into nine phases that are grouped into three stages:

I. Creation: This stage contemplates recruitment based on capacity, promotion mechanisms based on performance, design of the study plan, instances of encounter between experts to contribute in the training or updating, and development of a body of stable faculty members in the IS.

II. Institutionalization or formalization: This stage corresponds to the implementation of the curriculum, publication of specialized documents on intelligence, and the establishment of the desired culture on intelligence in democracy.

III. Consolidation or strengthening: This stage includes the evaluation of the IS management according to its proposed objectives; that is, it seeks to generate feedback on what has been done within the framework of a continuous improvement of the work carried out, having as a special matter the review of the contribution from the IS to the various factors present in a public intelligence policy.

The systematization of the indicated stages and phases, together with an explanation of each of them, is set out in figure 12.3. This identifies the phases in a way that makes possible the establishment of an IS that is sustainable in the short, medium, and long terms.

The Spanish experience can be beneficial to this line of thinking, since the Centro Nacional de Inteligencia (CNI), the internal and external intelligence service of the Kingdom of Spain, created an intelligence culture priority/unit in the year 2003.[31] As a result, the relationship between the CNI and several universities in Spain was the source of a number of academic activities, including publications and seminars.

The Latin American experience is varied due to the region's diverse history, but some common themes can be identified. One of them would be that certain academics do feel reluctant to include practitioners or former practitioners at universities due to the historical connection between the intelligence services and political police and oppression under military regimes. There is also an issue with the selection process for certain positions in which nonmeritocratic processes are followed, with the result of diminishing the quality of outcomes in the institution. That is why in this chapter, we have been very demanding, setting out clearly a profile and education levels for those who are part of the process.

The integration of practitioners or former practitioners also brings up questions regarding the actual freedom of expression regarding discussion of and publishing on sensitive topics that are part of a practitioner's professional engagement. An additional concern is whether practitioners would be forthcoming about past failures of intelligence without compromising national security. We do have to stress that in systems with low professional and institutional standards, there is a tendency to dismiss professionals due to political interests, and there is a lack of stability in the public sphere and among public workers. In many intelligence services in Latin America, a change in the government can mean a change within the service practitioners at a range of levels. It can also affect the service's capabilities in the short and medium run.

Time		Stage	Phase	Content
First Year	Semester 1	1- Creation	1- Recruitment	Implementation of a recruitment system: public and inclusive in its call, competitive and discreet in the selection. In short, meri-based while recognising the need for secrecy.
			2- Professional Career	Existence of a civil service career that encourages promotion based on merit. Contemplating tests that prove updating in the subjects of the position for promotion. In short, evolution in the professional career according to performance. As a way of assimilating to other recognized professions, create the day of the intelligence professional, as an instance to recognize this specialized work, take stock of achievements and identify challenges.
			3- Design of a Study Plan	Elaboration of a study plan for the training of the intelligence professional that considers the current skills and competencies required according to the different profiles or roles to be performed, taking into special consideration the current context in which the function is performed.
			4-Cooperation among specialists for intelligence professionals	Periodically develop meeting instances between national and international specialists that address topics of interest to the intelligence professional. This activity can be carried out in a structured format (Seminar, conference or workshops) or semi-structured (discussion), giving priority to sharing knowledge or dialogue and reflection, as deemed appropriate. This can lead to posts.
			5- Building up a team of Faculty who are experts in the field by training and experience	Convene a stable body of national and international instructors, whose knowledge in the field is ideally based on two categories simultaneously: A) teaching and / or academic management in intelligence or subjects associated with it; B) experience due to their condition of manager, analyst, operator, consumer or intelligence producer.

2nd Year	Semester 2	II- Institucionalización o formalización	6-Implement the study plan	Execution of the study plan, with special attention to the qualities that you want to develop or strengthen, such as, for example, multidisciplinary work capacity within the framework of interagency coordination processes.
			7-Publication in intelligence	Edit periodical publications in different formats that address topics of interest to the intelligence professional, as well as to the public specialized or not in these topics. Differentiated publications can be evaluated according to the segment of the public to which it is oriented (indexed or not open access or not).
			8-Establishment of an intelligence culture about intelligence and democracy	Promote an intelligence culture that allows the understanding of the foundations, role, characteristics and particularity of intelligence for producers and consumers of intelligence, as well as authorities of the different powers of state, the media and public opinion.
	Semester 1 and 2	III- Consolidación o fortalecimiento	9-Evaluation and feedback	Make visible to different audiences and evaluate (for continuous improvement) the contribution of the IS in the different factors that influence a public intelligence policy, that is, its institutionality, professionalization, cooperation, accountability and intelligence culture.

Figure 12.3.   Stages and Steps to Developing an Intelligence School.

Future Challenges

One of the most crucial gaps between theory and practice in intelligence studies or education is related to the challenges of training, specializing, or providing continuing education to future professionals. Substantive changes in the environment in which intelligence operates generate important challenges when planning studies or education in intelligence. In this sense, it is important to consider a solid base in principles and foundations because, in a changing context, it is important to be clear about the core of the discipline and to emphasize it as the main goal of the training.

While carefully studying the region, we have observed that the public's perception of the intelligence services is more linked to the latest scandals than to the past in the context of military dictatorships and repression of individual rights and freedoms. Thus, we observe recurrent problems linked to professionalization in the intelligence services of Latin American countries such as the ones already mentioned in this chapter, with massive layoffs and hirings when governments change, and lack of modern teaching methods, including the use of theoretical frameworks.[32] Having said that, we observe that there is freedom to research intelligence-related topics in those countries where there is freedom of expression. Thus, there is a correlation between general freedom of expression and academic freedom in intelligence and related fields.

CONCLUSION

In matters of intelligence studies and intelligence education, it is possible to identify a gap between theory and practice. This problem in Latin American countries with deficits in the institutionalization of the intelligence function and professionalization of its activity is partly related to inadequate professional profiles in charge of the leadership of academic centers, areas, and programs in intelligence. It is common to find an inappropriate alignment of their expertise and what should be taught in intelligence issues at universities. In the case of intelligence services, the deficiencies are in the academic rigor necessary to lead academic training programs. Thus, we propose a more suitable model that can lead studies or education in intelligence and training in universities or intelligence services. It can add to the enhancement of the professionalization and institutionalization of intelligence as developed in this chapter. Finally, we argue that education and training be imparted in a context of globalization and exponential change. This constitutes a challenge, and there is a need to emphasize fundamental aspects related to the studies of intelligence and the new trends in an increasingly digitized world that generates substantive impacts on the structural, process, and product dimensions of intelligence.

NOTES

We thank the peer reviewers for their comments, which contributed tremendously to the quality of our chapter.

1. This issue has been addressed in previous works; see, for example, Carolina Sancho Hirane, "Democracia, política pública de Inteligencia y desafíos actuales: Tendencias en países de Latinoamérica," in *Revisita Inteligencia y Seguridad: Revista de Análisis y Prospectiva*, no. 11 (Spain: Cátedra Servicios de Inteligencia y Sistemas democráticos [Universidad Rey Juan Carlos] e Instituto Juan Velázquez de Velasco de Investigación en Inteligencia para la Seguridad y Defensa, 2012); Carolina Sancho

Hirane, "Política publica de inteligencia," in *Conceptos Fundamentales de Inteligencia*, ed. Antonio M. Díaz Fernández, 287–94 (Valencia: Tirant lo Blanch, 2016); and Carlos Maldonado and Carolina Sancho, "Strategic Intelligence Cooperation in South America and the South American Defense Council," *Journal of Mediterranean and Balkan Intelligence* 7, no. 1 (2016), where the idea of institutionalization of the intelligence function has been explained.

2. Samuel Huntington, *El Soldado y el Estado* (Argentina: Grupo Editor Latinoamericano, 1995).

3. For example, political espionage, misuse of reserved funds, unauthorized dissemination of information, and the neglect of secret information, to name just a few.

4. Decreto Supremo 363/1991, Crea el Consejo Coordinador de Seguridad Pública, Ministerio del Interior, Chile.

5. Decreto Supremo 4/1992, Modifica el Consejo Coordinador de Seguridad Pública, Ministerio del Interior, Chile.

6. For additional information on Kelsen's pyramid, see https://plato.stanford.edu /entries/lawphil-theory.

7. Carolina Sancho Hirane, "Reflexion en Torno a la Comunidad de Inteligencia en Chile a Partir de la Cultura de Inteligencia Nacional: Los desafios pendientes," in *Democratizacion de la funcion de inteligencia: El nexo de la cultura nacional y la inteligencia estrategica*, ed. Russell G. Swenson and Susana C. Lemozy, 65–196 (Washington, DC: National Defense Intelligence College, 2009).

8. Peter Gill, "Democratic and Parliamentary Accountability of Intelligence Services after September 11th" (Working Paper No. 103, Geneva Center for the Democratic Control of Armed Forces [DCAF], 2003); Thomas Bruneau, *Controlling Intelligence in New Democracies in Strategic Intelligence* (Roxbury, 2004); Hans Born and Lan Leigh, *Hacia un control democrático de las actividades de inteligencia: Estándares legales y métodos de supervisión* (Switzerland: DCAF-EOS, 2005).

9. Like other professions such as the military or career diplomats, with regard to intelligence professionals it is possible to observe a cohesive group that shares a tradition and practices that distinguish them from other professions; in other words, which has an esprit de corps. Additionally, they even have a specific language, which is manifested in terms of the work they do, such as compartmentalization, the need to know, and secrecy. Some of these ideas have been previously developed by Huntington, *El Soldado y el Estado*, to refer to the military profession.

10. Intelligence officials must be recruited, assigned, and promoted according to known and previously disseminated criteria based on the merit and quality of their performance. In addition, there must be a separation and/or retirement mechanism that ensures possibilities of labor reintegration in other jobs, or a job retirement that ensures that basic needs can be satisfied, such as what occurs at the end of the career of a diplomat or a military career.

11. FLACSO, *Reporte del sector seguridad en América Latina y el Caribe* (Chile, 2007); Russell Swenson and Carolina Sancho Hirane, eds., "Intelligence Managenent in the Americas," National Intelligence University, 2015.

12. Nicolás Wiñazki, "La purga llegó a los camporistas de AFI, pero nadie los defendió," El Clarín de Argentina, January 30, 2016, https://www.clarin.com/politica

/gobierno-agencia_federal_de_inteligencia-la_campora-despidos-estado_0_Bkajpa ODXe.html; Santiago Dapelo, "Denuncian una purga contra los espías nombrados por Macri," *La Nación de Argentina*, February 15, 2020, https://www.lanacion.com .ar/politica/denuncian-purga-espias-nombrados-mauricio-macri-nid2334244.

13. Patricio Carrera and Héctor Rojas, "Gobierno despide a 13 analistas de la ANI," La Tercera de Chile, May 4, 2010, https://www.latercera.com/noticia/gobierno -despide-a-13-analistas-de-la-ani; Marcela Jiménez, "¿Qué pasa en la ANI?," *El Mostrador*, July 12, 2018, https://m.elmostrador.cl/noticias/pais/2018/07/12/que-pasa-en -la-a-n-i.

14. Carrera and Rojas, "Gobierno despide a 13 analistas de la ANI." Jiménez, "¿Qué pasa en la ANI?"

15. "La perspectiva del cambio en los servicios de inteligencia," *Plan V de Ecuador*, October 1, 2018, https://www.planv.com.ec/historias/politica/perspectivas-del-cambio -servicios-inteligencia.

16. "El DAS dejará de existir para dar paso a la Agencia Nacional de Inteligencia," *Semana de Colombia*, October 30, 2011, https://www.semana.com/politica/articulo /el-das-deja-existir-para-dar-paso-agencia-nacional-inteligencia/248740-3.

17. "Perú cierra su servicio de inteligencia en medio de un escándalo de espionaje," BBC Mundo, February 10, 2015, https://www.bbc.com/mundo/noticias/2015/02 /150210_peru_espiuonaje_cierre_porque_gl.

18. "Demissão de diretor da Abin é anunciada na CPMI," Càmara Dos Diputaodos de Brasil, July 13, 2005, https://www.camara.leg.br/noticias/68352-demissao-de -diretor-da-abin-e-anunciada-na-cpmi; "Governo faz mudanças em setor de Inteligência," August 8, 2020, https://istoe.com.br/governo-faz-mudancas-em-setor-de -inteligencia; Joanisval Brito Gonçalves, Ricardo Zonato Esteves, and Marcus Vinicius Reis, "Brasil, 2020 A Inteligência no Goberno Jair Bolsonaro: O imperativo da mudança," *Frumentarius, Blog de Joanisval Gonçalves*, 2020, https://iepecdg.com .br/wp-content/uploads/2020/08/INTELIGENCIA-NO-GOVERNO-BOLSONARO -FRUMENTARIUS.pdf.

19. https://www.esg.br/cursos-regulares/csie.

20. https://www.caen.edu.pe/wordpress/iv-maestria-en-inteligencia-estrategica.

21. https://www.flacso.edu.ec/maestrias/maestria_en_relaciones_internacionales _con_mencion_en_seguridad_y_conflicto.

22. https://www.jursoc.unlp.edu.ar/index.php/inteligencia-estrategica-nacional .html.

23. https://sceu.frba.utn.edu.ar/e-learning/detalle/experto-universitario/1373 /experto-universitario-en-seguridad-internacional-y-servicios-de-inteligencia.

24. https://mexico.anahuac.mx/licenciaturas/inteligencia-estrategica.

25. https://www.inap.mx/portal/images/pdf/enpg/misn.pdf.

26. http://esici.cemil.edu.co/index.php/maestria.

27. Sancho Hirane, "Política pública de inteligencia."

28. Peter Gill and Mark Phythian, *Intelligence in an Insecure World*, 274 (Cambridge: Polity Press, 2018).

29. Russell Swenson, "Intelligence Education in the Americas," *International Journal of Intelligence and CounterIntelligence* 16, no. 1 (2003): 108–30.

30. Sancho Hirane, "Política pública de inteligencia."

31. https://www.cni.es/es/culturainteligencia/introduccion.

32. Carlos Maldonado, "Desafíos de los Servicios de Inteligencia en la región andina," in *SIN Arcana Imperii*, ed. Andrés Gómez de la Torre (Peru: Foro Libertad & Seguridad, 2007); Carlos Maldonado, "La inteligencia estrategica en America del Sur: Persisten las falencias de profesionalism," in *Inteligencia Estrategica Contemporanea* (Ecuador: Universidad de las Fuerzas Armadas de Ecuador [ESPE], 2016); Maldonado and Sancho, "Strategic Intelligence Cooperation"; Gerardo Boimvaser, *Los sospechosos de siempre* (Argentina: Planeta, 2000); Gerardo Young, *SIDE: La Argentina secreta* (Argentina: Planeta, 2006); José Ugarte, "La cultura política y administrativa y su influencia en el desarrollo de estructuras de Inteligencia en Argentina," in *Democratización de la función de inteligencia: El nexo de la cultura nacional y la inteligencia estratégica*, Center for Strategic Intelligence Research, ed. Russell G. Swenson and Susana C. Lemozy, 437–56 (Washington, DC: National Defense Intelligence College, 2009); Claudio Savoia, *Espiados* (Argentina, 2015); Gerardo Young, *Código Stiuso* (Argentina: Planeta, 2015); Marcelo Saín, *La Casa que no cesa: Infortunios y desafíos en el proceso de reforma de la ex SIDE* (Argentina: Editorial Octubre, 2016). Peru: Enrique Obando, "La reestructuración de la inteligencia en el Perú: Sus avances y problemas," in *Inteligencia y Seguridad: Revista de análisis y prospectiva*, no. 5 (Universidad Rey Juan Carlos [Cátedra Servicios de Inteligencia y Sistemas democráticos] and Universidad Carlos III de Madrid [Instituto Juan Velásquez de Velasco de Investigación para la Seguridad y Defensa], Spain, 2008/2009); Andrés Gómez de la Torre, "Servicios de Inteligencia y Democracia en América Del Sur: ¿Hacia una Segunda Generación de Reformas Normativas?," RESDAL, 2009, http://www.resdal.org/producciones-miembros/trabajo-academico -gomez.pdf; Fernando Rospigliosi, "La DINI: Una alternativa," *El Comercio de Perú*, April 12, 2015, https://elcomercio.pe/opinion/mirada-de-fondo/dini-alternativa-fer nando-rospigliosi-351487-noticia; Andrés Gómez de la Torre, "Institucionalización y crisis de inteligencia: Perú en el contexto andino," in *Los macro y micro desafíos de la seguridad en democracia*, ed. Bertha García and José Ugarte (Ecuador: Centro de Publicaciones Pontificia Universidad Católica de Ecuador, 2018). Ecuador: Fredy Rivera, "Inteligencia estratégica y prospectiva. Editorial," FLACSO/SENAIN, Ecuador, 2011; Fredy Rivera, "Inteligencia estratégica e inteligencia política: Los claro-oscuros del caso ecuatoriano," in *Inteligencia Estratégica Contemporánea* (Ecuador: Universidad de las Fuerzas Armadas de Ecuador [ESPE], 2016), https://repositorio .espe.edu.ec/bitstream/21000/11692/1/INTELIGENICIA%20ESTRATEGICA.pdf; Katalina Barreiro, *Angostura: La inteligencia, el espejo oculto de la seguridad* (Quito, Ecuador: Instituto de Altos Estudios Nacionales, 2018); Fredy Rivera, Katalina Barreiro, and Gilda Guerrero, *¿Dónde está el pesquisa? Una historia de la Inteligencia de la Política en el Ecuador* (Ecuador: Centro de Publicaciones Pontificia Universidad Católica de Ecuador, 2018). Colombia: Hernando Salazar, "Uribe liquidará el DAS," BBC Mundo, September 19, 2009, http://www.bbc.co.uk/mundo /america_latina/2009/09/090918_0237_colombia_das_gm.shtml; Arturo Wallace, "Colombia y la revancha final de los espías del DAS," BBC Mundo, September 19, 2011, https://www.bbc.com/mundo/noticias/2011/09/110919_colombia_das

_escandalo_filtraciones_semana_aw; Álvaro J. Venegas, "En busca de inteligencia estratégica: Cuatro factores para el nacimiento y evolución de una inteligencia civil colombiana," *Ciencia Política* 13, no. 26 (2018): 287–318; Cesar Niño, "Chuzadas: Las tenues líneas entre la seguridad y la inseguridad," *Razón Pública*, January 27, 2020, https://razonpublica.com/chuzadas-las-tenues-lineas-la-seguridad-la-inseguridad.

13

Teaching Ethical Intelligence in a World That Doesn't Think It Needs It

Jan Goldman

The proposition that espionage corrupts the people who practice it, or at least corrupts the people who recruit, induce, or handle the spies who are betraying their trusts, has a lot of weight. I think it is corrupting; it is corrupting for men and women to . . . induce and to pander to the kinds of betrayals and personal tragedies that result from these betrayals. In any open-eyed view of things, it is corrupting to engage in such activities: corrupting to the person who does it, it's corrupting to the people or institutions that sponsor it. This is why espionage has never been respectable; this is why espionage has always been disreputable because people instinctively understand it. And it's deeply compromising to the people in institutions that practice it. But does it lead to a later betrayal? No, I don't think so, I don't think so. I don't think that a KGB officer, a CIA officer, an SIS officer, out pandering to betrayals on the part of the people that he's recruiting and handling—I don't think that the corruption and perversion of ethics, and the way you believe that happens to him—expresses itself in any natural way in a willingness for him to go out and do it. I don't think so. I think what it does is, it makes a person callused. I mean, I take it for granted that doing these things has to have an effect on you, just as a professional soldier who has overseen the deaths of thousands of people, you know, for this great cause, as his professional duty, it has an effect on him. It doesn't turn him into a sadistic killer, or at least for most it doesn't, but it has a deeply forming and shaping effect on character. And I'll just have to leave it for others to try and figure that out.[1]

Aldrich Ames, an American intelligence professional, was convicted of spying for another country and sentenced to life in prison. According to the CIA Inspector General's Report, Ames's primary motivating factor for his decision to commit espionage was financial indebtedness, and "his fading respect for the value of his Agency work . . . and his belief that the rules that governed others did not apply to him."[2]

We do not need saints working in the intelligence community, nor do we need people who will betray their loyalty to the country. The world of espionage is like any other profession, mostly occupied by people who believe in and are proud of what they are doing—beyond receiving a paycheck. However, there are few professions where the corruption of secrecy, autonomy, and conviction can overtake and burden an individual if they are ill equipped to handle it. The intelligence community needs people with a "moral compass" and an ethical understanding of "who they are and what they are doing." This requirement applies to the intelligence analyst, the field agent, and those conducting intelligence operations here and abroad. This raises the much larger issue: How do you teach in this environment? How do you teach individuals hired for their ethics and morals to work in a profession that (on the surface) can be considered a character weakness? How do you consider human dignity in a field that includes manipulation and deceit? If you are a case officer recruiting new informants, you are working in a relationship of both deception and trust. For example, human intelligence (HUMINT) collection is the process of building relationships with potential spies to become disloyal to their country, yet find purpose in doing what you want them to do.[3] According to one CIA case officer, working in this environment involves three stages: deception, manipulation, and corruption. At the heart of espionage is always a paradox: a relationship formed on the basis of deception has to be a relationship of absolute trust both ways.[4]

LOOKING FOR ANSWERS

While working on my master's degree at a Jesuit college in 1989, I enrolled in a course on ethics and the professions. It changed my life. The graduate course focused on the ethical conduct of hundreds of professions. The concept of a "profession" has a moderately complicated sociological definition with several factors. These factors include extensive training or education, a significant intellectual component, a service that is deemed important, credentialing, autonomy of work, and a code of ethics. For any work to be deemed a profession, there is a need to score fairly high on several, if not all, of these factors. No single factor is regarded as a necessary condition; a low score in one factor can be compensated by high scores in other factors. The intelligence (domestic and foreign) community scores fairly high in extensive training and education (e.g., learning a new method for analysis or learning a language). Teaching professional ethics needs to go beyond personal beliefs.

A code of professional conduct is a necessary component to maintain standards for those individuals working within a profession. To be called "a professional" means that this person can be accountable, responsible, and worthy of trust, in addition to being skilled, educated, and current on the knowledge in their profession.

At the time, I was an intelligence analyst working in the Washington, DC, area. Although I considered myself a professional with a decade of experience, I was not sure what my professional ethics meant. The most prominent professions include law, medicine, and religion, but other less prominently known professions include plumbing, landscaping, real estate, furniture building, and hairstyling.[5] A profession has accountability and individual responsibility. Missing from the list was the "intelligence professional."

Additionally, a major component of being called a professional is a "code of ethics." Simply put, a code of ethics is a guide of principles designed to help professionals conduct their work honestly and with integrity. Also, a code of ethics document may outline the mission and values of the organization, which can describe how professionals approach problems. More importantly, they are the ethical principles based on the organization's core values and the standards to which the professional is held. Consequently, over the next forty years, I became obsessed with defining "professionalism" in the intelligence community.

I decided to pursue a doctorate with a dissertation that would focus on the development of the core knowledge needed to establish an ethics curriculum for the US intelligence community. Unfortunately, I ran into some problems. At one school, the chairman of my committee wanted the research to focus on Supreme Court cases as the basis of core ethical concerns in the US intelligence community. According to the chairman of my dissertation committee, it is important to understand the difference in legal guidelines to solve ethical and moral dilemmas in the intelligence community. Of course, not everything legal is ethical. I explained to him that legal rulings might not constitute ethical concerns, and on the contrary, they may exacerbate those anxieties. For example, court cases on abortion, gun control, and the death penalty are continually revisited and modified by the political leanings that constitute the majority of the court. Maybe that's why they call the writings of court justices "opinions." Ethical teachings need to be above faith in the law as well as faith in religion.

One school has as part of its core requirements an ethics and intelligence course based distinctly on a "Christian worldview and the implications for the collection, analysis, and production of information." The course is designed to critically examine assumptions and alternatives and address issues of social, political, and environmental perspectives in support of national security objectives.[6]

Religious congregations rely on a leader's interpretation of their religious doctrine to interpret their adherence to the faith to avoid "sin." Consequently, does this mean an atheist would be incapable of making a determination between "good and evil"? During World War II, the personnel that composed the newly formed Office of Strategic Services (OSS) were mostly recruited from upper-middle-class to wealthy families. This was vividly captured in the fictional movie *The Good Shepherd*.[7] Although women and minorities were also involved in the founding of the OSS (which after the war would become the CIA), it was predominately male, Protestant, and well-educated individuals with their accompanying value system (notably referred to as "pale, male, and from Yale"). For many years after the war, reportedly, background checks for security clearances would inquire, "How often do you attend a house of worship?"

Ethics simply is a standard of conduct ideally grounded in virtue and morals; a determination of "what is good" and "what is evil" in order to develop an ethos. For most professions, a key component is to develop a "code of ethics." This is because being a professional includes various attributes. If intelligence professionals want to think of themselves as more than mere intelligence "workers," then becoming a professional and defining intelligence as a profession is paramount to this objective.

The US intelligence community's mission satisfies the requirement for a service deemed important. An example of autonomy of work is the unbiased and objective nature of our methods employed to collect, analyze, and produce intelligence. Three well-established professions that have codes of ethics include law, medicine, and religion. The American Bar Association promulgates the lawyer's code of ethics, and a medical doctor's code of ethics can be found in the Hippocratic oath. Theologians and clerics are guided by the tenets of their faith (not to include the oldest code of ethics—the Ten Commandments). Other professions that have a code of ethics include home inspectors, construction workers, engineers, anthropologists, librarians, hypnotists, photographers, foresters, wedding organizers, funeral directors, and yacht builders.

All of these codes of ethics have some commonality. Typically, a code of ethics includes defining acceptable and unacceptable behavior; seeking to promote high standards of practice; providing a benchmark for member self-evaluation; establishing a framework for professional behavior and responsibilities, to be used as a vehicle for occupational identity; and marking occupational maturity as part of an integral element of society.

SEEKING ETHICAL BOUNDARIES TO TEACH

The work of the intelligence community has never been understood by the public or politicians, which are dictated by extreme views. In 1929, Secretary of State Henry L. Stimson made his oft-quoted comment, "Gentlemen do not read each other's mail."[8] However, Stimson's ethical reservations focus on the targeting of diplomats from America's close allies, not on spying in general. Later, when he became secretary of war during World War II, he relied heavily on decrypted enemy communications. Mass media craves the intelligence worker in an "unhinged" profession. The public wants (and enjoys) the intelligence professional to be without ethical boundaries and possibly beyond the law, which may explain why James Bond has a "license to kill." In 1940, the US Navy was looking for people to work in their newly created intelligence collection unit. The requirement was that they were to have no moral or ethical boundaries. Less than a year before the United States entered World War II, the Office of Naval Intelligence decided it needed to create an organization for an overseas espionage system.[9] According to a classified February 3, 1941, memorandum, in order to accomplish this mission, "certain self-evident fundamental facts must be faced: Espionage by its very nature is not to be considered as 'honorable' or 'clean' or 'fair' or 'decent.'"[10] The memorandum goes on to outline the "type" of individual needed to conduct intelligence collection: "By far the largest number of Agents or Employees are taken from the petty criminal class; malcontents, revolutionaries; refugees or psychopaths."[11] Teaching ethical conduct, much less defining an intelligence collector as a professional, was far from something that was expected of these individuals.

John le Carré, a former practitioner and famous author, broke the absolute moral barriers and wrote of the sometimes conflicting values intelligence professionals have to endure.[12] On the other hand, he was able to show the human side of an intelligence professional. This has always played well with the public, rather than the robotic amoral government agent. According to some cinematic experts, the best spy movies seemingly come from overseas, to include John le Carré's *The Spy Who Came in from the Cold* in 1965, Alfred Hitchcock's *North by Northwest* in 1959, and the more recently released Dutch director Paul Verhoeven's *Black Book* in 2006. According to reviews, Verhoeven's movie accurately portrays the ethical and moral quandaries in the acceptance that immoral acts can be found in even the most righteous cause, balancing the work ethic and personal morals, "alternately depicting espionage as thrilling and sexy, and as a harrowing pursuit that puts spies in constant danger of losing their lives and souls."[13]

2006: ETHICAL INTELLIGENCE BREAKTHROUGH

So, how does one teach ethical intelligence without going to the extremes of being immoral (anything goes to accomplish the job) or a believer that spying is a sin? In 2004, reports began to appear of torture and prison abuse at Abu Ghraib, Iraq, and I sought to hold an ethics and intelligence conference to answer this question. Over the next two years, no one in the government was interested in discussing professionalism, ethics, or morals in analyzing information, much less how that information should be collected.

In 2006, I organized and self-sponsored my first ethics and intelligence conference, which appeared on the front page of the *New York Times*, with the headline "Pursuing an Exotic Tool for Espionage: A Moral Compass."[14] Although the academic conference sought to find out if ethics should be considered a part of the work in the intelligence community, some people were not interested in finding out. "It doesn't make much sense to me," said Duane R. Clarridge, who retired in 1988 after thirty-three years as a CIA operations officer and who could not attend the conference. "Depending on where you're coming from, the whole business of espionage is unethical. . . . Intelligence ethics is an oxymoron. It's not an issue. It never was and never will be, not if you want a real spy service."[15]

It should be noted that Clarridge was indicted on perjury charges in 1991, accused of lying to Congress about the Iran-Contra affair. He was later pardoned by President George H. W. Bush.

What is most telling in this article is that farther down the page, a CIA spokesperson says, "The agency had a robust ethics training program that focused on 'integrity, honesty, and accountability' and included the use of case studies."[16] In pulling together an ethics course in the government, it would normally focus on the characteristics of a good employee. Thus, it would be easy to understand that with employees in the intelligence field, most with top-secret clearances, you want people that are responsible and will not lie when trusted with the nation's secrets. But is that enough? Do an individual's good values transfer to being a good employee?

Ten years earlier, in 1996, a group looked into how ethics education is conducted at the CIA.[17] Among their findings in developing an ethics curriculum for the CIA, employees mentioned that the challenges to integrity include "a belief that within the Agency open discussion and dissent are often discouraged, making it less likely that people will speak out about ethical problems; a concern that an unwillingness to acknowledge failure as an acceptable outcome creates an incentive to cover up honest mistakes and to avoid risk; and a belief that promotions and performance appraisals regularly reward those who acted without integrity."[18]

The author of the article, and a member of the group, offered some suggestions on a CIA program of ethics education. These includes:

- The CIA should develop its own ethics education, to include a number of "intelligence ethicists" capable of understanding the type of work required by the agency.
- An evolving framework of values should connect personal and professional ethics and an understanding of the difference between them.
- Encourage debate on the ideals upon which the agency's mission is based.
- Accept failure and the commitment to learn from it.
- Case studies should include conflicting values.
- Celebrate the "heroes of integrity" who stood by the agency's core values in the face of pressure.

Furthermore, in 2018, the Congressional Research Service found that CIA ethics education "includes familiarization with the legal authorities for the conduct of intelligence activities, principally Executive Order 12333, The Intelligence Community, as amended, and CIA's AR 2-2, Law and Policy Governing the Conduct of Intelligence Activities. However, while these baseline references spell out dos and don'ts from a legal standpoint, there is little mention of ethics per se."[19]

PARAMETERS FOR TEACHING ETHICS

Overall, national security and law enforcement communities fall short in the promotion, training, and education of professionals relying on such material.

Most individuals who teach ethical conduct may be ill equipped and thus unprepared to discuss the many unique ethical dilemmas faced by those in the intelligence community. Instead, institutions rely on ethical conduct based on personal beliefs rather than professional characteristics and conduct required by intelligence work. Additionally, according to many individuals, the role of ethics in intelligence operations *depends on the culture of the department within an organization that should determine "right" from "wrong."* At an ethics and intelligence conference, it was reported,

HUMINT collectors in the CIA may have more ethical concerns in common with collectors in the Defense Intelligence Agency (DIA) than they do with analysts or other administrative personnel in their own Agency. The participants noted that any such "functional" community code(s) would not necessarily replace any existing codes at the agency level; different agencies have varying mission requirements and cultures and will likely need different codes. In any case, while there may be strength in varying agency approaches to the central identity issues (who we "are" as professionals), any existing agency codes in the community should be clearly "nested" within the overarching communitywide concepts.[20]

Over the last few years, there has been a rash of unethical behavior by intelligence and law enforcement professionals. Appearing in the media are reports of unethical behavior by civil servants serving national security both at home and abroad. These reports appear worldwide. They include undercover agents having children with the people they were assigned to collect information on, government security officials seeking to be exempt from the law for performing unethical and illegal actions, and ethics training that is required *only* for employees holding certain positions in the organization. All of these instances can probably be summed up with a fundamental understanding of all ethics training and education: "What may be legal may not be ethical." Ethics should be taught at all levels and to all members of the intelligence community, from the most senior officials to those at the entry level of apprentice in the intelligence cycle. Collection, analysis, and the production of information and intelligence should be covered by all aspects of the philosophy and law of moral and ethical conduct.

OVERSEAS ETHICS INTELLIGENCE EDUCATION MAY NOT BE ANY BETTER

In the United Kingdom, from 1987 to 2010, eight women were reportedly duped into forming long-term intimate relationships in a covert operation that lasted up to nine years, with five undercover law enforcement officials.[21] If the accusations are correct, these police officers had sexual relations with the targets of their surveillance. According to one government spy, he admitted to tricking the woman into having a long-term relationship with him as part of an intricate attempt to bolster his credibility in the group under surveillance. At least one child was born out of this government surveillance operation, in which the government official was already married during his secret mission.

Meanwhile, the Norwegian spy service is seeking legislation that would "offer immunity from prosecution to intelligence officials and informants who are authorized by the country's spy service to conduct espionage."[22] According to supporters of this legislation, the country's intelligence service is the only institution authorized by the government to break laws in foreign countries; however, the new bill will also allow officials and the people who work for them in overseas operations to break Norwegian law.

In the United States, the Department of Justice's (DOJ) *Ethics Handbook for On and Off-Duty Conduct* discusses the ethical obligations of its members.[23] Some of the ethical considerations while on duty include a prohibition of gambling activity; engaging in commercial sex; using alcohol and other intoxicants to excess; and engaging in "criminal, infamous, dishonest, immoral or disgraceful conduct or other conduct prejudicial to the government."[24] In other words, if the evidence points to the fact that you broke one of these rules, you can be suspended and terminated as a member of the department. The DOJ focus on sexual activity explicitly says,

> An employee is at all times prohibited from soliciting, procuring, or accepting commercial sex, whether on or off-duty or on personal leave and regardless of whether the activity is legal or tolerated in a particular jurisdiction, foreign or domestic.[25]

Clearly, based on this guidance, does it address whether DOJ undercover agents can commit sexual relations while on duty, similar to what occurred in the United Kingdom?

Beyond intelligence operations, intelligence analysts may face ethical pressures. Thus, the question must be asked, what are educators and trainers in the intelligence community doing to combat the politicization of intelligence? In the Department of Homeland Security's *Learning Roadmaps for Intelligence Professionals—Analytics*, the chief intelligence officer Charles Allen writes, "Professional development must prepare you for the diverse and complex challenges intelligence analysts face across the DHS Intelligence Enterprise, and within the larger Intelligence Community."[26] This 2005 publication is designed to persuade employees of the new organization to identify with the necessary skills needed to be part of the country's domestic security infrastructure. For example, an entry-level intelligence analyst is told to acquire fourteen areas of knowledge, to include how to handle classified information and understand how to use techniques for critical thinking. In contrast, a midlevel analyst (i.e., supervisor) is asked to acquire knowledge in thirteen areas, to include knowing how to utilize the collection requirement process and exposure to structured analytic methods and techniques. However, it is not until a person reaches the senior level (i.e., management) of intelligence analysis that they are asked to *demonstrate an ability to identify attempts to politicize intelligence analysis*. Consequently, it is not until an analyst moves into a senior analytical position or management position that the individual gets exposed to the unethical use of intelligence for political gain.

Ten years later, the DOJ produced *Analyst Professional Development Road Map*, which does much better in acknowledging the importance of ethics.[27] According to this training document, a forty-hour entry-level course for intelligence analysts should consist of two to three hours of instruction on the legal, privacy, and *ethical* issues of intelligence.[28] However, upon closer examination, this learning objective includes teaching adherence to the policies and procedures of privacy and liability issues in the intelligence process and ethics training that is limited to "providing a scenario to illustrate its importance."[29] This lack of professional ethics has led to an explosion of recent ethics violations. According to a nonpartisan committee at the Center for Ethics and the Rule of Law,

> The Working Group concluded that there is a grave danger to the Intelligence Community from politicized DOJ investigations, intimidation, and potential prosecutions and that this danger poses, in turn, a grave risk of harm to U.S. national security, which depends heavily upon effective intelligence operations and a collaborative relationship between the president and the IC.[30]

Most ethics courses taught inside and outside of the government remain law based. Overwhelmingly, faculty teaching ethics courses have mostly legal backgrounds, if they are not outright holding law degrees. These courses delve into understanding the rules and regulations that govern ethical conduct in the US intelligence community. Most prominently, this includes Supreme Court rulings, executive orders, US Code, and assorted legislation. A full list of the over forty documents, from the US Constitution to Executive Order 12333, is available at the Office of the Director of National Intelligence website.[31] A typical "ethics" and intelligence course includes learning objectives such as understanding the permissions and restrictions on US national intelligence community activities as prescribed by federal law and executive and agency directives, key aspects of the post-9/11 intelligence reform (more legal), knowing the difference between legal and ethical personal considerations in making decisions, and looking at some case studies.

ASSESSING ETHICAL CONDUCT FOR THE WORKFORCE

Today's future workforce of the intelligence community should not go into positions of employment "morally blind," but rather understand what is considered professional conduct by the specific intelligence agency and the IC as a community. In other words, before seeking employment at any intelligence organization, the applicant must ask, "What is the culture of the organization?" Faculty teaching intelligence courses have a responsibility to discuss at the outset the moral obligations and responsibilities that individuals may be called upon to support or exercise in their potential line of work.

There is a misperception that teaching ethics to any person in an intelligence program is similar to teaching a war fighter to be mindful of human rights during wartime. Except, that is exactly what occurs at all military academies and senior war colleges. It is what defines a "professional soldier" and allows the prosecution of war crimes. Just war theory is an integral part of a professional military member's training and education curriculum. According to statements posted at the Naval Academy, it's no coincidence that "moral development" is listed first, for, in a profession where members may confront issues of who lives and who dies, future military officers must be persons of character. In that vein, during their sophomore year in Annapolis, all midshipmen spend a semester in a dedicated study of ethics and moral reasoning for the naval officer. But a single semester's study almost certainly is not enough.[32]

Today ethics is almost parochial to each agency. Where you work will define how ethical you are expected to be. Or, if you take the other extreme, you bring personal ethics to the job. These are based on experience, family, religion, and education. Surprisingly, of the intelligence community members, some of these agencies would not admit that they had ethical standards. One person whom I called to inquire about her agency's code of ethics responded, "Why would we want to display and acknowledge that we have ethics?" One agency official said that I would have to apply under the Freedom of Information Act to view their code of ethics; another agency official questioned my intent to find their code of ethics. One agency official said their code of ethics requires a password available only to members of that agency. Most agency ethics officers rely on employees' legal rights, cultural diversity policies, or the effective and efficient use of a worker's space. Clearly, there is some confusion as to what ethics are, and there is no standard code of ethics per se for US intelligence professionals; we do have standards of conduct, codes of conduct, creeds, value statements for employees, and, of course, regulations and laws.

The Office of the Director of National Intelligence, when it comes to promoting ethics, lists the 2014 National Intelligence Strategy to "recognize and reinforce the principles as fundamental to the Intelligence Community's mission and vision."[33] These principles of professional ethics include "mission, truth, lawfulness, integrity, stewardship, excellence, and diversity." Unfortunately, these aspirational attributes speak of the individual's worth to their agency, organization, or the US government. Meanwhile, the US Office of Government Ethics focuses on an employee's failure to adhere to legal requirements and provides advice in the interpretation of government regulations, which could result in administrative or judicial punishment. (I remember when I invited an official to speak at one of my half-dozen ethics conferences, the Office of Government Ethics spokesperson jokingly mentioned, "We're all lawyers; what do we know about ethics?")

A code of ethics is what is expected of all employees doing similar work. It should help provide the development of ethical reasoning that can be applied to the practice of intelligence. General principles, based on accepted values in Western society, lead to guidelines for ethical behavior; such essential values include personal autonomy, democracy, and solidarity. The principle of nonmalfeasance can also be derived from these guidelines.[34]

Today, we have no systematic training program in the intelligence community. Each agency or department has its own method or avenue of dealing with intelligence. Some organizations will bring in defense contractors, while others will rely on in-house lawyers. Stories will be told, and the laws pertaining to the conduct of a government employee will be discussed. Most of it will not pertain to professional ethics as it should involve collecting, processing, and disseminating information and intelligence.

DEVELOPING AN ETHICS AND INTELLIGENCE COURSE

In any course focusing on ethics in the context of intelligence work, several foundational lessons must be established for students. First, they must understand the difference between law and philosophy. Law in the United States is governed, as all legislation, under the rubric of the Constitution. However, legal rulings by the judicial branch of government do not mean it may be morally the correct decision. A quick review of such "hot-button" issues as abortion, gun control, and the death penalty proves this point. Secondly, students need to be exposed to the philosophical tenets of Kant, consequentialism, utilitarianism, and others. This allows students to view ethical discussions from different perspectives. Some students may want to use theological teachings as their moral code, which is certainly permissible. But, given the diverse religions and for students who may be atheists, religion cannot be a universally accepted moral code. Thirdly, the role of logic and reason needs to be emphasized. In other words, why is it the "right thing" to do if you needed to explain it to a third party? It is here where moral theory comes in contact with the practicality of any decision. For example, you can discuss the five steps of the decision-making process (problem recognition, search process, alternatives, selection, evaluation). The fourth and final step in teaching a course in ethics and intelligence is the ethical dilemma case study. These are problems that should be posted to the class, allowing them to work either in groups or alone. In the past, many governmental ethics classes were nothing but case studies. Usually, these case studies were highlighted by stories of what happened, with a clear definition of finding a good choice. These classes are also interspersed with laws, rules, and regulations, with a spokesperson from the agency's inspector general's office describing the punishment should an employee decide to "do the wrong thing."

One of the greatest instruments of teaching ethics and intelligence is knowing how to define an ethical dilemma. During my years of teaching this course, most students think they know what an ethical dilemma is, but in fact there is no ethical dilemma. For example, while working at an agency, certain websites were off-limits for various reasons. One analyst went home and accessed one of these "forbidden" websites, which he had a perfect right to do. The next day, this analyst reportedly had an "ethical dilemma" because he wanted to use some of the information from the website in his assessment. Thus, does the analyst use this information or not? That is the ethical dilemma. Of course, this is not an ethical dilemma, since that site is reportedly off-limits to the analyst. And unless there is some pressure to include this information, there is no ethical dilemma. An ethical dilemma occurs when you must choose between "two rights" or "two wrongs." Ethics does not allow you to disobey rules, regulations, and procedures when there is no pressure and the consequences are minimal.

WHERE DO WE GO FROM HERE?

In the United States, instead of developing bromides and empty platitudes on the value of principles, relying on religion, or, at worst, the law, we need to establish and support ethical conduct—maybe the development of a National Intelligence Council on Ethics. This council would be staffed by intelligence professionals from all levels (entry, supervisory, executive) as well as administrators, citizens, and clergy. It would operate similar to how some hospitals seek advice on the determination of end-of-life care. Rather than a community being governed and dictated by law, this would be a council of professionals and nonprofessionals seeking to balance real-world requirements in meeting threats with upholding the values we subscribe to as a nation. The most powerful force for ethics in the intelligence profession is open and honest reflection. We must begin to discuss and debate ethics in order to educate new intelligence personnel. Self-criticism will both strengthen good behavior and serve to correct previous ethical and moral lapses. Individuals who work in intelligence and the society that depends on their work must have an open discussion regarding the values and standards that will make this nation safe. Today we are at an auspicious moment. The way forward is not entirely clear, but it will be up to men and women of goodwill and moral sensibility to lead the way. Once that is established, we can begin to teach professional ethics in the intelligence community.

NOTES

1. Interview with Aldrich Ames, *CNN's Declassified: Cold War*, episode 21, "Spies," aired March 14, 1999.

2. CIA Inspector General's Report on the Aldrich H. Ames Case, "Unclassified Abstract—Preface to the Report from the I.G.," 14, https://apps.dtic.mil/dtic/tr/full text/u2/a311780.pdf.

3. Catholic University Newsletter, "The Humanity of Espionage," March 6, 2019.

4. For one of the most complete lists of professional codes of conduct, see the Illinois Institute of Technology's "Ethics Codes Collection" at http://ethicscodescol lection.org.

5. School identification withheld.

6. *The Good Shepherd* is a 2006 American spy film produced and directed by Robert De Niro and starring Matt Damon, Angelina Jolie, and De Niro, with an extensive supporting cast. This fictional account does capture the white, Anglo-Saxon Protestant ethos at the birth of the intelligence community, specifically the CIA.

7. Henry L. Stimson and McGeorge Bundy, *On Active Service in Peace and War* (New York: Harper, 1948), 188.

8. The memorandum can be found in Jan Goldman, *Ethics of Spying*, vol. 2 (Lanham: Rowman & Littlefield, 2010), 15–18.

9. Goldman, *Ethics of Spying*, 15.

10. Goldman, *Ethics of Spying*, 15.

11. Goldman, *Ethics of Spying*, 16.

12. Consider using fictional books in teaching an ethics and intelligence course. If you do use John le Carré novels, they should be supplemented with *The Spy Novels of John le Carré: Balancing Ethics and Politics*, by Myron J. Aronoff (New York: Palgrave Macmillan, 1999).

13. Keith Phipps, "The 50 Best Spy Movies of All Time," *Vulture*, March 14, 2019, https://www.vulture.com/article/best-spy-movies-ranked.html.

14. Scott Shane, "Pursuing an Exotic Tool for Espionage: A Moral Compass," *New York Times*, January 28, 2006, A1.

15. Shane, "Pursuing an Exotic Tool."

16. Shane, "Pursuing an Exotic Tool."

17. Kent Pekel, "The Need for Improvement: Integrity, Ethics, and the CIA," *Studies in Intelligence*, 1996, 85–94, https://www.cia.gov/static/c053b4680f58a4b88c 9863201c90e6a0/Integrity-Ethics-the-CIA.pdf.

18. Pekel, "The Need for Improvement."

19. Michael Devine, "CIA Ethics Education: Background and Perspective," Congressional Research Service, June 11, 2018, https://fas.org/sgp/crs/intel/IF10906.pdf.

20. Christopher Bailey and Susan M. Galich, "Codes of Ethics: The Intelligence Community," *International Journal of Intelligence Ethics* 3, no. 2 (Fall/Winter 2012): 77–99.

21. Rob Evans and Paul Lewis, "Undercover Police Had Children with Activists," *Guardian*, January 12, 2012, https://www.theguardian.com/uk/2012/jan/20/undercover-police-children-activists.

22. Joseph Fitsanakis, "Norwegian Spy Service Seeks Right to Break Law during Espionage Operations," IntelNews.org, November 21, 2018, https://intelnews.org/2018/11/21/01-2441.

23. US Department of Justice, *Ethics Handbook for On and Off-Duty Conduct*, January 2016, https://www.justice.gov/usao-sdny/page/file/1153451/download.

24. US Department of Justice, *Ethics Handbook*, 4.

25. Eric H. Holder, Attorney General Memorandum, April 10, 2015, https://www.justice.gov/file/1047646/download. A closer look at the reference is the solicitation of prostitution, for fear that "it invites extortion, blackmail, and leaks of sensitive or classified information" and undermines the department's efforts to eradicate human trafficking. The memo further states, "This rule applies at all times during an individual's employment, including while off duty or on personal leave, and applies regardless of whether the activity is legal or tolerated in a particular jurisdiction, foreign or domestic."

26. Department of Homeland Security, *Learning Roadmaps for Intelligence Professionals—Analytics*, 2005.

27. Department of Justice, *Analyst Professional Development Road Map*, June 2015, https://www.ojp.gov/library/publications/analyst-professional-development-road-map.

28. Department of Justice, *Analyst Professional Development*, 9.

29. Department of Justice, *Analyst Professional Development*, 12.

30. Center for Ethics and the Rule of Law at the University of Pennsylvania, *Report on the Department of Justice and the Rule of Law*, October 12, 2020, https://www.law.upenn.edu/live/files/10900-report-on-the-doj-and-the-rule-of-law.

31. Office of the Director of National Intelligence, Office of General Counsel, *Intelligence Community Legal Reference Book*, 2020, https://www.dni.gov/files/documents/OGC/IC%20Legal%20Reference%20Book%202020.pdf.

32. US Naval Academy, "Ethics across the Curriculum," Stockdale Center for Ethical Leadership, https://www.usna.edu/Ethics/blog/2020/ethics_across_the_curriculum.php.

33. Office of the Director of National Intelligence, "Principles of Professional Ethics for the Intelligence Community," https://www.dni.gov/index.php/how-we-work/ethics.

34. Michael M. Andregg, *Intelligence Ethics: The Definitive Work of 2007*, Center for the Study of Intelligence and Wisdom (St. Paul, MN: Ground Zero Publishing, 2007).

14

Bridging the Divide

Rubén Arcos, Nicole K. Drumhiller, and Mark Phythian

We have been presented with a number of different perspectives on and approaches to the question of the academic-practitioner divide in this book. What, then, are the key conclusions that can be drawn from the ideas and experiences set out by the authors? First of all, even though the authors write from a range of intelligence and educational contexts, all see clear advantages in, and share a commitment to, thinking about the divide and how academic-practitioner relations in the field can be developed in pursuit of shared goals based around increasing knowledge and improving understanding of intelligence. Second, there is, in various forms, a recognition of essential differences in the two professions. These differences impose limits on the nature and extent of academic-practitioner engagement. This recognition, coupled with the shared belief in the benefits of addressing the divide, point us to the key question, that of "how close?" In this concluding chapter, we begin by building on the ideas presented by authors in the earlier chapters to discuss a menu of ways in which the academic-practitioner divide can be mitigated (indeed, *is being* mitigated) before turning our attention to remaining challenges and addressing the "how close?" question.

MUTUALLY BENEFICIAL COLLABORATIONS

There is a risk that by highlighting the divide, something that is a necessary first step in thinking about approaches to bridging it, we give the impression that there is only very limited interaction between academics and practitioners in this area. However, as the authors of the earlier chapters show, there is much activity that currently takes place designed to bring academics and practitioners together. Here, we outline key initiatives that can be used to take this work forward and further develop mutually beneficial collaborations.

The contributions of practitioners and practitioner-scholars to the specialist intelligence literature. As noted earlier, the production and development of the intelligence studies literature is a collaborative endeavor that draws on contributions by academics, practitioner-scholars, and practitioners, sometimes working separately and sometimes coauthoring work. The practitioner contribution appears in both academic journals and in journals that are published by or for intelligence organizations (and in which contributions by academics also appear), but which are made publicly available in some form (e.g., the Center for the Study of Intelligence *Studies in Intelligence*, the *Romanian Intelligence Studies Review*).[1] The specialist intelligence literature, then, is a coproduction involving academics and practitioners. It could not have developed to the extent and in the ways it has without the contributions of both. Facilitating cooperation designed to further develop this literature should be seen as a priority by all involved.

Even when direct contribution through the publication of peer-reviewed work is not possible, practitioners can support academics in other ways, such as by "granting interviews . . . responding to academic queries or making scarce research materials available," and through the writing of "memoirs or accounts of particular intelligence activities, episodes or actors."[2]

Participating in academic conferences that bring together academics, practitioners, and practitioner-scholars. International conferences provide opportunities for community making (i.e., developing the international intelligence studies community) and trust building with stakeholders, something that is particularly relevant when it comes to intelligence issues. They become a framework for gathering together a set of stakeholders with different organizational and professional backgrounds, including scholars but also security and intelligence practitioners and even policy makers or their advisers, to share insights and perspectives on particular issues.[3] These interactions promote relationship building and the sharing of information and knowledge, and, as with other disciplines, they provide opportunities to engage with and resolve academic controversies between peers around questions that are key to advancing the field.[4] From a knowledge network perspective, events become a sort of hub, connecting nodes and weaving together networks of researchers involved in the study of intelligence.

Examples of unclassified forums that provide opportunities to bring these groups together include the International Studies Association's Intelligence Studies Section, the American Political Science Association's Intelligence Studies Group, the International Association for Intelligence Education (IAFIE), and the Intelligence and National Security Association (INSA), to name a few. Additionally, conferences that hold discussions in classified formats include the Armed Forces Communications and Electronics Association, as well as the INSA. Within the United Kingdom, intelligence scholars have opportunities to exchange ideas in forums such as the Cambridge Intelligence Seminars, the Oxford Intelligence Group, the Study Group on Intelligence, and the Greynog Conference organized from Aberystwyth University.[5] European examples of regular conferences engaging academics and practitioners include the international conference held in Romania, Intelligence in the Knowledge Society, which aims to encourage "interdisciplinary communication and exchanges between the academic field and practitioners interested in intelligence and security-related issues, so as to identify and assess the innovation degree, practices, policies, and trends governing these fields."[6]

Additionally, events conducted under Chatham House rules, or under modified versions for an era of social media, encourage the sharing of information and, over time, strengthen trust.[7] These can also provide an opportunity to engage in scenario-based discussions related to security topics involving practitioners and academics. In this kind of event, the combined experiences and knowledge of government, academia, and the private sector are put together for the purpose of exploring scenarios or answering research/policy questions in the face of security threats. The information shared is unclassified, but the outcome is not necessarily put in the public domain, although it is usually disseminated to a limited number of stakeholders.

Conferences and symposia that bring together academics and practitioners can also be *focused on teaching intelligence*. Examples include the 1993 US Central Intelligence Agency Symposium on Teaching Intelligence and the follow-on conference held in 1999 by the Joint Military Intelligence College.[8] The goal of the conference was to bring together intelligence practitioners and academics to enhance the integration of intelligence studies topics into programs of study. Conferences such as this can serve as a useful resource in identifying effective teaching practices but also helping to resolve programming gaps. Issues related to the teaching of intelligence are also at the core of the IAFIE mission and its conference programs. The development of IAFIE's Europe Chapter and its commitment to holding conferences outside (as well as inside) the United States—for example, in Europe and Australia—has made a major contribution in this area of bridging the academic-practitioner divide.

Additionally, *the funding of academic centers of excellence* should also be mentioned, as these centers help provide financial resources to students and faculty conducting research on problems relevant to the intelligence community and further build long-term relationships between government organizations and academia.[9] Linked to this, government research grants provide opportunities for collaboration. Historically, such grant programs have included the development of academic intelligence centers of excellence, the MacArthur and Ford foundation grants, and also the Minerva Initiative through the US defense community.[10]

Additional sources of funding for academic and collaborative projects have facilitated research into intelligence themes. In the European context, research collaborations framed under the North Atlantic Treaty Organization's Science and Technology Organization have included research task groups addressing intelligence topics such as "intelligence exploitation of social media," "automation in the intelligence cycle," "high-level fusion of hard and soft information for intelligence," and "assessment and communication of intelligence to support decision making."[11]

European Union (EU)-funded security research includes funded research projects addressing themes on or related to intelligence. Results from basic queries (keyword = *intelligence*) to the CORDIS database show how the EU has funded consortiums conducting research on a number of intelligence issues, such as criminal intelligence (EUCRIMTEL), law enforcement intelligence (LEILA), cognitive biases in intelligence analysis (RECOBIA), informal security cooperation and intelligence sharing (LINSEC), and cyber threat intelligence (CYBER-TRUST), to name a few.[12]

Student internships and practicums also provide students seeking to become practitioners, or in the case of practicums, students seeking to transition from the intelligence community into academia, with an opportunity to help address problems of practice within the intelligence field.

Another bridge developed within the US education system is the Central Intelligence Agency's (CIA) *officer-in-residence program* (which began in the fall of 1985).[13] Under this program, practitioners are placed in university settings to help enhance exposure to the topic both within the classroom, through guest lectures and seminar discussions, and also among academic colleagues.

Example Areas Where Academic Contributions Can Help Practitioners

As noted above, the specialist literature on which intelligence education and training depends is now a coproduction drawing on academic and practitioner contributions. Academics have made significant contributions to understanding across the field. Here, we outline a few areas where academic contributions have helped and can help in shaping practice.

Structured Analytic Techniques (SATs)

One area where academics contribute and inform practice is by conducting research on different analytical methods to help ensure that they result in unbiased and accurate reports. As discussed in earlier chapters, intelligence practitioners often rely on structured analytic techniques (SATs). However, the reliability of these techniques has been called into question.[14] One way that academics can assist practitioners in closing this gap is via continued research into SATs with the goal of providing recommendations for improvement. Of course, it would then be the responsibility of practitioners within intelligence organizations to implement any recommended changes (something academics might not be privy to in the end). Additionally, academics can be engaged by intelligence professionals in "developing and validating foresight techniques to map out the range of possible future threat and contingencies, or they could contribute subject-matter expertise in foresight exercises conducted by intelligence services."[15]

Developing Process Knowledge

Another area where academics can contribute to practice and so help bridge the divide is by focusing on the development of process knowledge. In this manner, research can be carried out on "how to structure and manage the analytical process" to increase the production of more accurate and higher-quality analysis.[16] Likewise, academics from a variety of disciplines can help provide insights into the development of "nonliteral collection systems (mapping, sensing, measuring, etc.)" and also through the development or improvement of knowledge management systems.[17]

Understanding Intelligence Failure

In addition to this, studying past intelligence failures is a major area of academic contribution. Here the focus should be on gaining "a deeper appreciation of the complexities of the analytic task, the wide range of obstacles and hurdles that analysts must overcome in order to succeed, and positive recommendations regarding what they can do to avoid future failure."[18] Academic work has done much to improve understanding of the various causes and complexity of intelligence failure.

Case Studies and Modeling

Linked to this, case studies and modeling are another means by which academics can assist intelligence practitioners. As Miller has observed,

> Government experts seldom, if ever, have the time or panoply of skills and backgrounds to effectively describe and model risk analysis solutions, structural indicator approaches, experimental diagnostic models for conflict anticipation

and analysis, econometrics, and more. This is an area which outside expertise is frequently called on, mined, and/or deployed for purposes of trying both to better manage information volume and to map and track intelligence indicators.[19]

US Northern Command's (NORAD) North American Defense and Security Academic Alliance is a unique program that allows any institution, student, or faculty to participate in problem-oriented research. Their website promotes the need for problem-oriented research that helps serve the Aerospace Defense, Homeland Defense, Security Cooperation, and Defense Support of Civil Authorities communities. In this manner, NORAD lists research topics of interest and allows interested parties to connect with their education team. Something like this, even without the support of grant money, can help further develop the field of intelligence as eager students are able to utilize the topics as inspiration for their own research.

Organizational Efficiencies

Other areas that can benefit from additional academic exploration include research on the operations and efficiencies of intelligence organizations themselves in order to help ensure that organizational processes do not negatively impact the overall mission. The nature and bases of foreign intelligence liaison is another area where academics have made important contributions.[20]

REMAINING CHALLENGES

Despite these promising bases for bridge building, it is clear from the discussions in this book that gaps remain. Additional strategies for bridging the academic-practitioner divide in intelligence studies include addressing the following.

Working in Isolation

A common theme within the literature, also evident in the chapters here, is the notion that academics and practitioners often operate in isolation from one another. To help bridge this gap, additional opportunities need to be created for the more extensive exchange of ideas and increased collaboration between intelligence practitioners and academics to resolve problems of practice.[21] As noted earlier, participation in conferences and various fellows programs is already among the mutually beneficial links available to scholars and practitioners. However, as Anthony Glees has pointed out, among the more difficult challenges for the study of intelligence "is to surmount intellectual isolation by working together more systematically and less hierarchically—more workshops, more study groups, fewer large showcasing conferences."[22] While large conferences offer opportunities for researchers to present their work, Glees makes the case for more intimate settings where the two camps can use their time away from day-to-day activities to dig into issues and problems that need to be addressed.[23] Furthermore, in thinking about how gaps can be addressed in this field, consideration needs to be given to the intelligence community's need for secrecy, quick results, and rapid shifting of topics. To help navigate these needs, Dover and Goodman argue that small "in-house talks, lectures and discussions either held at a location in the academic community, or within the national security community," are needed.[24] In such a setting, practitioners are better able to ensure their need for secrecy, establish an agenda, and set the pace of conversation in order to achieve actionable results.

Intelligence Studies Staffing and Placement in Universities

Another targeted way to help bridge the intellectual isolation gap in intelligence studies is through the staffing and placement of intelligence studies programs within universities. Staffing addresses directly one of the key challenges to enhancing the field of intelligence studies, namely the recruitment of experienced, qualified, and interested faculty.[25] Faculty qualifications emerge as a hot-button issue for those writing on the academic-practitioner divide in intelligence studies, as can be seen in the preceding chapters. In some cases, university leadership might have an ideal type in mind that seems to leave little room for individuals with only an academic background to participate in the discussion. For others, academic researchers are acknowledged to be valuable in developing the field. There is no doubt that the hiring of faculty that have prior government experience is an asset to any intelligence studies program and is something advocated for within the field.[26] In this regard, intelligence practitioners are thought to help put "a face on the profession," remove some of the misperceptions surrounding the work taking place in the intelligence community, "give added meaning to academic theories," and further enrich the student experience.[27] One caution from Glees specific to the involvement of practitioners in the classroom is that they may inadvertently stifle discussion "on the grounds that they know the truth and that is that."[28]

One overarching theme that does emerge is that in order for the field to advance, academic departments need to focus on bringing together a healthy blend of both those who have intelligence field experience and those who do not but who specialize in areas relevant to the topics of interest. This would replicate at the teaching level the respective contributions that have resulted in the coproduction of the specialist literature. Having a balance of academics and practitioners teaching in an intelligence studies program is important. However, so too is the need to ensure that the programs are not "too heavily imbalanced towards part-time" faculty, as the "resulting program impact is negative."[29] Even in a program featuring a relatively high proportion of (former) practitioners, the professional expectations that apply should be similar to those of academic professional requirements in terms of adding to the field. Former practitioners should not be employed in university settings solely for their ability to reminisce.

It is important to keep in mind that staffing is one component that will make up an intelligence program's identity. Given the interdisciplinary nature that is the intelligence field, a program's identity will emerge not just from the faculty that teach within the program, but also where that program is located within the greater university. In this manner, an intelligence studies program that is housed within a larger history program will likely take on a historical approach to the classes taught and the research carried out. Likewise, an intelligence program housed within the sciences will likely take on a more technical identity. As has been discussed within this book and the wider literature, there is value in developing an intelligence studies program made up of diverse perspectives. Along these lines, Willmetts makes the case that in order for the field of intelligence studies to further develop, it needs to embrace "new methodologies and theoretical paradigms" from within cultural studies (including media representations of espionage and anthropological attempts to determine intelligence culture or cultures), literary theory, and the philosophy of history.[30] One challenge within the United States is the way in which accrediting bodies review faculty qualifications.[31] In this regard, because there are very few faculty with doctoral degrees in intelligence, a majority of faculty will come from a variety of disciplines as a result of the multidisciplinary nature that is this field. To get here, university leadership needs to work with their faculty human resources and accreditation teams to ensure that an understanding is reached regarding the kind of backgrounds the intelligence studies faculty will have. Failing to allow faculty from diverse backgrounds to teach within an intelligence studies department will negatively impact the learning outcomes of students and stifle the growth of the field.

However, even a balanced portfolio made up of practitioners, academics, and hybrid personas may still not be enough if there is no engagement across these different backgrounds. Joseph Nye, an academic-practitioner within international relations, has mentioned that the key to ensuring a department's success stems from "the ability and willingness of members to interact and communicate with each other."[32] Clearly, this cross-scope communication is something that is not only relevant within the international relations and policy arena, but also particularly relevant within the study of intelligence.

Supporting Faculty in Government/Policy Research

In relation to developing a blended faculty made up of practitioners, academics, and practitioner-scholars, university leadership needs to think critically about and address how they can cultivate an environment that is supportive of faculty participation in policy-relevant research. Often academics are punished or overlooked during their rank-advancement process when they spend time in government service rather than within academia seemingly contributing to the discipline.[33] This is something that ultimately discourages people from moving from academia into intelligence and from intelligence into academia.[34]

Instead of creating barriers to government service, a shift in mentality needs to occur that allows for contributions to the discipline that include periods of military or government service, as well as publication within professional or policy-related journals. Culturally there are differences in job mobility and advancement when it comes to distinctions between academics and practitioners in intelligence. Scholars "are rated and promoted by their contributions to refereed academic journals. . . . They get little credit for contributions to policy journals edited for a broader audience."[35] However, intellectual involvement in these forums can directly contribute to resolving problems of practice in the intelligence studies field, as they reach a wider practitioner audience.[36]

Similar to academics needing assistance in making their research more accessible to wider audiences, so too might practitioners require assistance from academic mentors, research offices, or university professional development units in carrying out academic research.

Need for Greater University Resources and Partnerships

Faculty qualifications have been discussed throughout the book as a key area of focus that will not only help to bridge the academic-practitioner gap but also help in the continued development of the field internationally. Part of the challenge surrounding this involves the limited resources available dedicated to its study. Two concerns in particular include the lack of private endowments or gifts specific to intelligence faculty positions and that academic resources typically do not correspond with government agency needs.[37] However, in the United States, the CIA's Intelligence Center of Excellence program may be one way to overcome this. Likewise, something along the lines of the NORAD North American Defense and Security Academic Alliance[38] coupled with grant money to support research teams could go a long way in this area—both within the United States and more widely.

Focus on the Anglosphere

One of the key distinctions or challenges when considering the academic-practitioner divide in intelligence stems from the areas on which researchers focus. In particular, Crosston argues that the academic-practitioner divide in intelligence suffers from an overemphasis on the "Anglosphere" and the discounting and nonengagement of non-Western perspectives of the intelligence field.[39] He argues that this Western-oriented focus stems from a keen bias that intelligence is foreign facing rather than an activity that also looks at domestic affairs. In this manner, "embracing intelligence as an exclusively foreign-policy domain and not engaging domestic concerns . . . creates analyses that miss whole swathes of information, pushed aside as internal security measures or law enforcement issues."[40]

Moving away from an outward-facing perspective of intelligence, Crosston argues that intelligence must be studied as a means of "gaining insight from information, often by any means necessary."[41] This is a sentiment that is echoed by Glees in that academia should have a greater understanding of intelligence agencies in the developing world.[42] Failing to consider these non-Western approaches "produces research that deforms the body of knowledge (a debilitating error for any emerging discipline) and creates analyses blind to on-the-ground realities."[43] Despite this call, some may perceive this area of study to lack immediate policy relevance, even though this kind of research is critically valuable in the development of area expertise, which intelligence organizations often seek assistance in developing.

Overcoming a Lack of Diversity

While great strides have been made toward the development of the field, intelligence studies continues to be under scrutiny for its lack of diversity.[44] Historically, both the US and the UK intelligence communities have been made up of predominantly white males. This lack of diversity has led to phrases such as "white, male, and Yale" being associated with the US intelligence community (or CIA specifically), and "Oxbridge" in reference to the UK intelligence community stereotype of having studied at either Oxford or Cambridge.[45] As a result of their historical developments, the lack of diversity in the intelligence communities is also a factor in the lack of diversity within the academic arena. In their research, Puyvelde and Curtis assessed the state of the field by reviewing two flagship intelligence journals and found that much like at intelligence and national security conferences, among those publishing, approximately 90 percent are males, while females make up 9 percent of the population.[46] Likewise a majority of publications come from authors based in the United States, the United Kingdom, or Canada.

This lack in author diversity has also led to a gap in the kind of research that is being carried out, as the US and British intelligence communities serve as the subject in approximately 71 percent of the publications.[47] This has led to over ninety countries having little to no research carried out on them, so Crosston's concerns regarding the heavy focus on the Anglosphere remain relevant.[48] However, as mentioned in the introduction, some recent publications have taken on a more critical approach to the study of intelligence, which will ultimately enhance the intellectual diversity of the field.[49] Arguments for enhancing the diversity of the intelligence community go beyond the traditional equity, diversity, and inclusion initiatives making headlines in the United States and in other parts of the globe. As it relates to the diversity of the intelligence community, a more diverse workforce helps to ensure that the analysis being carried out on real-world problems does not suffer from mirror-imaging or ethnocentric biases. In particular, in discussing the need for diversity in the US intelligence community, Robert Callum explains,

> To understand an increasingly complex world, an increasingly diverse work force is needed. As Angelo Codevilla has written, "No one profession, one nationality, one state of life, one *curriculum vitae*, allows one kind of person to understand all others and solicit all others." . . . Continued reliance on a culturally homogeneous pool of analysts will doom the United States to future "intelligence failures" caused by the projection of "our logic" onto the actions and tactics of antagonists.[50]

In order to foster mentorship and persistence within the intelligence community, special-interest organizations and government agency activities have been developed to help ensure that a greater diversity of voices are heard within the field. For example, groups such as the Women's Intelligence Network, Women in International Security, and the Amazing Women of the Intelligence Community all serve to help ensure female voices are not lost in a male-dominated field. Likewise, the Leadership Summit for Women in National Security Careers has helped with skills development and job mobility, while the International Spy Museum hosts an annual event, "Mother, Daughter, Sister, Spy," which helps celebrate female roles within the intelligence community. Continued alternative recruitment practices, networking opportunities, dialogue on diversity, and gender dynamics in the field continue to be a relevant component in helping to enhance the diversity of perspectives in the field.[51]

HOW CLOSE? RECOGNIZING THE REALITY OF LIMITS

Intelligence and academia share similar goals—to increase knowledge and improve understanding. Given that academics are in the knowledge business, it would be natural for them to collaborate with intelligence as intelligence reflects on how it can improve its quest for timely knowledge and understanding. In the last two decades, there has been evidence of increasingly systematic use of some academic expertise by national intelligence bodies aimed at improving the analytical function. This supplanted the more ad hoc approach that characterized earlier academic-practitioner interactions and reflected the increasing professionalization of the intelligence analyst role internationally. In the United Kingdom at least, this shift was a consequence of the Iraq weapons of mass destruction (WMD) intelligence failure and, specifically, the recommendations of the Butler Report that investigated WMD intelligence in its wake.[52] Its recommendations underscored the importance of intelligence professionals inside government having access to a wide range of information and perspectives in arriving at their assessments. Butler found that

> the JIC [Joint Intelligence Committee] may, in some assessments, also have misread the nature of Iraqi governmental and social structures. The absence of intelligence in this area may also have hampered planning for the post-war phase on which departments did a great deal of work. We note that the collection of intelligence on Iraq's prohibited weapons programmes was designated as being a JIC First Order of Priority whereas intelligence on Iraqi political issues was designated as being Third Order. The membership of the JIC is broad enough to allow such wider evidence to be brought to bear. *We emphasise the importance of the Assessments Staff and the JIC having access to a wide range of information, especially in circumstances (e.g. where the UK is likely to become involved in national reconstruction and institution-building) where information on political and social issues will be vital.*[53]

It also recommended a review of "the size of the Assessments Staff, and in particular . . . whether they have available the volume and range of resources to ask the questions which need to be asked in fully assessing intelligence reports and in thinking radically."[54]

All of this suggested that academics could play a role in offering external perspectives and challenge emerging conventional wisdom being derived from intelligence—that is, provide open-source challenges to intelligence analysts. This idea was reinforced by the recommendations of the 2011 Blackett Review. This was commissioned by the Cabinet Office and Ministry of Defence to recommend ways of identifying, assessing, and managing high-impact, low-probability risks, and involved outside experts. Recommendation one of eleven was that "government should make greater use of external experts to inform risk assumptions, judgements and analyses."[55]

However, while intelligence and academia share similar goals linked to knowledge and understanding, there are key differences. As Robert Dover has noted, governmental intelligence analysis "is not a foundational science and therefore does not seek to posit fundamental truths in an environment that exists outside of the context in which it is made."[56] This gives rise to a fundamental question: "Is there genuinely the appetite within senior public policy circles for uncomfortable or paradigm breaking truths?"[57] In addition, is there the time or space to accommodate them in the analytical process?

There has been evidence of intelligence-related closed areas of government opening up and welcoming academic input in the United Kingdom, although there is enormous scope to make more of this resource. However, the scale of this in the future is likely to be limited by the related issues of secrecy and trust and also the need for speed and the changing requirements of the intelligence community.[58] Other significant factors include money and how far intelligence insiders think that liaison with academic outsiders is worth the time and effort.

In a further sign of increasing engagement with academia, the UK security and intelligence agencies did find the money to set up the National Centre for Research and Evidence on Security Threats (CREST), based at the University of Lancaster but drawing in other universities. Its mission is to "deliver a world-class, interdisciplinary portfolio of activity that maximizes the value of economic and social science research in countering threats to national security."[59] A 2019 external review of CREST's impact identified three different types of impact arising from its work: instrumental impact, conceptual impact, and capacity building. At the same time, the review's recommendations suggested that practitioners did not always see CREST's work as being useful and that CREST could go further in demonstrating "what research adds most value to stakeholders, and why."[60] Moreover, even in the context of a research institute funded by the security and intelligence agencies, reporting to them and designed to benefit them, issues of secrecy and trust remained barriers that limited academic-practitioner engagement.[61]

Hence, even within examples of closer cooperation, secrecy and trust are inevitable limiting factors.[62] Academics need to accept that this fundamental divide cannot be eliminated. At the same time, its existence does limit the benefits of engagement from the external academic perspective.[63] Intelligence and security academic Robert Dover has written of how his own experience suggests that the expectations of practitioners are that this engagement is something that external experts should *want* to do for the government as an end in and of itself, and further should be willing to do so to the partial detriment of other professional duties. This is not as unreasonable a position as it might seem at first glance. Motivation has always been an important factor for intelligence officers measuring the potential reliability of human sources, and my sense is that the attitude towards external experts fits on this spectrum for security officials.[64]

One question that all of this begs is how unrealistic the expectations are on both sides of the academic-practitioner divide around the possibilities of closer engagement. This question of expectations also arises in the related research fields discussed earlier. Practitioners need to understand that outside social science and historical perspectives are unlikely to provide them with "silver bullet" solutions. As Preble cautions, "We can expect foreign policy to have its healthy share of mistakes, misjudgments, and simple bad luck, with or without substantial and systematic input from serious and credentialed scholars."[65] For their part, academics need to realize that not all research or expertise that they consider helpful to the practitioner will be viewed in the same way by the practitioner. As Richards J. Heuer Jr. noted back in the 1970s, "Social scientists commonly define policy-relevant research far more broadly than the foreign policy community does."[66] Moreover, as in cognate fields, where practitioners do regard this research as relevant, the influence of academics may be more indirect than direct.[67] Given all of this, is it the case that the ability to pursue limited forms of engagement with greater frequency would be the optimal solution to the problem of bringing the benefits of outside academic expertise into the closed world of intelligence and security?

Concerns that academics could compromise their independence, or even their values, if they become too close to the world of practice remain, alongside a sense that some academic approaches are of limited use to practitioners, including policy makers. Within the social sciences, there has been some historic hesitancy for academic researchers to cross over and work on government, military, or intelligence-related topics. In some cases, like the human terrain research mentioned in chapter 1 of this book, deadly outcomes resulted as academic researchers were placed directly into war zones.[68] The challenge stems from the worry that academic knowledge or insight might be used in unintended ways, like a sort of weaponized social science research.[69]

Questions within academia arise over the "intellectual integrity, morality, or professional or ethical obligations to their given discipline," and the potential negative long-term effects of the research being conducted.[70] This has especially been the case for scholars within anthropology, psychology, and medicine, to name just a few. For example, one area that has caused anthropologists and other social scientists concern in working with government and intelligence organizations is "cultural intelligence," or the provision of insight into the intergroup dynamics of a society.[71] Though government research or work produced as part of a human terrain team might be conducted under the guise of secrecy, this policy itself does not raise ethical concerns. Instead, of concern is how the information will come to be used, as there "is a chance that information gathered by social scientists might be used improperly."[72] This is especially troublesome when researchers and scientists must abide by policies like that of the Nuremberg Code as well as other human subjects review board requirements that serve to protect the populations being studied. Likewise, psychiatrists have questioned the ethics behind participation in interrogations as a potential violation of their Hippocratic oath to do no harm. This was especially the case in the wake of the Abu Ghraib scandal in the United States and the interrogation practices that were in use.[73]

Much like the concerns regarding the use of research in off-campus settings, concerns also emerge over the conduct of intelligence or security-related research on university campuses. The idea of academics conducting research in government facilities places the protection of that work in the hands of the government organizations contracting the work. However, when the research is being conducted on college campuses, questions arise over the increased security needs given the "unpredictable features of international terrorism."[74]

Efforts aimed at bridging the divide may also raise concerns from both communities on issues that have not been discussed sufficiently in intelligence studies forums, such as red lines and gray zones in collaboration, which might elicit nonhomogeneous responses from scholars and practitioners with different cultural backgrounds.

Ethical committees in universities may suffice in the case of granting approval for research procedures in particular projects, but perhaps not for other issues. Regional diversity may influence perceptions of the dos and don'ts in engaging in research projects with scholars employed in academic institutions from countries that do not meet the standards of Western-style liberal democracies. On the one hand, such hypothetical collaborations might bring an opportunity for advancing the field through findings on intelligence communities from those countries. However, this might also put scholars in an uncomfortable position at home. At the end of the day, intelligence and security are regarded as sensitive topics, and tensions and existing issues between countries and allies can affect perceptions of what is appropriate. For example, would it be acceptable to engage in intelligence-related education and research with scholars from authoritarian countries or adversaries? Does the scholar's affiliation necessarily mean that they embrace the foreign policy objectives or activities of a particular country? How would this affect the academic reputation of an intelligence scholar in the eyes of intelligence practitioners from that scholar's country of origin? Similarly, collaboration agreements for education programs and research on security and intelligence issues with academic institutions from countries with low democratic standards might raise ethical concerns from other members of the academic community, even if academic scholars are entitled "to full freedom in research and in the publication of the results."[75]

Also, even if academic intelligence studies forums are formally open to participation with no country restrictions, the fact is that the participation of academic researchers from countries not meeting democratic standards would likely affect the degree of comfort of academics when discussing intelligence topics, not to say the future presence of practitioners in the academic forum. This suggests the existence of latent informal rules of engagement in intelligence studies events such as conferences that frame participation and interactions within those events and intelligence studies communities. At the same time, this also suggests that the academic-practitioner divide may get narrower in these contexts and be subject to events and developments in the international arena.

When considering how close is too close, one might consider if an intelligence studies organization or body within the epistemological community could help establish some guidelines for professional conduct. As opposed to the reactive guidance developed by the American and Australian anthropological associations, this effort would be proactive in providing guidance on the forging of relationships between intelligence organizations and academia. For example, in discussing the relationship between universities in the United States and the US intelligence community, Loch Johnson mentions the following as a starting point for the kinds of activities that should be prohibited: "agency cover recruitment on campus, covert research relationships, the use of academic cover by intelligence officers, the tasking of faculty and students to collect intelligence, and the tapping of academicians for counterintelligence or covert action operations."[76] Though this only covers a few of the concerns mentioned above, it provides a foundation for future discussions on this topic. The International Studies Association's Intelligence Section, the IAFIE, and their sister organization, IAFIE Europe, would serve as instrumental organizations in furthering this discussion.

All of this begs questions of the appropriate distance that should be maintained and of just what "too close" would look like in relation to intelligence studies. In general, it seems that here both academics and practitioners can be highly sensitive to the risk that the other side does not value them sufficiently.[77] Moreover, many academics working in the field are predisposed to offer their input to discussions about national security intelligence, precisely because it is concerned with national security and citizen protection. Nevertheless, ethical red lines that are fundamental to the academic profession exist. In this sense, the shift from the national security state of the Cold War era to the "protective" state of the twenty-first century has played its part. Thus, there are always likely to be limits as a result of diverging interests on each side of the divide.

A useful illustration of this is provided by the exposure of the Western intelligence involvement in Crypto AG and Operation Rubicon, via which the CIA together with the West German BND secretly owned the internationally market-leading company in encryption devices, enabling it to break the codes and so monitor communications from governments.[78] This was the result of a joint effort on the part of journalists and academics.[79] Clearly, this knowledge existed inside relevant intelligence organizations where the national interest in maintaining the secret was held to outweigh the public interest in knowing about it.

In making this public and seeking to explain it, academics working on intelligence can be considered to be carrying out a form of oversight and public education. This role—academics as contributors to the architecture of intelligence oversight in liberal democracies—involves them seeking to find out as much as possible about this secret part of government so as to be able to explain its role, as well as effectiveness, in government and international affairs; to generate models that help explain these things; to help frame and develop debates in this area; and so to inform the public concerning key questions for intelligence like the following: Does the current level of investment in intelligence provide value for money? Would further investment result in greater security? Why does intelligence fail, and how far can failure be avoided? How can oversight of intelligence best be performed? Intelligence bureaucracies are not the best places to look for answers to these questions. An outside perspective is called for.

However, the key questions to be addressed are not just limited to intelligence practice per se, but to its implications for thinking about the nature of the contemporary liberal state and the relationship between state and citizen. Beyond this, there are questions about the multilevel nature of intelligence beyond the state; about the role intelligence could play in relation to human security, as well as around public-private partnerships; and about the nature, role, and even limits of secrecy in relation to intelligence practice, which either are not an obvious focus of intelligence education as preprofessional training or do not benefit from external input. Academics working on intelligence have an important contribution to make in terms of such normative issues, and this is especially the case in countries that are still involved in building national cultures of intelligence in posttransitional contexts where previously intelligence-citizen relations were marked by distance, suspicion, and fear.

NOTES

1. See, for example, the *Romanian Intelligence Studies Review*, https://animv.ro /revista-romana-de-studii-de-intelligence; and the Center for the Study of Intelligence, https://www.cia.gov/resources/csi/studies-in-intelligence.

2. Stéphane Lefebvre, "Academic-Intelligence Relationships: Opportunities, Strengths, Weaknesses and Threats," *Journal of Policing, Intelligence and Counter Terrorism* 16, no. 1 (2021): 99.

3. See Rubén Arcos, "Understanding the Relationships between Academia and National Security Intelligence in the European Context," in *The Routledge International Handbook of Universities, Security and Intelligence Studies*, ed. Liam Francis Gearon, 161–62 (New York: Routledge, 2020).

4. Arcos, "Understanding the Relationships"; Martin Rudner, "Intelligence Studies in Higher Education: Capacity-Building to Meet Societal Demand," *International Journal of Intelligence and CounterIntelligence* 22, no. 1 (2009): 110–30; Damien Van Puyvelde and Sean Curtis, "'Standing on the Shoulders of Giants': Diversity and Scholarship in Intelligence Studies," *Intelligence and National Security* 31, no. 7 (2016): 1040–54.

5. See Damien Van Puyvelde's section on the United Kingdom in Van Puyvelde et al., "Comparing National Approaches to the Study of Intelligence," *International Studies Perspectives* 21, no. 3 (2020): 1–40.

6. See ANIMV's "International Conferences and Training Programs," https:// animv.ro/en/conferinte-internationale. See also Arcos, "Understanding the Relationships," 162.

7. Rubén Arcos, Mark Phythian, and Stephen Marrin, "Building the Intelligence Studies Community: The Role of International Conferences and Events" (paper presented at the Fifty-Ninth Annual Convention of the International Studies Association, San Francisco, CA, April 4–7, 2018). According to the rule, "When a meeting, or part thereof, is held under the Chatham House Rule, participants are free to use the information received, but neither the identity nor the affiliation of the speaker(s), nor that of any other participant, may be revealed"; https://www.chathamhouse.org /chatham-house-rule.

8. Rudner, "Intelligence Studies in Higher Education."

9. Lefebvre, "Academic-Intelligence Relationships."

10. Michael Mosser, "Puzzles versus Problems: The Alleged Disconnect between Academics and Military Practitioners," *Perspectives on Politics* 8, no. 4 (2016): 1077–86; Stephen Marrin, "Intelligence Studies Centers: Making Scholarship on Intelligence Analysis Useful," *Intelligence and National Security* 27, no. 3 (2012): 398–422.

11. North Atlantic Treaty Organization Science and Technology Organization, "Science Connect," https://www.sto.nato.int/Pages/scienceconnect.aspx.

12. See, for example, Cordis, https://cordis.europa.eu/en.

13. Rudner, "Intelligence Studies in Higher Education"; Bowman H. Miller, "Soldiers, Scholars, and Spies: Combining Smarts and Secrets," *Armed Forces & Society* 36, no. 4 (2010): 695–715; Marrin, "Intelligence Studies Centers"; Christopher Moran, "Note on Teaching Intelligence," *Intelligence and National Security* 31, no. 1 (2016): 118–30; Van Puyvelde and Curtis, "'Standing on the Shoulders of Giants.'"

14. As demonstrated in David Mandel's chapter herein. See also David R. Mandel, "Can Decision Science Improve Intelligence Analysis?," in *Researching National Security Intelligence: Multidisciplinary Approaches*, ed. Stephen M. Coulthart, Michael Landon-Murray, and Damien Van Puyvelde, 117–40 (Washington, DC: Georgetown University Press, 2019); Christopher W. Karvetski, David R. Mandel, and Daniel Irwin, "Improving Probability Judgment in Intelligence Analysis: From Structured Analysis to Statistical Aggregation," *Risk Analysis* 40, no. 5 (2020): 1040–57.

15. Lefebvre, "Academic-Intelligence Relationships," 93.

16. Marrin, "Intelligence Studies Centers," 212.

17. Lefebvre, "Academic-Intelligence Relationships," 94, 97.

18. Marrin, "Intelligence Studies Centers," 412.

19. Miller, "Soldiers, Scholars, and Spies," 708.

20. Adam D. M. Svendsen, "Connecting Intelligence and Theory: Intelligence Liaison and International Relations," *Intelligence and National Security* 24, no. 5 (October 2009): 700–729.

21. Matthew Crosston, "Occam's Follies: Real and Imagined Biases Facing Intelligence Studies," *Journal of Strategic Security* 6, no. 3 (2013): 40–53.

22. Anthony Glees, "The Future of Intelligence Studies," *Journal of Strategic Security* 6, no. 3 (2013): 127.

23. Glees, "The Future of Intelligence Studies."

24. Robert Dover and Michael S. Goodman, "Impactful Scholarship in Intelligence: A Public Policy Challenge," *British Politics* 13, no. 3 (September 2018): 387. See also Lefebvre, "Academic-Intelligence Relationships."

25. Rudner, "Intelligence Studies in Higher Education"; Crosston, "Occam's Follies"; Patrick F. Walsh, "Teaching Intelligence in the Twenty-First Century: Towards an Evidence-Based Approach for Curriculum Design," *Intelligence and National Security* 32, no. 7 (2017): 1005–21.

26. Tickner et al., "Risks and Opportunities of Crossing the Academic/Policy Divide," *International Studies Review* 10, no. 1 (2008): 155–77; Miller, "Soldiers, Scholars, Spies"; Marrin, "Intelligence Studies Centers."

27. Moran, "Note on Teaching Intelligence," 118.

28. Glees, "The Future of Intelligence Studies," 125.

29. Crosston, "Occam's Follies," 46.

30. Simon Willmetts, "The Cultural Turn in Intelligence Studies," *Intelligence and National Security* 34, no. 6 (September 2019): 800.

31. Stephen Coulthart and Matthew Crosston, "Terra Incognita: Mapping American Intelligence Education Curriculum," *Journal of Strategic Security* 8, no. 3 (2015):

46–68; Kobi Michael and Aaron Kornbluth, "The Academization of Intelligence: A Comparative Overview of Intelligence Studies in the West," *Cyber, Intelligence, and Security* 3, no. 1 (2019): 117–40.

32. Tickner et al., "Risks and Opportunities," 157.

33. Mosser, "Puzzles versus Problems."

34. Marrin, "Intelligence Studies Centers."

35. Tickner et al., "Risks and Opportunities," 158.

36. Ann Marie Murphy and Andreas Fulda, "Bridging the Gap: Pracademics in Foreign Policy," *PS: Political Science and Politics* 44, no. 2 (2011): 279–83.

37. Rudner, "Intelligence Studies in Higher Education."

38. US Northern Command, "North American Defense and Security Academic Alliance," 2021, accessed April 20, 2021, https://www.northcom.mil/Educational /North-American-Defense-and-Security-Academic-Alliance/North-American-De fense-and-Security-Academic-Alliance-Research-Topics.

39. Crosston, "Occam's Follies."

40. Crosston, "Occam's Follies," 41.

41. Crosston, "Occam's Follies," 41.

42. Glees, "The Future of Intelligence Studies."

43. Crosston, "Occam's Follies," 42.

44. Robert Callum, "The Case for Cultural Diversity in the Intelligence Community," *International Journal of Intelligence and CounterIntelligence* 14, no. 1 (2001): 25–48; Van Puyvelde and Curtis, "'Standing on the Shoulders of Giants'"; Daniela Bacheş-Torres and Efen Torres-Bacheş, "Intelligence Studies: An Ironic Tale of Politicization, Failure of Imagination, Lack of Collaboration, and Exclusion," *Journal of European and American Intelligence Studies* 1, no. 1 (2018): 15–24; Damien Van Puyvelde, "Women and Black Employees at the Central Intelligence Agency: From Fair Employment to Diversity Management," *Cambridge Review of International Affairs* 34, no. 5 (2021): 673–703, https://doi.org/10.1080/09557571.2020.1853052; Daniel W. B. Lomas, "#ForgetJamesBond: Diversity, Inclusion and the UK's Intelligence Agencies," *Intelligence and National Security* 36, no. 7 (2021): 995–1017, https://doi.org/10.1080/02684527.2021.1938370.

45. Callum, "The Case for Cultural Diversity"; Lomas, "#ForgetJamesBond."

46. Van Puyvelde and Curtis, "'Standing on the Shoulders of Giants.'"

47. Van Puyvelde and Curtis, "'Standing on the Shoulders of Giants.'"

48. Crosston, "Occam's Follies."

49. See, for example, Hamilton Bean, "Intelligence Theory from the Margins: Questions Ignored and Debates Not Had," *Intelligence and National Security* 33, no. 4 (2018): 527–40; Hamilton Bean and Mia Fischer, "Queering Intelligence Studies," *Intelligence and National Security* 36, no. 4 (2021): 584–98.

50. Callum, "The Case for Cultural Diversity."

51. Nicole K. Drumhiller and Kate Brannum, "Women in Global Security and Intelligence," *Journal of European and American Intelligence Studies* 1, no. 1 (2018): 303–9.

52. Lord Butler, *Review of Intelligence on Weapons of Mass Destruction: Report of a Committee of Privy Counsellors*, HC 898 (London: Her Majesty's Stationery Office, 2004).

53. Butler, para. 459 (emphasis in original).

54. Butler, para. 600.

55. *Blackett Review of High Impact Low Probability Risks* (London: Government Office for Science, 2011), 7, https://assets.publishing.service.gov.uk/government /uploads/system/uploads/attachment_data/file/278526/12-519-blackett-review-high -impact-low-probability-risks.pdf.

56. Robert Dover, "Adding Value to the Intelligence Community: What Role for Expert External Advice?," *Intelligence and National Security* 35, no. 6 (2020): 859.

57. Dover, "Adding Value," 859.

58. Robert Dover and Michael S. Goodman, "Between Lucky Jim and George Smiley: The Public Role of Intelligence Scholars," in *The Routledge International Handbook of Universities, Security and Intelligence Studies*, ed. Liam Francis Gearon, 343–51 (Abingdon: Routledge, 2020).

59. Jo Edwards, *Impact Review: A Review of the Impact of CREST Research Projects* (Lucidity Solutions Ltd., September 2019), 7, https://crestresearch.ac.uk/site /assets/files/3427/impact-report-19-028-03.pdf. See also https://crestresearch.ac.uk /about.

60. Edwards, *Impact Review*, 18.

61. Edwards, *Impact Review*, 9.

62. Edwards, *Impact Review*, 18.

63. See also Lawrence Freedman, "Academics and Policy-Making: Rules of Engagement," *Journal of Strategic Studies* 40, nos. 1–2 (2017): 263–68.

64. Dover, "Adding Value to the Intelligence Community," 856 (italics in original).

65. Christopher Preble, "Bridging the Gap: Managing Expectations, Improving Communications," *Journal of Strategic Studies* 40, nos. 1–2 (2017): 278.

66. Richards J. Heuer Jr. "Adapting Academic Methods and Models to Government Needs," in *Quantitative Approaches to Political Intelligence: The CIA Experience*, ed. Richards J. Heuer Jr., 3 (Boulder, CO: Westview Press, 1978). Although his focus here was on quantitative research, the point applies more generally.

67. See, for example, Roland Paris, "Ordering the World: Academic Research and Policymaking on Fragile States," *International Studies Review* 13, no. 1 (2011): 58–71.

68. Miller, "Soldiers, Scholars, and Spies."

69. Craig Calhoun, "Social Science Research and Military Agendas: Safe Distance or Bridging a Troubling Divide?," *Perspectives on Politics* 8, no. 4 (2010): 1101–6.

70. Miller, "Soldiers, Scholars, and Spies," 696.

71. Miller, "Soldiers, Scholars, and Spies," 696.

72. Michał Pawiński, "Going Beyond Human Terrain System: Exploring Ethical Dilemmas," *Journal of Military Ethics* 17, nos. 2–3 (2018): 122–39.

73. Peter A. Clark, "Medical Ethics at Guantanamo Bay and Abu Ghraib: The Problem of Dual Loyalty," *Journal of Law, Medicine & Ethics* 34, no. 3 (2006): 570–80.

74. Liam F. Gearon and Scott Parsons, "Research Ethics in the Securitised University," *Journal of Academic Ethics* 17 (2019): 75.

75. American Association of University Professors, "1940 Statement of Principles on Academic Freedom and Tenure: With 1970 Interpretive Comments," https://www .aaup.org/file/1940%20Statement.pdf.

76. Loch K. Johnson, "Spies and Scholars in the United States: Winds of Ambivalence in the Groves of Academe," *Intelligence and National Security* 34, no. 1 (2019): 17.

77. See, for example, some of the responses recorded by Loch K. Johnson and Alison M. Shelton, "Thoughts on the State of Intelligence Studies: A Survey Report," *Intelligence and National Security* 28, no. 1 (2013): 109–20.

78. Greg Miller, "The Intelligence Coup of the Century," *Washington Post*, February 11, 2020.

79. See Richard J. Aldrich, Peter F. Müller, David Ridd, and Erich Schmidt-Eenboom, "Operation Rubicon: Sixty Years of German-American Success in Signals Intelligence," *Intelligence and National Security* 35, no. 5 (2020): 603–7. See also Melina J. Dobson, "Operation Rubicon: Germany as an Intelligence 'Great Power'?," *Intelligence and National Security* 35, no. 5 (2020): 608–22; Sarah Mainwaring, "Division D: Operation Rubicon and the CIA's Secret SIGINT Empire," *Intelligence and National Security* 35, no. 5 (2020): 623–40; Jason Dymydiuk, "Rubicon and Revelation: The Curious Robustness of the 'Secret' CIA-BND Operation with Crypto AG," *Intelligence and National Security* 35, no. 5 (2020): 641–58.

Bibliography

Académie du renseignement. "L'académie du renseignement." http://www.academie
-renseignement.gouv.fr/academie.html.

Academy of the Social Sciences in Australia Inc. *Social Science Research and Intelligence in Australia.* September 2019. https://socialsciences.org.au/publications
/social-science-research-intelligence-in-australia.

Acharya, Amitav. "Engagement or Entrapment? Scholarship and Policymaking on Asian Regionalism." *International Studies Review* 13, no. 1 (2011): 12–17.

Agrell, Wilhelm, and Gregory F. Treverton. *National Intelligence and Science: Beyond the Great Divide in Analysis and Policy.* New York: Oxford University Press, 2014.

Aldrich, Richard J. "Whitehall and the Iraq War: The UK's Four Intelligence Enquiries." *Irish Studies in International Affairs* 16 (2005): 73–88.

Aldrich, Richard J., Peter F. Müller, David Ridd, and Erich Schmidt-Eenboom. "Operation Rubicon: Sixty Years of German-American Success in Signals Intelligence." *Intelligence and National Security* 35, no. 5 (2020): 603–7.

Alem, Jean-Pierre. *L'Espionnage et le Contre-Espionnage.* Paris: Presses Universitaires de France, 1980.

American Association of University Professors. "1940 Statement of Principles on Academic Freedom and Tenure: With 1970 Interpretive Comments." https://www
.aaup.org/file/1940%20Statement.pdf.

American Public University System. "Catalog—2002." Richard G. Trefry Archives. Accessed July 2, 2021. https://exhibit.apus.edu/items/show/1121.

Anderson, Janna, and Lee Rainie. "Artificial Intelligence and the Future of Humans." Pew Research Center, December 10, 2018. https://www.pewresearch.org/internet
/2018/12/10/artificial-intelligence-and-the-future-of-humans.

Andregg, Michael M. *Intelligence Ethics: The Definitive Work of 2007.* Center for the Study of Intelligence and Wisdom. St. Paul, MN: Ground Zero Publishing, 2007.

Andrew, Christopher. *The Defence of the Realm: The Authorized History of MI5.* London: Allen Lane, 2009.

———. "Intelligence, International Relations and 'Under-Theorisation.'" *Intelligence and National Security* 19, no. 2 (2004): 170–84.

———. *The Secret World: A History of Intelligence.* London: Allen Lane, 2018.

Andrew, Christopher, and David Dilks, eds. *The Missing Dimension: Governments and Intelligence Communities in the Twentieth Century.* London: Macmillan, 1984.

Arcos, Rubén. "Academics as Strategic Stakeholders of Intelligence Organizations: A View from Spain." *International Journal of Intelligence and CounterIntelligence* 26, no. 2 (2013): 332–46.

———. "Reservas de Inteligencia." In *Conceptos Fundamentales de Inteligencia*, edited by Antonio M. Díaz Fernández, 329–34. Valencia: Tirant lo Blanch, 2016.

———. "Understanding the Relationships between Academia and National Security Intelligence in the European Context." In *The Routledge International Handbook of Universities, Security and Intelligence Studies*, edited by Liam Francis Gearon, 156–67. New York: Routledge, 2020.

Arcos, Rubén, and Joan Antón. "Reservas de Inteligencia: Hacia una Comunidad Ampliada de Inteligencia." *Inteligencia y Seguridad: Revista de Análisis y Prospectiva* 8 (2010): 11–38.

Arcos, Rubén, and José-Miguel Palacios. "EU INTCEN: A Transnational European Culture of Intelligence Analysis?" *Intelligence and National Security* 35, no. 1 (2020): 72–94.

Arcos, Rubén, Mark Phythian, and Stephen Marrin. "Building the Intelligence Studies Community: The Role of International Conferences and Events." Paper presented at the Fifty-Ninth Annual Convention of the International Studies Association, San Francisco, CA, April 4–7, 2018.

Aronoff, Myron J. *The Spy Novels of John le Carré: Balancing Ethics and Politics.* New York: Palgrave Macmillan, 1999.

Artner, Stephen, Richard S. Girven, and James B. Bruce. "Assessing the Value of Structured Analytic Techniques in the U.S. Intelligence Community." RAND Corporation, 2016.

Association Français de Droit de la Sécurité et de la Défense. "Actualités." http://www.afdsd.fr.

Association Pour les Études Sur la Guerre et la Stratégie. "Renseignement." http://www.aeges.fr/groupes-travail/gt-renseignement.

Australian Institute of Professional Intelligence Officers. *AIPIO Journal.* Accessed January 11, 2021. https://www.aipio.asn.au/aipio-journal.

Australian Qualifications Framework. "What Is the AQF?" Accessed 2020. https://www.aqf.edu.au/what-is-the-aqf.

Bacheş-Torres, Daniela, and Efren Torres-Bacheş. "Intelligence Studies: An Ironic Take of Politicization, Failure of Imagination, Lack of Collaboration and Exclusion." *Journal of European and American Intelligence Studies* 1, no. 1 (2018): 15–24.

Bailey, Christopher, and Susan M. Galich. "Codes of Ethics: The Intelligence Community." *International Journal of Intelligence Ethics* 3, no. 2 (Fall/Winter 2012): 77–99.

Barna, Cristian. "From Profession to Discipline: The Development of Romanian Intelligence Studies." *International Journal of Intelligence and CounterIntelligence* 27, no. 4 (2014): 772–84. https://doi.org/10.1080/08850607.2014.924817.

Barnes, Alan. "Making Intelligence Analysis More Intelligent: Using Numeric Probabilities." *Intelligence and National Security* 31, no. 3 (2016): 327–44.

Barreiro, Katalina. *Angostura: La inteligencia, el espejo oculto de la seguridad.* Quito, Ecuador: Instituto de Altos Estudios Nacionales, 2018.

Bartolomé, Mariano, et al. *Inteligencia Estratégica Contemporánea.* Ecuador: Universidad de las Fuerzas Armadas de Ecuador (ESPE), 2016. http://repositorio.espe .edu.ec/bitstream/21000/11692/1/INTELIGENICIA%20ESTRATEGICA.pdf.

Bean, Hamilton. "Intelligence Theory from the Margins: Questions Ignored and Debates Not Had." *Intelligence and National Security* 33, no. 4 (2018): 527–40. https://doi.org/10.1080/02684527.2018.1452544.

Bean, Hamilton, and Mia Fischer. "Queering Intelligence Studies." *Intelligence and National Security* 36, no. 4 (2021): 584–98.

Bearden, Milton, and James Risen. *The Main Enemy.* New York: Random House, 2003.

Beck, Catherine A. "Bureau of Intelligence and Research and Washington Politics." MA thesis, University of Georgia, 2005. https://getd.libs.uga.edu/pdfs/beck _catherine_a_200505_ma.pdf.

Behn, Robert D. "Why Measure Performance? Different Purposes Require Different Measures." *Public Administration Review* 63, no. 5 (2003): 586–606.

Bessarabova, Elena, Cameron W. Piercy, Shawn King, Cindy Vincent, Norah E. Dunbar, Judee K. Burgoon, Claude H. Miller, et al. "Mitigating Bias Blind Spot via a Serious Video Game." *Computers in Human Behavior* 62 (2016): 452–66.

Betts, Richard K. *The Enemies of Intelligence: Knowledge and Power in American National Security.* New York: Columbia University Press, 2007.

Bew, John. *Realpolitik: A History.* Oxford: Oxford University Press, 2016.

Bigo, Didier. "Shared Secrecy in a Digital Age and a Transnational World." *Intelligence and National Security* 34, no. 3 (2019): 379–94.

Blackett Review of High Impact Low Probability Risks (London: Government Office for Science, 2011).

Boimvaser, Gerardo. *Los sospechosos de siempre.* Argentina: Planeta, 2000.

Booth, Ken. "Discussion: A Reply to Wallace." *Review of International Studies* 23, no. 3 (1997): 371–77.

Born, Hans, and Lan Leigh. *Hacia un control democrático de las actividades de inteligencia: Estándares legales y métodos de supervisión.* Switzerland: DCAF-EOS, 2005.

Box, G. E. P. "Robustness in the Strategy of Scientific Model Building." In *Robustness in Statistics*, edited by Robert L. Launer and Graham N. Wilkinson, 201–36. New York: Academic Press, 1979.

Brito Gonçalves, Joanisval, Ricardo Zonato Esteves, and Marcus Vinicius Reis. "Brasil, 2020 A Inteligência no Governo Jair Bolsonaro: O imperativo da mudança." *Frumentarius, Blog de Joanisval Gonçalves*, 2020. https://iepecdg.com.br/wp-content/uploads/2020/08/INTELIGENCIA-NO-GOVERNO-BOLSONARO-FRUMENTARIUS.pdf.

Bromiley, Matt. "Effectively Addressing Advanced Threats." SANS, July 2019.

Bruneau, Thomas. *Controlling Intelligence in New Democracies in Strategic Intelligence*. Roxbury, 2004.

Budescu, David V., Han-Hui Por, Stephen B. Broomell, and Michael Smithson. "The Interpretation of IPCC Probabilistic Statements around the World." *Nature Climate Change* 4 (2014): 508–12.

Butler, Lord. *Review of Intelligence on Weapons of Mass Destruction: Report of a Committee of Privy Counsellors.* HC 898. London: Her Majesty's Stationery Office, 2004.

Calhoun, Craig. "Social Science Research and Military Agendas: Safe Distance or Bridging a Troubling Divide?" *Perspectives on Politics* 8, no. 4 (2010): 1101–6.

Callum, Robert. "The Case for Cultural Diversity in the Intelligence Community." *International Journal of Intelligence and CounterIntelligence* 14, no. 1 (2001): 25–48.

Carew Hunt, R. N. *The Theory and Practice of Communism.* London: Penguin, 1966.

Carrera, Patricio, and Héctor Rojas. "Gobierno despide a 13 analistas de la ANI." La Tercera de Chile, May 4, 2010. https://www.latercera.com/noticia/gobierno-despide-a-13-analistas-de-la-ani.

Catholic University Newsletter. "The Humanity of Espionage." March 6, 2019.

Center for Ethics and the Rule of Law at the University of Pennsylvania. *Report on the Department of Justice and the Rule of Law.* October 12, 2020. https://www.law.upenn.edu/live/files/10900-report-on-the-doj-and-the-rule-of-law.

Chang, Welton, Elissabeth Berdini, David R. Mandel, and Philip E. Tetlock. "Restructuring Structured Analytic Techniques in Intelligence." *Intelligence and National Security* 33, no. 3 (2018): 337–56.

Chao Rong Phua, Charles. "Towards One-Ness of International Relations and Intelligence 2028." *Journal of European and American Intelligence Studies* 1, no. 1 (2018): 319–24.

Chapleau, Philippe. "Un Master Géopolitique-Geoint, à la rentrée, à Sorbonne Université." *Lignes de défense* (blog), June 5, 2020. http://lignesdedefense.blogs.ouest-france.fr/archive/2020/06/04/master-geopolitique-geoint-a-la-rentree-a-sorbonne-universit-21217.html.

Chomsky, Noam. "The Responsibility of the Intellectuals." *New York Review of Books*, February 23, 1967. https://chomsky.info/19670223.

Chopin, Olivier. "Intelligence Reform and the Transformation of the State: The End of a French Exception." *Journal of Strategic Studies* 40, no. 4 (2017): 532–53.

CIA Inspector General's Report on the Aldrich H. Ames Case. "Unclassified Abstract—Preface to the Report from the I.G." https://apps.dtic.mil/dtic/tr/fulltext/u2/a311780.pdf.

Clark, Peter A. "Medical Ethics at Guantanamo Bay and Abu Ghraib: The Problem of Dual Loyalty." *Journal of Law, Medicine & Ethics* 34, no. 3 (2006): 570–80.

Clark, Robert M. *Intelligence Analysis: A Target-Centric Approach.* Washington, DC: CQ Press, 2010.

Clauser, Jerome K., and Sandra M. Weir. *Intelligence Research Methodology: An Introduction to Techniques and Procedures for Conducting Research in Defense Intelligence.* Washington, DC: Defense Intelligence School, 1976.

Clemis, Martin G. "Crafting Non-kinetic Warfare: The Academic-Military Nexus in US Counterinsurgency Doctrine." *Small Wars & Insurgencies* 20, no. 1 (2009): 160–84.

Coordination Nationale du Renseignement et de la Lutte contre le Terrorisme. *La Stratégie Nationale du renseignement.* July 2019.

CORDIS. "Final Report Summary—RECOBIA (REduction of COgnitive BIAses in Intelligence Analysis)." November 26, 2015. https://cordis.europa.eu/project /id/285010/reporting/es.

Corvaja, Alessandro Scheffler, Brigita Jeraj, and Uwe M. Borghoff. "The Rise of Intelligence Studies: A Model for Germany." *Connections: The Quarterly Journal* 15, no. 1 (2016): 79–106.

Coulthart, Stephen. "From Laboratory to the WMD Commission: How Academic Research Influences Intelligence Agencies." *Intelligence and National Security* 34, no. 6 (2019): 818–32.

———. "Why Do Analysts Use Structured Analytic Techniques? An In-Depth Study of an American Intelligence Agency." *Intelligence and National Security* 31, no. 7 (2016): 933–48.

Coulthart, Stephen, and Matthew Crosston. "Terra Incognita: Mapping American Intelligence Education Curriculum." *Journal of Strategic Security* 8, no. 3 (2015): 46–68.

Crawley, Rhys, and Shannon Brandt Ford. "The Current State of Intelligence Studies." In *Intelligence and the Function of Government*, edited by Daniel Baldino and Rhys Crawley. Melbourne: Melbourne University Press, 2018.

Crossley, John N. "Unofficial Advice and Official Policy: Sir Maurice Oldfield and All Souls College, Oxford, 1978–9." *Intelligence and National Security* 35, no. 3 (2020): 424–37.

Crosston, Matthew. "Occam's Follies: Real and Imagined Biases Facing Intelligence Studies." *Journal of Strategic Security* 6, no. 3 (2013): 40–53.

Dapelo, Santiago. "Denuncian una purga contra los espías nombrados por Macri." *La Nación de Argentina*, February 15, 2020. https://www.lanacion.com.ar/politica /denuncian-purga-espias-nombrados-mauricio-macri-nid2334244.

Davies, Philip H. J., and Kristian C. Gustafson, eds. *Intelligence Elsewhere: Spies and Espionage Outside the Anglosphere.* Washington, DC: Georgetown University Press, 2013.

Davis, Jack. "The Kent-Kendall Debate of 1949." *Studies in Intelligence* 36, no. 5 (1992): 91–103.

———. "Sherman Kent and the Profession of Intelligence Analysis." Occasional Papers 1, no. 5, Sherman Kent Center for Intelligence Analysis, 2002. https://

www.cia.gov/static/aa47b490ac1c52c04c467a248c5cbace/Kent-Profession-Intel -Analysis.pdf.

Davydoff, Daniil. "How Intelligence Analysis Can Drive Corporate ROI." *Security Magazine*, July 1, 2018. https://www.securitymagazine.com/articles/89193-how -intelligence-analysis-can-drive-corporate-roi.

Decreto Supremo 363/1991. Crea el Consejo Coordinador de Seguridad Pública. Ministerio del Interior, Chile.

Decreto Supremo 4/1992. Modifica el Consejo Coordinador de Seguridad Pública. Ministerio del Interior, Chile.

de Marenches, Alexandre, and Christine Ockrent. *Dans le secret des princes.* Paris: Stock, 1986.

"Demissão de diretor da Abin é anunciada na CPMI." *Càmara Dos Diputaodos de Brasil*, July 13, 2005. https://www.camara.leg.br/noticias/68352-demissao-de -diretor-da-abin-e-anunciada-na-cpmi.

Denécé, Eric, and Gérald Arboit. "The Development of Intelligence Studies in France." *African Yearbook of Rhetoric* 3, no. 1 (2012): 23–35.

Department of Prime Minister and Cabinet. "Statement on Malicious Cyber Activity against Australian Networks." June 19, 2020. https://www.pm.gov.au/media /statement-malicious-cyber-activity-against-australian-networks.

Desch, Michael C. *Cult of the Irrelevant: The Waning Influence of Social Science on National Security.* Princeton, NJ: Princeton University Press, 2019.

Deuve, Jean. *La Guerre secrète au Laos contre les communistes.* Paris: L'Harmattan, 1995.

Devine, Michael. "CIA Ethics Education: Background and Perspective." Congressional Research Service, June 11, 2018. https://fas.org/sgp/crs/intel/IF10906.pdf.

de Werd, Peter. *US Intelligence and Al Qaeda: Analysis by Contrasting Narratives.* Edinburgh: Edinburgh University Press, 2020.

Dewerpe, Alain. *Espion: Une anthropologie historique du Secret d'Etat contemporain.* Paris: Gallimard, 1994.

Dhami, Mandeep K., and David R. Mandel. "Words or Numbers? Communicating Probability in Intelligence Analysis." *American Psychologist* 76, no. 3 (2020): 549–60.

Dhami, Mandeep K., David R. Mandel, Barbara A. Mellers, and Philip E. Tetlock. "Improving Intelligence Analysis with Decision Science." *Perspectives on Psychological Science* 106, no. 6 (2015): 753–57.

Dhami, Mandeep K., Ian K. Belton, and David R. Mandel. "The 'Analysis of Competing Hypotheses' in Intelligence Analysis." *Applied Cognitive Psychology* 33, no. 6 (2019): 1080–90.

Díaz, Antonio, ed. *Conceptos Fundamentales de Inteligencia.* Valencia: Tirant lo Blanch, 2016.

Díaz Fernández, Antonio. "El Papel de la Comunidad de Inteligencia en la Toma de Decisiones de la Política Exterior y de Seguridad de España." Working Paper 3, Fundación Alternativas, Opex, 2006. https://www.fundacionalternativas. org/observatorio-de-politica-exterior-opex/documentos/documentos-de-trabajo

/el-papel-de-la-comunidad-de-inteligencia-en-la-toma-de-decisiones-de-la-polit
ica-exterior-y-de-seguridad-de-espana.

Dobson, Melina J. "Operation Rubicon: Germany as an Intelligence 'Great Power'?" *Intelligence and National Security* 35, no. 5 (2020): 608–22.

Dokos, Thonos. "The Ukraine Crisis: A Story of Misperceptions, Miscalculations & Mismanagement; Is There Still Time to Avoid Permanent Damage to the European Security Order?" *Eliamep Thesis*, December 2014. https://www.files.ethz.ch /isn/186245/ELIAMEP-Thesis-1-2014_Th.Dokos-1.pdf.

Dorronsoro, Gilles. "Quand le CNRS met en danger les chercheurs." *AOC*, June 21, 2018. https://aoc.media/opinion/2018/06/21/cnrs-met-danger-chercheurs.

Dover, Robert. "Adding Value to the Intelligence Community: What Role for Expert External Advice?" *Intelligence and National Security* 35, no. 6 (2020): 852–69.

Dover, Robert, and Michael S. Goodman. "Between Lucky Jim and George Smiley: The Public Role of Intelligence Scholars." In *The Routledge International Handbook of Universities, Security and Intelligence Studies*, edited by Liam Francis Gearon, 343–51. Abingdon: Routledge, 2020.

———. "Impactful Scholarship in Intelligence: A Public Policy Challenge." *British Politics* 13, no. 3 (2018): 374–91.

Drumhiller, Nicole K., and Kate Brannum. "Women in Global Security and Intelligence." *Journal of European and American Intelligence Studies* 1, no. 1 (2018): 303–9.

Drumhiller, Nicole, Mark Phythian, and Rubén Arcos. "IntelHub." https://www.apus .edu/academic-community/intelhub/index.

Dujmović, Nicholas. "Colleges Must Be Intelligent about Intelligence Studies." *Washington Post*, December 30, 2016. https://www.washingtonpost.com/news /grade-point/wp/2016/12/30/colleges-must-be-intelligent-about-intelligence-studies.

———. "Elegy of Slashes: A Review of *Legacy of Ashes: The History of the CIA*." *Studies in Intelligence* 51, no. 3 (2007): 33–43.

———. "Hollywood: Don't You Go Disrespectin' My Culture; The Good Shepherd versus Real CIA History." *Intelligence and National Security* 23, no. 1 (2008): 25–41.

———. "Less Is More, and More Professional: Reflections on Building an 'Ideal' Intelligence Program." *Intelligence and National Security* 32, no. 7 (2017): 935–43.

Dulles, Allen W. *The Craft of Intelligence*. New York: Harper & Row, 1963.

Dymydiuk, Jason. "Rubicon and Revelation: The Curious Robustness of the 'Secret' CIA-BND Operation with Crypto AG." *Intelligence and National Security* 35, no. 5 (2020): 641–58.

Edwards, Jo. *Impact Review: A Review of the Impact of CREST Research Projects.* Lucidity Solutions, 2019. https://crestresearch.ac.uk/site/assets/files/3427/impact -report-19-028-03.pdf.

Edwards, Ward. "Conservatism in Human Information Processing." In *Formal Representation of Human Judgment*, edited by Benjamin Kleinmuntz, 17–52. New York: Wiley, 1968.

"El DAS dejará de existir para dar paso a la Agencia Nacional de Inteligencia." *Semana de Colombia*, October 30, 2011. https://www.semana.com/politica/articulo/el-das-deja-existir-para-dar-paso-agencia-nacional-inteligencia/248740-3.

Engel, Pascal. "Alain Dewerpe et l'histoire dormante du secret." *L'Atelier du Centre de Recherches Historiques* 17 (2017). https://doi.org/10.4000/acrh.7996.

European Centre of Excellence for Countering Hybrid Threats. "Hybrid CoE." https://www.hybridcoe.fi.

European Commission. "The EU's Cybersecurity Strategy for the Digital Decade." Joint Communication to the European Parliament and the Council, December 16, 2020. https://eur-lex.europa.eu/legal-content/EN/TXT/PDF/?uri=CELEX:52020JC0018&from=EN.

———. "Joint Framework on Countering Hybrid Threats: A European Response." Joint Communication to the European Parliament and the Council, April 6, 2016. https://eur-lex.europa.eu/legal-content/EN/TXT/?uri=CELEX%3A52016JC0018.

European External Action Service (EEAS). "2011 Discharge to the EEAS." Answers by the High Representative/Vice President Catherine Ashton to the Written Questions of the Committee on Budgetary Control, January 1, 2013. https://www.europarl.europa.eu/meetdocs/2009_2014/documents/cont/dv/eeasreplies_/eeasreplies_en.pdf.

Evans, Rob, and Paul Lewis. "Undercover Police Had Children with Activists." *Guardian*, January 12, 2012. https://www.theguardian.com/uk/2012/jan/20/undercover-police-children-activists.

Fägersten, Björn. "Intelligence and Decision-Making within the Common Foreign and Security Policy." Swedish Institute for European Policy Studies, *European Policy Analysis* 22 (2015). https://www.sieps.se/en/publications/2015/intelligence-and-decision-making-within-the-common-foreign-and-security-policy-201522epa.

Faligot, Roget, and Pascal Krop. *La Piscine.* Paris: Seuil, 1985.

Federal Emergency Management Agency. National Incident Management System. 2017, 24–34.

Feng, Emily. "FBI Urges Universities to Monitor Some Chinese Students and Scholars in the US." NPR, June 28, 2019. https://www.npr.org/2019/06/28/728659124/fbi-urges-universities-to-monitor-some-chinese-students-and-scholars-in-the-u-s?t=1623746295539.

Ferris, John. *Behind the Enigma: The Authorised History of GCHQ, Britain's Secret Cyber-Intelligence Agency.* London: Bloomsbury, 2020.

Fewster, Kerryn, and Peter O'Connor. "Embracing Ambiguity in the Workplace." Queensland University of Technology, May 2017. https://eprints.qut.edu.au/108255/1/Industry%20Report%20TOA.pdf.

Fingar, Thomas. *Reducing Uncertainty: Intelligence Analysis and National Security.* Palo Alto, CA: Stanford University Press, 2011.

Firehock, Raymond B., John A. Gentry, Julia W. Rogers, and James M. Simon Jr. "Negotiating the Review Process: A CIA Guide to Intelligence Analysis, 1970." *Intelligence and National Security* 33, no. 5 (2018): 774–83.

Fischer, Robert J., Edward Halibozek, and Gion Green. *Introduction to Security*. 8th ed. Burlington, MA: Elsevier, 2008.

Fisher, Rebecca, Rob Johnston, and Peter Clement. "Is Intelligence Analysis a Discipline?" In *Analyzing Intelligence: National Security Practitioners' Perspectives*, edited by Roger Z. George and James B. Bruce, 57–77. Washington, DC: Georgetown University Press, 2014.

Fitsanakis, Joseph. "Norwegian Spy Service Seeks Right to Break Law during Espionage Operations." IntelNews.org, November 21, 2018. https://intelnews.org /2018/11/21/01-2441.

FLACSO. *Reporte del sector seguridad en América Latina y el Caribe*. Chile, 2007.

Foccart, Jacques. *Journal de l'Elysée. Tome 1. Tous les Soirs Avec de Gaulle (1965–1967)*. Paris: Fayard, 1995.

Folsom, Suzanne, and Robert Garretson. "The Continuing Danger of Academic Espionage." *Inside Higher Ed*, May 5, 2020. https://www.insidehighered.com /views/2020/05/05/threat-academic-espionage-should-not-be-overlooked-even -time-pandemic-opinion.

Forcade, Olivier. *La République Secrète: Histoire des Services Spéciaux français de 1918 à 1939*. Paris: Nouveau Monde, 2008.

Forcade, Olivier, and Bertrand Warusfel, eds. *Le droit du renseignement*. Paris: La Documentation Française, 2020.

Forcade, Olivier, and Maurice Vaïsse, eds. *Le Renseignement au début de la Guerre Froide, 1945–1955*. Paris: La Documentation Française, 2016.

Freedman, Lawrence. "Academics and Policy-Making: Rules of Engagement." *Journal of Strategic Studies* 40, nos. 1–2 (2017): 263–68.

———. "Review Essay: Cult of the Irrelevant." *Journal of Strategic Studies* 42, no. 7 (2019): 1027–37.

Frerichs, Rebecca L., and Stephen R. Di Rienzo. "Establishing a Framework for Intelligence Education and Training." *Joint Force Quarterly* 62 (2011): 68–73.

Friedman, Jeffrey A. *War and Chance: Assessing Uncertainty in International Politics*. New York: Oxford University Press, 2019.

Friedman, Jeffrey A., and Richard Zeckhauser. "Assessing Uncertainty in Intelligence." *Intelligence and National Security* 27, no. 6 (2012): 824–47.

Fry, Michael G., and Miles Hochstein. "Epistemic Communities: Intelligence Studies and International Relations." *Intelligence and National Security* 8, no. 3 (1993): 14–28. https://doi.org/10.1080/02684529308432212.

Fussell, Christopher, Trevor Hough, and Matthew Pedersen. "What Makes Fusion Cells Effective?" MSc thesis, Naval Postgraduate School, Monterey, CA, 2009. https://apps.dtic.mil/dtic/tr/fulltext/u2/a514114.pdf.

Gaillard, Philippe. *Foccart Parle*. Paris: Fayard, 1995.

Gearon, Liam Francis, ed. *Routledge International Handbook of Universities, Security and Intelligence Studies*. New York: Routledge, 2020.

Gearon, Liam F., and Scott Parsons. "Research Ethics in the Securitised University." *Journal of Academic Ethics* 17 (2019): 73–93.

Gentry, John A., ed. "An INS Special Forum: US Intelligence Officers' Involvement in Political Activities in the Trump Era." *Intelligence and National Security* 35, no. 1 (2020): 1–19.

———. "Intelligence in War: How Important Is It? How Do We Know?" *Intelligence and National Security* 34, no. 6 (2019): 833–50.

———. "'Truth' as a Tool of the Politicization of Intelligence." *International Journal of Intelligence and CounterIntelligence* 32, no. 2 (2019): 217–47.

Gentry, John A., and Joseph S. Gordon. *Strategic Warning Intelligence: History, Challenges, and Prospects.* Washington, DC: Georgetown University Press, 2019.

George, Roger Z. *Intelligence in the National Security Enterprise.* Washington, DC: Georgetown University Press, 2020.

George, Roger Z., and James B. Bruce, eds. *Analyzing Intelligence: National Security Practitioners' Perspectives.* Washington, DC: Georgetown University Press, 2014.

Giannopoulos, Georgios, Hanna Smith, and Marianthi Theocharidou, eds. *The Landscape of Hybrid Threats: A Conceptual Model.* EUR 30585 EN. Luxembourg: Publications Office of the European Union, 2021.

Gill, Peter. "Democratic and Parliamentary Accountability of Intelligence Services after September 11th." Working Paper No. 103. Geneva Centre for the Democratic Control of Armed Forces (DCAF), 2003. https://warwick.ac.uk/fac/soc/pais/people/aldrich/vigilant/gill_103.pdf.

Gill, Peter, and Mark Phythian. *Intelligence in an Insecure World.* Cambridge: Polity Press, 2006.

———. "What Is Intelligence Studies?" *The International Journal of Intelligence, Security, and Public Affairs* 18, no. 1 (2016): 5–19.

Glasgow, Ralph I. "Planning and Intelligence." *Army Transportation Journal* 4, no. 3 (1948): 14–59. Accessed May 4, 2021. http://www.jstor.org/stable/44094752.

Glees, Anthony. "The Future of Intelligence Studies." Supplement, *Journal of Strategic Security* 6, no. 3 (2013): 124–27. https://doi.org/10.5038/1944-0472.6.3S.13.

Goldman, Jan. *Ethics of Spying.* Vol. 2. Lanham: Rowman & Littlefield, 2010.

———. "Foreword to Previous Edition." In *Handbook of Warning Intelligence: Complete and Declassified Edition*, edited by Cynthia Grabo with Jan Goldman, xi–xviii. Lanham, MD: Rowman & Littlefield, 2015.

Gómez de la Torre, Andrés. "Institucionalización y crisis de inteligencia: Perú en el contexto andino." In *Los macro y micro desafíos de la seguridad en democracia*, edited by Bertha García and José Ugarte. Centro de Publicaciones Pontificia Universidad Católica de Ecuador. Ecuador, 2018.

———. "¿Quién vigilará a nuestros vigilantes? (reinventando a Juvenal ante el foro de Roma, en Perú y Sudamérica)." In *Inteligencia y Seguridad: Revista de análisis y prospectiva*, no. 5. Universidad Rey Juan Carlos (Cátedra Servicios de Inteligencia y Sistemas democráticos) and Universidad Carlos III de Madrid (Instituto Juan Velásquez de Velasco de Investigación para la Seguridad y Defensa), Spain, 2008/2009.

———. "Servicios de Inteligencia y Democracia en América Del Sur: ¿Hacia una Segunda Generación de Reformas Normativas?" RESDAL, 2009. http://www.resdal.org/producciones-miembros/trabajo-academico-gomez.pdf.

Goodman, Michael S. *The Official History of the Joint Intelligence Committee*. Vol. 1, *From the Approach of the Second World War to the Suez Crisis*. Abingdon: Routledge, 2014.

Goodman, Michael S., and David Omand. "What Analysts Need to Understand: The King's Intelligence Studies Program." *Studies in Intelligence* 52, no. 4 (2008): 1–12. https://www.cia.gov/resources/csi/studies-in-intelligence/volume-52-no-4/what -analysts-need-to-understand-the-kings-intelligence-studies-program.

Goslin, Charles E. *Understanding Personal Security and Risk: A Guide for Business Travelers*. Boca Raton, FL: CRC Press, 2017.

"Governo faz mudanças em setor de Inteligência." Estado de Minas de Brasil, August 8, 2020. https://istoe.com.br/Governo-faz-mudancas-em-setor-de-inteligencia.

Grabo, Cynthia, and Jan Goldman. *Handbook of Warning Intelligence: Complete and Declassified Edition*. Lanham, MD: Rowman & Littlefield, 2015.

Greenberg, Andy. "The Untold Story of NotPetya, the Most Devastating Cyberattack in History." *Wired*, August 22, 2018. https://www.wired.com/story/notpetya -cyberattack-ukraine-russia-code-crashed-the-world.

Groysberg, Boris, Jeremiah Lee, Jesse Price, and J. Yo-Jud Cheng. "The Leader's Guide to Corporate Culture." *Harvard Business Review*, January–February 2018. https://hbr.org/2018/01/the-leaders-guide-to-corporate-culture.

Guisnel, Jean. *Histoire secrète de la DGSE. Au cœur du véritable bureau des légendes*. Paris: Robert Laffont, 2019.

Guisnel, Jean, and Bernard Violet. *Services secrets: Les services de renseignement sous François Mitterrand*. Paris: La Découverte, 1988.

Guisnel, Jean, Roger Faligot, and Rémi Kauffer. *Histoire politique des services secrets français: De la Seconde Guerre mondiale à nos jours*. Paris: La Découverte, 2013.

Gusterson, Hugh. "Project Minerva and the Militarization of Anthropology." *Radical Teacher* 86 (2009): 4–16.

Haas, Peter M. "Introduction: Epistemic Communities and International Policy Coordination." *International Organization* 46, no. 1 (1992): 1–35.

Hamm, Mark S. "'High Crimes and Misdemeanors': George W. Bush and the Sins of Abu Ghraib." *Crime, Media, Culture* 3, no. 3 (2007): 259–84.

Handel, Michael I., ed. *Intelligence and Military Operations*. Portland, OR: Frank Cass, 1990.

———. "Leaders and Intelligence." *Intelligence and National Security* 3, no. 3 (1988): 3–39.

Harari, Yuval Noah. *Sapiens: A Brief History of Humankind*. New York: Harper, 2014.

Harrison, Mark, Patrick F. Walsh, Shane Lysons-Smith, David Truong, Catherine Horan, and Ramzi Jabbour. "Tradecraft to Standards: Moving Criminal Intelligence Practice to a Profession through the Development of a Criminal Intelligence Training and Development Continuum." *Policing* 14, no. 2 (June 2020): 312–24.

Hastedt, Glenn P. "Towards the Comparative Study of Intelligence." *Journal of Conflict Studies* 11, no. 3 (1991): 55–72.

Hayden, Michael V. *Playing to the Edge: American Intelligence in the Age of Terror.* New York: Penguin, 2016.

Hayez, Philippe. "*'Renseignement'*: The New French Intelligence Policy." *International Journal of Intelligence and CounterIntelligence* 23, no. 3 (2010): 474–86.

Hedley, John. "Twenty Years of Officers in Residence." *Studies in Intelligence* 49, no. 4 (2005): 31–39.

Heibel, Robert J. "Catalyst and Enabler." *Liberal Studies at Georgetown* 3, no. 2 (2005): 13–15.

Helms, Richard, with William Hood. *A Look over My Shoulder: A Life in the Central Intelligence Agency.* New York: Random House, 2003.

Hendrickson, Noel. "Critical Thinking in Intelligence Analysis." *International Journal of Intelligence and CounterIntelligence* 21, no. 4 (2008): 679–93.

Herman, Michael. *Intelligence Power in Peace and War.* Cambridge: Cambridge University Press, 1996.

———. *Intelligence Services in the Information Age: Theory and Practice.* London: Frank Cass, 2001.

Herrero de Castro, Rubén. "La influencia de variables políticas y psicológicas en los procesos de información y decisión." In *Inteligencia y Seguridad: Revista de análisis y prospectiva*, no. 2. Universidad Rey Juan Carlos (Cátedra Servicios de Inteligencia y Sistemas democráticos) and Universidad Carlos III de Madrid (Instituto Juan Velázquez de Velasco de Investigación para la Seguridad y Defensa), Spain, 2007.

Heuer, Richards J., Jr. "Adapting Academic Methods and Models to Government Needs." In *Quantitative Approaches to Political Intelligence: The CIA Experience*, edited by Richards J. Heuer Jr. Boulder, CO: Westview Press, 1978.

———. "The Evolution of Structured Analytic Techniques." Presentation to the National Academy of Sciences, Washington, DC, December 8, 2009. https://www.e-education.psu.edu/geog885/sites/www.e-education.psu.edu.geog885/files/file/Evolution_SAT_Heuer.pdf.

———. *Psychology of Intelligence Analysis.* Washington, DC: Center for the Study of Intelligence, 1999.

———, ed. *Quantitative Approaches to Political Intelligence: The CIA Experience.* New York: Routledge, 1978.

Heuer, Richards J., Jr., and Randolph H. Pherson. *Structured Analytic Techniques for Intelligence Analysis.* Washington, DC: CQ Press, 2014.

Hewitt, Steve. *Spying 101: The RCMP's Secret Activities at Canadian Universities, 1917–1997.* Toronto: University of Toronto Press, 2002.

Hill, Christopher. "Academic International Relations: The Siren Song of Policy Relevance." In *The Two Worlds of International Relations: Academics, Practitioners and the Trade in Ideas*, edited by Christopher Hill and Pamela Beshoff. London: Routledge, 1994.

Hill, Christopher, and Pamela Beshoff, eds. *The Two Worlds of International Relations: Academics, Practitioners and the Trade in Ideas.* London: Routledge, 1994.

Hilsman, Roger. *Strategic Intelligence and National Decisions.* Glencoe, IL: Free Press, 1956.

Hilsman, Roger, Jr. "Intelligence and Policy-Making in Foreign Affairs." *World Politics* 5, no. 1 (October 1952): 1–45. https://doi.org/10.2307/2009086.

Hinsley, F. H., et al. *British Intelligence in the Second World War*. 5 vols. London: HMSO, 1979–1990.

Hinton, Peter. "The 'Thailand Controversy' Revisited." *Australian Journal of Anthropology* 13, no. 2 (2002): 155–77.

Ho, Emily, David V. Budescu, Mandeep K. Dhami, and David R. Mandel. "Improving the Communication of Uncertainty in Climate Science and Intelligence Analysis." *Behavioral Science & Policy* 1, no. 2 (2015): 43–55.

Holder, Eric H. Attorney General Memorandum. April 10, 2015. https://www.justice .gov/file/1047646/download.

Holeindre, Jean-Vincent, and Benjamin Oudet. "Intelligence Studies in France: History, Structure and Proposals." IRSEM Research Note 67, November 27, 2018, 4–5.

Hood, Christopher. *The Blame Game: Spin, Bureaucracy, and Self-Preservation in Government*. Princeton, NJ: Princeton University Press, 2011.

Hubbard, Douglas W. *The Failure of Risk Management: Why It's Broken and How to Fix It*. Hoboken, NJ: Wiley, 2009.

Hughes, Gwilym. "The Oxford Intelligence Group." In *The Routledge International Handbook of Universities, Security and Intelligence Studies*, edited by Liam Francis Gearon, 231–42. Abingdon: Routledge, 2020.

Huntington, Samuel. *El Soldado y el Estado*. Argentina: Grupo Editor Latinoamericano, 1995.

Hyvönen, Ari-Elmeri, Tapio Juntunen, Harri Mikkola, Juha Käpylä, Harri Gustafsberg, Markku Nyman, Tiina Rättilä, Sirpa Virta, and Johanna Liljeroos. *Kokonaisresilienssi ja turvallisuus: Tasot, prosessit ja arviointi*. Finland: Prime Minister's Office, 2019. https://julkaisut.valtioneuvosto.fi/bitstream/handle/10024/161358/17 -2019-Kokonaisresilienssi%20ja%20turvallisuus.pdf.

Independent Surveillance Review. *A Democratic Licence to Operate: Report of the Independent Surveillance Review*. London: Royal United Services Institute (RUSI), 2015. https://rusi.org/sites/default/files/20150714_whr_2-15_a_democratic _licence_to_operate.pdf.

Institut de Recherche Stratégique de l'Ecole Militaire. "La Lettre de l'IRSEM." July–September 2020. https://www.irsem.fr/media/5-publications/la-lettre/lettre -irsem-07-08-09-2020.pdf.

Intelligence Online. "La bataille des master 'renseignement' est lancée." September 14, 2020. https://www.intelligenceonline.fr/renseignement-d-etat/2020/09/14 /la-bataille-des-masters-renseignement-est-lancee,109606432-art.

———. "La DGSI met les bouchées doubles sur les universités." September 9, 2020. https://www.intelligenceonline.fr/renseignement-d-etat/2020/09/09/la-dgsi-met -les-bouchees-doubles-sur-les-universites,109604975-bre.

———. "La DGSI revoit son lien avec l'université." July 22, 2020. https://www .intelligenceonline.fr/renseignement-d-etat/2020/07/22/la-dgsi-revoit-son-lien -avec-l-universite,109596173-bre.

Irwin, Daniel, and David R. Mandel. "Improving Information Evaluation for Intelligence Production." *Intelligence and National Security* 34, no. 4 (2019): 503–25.

Izambard, Antoine. "Sciences Po Aix va créer la première chaire française 100% dédiée au renseignement." *Challenges*, July 3, 2020. https://www.challenges.fr /education/sciences-po-aix-va-creer-la-premiere-chaire-francaise-100-dediee-au -renseignement_717661.

Jackson, Peter. "Intelligence and the State: An Emerging 'French School' of Intelligence Studies." *Intelligence and National Security* 21, no. 6 (2006): 1061–65.

Jamieson, Kathleen Hall. *Cyberwar: How Russian Hackers and Trolls Helped Elect a President*. New York: Oxford University Press, 2018.

Jeffery, Keith. *MI6: The History of the Secret Intelligence Service, 1909–1949*. London: Bloomsbury, 2010.

Jeffreys-Jones, Rhodri. "Commentary: Loch Johnson's Oral History Interview with William Colby, and Johnson's Introduction to That Interview." In *Exploring Intelligence Archives: Enquiries into the Secret State*, edited by R. Gerald Hughes, Peter Jackson, and Len Scott, 270–72. London: Routledge, 2008.

Jentleson, Bruce W., and Ely Ratner. "Bridging the Beltway—Ivory Tower Gap." *International Studies Review* 13, no. 1 (2011): 6–11.

Jervis, Robert. *Why Intelligence Fails: Lessons from the Iranian Revolution and the Iraq War*. Ithaca, NY: Cornell University Press, 2010.

Jibilian, Isabella, and Katie Canales. "The US Is Readying Sanctions against Russia over the SolarWinds Cyber Attack: Here's a Simple Explanation of How the Massive Hack Happened and Why It's Such a Big Deal." *Insider*, April 15, 2021. https://www.businessinsider.com/solarwinds-hack-explained-government -agencies-cyber-security-2020-12.

Jiménez, Marcela. "¿Qué pasa en la ANI?" *El Mostrador*, July 12, 2018. https://m .elmostrador.cl/noticias/pais/2018/07/12/que-pasa-en-la-a-n-i.

Johnson, Loch K. *A Season of Inquiry: The Senate Intelligence Investigation*. Lexington: University of Kentucky Press, 1985.

Johnson, Loch K. "Spies and Scholars in the United States: Winds of Ambivalence in the Groves of Academe." *Intelligence and National Security* 34, no. 1 (2019): 1–21.

Johnson, Loch K., and Alison M. Shelton. "Thoughts on the State of Intelligence Studies: A Survey Report." *Intelligence and National Security* 28, no. 1 (2013): 109–20.

Johnston, Rob. *Analytic Culture in the US Intelligence Community: An Ethnographic Study*. Washington, DC: Center for the Study of Intelligence, 2005. https://fas.org /irp/cia/product/analytic.pdf.

Joint Chiefs of Staff. *Developing Today's Joint Officers for Tomorrow's Ways of War: The Joint Chiefs of Staff Vision and Guidance for Professional Military Education & Talent Management*. Washington, DC: Joint Chiefs of Staff, 2020. https:// www.jcs.mil/Portals/36/Documents/Doctrine/education/jcs_pme_tm_vision.pdf.

Joint Chiefs of Staff. Joint Doctrine Note 1-18. *Strategy*. Washington, DC: Joint Chiefs of Staff, 2018. https://www.jcs.mil/Portals/36/Documents/Doctrine/jdn_jg /jdn1_18.pdf.

Joyner, James. "Soldier-Scholar [Pick One]: Anti-Intellectualism in the American Military." *War on the Rocks*, August 25, 2020. https://warontherocks.com/2020/08/soldier-scholar-pick-one-anti-intellectualism-in-the-american-military.

Kagan, Donald. *Pericles of Athens and the Birth of Democracy: The Triumph of Vision in Leadership.* New York: Simon & Schuster, 1991.

Kahn, David. "Intelligence Studies on the Continent." *Intelligence and National Security* 23, no. 2 (2008): 249–62.

Kahneman, Daniel. *Thinking, Fast and Slow.* New York: Farrar, Straus and Giroux, 2011.

Karvetski, Christopher W., and David R. Mandel. "Coherence of Probability Judgments from Uncertain Evidence: Does ACH Help?" *Judgment and Decision Making* 15, no. 6 (2020): 939–58.

Karvetski, Christopher W., David R. Mandel, and Daniel Irwin. "Improving Probability Judgment in Intelligence Analysis: From Structured Analysis to Statistical Aggregation." *Risk Analysis* 40, no. 5 (2020): 1040–57.

Kelly, John E. "Computing, Cognition and the Future of Knowing: How Humans and Machines Are Forging a New Age of Understanding." IBM Research, 2015. http://publicservicesalliance.org/wp-content/uploads/2015/10/Computing_Cognition_WhitePaper.pdf.

Kendall, Willmoore. "The Function of Intelligence." *World Politics* 1, no. 4 (1949): 542–52.

Kent, Sherman. "The Need for an Intelligence Literature." *Studies in Intelligence* 1, no. 1 (1955): 1–11. https://www.cia.gov/static/539a695e2365ed5a17422139fa14e3cf/Need-for-Intelligence-Literature.pdf.

———. *Strategic Intelligence for American World Policy.* Princeton, NJ: Princeton University Press, 1949.

———. "Words of Estimative Probability." *Studies in Intelligence* 8, no. 4 (1964): 49–65.

Kent, Thomas. *Striking Back: Overt and Covert Options to Combat Russian Disinformation.* Washington, DC: Jamestown Foundation, 2020.

Kerbel, Josh, and Anthony Olcott. "Synthesizing with Clients, Not Analyzing for Customers." *Studies in Intelligence* 54, no. 4 (2010): 11–27.

Keršanskas, Vytautas. "Deterrence: Proposing a More Strategic Approach to Countering Hybrid Threats." Hybrid CoE Paper 2. March 2020. https://www.hybridcoe.fi/wp-content/uploads/2020/07/Deterrence_public.pdf.

Klayman, Joshua, and Young-won Ha. "Hypothesis Testing in Rule Discovery: Strategy, Structure, and Content." *Journal of Experimental Psychology: Learning, Memory, and Cognition* 15, no. 4 (1989): 596–604.

Knorr, Klaus. "Failures in National Intelligence Estimates: The Case of the Cuban Missiles." *World Politics* 16, no. 3 (1964): 455–67.

Knorr, Klaus E. "Foreign Intelligence and the Social Sciences." Research Monograph No. 17. Center of International Studies, Woodrow Wilson School of Public and International Affairs, Princeton University, NJ, 1964.

Kojm, Christopher A. "Change and Continuity: The National Intelligence Council, 2009–2014." *Studies in Intelligence* 59, no. 2 (2015): 1–11.

Kreuter, Nate. "The US Intelligence Community's Mathematical Ideology of Technical Communication." *Technical Communication Quarterly* 24, no. 3 (April 2015): 217–34.

Kuhn, Thomas S. *The Structure of Scientific Revolutions*. Chicago, IL: University of Chicago Press, 1962.

Kunda, Ziva. "The Case for Motivated Reasoning." *Psychological Bulletin* 108, no. 3 (1990): 480–98.

Laal, Marjan. "Benefits of Lifelong Learning." *Procedia—Social and Behavioral Sciences* 46 (2012): 4268–72.

Lacoste, Pierre. "Trois ans de séminaire sur la culture française du renseignement." In *Le Renseignement à la française*, edited by Pierre Lacoste. Paris: Economica, 1998.

Lagneau, Laurent. "La Direction du renseignement militaire a signé une convention de partenariat avec le CNRS." *OPEX 360*, June 10, 2018. http://www.opex360.com/2018/06/10/direction-renseignement-militaire-a-signe-convention-de-parte nariat-cnrs.

Lagrone, James J. "The Hotel in Operations." *Studies in Intelligence* 9, no. 4 (1965). https://www.cia.gov/resources/csi/studies-in-intelligence/archives/vol-9-no-4/the -hotel-in-operations.

"La perspectiva del cambio en los servicios de inteligencia." *Plan V de Ecuador*, October 1, 2018. https://www.planv.com.ec/historias/politica/perspectivas-del -cambio-servicios-inteligencia.

Lasoen, Kenneth L. "For Belgian Eyes Only: Intelligence Cooperation in Belgium." *International Journal of Intelligence and CounterIntelligence* 30, no. 3 (2017): 464–90.

Lasswell, Harold D. "On the Policy Sciences in 1943." In "Professional Insecurities," special issue, *Policy Sciences* 36, no. 1 (2003): 71–98.

Lasswell, Harold D. "The Relation of Ideological Intelligence to Public Policy." *Ethics* 53, no. 1 (October 1942): 25–34.

Laurent, Sébastien. *Politiques de l'Ombre.* Paris: Fayard, 2009.

———. "Renseignement militaire et action politique, le BCRA et les services spéciaux de l'armée d'armistice." In *Le Renseignement à la française*, edited by Pierre Lacoste, 79–100. Paris: Economica, 1998.

Lefebvre, Stéphane. "Academic-Intelligence Relationships: Opportunities, Strengths, Weaknesses and Threats." *Journal of Policing, Intelligence and Counter Terrorism* 16, no. 1 (2021): 92–103.

Legge, J. Michael. *Theatre Nuclear Weapons and the NATO Strategy of Flexible Response*. Santa Monica, CA: RAND Corporation, 1983. https://www.rand.org /content/dam/rand/pubs/reports/2007/R2964.pdf.

L'Estrange, Michael, and Stephen Merchant. *Independent Intelligence Review*. June 2017. Canberra: Commonwealth of Australia. June 2019. https://www.pmc.gov .au/resource-centre/national-security/report-2017-independent-intelligence-review.

Lewis, Paul, and Owen Bowcott. "Brexit Advice: Are Ministers Obliged to Comply with International Law?" *Guardian*, September 10, 2020. https://www.the

guardian.com/politics/2020/sep/10/brexit-letter-are-mps-obliged-to-comply-with -international-law.

Ley 19212/1993. Crea la Dirección de Seguridad Pública e Informaciones. Ministerio del Interior, Chile.

Ley 19.696/2018. Crea el Sistema de Inteligencia del Estado. Uruguay.

Ley 5241/2016. Crea el Sistema de Inteligencia Nacional. Paraguay.

Lichtenstein, Sarah, Baruch Fischhoff, and Lawrence D. Phillips. "Calibration of Probabilities: The State of the Art to 1980." In *Judgment under Uncertainty: Heuristics and Biases*, edited by Daniel Kahneman, Paul Slovic, and Amos Tversky, 306–34. Cambridge: Cambridge University Press, 1982.

Lippmann, Walter. 1922. *Public Opinion*. New Brunswick: Transaction Publishers, 1998.

Löjdquist, Fredrik. "An Ambassador for Countering Hybrid Threats." Royal United Services Institute (RUSI), September 6, 2019. https://www.rusi.org/explore-our -research/publications/commentary/ambassador-countering-hybrid-threats.

Lomas, Daniel W. B. "#ForgetJamesBond: Diversity, Inclusion and the UK's Intelligence Agencies." *Intelligence and National Security* 36, no. 7 (2021): 995–1017. https://doi.org/10.1080/02684527.2021.1938370.

Lowenthal, Mark M. "Is the US Intelligence Community Anti-Intellectual?" In *The Future of Intelligence*: *Challenges in the 21st Century*, edited by Isabelle Duyvesteyn, Ben de Jong, and Joop van Reijn, 39–47. New York: Routledge, 2014.

Mackenzie, Compton. *Water on the Brain*. London: Cassell, 1933.

Macquarie University. *Journal of Policing, Intelligence and Counter Terrorism.* Accessed January 11, 2021. https://www.mq.edu.au/faculty-of-arts/departments -and-schools/department-of-security-studies-and-criminology/our-research /journal-of-policing,-intelligence-and-counter-terrorism.

Mainwaring, Sarah. "Division D: Operation Rubicon and the CIA's Secret SIGINT Empire." *Intelligence and National Security* 35, no. 5 (2020): 623–40.

Maldonado, Carlos. "Desafíos de los Servicios de Inteligencia en la región andina." In *SIN Arcana Imperii*, ed. Andrés Gómez de la Torre. Peru: Foro Libertad & Seguridad, 2007.

Maldonado, Carlos. "La inteligencia estratégica en América del Sur: Persisten las falencias de profesionalismo." In *Inteligencia Estratégica Contemporánea*. Ecuador: Universidad de las Fuerzas Armadas de Ecuador (ESPE), 2016. https:// repositorio.espe.edu.ec/bitstream/21000/11692/1/INTELIGENICIA%20ESTRA TEGICA.pdf.

Maldonado, Carlos, and Carolina Sancho. "Strategic Intelligence Cooperation in South America and the South American Defense Council." *Journal of Mediterranean and Balkan Intelligence* 7, no. 1 (2016).

Maldonado Prieto, Carlos. "Dilemas antiguos y modernos en la inteligencia estratégica en Sudamérica." *Security and Defense Studies Review* 9, nos. 1–2 (2009).

Mandel, David R. "Can Decision Science Improve Intelligence Analysis?" In *Researching National Security Intelligence: Multidisciplinary Approaches*, edited by Stephen M. Coulthart, Michael Landon-Murray, and Damien Van Puyvelde, 117–40. Washington, DC: Georgetown University Press, 2019.

———. "The Occasional Maverick of Analytic Tradecraft." *Intelligence and National Security* 35, no. 3 (2020): 438–43.

Mandel, David R., and Alan Barnes. "Accuracy of Forecasts in Strategic Intelligence." *Proceedings of the National Academy of Sciences* 111, no. 30 (2014): 10984–89.

———. "Geopolitical Forecasting Skill in Strategic Intelligence." *Journal of Behavioral Decision Making* 31, no. 1 (2018): 127–37.

Mandel, David R., and Daniel Irwin. "Facilitating Sender-Receiver Agreement in Communicated Probabilities: Is It Best to Use Words, Numbers or Both?" *Judgment and Decision Making* 16, no. 2 (2021): 363–93.

———. "On Measuring Agreement with Numerically Bounded Linguistic Probability Schemes: A Re-analysis of Data from Wintle, Fraser, Wills, Nicholson, and Fidler (2019)." *PLoS ONE* 16, no. 3 (2021): e0248424. https://doi.org/10.1371/journal.pone.0248424.

———. "Uncertainty, Intelligence, and National Security Decisionmaking." *International Journal of Intelligence and CounterIntelligence* 34, no. 3 (2020): 558–82. https://doi.org/10.1080/08850607.2020.1809056.

Mandel, David R., and Philip E. Tetlock. "Correcting Judgment Correctives in National Security Intelligence." *Frontiers in Psychology* 9, article 2640 (2018): 1–5. https://doi.org/10.3389/fpsyg.2018.02640.

———. "Debunking the Myth of Value-Neutral Virginity: Toward Truth in Scientific Advertising." *Frontiers in Psychology* 7, article 451 (2016): 1–5. https://doi.org/10.3389/fpsyg.2016.00451.

Mandel, David R., Christopher W. Karvetski, and Mandeep K. Dhami. "Boosting Intelligence Analysts' Judgment Accuracy: What Works, What Fails?" *Judgment and Decision Making* 13, no. 6 (2018): 607–21.

Mandel, David R., Tonya L. Hendriks, and Daniel Irwin. "Policy for Promoting Analytic Rigor in Intelligence: Professionals' Views and Their Psychological Correlates." *Intelligence and National Security*, October 2021. https://www.tandfonline.com/doi/full/10.1080/02684527.2021.1999621.

Marchio, Jim. "'How Good Is Your Batting Average?' Early IC Efforts to Assess the Accuracy of Estimates." *Studies in Intelligence (Extracts)* 60, no. 4 (2016): 3–13.

Marcoci, Alexandru, Mark Burgman, Ariel Kruger, Elizabeth Silver, Marissa McBride, Felix Singleton Thorn, Hannah Fraser, Bonnie C. Wintle, Fiona Fidler, and Ans Vercammen. "Better Together: Reliable Application of the Post-9/11 and Post-Iraq US Intelligence Tradecraft Standards Requires Collective Analysis." *Frontiers in Psychology* 9, article 2634 (2019): 1–9. https://doi.org/10.3389/fpsyg.2018.02634.

Marion, Pierre. *La mission impossible: À la tête des Services Secrets.* Paris: Calman-Lévy, 1991.

Marrin, Stephen. "Evaluating the Quality of Intelligence Analysis: By What (Mis) Measure?" *Intelligence and National Security* 27, no. 6 (2012): 896–912.

———. *Improving Intelligence Analysis: Bridging the Gap between Scholarship and Practice.* Abingdon: Routledge, 2012.

———. "Improving Intelligence Studies as an Academic Discipline." *Intelligence and National Security* 31, no. 2 (2016): 266–79.

———. "Intelligence Analysis: Structured Methods or Intuition?" *American Intelligence Journal* 25, no. 1 (2007): 7–16.

———. "Intelligence Studies Centers: Making Scholarship on Intelligence Analysis Useful." *Intelligence and National Security* 27, no. 3 (2012): 398–422.

———. "Training and Educating U.S. Intelligence Analysts." *International Journal of Intelligence and CounterIntelligence* 22, no. 1 (2009): 131–46.

Marrin, Stephen, and Sophie Cienski. "Experimenting with Intelligence Education: Overcoming Design Challenges in Multidisciplinary Intelligence Analysis Programmes." In *The Routledge International Handbook of Universities, Security and Intelligence Studies*, edited by Liam Francis Gearon, 287–99. Abingdon: Routledge, 2020.

Matei, Mihaela, and Ionel Nițu. "Intelligence Analysis in Romania's SRI: The Critical 'Ps'—People, Processes, Products." *International Journal of Intelligence and CounterIntelligence* 25, no. 4 (2012): 700–726.

Matey, Gustavo Díaz. "The Development of Intelligence Studies in Spain." *International Journal of Intelligence and CounterIntelligence* 23, no. 4 (2010): 748–65.

Matheny, Michael R. *Carrying the War to the Enemy: American Operational Art to 1945*. Norman: University of Oklahoma Press, 2011.

Maugham, W. Somerset. *Ashenden, or the British Agent*. London: Heinemann, 1928.

McCarthy, David S. "'The Sun Never Sets on the Activities of the CIA': Project Resistance at William and Mary." *Intelligence and National Security* 28, no. 5 (2013): 611–33.

Meleagrou-Hitchins, Alexander. *Incitement: Anwar al-Awlaki's Western Jihad*. Cambridge, MA: Harvard University Press, 2020.

Melnik, Constantin. *1000 Jours à Matignon*. Paris: Grasset, 1988.

———. *La mort était leur mission: Le service Action pendant la guerre d'Algérie*. Paris: Plon, 1996.

Michael, Kobi, and Aaron Kornbluth. "The Academization of Intelligence: A Comparative Overview of Intelligence Studies in the West." *Cyber, Intelligence, and Security* 3, no. 1 (2019): 117–40.

Mill, John Stuart. *On Liberty*. London: John W. Parker & Son, 1859.

Miller, Bowman H. "Soldiers, Scholars, and Spies: Combining Smarts and Secrets." *Armed Forces & Society* 36, no. 4 (2010): 695–715.

Miller, Greg. "The Intelligence Coup of the Century." *Washington Post*, February 11, 2020.

Ministère de la Défense. *Livre Blanc sur la Défense*. Paris, 1994.

Ministère des Armées. "Interaxions." September 24, 2018. https://www.defense .gouv.fr/dgse/tout-le-site/interaxions.

Mittelstadt, Jennifer. "Too Much War, Not Enough College." *War Room*, June 20, 2018. https://warroom.armywarcollege.edu/articles/too-much-war-not-enough -college.

Moore, Don A., and Paul J. Healy. "The Trouble with Overconfidence." *Psychological Review* 115, no. 2 (2008): 502–17.

Moran, Christopher. "Note on Teaching Intelligence." *Intelligence and National Security* 31, no. 1 (2016): 118–30. https://doi.org/10.1080/02684527.2014.989687.

Morgenthau, Hans J. *Truth and Power: Essays of a Decade, 1960–70.* London: Pall Mall Press, 1970.

Morris, Errol, dir. *The Unknown Known.* 2013.

Mosser, Michael. "Puzzles versus Problems: The Alleged Disconnect between Academics and Military Practitioners." *Perspectives on Politics* 8, no. 4 (2010): 1077–86.

Moynihan, Donald P. "The Network Governance of Crisis Response: Case Studies of Incident Command Systems." *Journal of Public Administration Research and Theory* 19, no. 4 (2009): 895–915.

Mueller, John, and Mark G. Stewart. *Terror, Security and Money: Balancing the Risks, Benefits, and Costs of Homeland Security.* New York: Oxford University Press, 2011.

Muggah, Robert. "Why the Latest Cyberattack Was Different." *Foreign Policy,* January 11, 2021. https://foreignpolicy.com/2021/01/11/cyberattack-hackers-russia-svr-gru-solarwinds-virus-internet.

Murphy, Ann Marie, and Andreas Fulda. "Bridging the Gap: Pracademics in Foreign Policy." *PS: Political Science and Politics* 44 (2011): 279–83.

National Research Council. *Intelligence Analysis for Tomorrow: Advances from the Behavioral and Social Sciences.* Washington, DC: National Academies Press, 2011. https://www.nap.edu/catalog/13040/intelligence-analysis-for-tomorrow-advances-from-the-behavioral-and-social.

Needell, Allan A. "'Truth Is Our Weapon': Project TROY, Political Warfare, and Government-Academic Relations in the National Security State." *Diplomatic History* 17, no. 3 (1993): 399–420.

Nemfakos, Charles, Bernard D. Rostker, Raymond E. Conley, Stephanie Young, William A. Williams, Jeffrey Engstrom, Barbara Bicksler, et al. *Workforce Planning in the Intelligence Community: A Retrospective.* Santa Monica, CA: RAND Corporation, 2013. https://www.rand.org/pubs/research_reports/RR114.html.

Nicholson, Michael. "What's the Use of International Relations?" *Review of International Studies* 26, no. 2 (2000): 183–98.

Niño, Cesar. "Chuzadas: Las tenues líneas entre la seguridad y la inseguridad." *Razón Pública,* January 27, 2020. https://razonpublica.com/chuzadas-las-tenues-lineas-la-seguridad-la-inseguridad.

Obando, Enrique. "La reestructuración de la inteligencia en el Perú: Sus avances y problemas." In *Inteligencia y Seguridad: Revista de análisis y prospectiva,* no. 5. Universidad Rey Juan Carlos (Cátedra Servicios de Inteligencia y Sistemas democráticos) and Universidad Carlos III de Madrid (Instituto Juan Velásquez de Velasco de Investigación para la Seguridad y Defensa), Spain, 2008/2009.

Office of National Intelligence. *The National Intelligence Community.* Accessed October 5, 2020. https://www.oni.gov.au/national-intelligence-community.

Office of the Director of National Intelligence. *Intelligence Community Directive 203: Analytic Standards.* Washington, DC: DNI, 2015. https://fas.org/irp/dni/icd/icd-203.pdf.

———. "Principles of Professional Ethics for the Intelligence Community." https://www.dni.gov/index.php/how-we-work/ethics.

Office of the Director of National Intelligence, Office of General Counsel. *Intelligence Community Legal Reference Book*. 2020. https://www.dni.gov/files/documents/OGC/IC%20Legal%20Reference%20Book%202020.pdf.

Omand, David. "Intelligence Secrets and Media Spotlights." In *Spinning Intelligence*, edited by Robert Dover and Michael S. Goodman, 37–56. London: Hurst, 2009.

———. *Securing the State*. London: Hurst, 2010.

Otis, Pauletta. "The Intelligence Pro and the Professor: Toward an Alchemy of Applied Arts and Sciences." In *Bringing Intelligence About: Practitioners Reflect on Best Practices*, edited by Russell G. Swenson, 7–18. Washington, DC: Joint Military Intelligence College, 2003.

Paiolle, Pau. *Services spéciaux (1935–1945)*. Paris: Robert Laffont, 1975.

Palacios, José-Miguel. "EU Intelligence: On the Road to a European Intelligence Agency?" In *Intelligence Law and Policies in Europe*, edited by Jan-Hendrik Dietrich and Satish Sule, 201–34. Munich: C. H. Beck, 2019.

———. "Intelligence Analysis Training: A European Perspective." *International Journal of Intelligence, Security, and Public Affairs* 18, no. 1 (2016): 34–56.

Paris, Roland. "Ordering the World: Academic Research and Policymaking on Fragile States." *International Studies Review* 13, no. 1 (2011): 58–71.

Parrett, William G. *The Sentinel CEO: Perspectives on Security, Risk, and Leadership in the Post-9/11 World*. Hoboken, NJ: Wiley, 2007.

Parsons, Scott. "Intelligent Studies: Degrees in Intelligence and the Intelligence Community." In *The Routledge International Handbook of Universities, Security and Intelligence Studies*, edited by Liam Francis Gearon, 272–86. New York: Routledge, 2020.

Pashler, Harold, Patrice M. Bain, Brian A. Bottge, Arthur Graesser, Kenneth Koedinger, Mark McDaniel, and Janet Metcalfe. *Organizing Instruction and Study to Improve Student Learning*. IES Practice Guide. National Center for Education Research (NCER), September 2007. https://files.eric.ed.gov/fulltext/ED498555.pdf.

Passy, Colonel. *Souvenirs I. 2e Bureau Londres*. Monte-Carlo: Raoul Solar, 1947.

Patty, Anna, and Nigel Gladstone. "Spooks and Psychologists: Jobs of the Future." *Sydney Morning Herald*, August 12, 2019. https://www.smh.com.au/business/workplace/spooks-and-psychologists-jobs-of-the-future-20190802-p52dae.html.

Pawiński, Michał. "Going beyond Human Terrain System: Exploring Ethical Dilemmas." *Journal of Military Ethics* 17, nos. 2–3 (2018): 122–39.

Pedersen, Tore, and Pia Therese Jansen. "Seduced by Secrecy—Perplexed by Complexity: Effects of Secret vs Open-Source on Intelligence Credibility and Analytic Confidence." *Intelligence and National Security* 34, no. 6 (2019): 881–98.

Pekel, Kent. "The Need for Improvement: Integrity, Ethics, and the CIA." *Studies in Intelligence*, 1996. https://www.cia.gov/static/c053b4680f58a4b88c9863201c90e6a0/Integrity-Ethics-the-CIA.pdf.

Perla, Peter. *The Art of Wargaming: A Guide for Professionals and Hobbyists*. Annapolis, MD: United States Naval Institute, 2011.

"Perú cierra su servicio de inteligencia en medio de un escándalo de espionaje." BBC Mundo, February 10, 2015. https://www.bbc.com/mundo/noticias/2015/02/150210_peru_espiuonaje_cierre_porque_gl.

Petersen, Martin. "Making the Analytic Review Process Work." *Studies in Intelligence* 49, no. 1 (2005): 55–61. https://www.cia.gov/static/d70fbabbb72a3d2b490f758c96548ebf/Analytic-Review-Process-Work.pdf.

Pettee, George S. *The Future of American Secret Intelligence.* Washington, DC: Infantry Journal Press, 1946.

Phipps, Keith. "The 50 Best Spy Movies of All Time." *Vulture*, March 14, 2019. https://www.vulture.com/article/best-spy-movies-ranked.html.

Phythian, Mark. "Intelligence Analysis and Social Science Methods: Exploring the Potential for and Possible Limits of Mutual Learning." *Intelligence and National Security* 32, no. 5 (2017): 600–612.

Platt, Washington. *Strategic Intelligence Production: Basic Principles.* New York: F. A. Praeger, 1957.

Poncet, Guerric, and Emmanuel Durget. "La guerre hybride expliquée par le renseignement militaire." *Le Point*, November 25, 2019. https://www.lepoint.fr/societe/la-guerre-hybride-expliquee-par-le-renseignement-militaire-25-11-2019-2349437_23.php#.

Ponemon Institute. *2020 Cost of Global Threats Insider Report.* https://www.observeit.com/2020costofinsiderthreat.

Pool, Robert. *Field Evaluation in the Intelligence and Counterintelligence Context: Workshop Summary.* Washington, DC: National Academies Press, 2010.

Popper, Karl. *The Logic of Scientific Discovery.* New York: Routledge, 2002. Originally published in 1935 as *Logik der Forschung Verlag* by Julius Springer (Vienna, Austria).

Powers, Kevin, and James Burns. "The FBI, Cybersecurity and American Campuses: Academia, Government, and Industry as Allies in Cybersecurity Effectiveness." In *The Routledge International Handbook of Universities, Security and Intelligence Studies*, edited by Liam Francis Gearon, 94–107. Abingdon: Routledge, 2020.

Preble, Christopher. "Bridging the Gap: Managing Expectations, Improving Communications." *Journal of Strategic Studies* 40, nos. 1–2 (2017): 275–82.

Pronin, Emily, Daniel Y. Lin, and Lee Ross. "The Bias Blind Spot: Perceptions of Bias in Self versus Others." *Personality and Social Psychology Bulletin* 28, no. 3 (2002): 369–81.

Raitasalo, Jyri. "Hybrid Warfare: Where's the Beef?" *War on the Rocks*, April 23, 2015. https://warontherocks.com/2015/04/hybrid-warfare-wheres-the-beef.

Ransom, Harry Howe. "Being Intelligent about Secret Intelligence Agencies." *American Political Science Review* 74, no. 1 (1980): 141–48.

Rathmell, Andrew. "Towards Postmodern Intelligence." *Intelligence and National Security* 17, no. 3 (2002): 87–104. https://doi.org/10.1080/02684520412331306560.

Renz, Bettina. "Russia and 'Hybrid Warfare.'" *Contemporary Politics* 22, no. 3 (2016): 283–300.

Renz, Bettina, and Hanna Smith. "Russia and Hybrid Warfare—Going beyond the Label." *Aleksanteri Papers*, 2016. https://helda.helsinki.fi//bitstream/handle /10138/175291/renz_smith_russia_and_hybrid_warfare.pdf.

Rice, Condoleezza, and Amy B. Zegart. *Political Risk: How Businesses and Organizations Can Anticipate Global Insecurity*. New York: Hachette, 2018.

Rieber, Steven, and Neil Thomason. "Creation of a National Institute for Analytic Methods." *Studies in Intelligence* 49, no. 4 (2005): 71–77.

Riley-Smith, Tristram. "Men of the 'Professor Type' Revisited: Building a Partnership between Academic Research and National Security." In *The Routledge International Handbook of Universities, Security and Intelligence Studies*, edited by Liam Francis Gearon, 368–82. New York: Routledge, 2020.

Rivera, Fredy. "Inteligencia estratégica e inteligencia política: Los claro-oscuros del caso ecuatoriano." In *Inteligencia Estratégica Contemporánea*. Ecuador: Universidad de las Fuerzas Armadas de Ecuador (ESPE), 2016. https://repositorio.espe.edu .ec/bitstream/21000/11692/1/INTELIGENICIA%20ESTRATEGICA.pdf.

———. "Inteligencia estratégica y prospectiva." Editorial. FLACSO/SENAIN. Ecuador, 2011.

Rivera, Fredy, Katalina Barreiro, and Gilda Guerrero. *¿Dónde está el pesquisa? Una historia de la Inteligencia de la Política en el Ecuador.* Ecuador: Centro de Publicaciones Pontificia Universidad Católica de Ecuador, 2018.

Roberts, Karlene H. "Managing High Reliability Organizations." *California Management Review* 32, no. 4 (1990): 101–13.

Rospigliosi, Fernando. "La DINI: Una alternativa." *El Comercio de Perú*, April 12, 2015. https://elcomercio.pe/opinion/mirada-de-fondo/dini-alternativa-fernando -rospigliosi-351487-noticia.

Rudner, Martin. "Intelligence Studies in Higher Education: Capacity-Building to Meet Societal Demand." *International Journal of Intelligence and CounterIntelligence* 22, no. 1 (2009): 110–30.

Sageman, Marc. "The Stagnation in Terrorism Research." *Terrorism and Political Violence* 26 (2014): 565–80.

Saín, Marcelo. *La Casa que no cesa: Infortunios y desafíos en el proceso de reforma de la ex SIDE*. Argentina: Editorial Octubre, 2016.

Salazar, Hernando. "Uribe liquidará el DAS." BBC Mundo, September 19, 2009. http://www.bbc.co.uk/mundo/america_latina/2009/09/090918_0237_colombia _das_gm.shtml.

Salus Journal: A Journal of Law Enforcement, National Security, and Emergency Management. Accessed January 11, 2021. https://salusjournal.com.

Sancho Hirane, Carolina. "Democracia, política pública de Inteligencia y desafíos actuales: Tendencias en países de Latinoamérica." In *Revista Inteligencia y Seguridad: Revista de Análisis y Prospectiva*, no. 11. Spain: Cátedra Servicios de Inteligencia y Sistemas democráticos (Universidad Rey Juan Carlos) e Instituto Juan Velázquez de Velasco de Investigación en Inteligencia para la Seguridad y Defensa, 2012.

———. "Fuerzas Armadas y Crimen Organizado en países Latinoamericanos durante el siglo XXI: Describiendo el fenómeno y sus principales desafíos." In *Los macro y micro desafíos de la seguridad en democracia*, edited by Bertha García and José Ugarte. Ecuador: Centro de Publicaciones Pontificia Universidad Católica de Ecuador, 2018.

———. "Política pública de inteligencia." In *Conceptos Fundamentales de Inteligencia*, edited by Antonio M. Díaz Fernández, 287–94. Valencia: Tirant lo Blanch, 2016.

———. "Reflexión en Torno a la Comunidad de Inteligencia en Chile a Partir de la Cultura de Inteligencia Nacional: Los desafíos pendientes." In *Democratización de la función de inteligencia: El nexo de la cultura nacional y la inteligencia estratégica*, edited by Russell G. Swenson and Susana C. Lemozy, 65–196. Washington, DC: National Defense Intelligence College, 2009.

Sandu, Oana. "Academia—A Strategic Resource for the Intelligence Community." In *Strategies XXI*, no. 2, supplement, 286–94. Bucharest: Centre for Defense and Security Strategic Studies, National Defence University, 2014.

Savoia, Claudio. *Espiados*. Argentina, 2015.

Schapper, Jan, and Susan E. Mayson. "Research-Led Teaching: Moving from a Fracture Engagement to a Marriage of Convenience." *Higher Education Research & Development* 29, no. 6 (2010): 641–51.

Schneier, Bruce. *Beyond Fear: Thinking Sensibly about Security in an Uncertain World.* New York: Copernicus Books, 2003.

Schoemaker, Paul J. H., and Philip E. Tetlock. "Superforecasting: How to Upgrade Your Company's Judgment." *Harvard Business Review*, May 2016. https://hbr.org /2016/05/superforecasting-how-to-upgrade-your-companys-judgment.

Schramm, Wilbur. "The Forefathers of Communication Study in America." In *The Beginnings of Communication Study in America: A Personal Memoir by Wilber Schramm*, edited by Steven H. Chaffee and Everett M. Rogers, 3–121. Thousand Oaks, CA: Sage, 1997.

Schwartz, Peter. *The Art of the Long View: Planning for the Future in an Uncertain World.* New York: Crown Business, 1996.

Sciences Po. "Le DiReM—Diplôme d'établissement sur le Renseignement et les Menaces globales." March 2019. https://www.sciencespo-saintgermainenlaye.fr /wp-content/uploads/2019/03/DiReMVF.pdf.

Sciences Po. "PSIA Curriculum 2019–20." 2019, 58.

Sciences Po. "Uses of Technologies for the Surveillance of Communications (UTIC)." https://www.sciencespo.fr/ceri/en/content/uses-technologies-surveillance -communications-utic#equipe-tab.

"Sciences Po Aix: Création de la première chaire académique sur le renseignement en France." *L'Express*, July 16, 2020. https://www.lexpress.fr/actualite/societe /sciences-po-aix-creation-de-la-premiere-chaire-academique-sur-le-renseignement -en-france_2131084.html.

Sciences Po Centre d'Histoire. "Le renseignement: Planification, stratégie et prospective—Séminaire METIS—Programme saison 17—séance 5." 2015. http:// www.sciencespo.fr/newsletter/archive-e52eb0eeb8b076757c624e6c40edf033 .html.

Sciences Po Saint-Germain-en-Laye. "Synopsis-DiReM 2019–2020, Module technique." May 2020. https://www.sciencespo-saintgermainenlaye.fr/wp-content/uploads/2020/05/Les-pratiques-du-renseignement-op%C3%A9rationnel.pdf.

Scopelliti, Irene, Carey K. Morewedge, Erin McCormick, H. Lauren Min, Sophie Lebrecht, and Karim S. Kassam. "Bias Blind Spot: Structure, Measurement, and Consequences." *Management Science* 61, no. 10 (2015): 2468–86.

Scott, Len, and Peter Jackson. "The Study of Intelligence in Theory and Practice." *Intelligence and National Security* 19, no. 2 (2004): 139–69.

Shane, Scott. "Pursuing an Exotic Tool for Espionage: A Moral Compass." *New York Times*, January 28, 2006.

Silberzahn, Claude, with Jean Guisnel. *Au cœur du secret: 1500 Jours aux Commandes de la DGSE* (Paris: Fayard, 1995).

Smith, Hanna. "Hybrid Threats to Allied Decision-Making." In *NATO Decision-Making in the Age of Big Data and Artificial Intelligence*, edited by Sonia Lucarelli, Alessandro Marrone, and Francesco N. Moro, 44–56. Brussels: NATO HQ, 2021. https://www.iai.it/sites/default/files/978195445000.pdf.

Smith, Steve. "Power and Truth: A Reply to William Wallace." *Review of International Studies* 23, no. 4 (1997): 507–15.

Solovey, Mark. "Project Camelot and the 1960s Epistemological Revolution: Rethinking the Politics-Patronage-Social Science Nexus." *Social Studies of Science* 31, no. 2 (2001): 171–206.

Spracher, William C. "Teaching Intelligence in the United States, the United Kingdom, and Canada." *Oxford Research Encyclopedia of International Studies*, March 2010. https://oxfordre.com/internationalstudies/view/10.1093/acrefore/9780190846626.001.0001/acrefore-9780190846626-e-308?rskey=ZyzDHZ.

Stephan, Walter G. "Bridging the Research-Practitioner Divide in Intergroup Relations." *Journal of Social Issues* 62, no. 3 (2006): 597–605.

Stimson, Henry L., and McGeorge Bundy. *On Active Service in Peace and War.* New York: Harper, 1948.

Svendsen, Adam D. M. "Connecting Intelligence and Theory: Intelligence Liaison and International Relations." *Intelligence and National Security* 24, no. 5 (2009): 700–729. https://doi.org/10.1080/02684520903209456.

Swenson, Russell. "Intelligence Education in the Americas." *International Journal of Intelligence and CounterIntelligence* 16, no. 1 (2003): 108–30.

Swenson, Russell, and Carolina Sancho Hirane, eds. "Intelligence Management in the Americas." National Intelligence University, 2015.

Swenson, Russell G., and Susana C. Lemozy, eds. *Democratización de la función de inteligencia: El nexo de la cultura nacional y la inteligencia estratégica.* Washington, DC: National Defense Intelligence College, 2009.

———, eds. *Profesionalismo de Inteligencia en las Américas.* Center for Strategic Intelligence Research/Joint Military Intelligence College, 2004.

Syndicat National des Travailleurs de la Recherche Scientifique. "En Bref No. 476: Communique Presse SNTRS CGT: 'La Convention CNRS—Direction du Renseignement Militaire Nuit à l'Indépendance de la Recherche.'" July 5, 2018. https://sntrscgt.vjf.cnrs.fr/spip.php?article2537.

Taddeo, Mariarosaria. "How to Deter in Cyberspace." Hybrid CoE Strategic Analysis 9. June–July 2018. https://www.hybridcoe.fi/wp-content/uploads/2020/07/Strategic-Analysis-9-Taddeo.pdf.

Tanter, Raymond, and Richard H. Ullman. "Introduction: Theory and Policy in International Relations." In "Theory and Policy in International Relations." Supplement, *World Politics* 24 (1972): 3–6.

Tetlock, Philip E. "Social Functionalist Frameworks for Judgment and Choice: Intuitive Politicians, Theologians, and Prosecutors." *Psychological Review* 109, no. 3 (2002): 451–71.

———. "Theory-Driven Reasoning about Plausible Pasts and Probable Futures in World Politics: Are We Prisoners of Our Preconceptions?" *American Journal of Political Science* 43, no. 2 (1999): 335–66.

Tetlock, Philip E., and Barbara A. Mellers. "Intelligent Management of Intelligence Agencies: Beyond Accountability Ping-Pong." *American Psychologist* 66 (2011): 542–54.

Thiele, Ralph. "Hybrid Warfare: Future & Technologies." Inspiration Paper No. 2, Helsinki, May 14, 2019.

Thomas, Jorhena, and Nicholas Dujmović. "Educators Consider Alternative Approaches to US College Intelligence Programs." *Studies in Intelligence* 63, no. 4 (2019): 17–21.

Thomson, Elizabeth A., Greg Auhl, Kerri Hicks, Kerstin McPherson, Caroline Robinson, and Denise Wood. "Course Design as a Collaborative Enterprise: Incorporating Interdisciplinarity into a Backward Mapping Systems Approach to Course Design in Higher Education." In *Research and Development in Higher Education: Curriculum Transformation*, edited by R. G. Walker and S. B. Bedford, 356–67. Sydney, Australia: Higher Education Research and Development Society of Australasia Inc., 2017.

Tickner, J. Ann, Andrei Tsygankov, Joseph S. Nye, Henry R. Nau, Jane S. Jaquette, Craig N. Murphy, Natalie J. Goldring, et al. "Risks and Opportunities of Crossing the Academic/Policy Divide." *International Studies Review* 10, no. 1 (2008): 155–77.

Timms, Mark A. C., David R. Mandel, and Jonathan D. Nelson. "Applying Information Theory to Validate Commanders' Critical Information Requirements." In *Handbook of Military and Defence Operation Research*, edited by Natalie M. Scala and James P. Howard, 331–44. Boca Raton, FL: CRC Press, 2020.

Tomes, Robert R. *Apocalypse Then: American Intellectuals and the Vietnam War, 1954–1975.* New York: New York University Press, 2000.

Treverton, Gregory F. *Covert Action: The Limits of Intervention in the Postwar World.* New York: Basic Books, 1987.

Tversky, Amos, and Daniel Kahneman. "Extensional versus Intuitive Reasoning: The Conjunction Fallacy in Probability Judgment." *Psychological Review* 90, no. 4 (1983): 293–315.

———. "Judgment under Uncertainty: Heuristics and Biases." *Science* 185 (1974): 1124–31.

Ugarte, José. "El control público de la actividad de inteligencia en América Latina." Argentina: Ediciones CICCUS, 2012.

―――. "La cultura política y administrativa y su influencia en el desarrollo de estructuras de Inteligencia en Argentina." In *Democratización de la función de inteligencia: El nexo de la cultura nacional y la inteligencia estratégica*, edited by Russell G. Swenson and Susana C. Lemozy, 437–56. Center for Strategic Intelligence Research. Washington, DC: National Defense Intelligence College, 2009.

UK Chiefs of Staff. *Joint Doctrine Publication 2-00: Understanding and Intelligence Support to Joint Operations*. 3rd ed. London: Ministry of Defence, 2011. https://www.gov.uk/government/publications/jdp-2-00-understanding-and-intelligence-support-to-joint-operations.

University Foreign Interference Task Force. "Guidelines to Counter Foreign Interference in the Australian University Sector." November 2019.

US Department of Defense. *Summary of the 2018 National Defense Strategy of the United States of America: Sharpening the American Military's Competitive Edge*. Washington, DC: Department of Defense, 2018. https://dod.defense.gov/Portals/1/Documents/pubs/2018-National-Defense-Strategy-Summary.pdf.

US Department of Homeland Security. *Learning Roadmaps for Intelligence Professionals—Analytics*. 2006.

―――. *Risk Management Fundamentals*. April 2011.

US Department of Justice. *Analyst Professional Development Road Map for Analysts*. June 2015. https://www.ojp.gov/library/publications/analyst-professional-development-road-map.

―――. *Ethics Handbook for On and Off-Duty Conduct*. January 2016. https://www.justice.gov/usao-sdny/page/file/1153451/download.

US Naval Academy. "Ethics across the Curriculum." Stockdale Center for Ethical Leadership. https://www.usna.edu/Ethics/blog/2020/ethics_across_the_curriculum.php.

US Northern Command. "North American Defense and Security Academic Alliance." 2021. Accessed April 20, 2021. https://www.northcom.mil/Educational/North-American-Defense-and-Security-Academic-Alliance/North-American-Defense-and-Security-Academic-Alliance-Research-Topics.

Valaskivi, Katja. "Beyond Fake News: Content Confusion and Understanding the Dynamics of the Contemporary Media Environment." Hybrid CoE Strategic Analysis 5. February 2018. https://www.hybridcoe.fi/wp-content/uploads/2020/07/Strategic-Analysis-5-Valaskivi.pdf.

Vandepeer, Charles. *Applied Thinking for Intelligence Analysis: A Guide for Practitioners*. Air Power Development Centre, 2014. https://airpower.airforce.gov.au/APDC/media/PDF-Files/Air%20Force%20Publications/AF13-Applied-Thinking-for-Intelligence-Analysis.pdf.

―――. "Increasing Student-to-Student (Peer) Learning through Deep Questions and Online Blogs." *iTeach* (blog), Charles Sturt University, July 15, 2019. https://iteach.csu.edu.au/2019/07/15/increasing-student-to-student-peer-learning-through-deep-questions-and-online-blogs.

———. "Intelligence and Knowledge Development: What Are the Questions Intelligence Analysts Ask?" *Intelligence and National Security* 33, no. 6 (2018): 785–803.

———. "Question-Asking in Intelligence Analysis: Competitive Advantage or Lost Opportunity?" *Air & Space Power Journal: Afrique et Francophonie* 7, no. 4 (2016): 24–43.

Vandepeer, Charles, and James L. Regens. "Teaching and Mentoring in Intelligence Education: Preparing Intelligence Professionals for Asking Better Questions." Paper presented at the Fourteenth Annual Intelligence Association for Intelligence Education Conference. Sydney, Australia, July 2018.

Van Puyvelde, Damien. *Outsourcing US Intelligence: Contractors and Government Accountability.* Edinburgh: Edinburgh University Press, 2019.

———. "Women and Black Employees at the Central Intelligence Agency: From Fair Employment to Diversity Management." *Cambridge Review of International Affairs* 34, no. 5 (2020): 673–703. https://doi.org/10.1080/09557571.2020.1853052.

Van Puyvelde, Damien, and Sean Curtis. "'Standing on the Shoulders of Giants': Diversity and Scholarship in Intelligence Studies." *Intelligence and National Security* 31, no. 7 (2016): 1040–54. https://doi.org/10.1080/02684527.2016.1185323.

Van Puyvelde, Damien, James J. Wirtz, Jean-Vincent Holeindre, Benjamin Oudet, Uri Bar-Joseph, Ken Kotani, Florina Cristiana Matei, and Antonio M. Díaz Fernández. "Comparing National Approaches to the Study of Intelligence." *International Studies Perspectives* 21, no. 3 (2020): 298–337.

Venegas, Álvaro J. "En busca de inteligencia estratégica: Cuatro factores para el nacimiento y evolución de una inteligencia civil colombiana." *Ciencia Política* 13, no. 26 (2018): 287–318. https://doi.org/10.15446/cp.v13n26.71938.

Villarreal, Alexandra. "Russian SolarWinds Hackers Launch Email Attack on Government Agencies." *Guardian*, May 28, 2021. https://www.theguardian.com/technology/2021/may/28/russian-solarwinds-hackers-launch-assault-government-agencies.

Vilmer, Jean-Baptiste Jeangène, Jean-Vincent Holeindre, and Paul Charon, eds. *Le Renseignement: Approches, acteurs et enjeux.* Paris: Presses Universitaires de France, forthcoming.

von Hippel, William, and Robert Trivers. "The Evolution and Psychology of Self-Deception." *Behavioral and Brain Sciences* 34, no. 1 (2011): 1–16.

Wallace, Arturo. "Colombia y la revancha final de los espías del DAS." BBC Mundo, September 19, 2011. https://www.bbc.com/mundo/noticias/2011/09/110919_colombia_das_escandalo_filtraciones_semana_aw.

Wallace, Robert, and Keith Melton. *Spycraft: The Secret History of the CIA's Spytechs from Communism to Al-Qaeda.* New York: Dutton/Penguin, 2009.

Wallace, William. "Truth and Power, Monks and Technocrats: Theory and Practice in International Relations." *Review of International Studies* 22, no. 3 (1996): 301–21.

Walsh, Patrick F. "Improving 'Five Eyes' Health Security Intelligence Capabilities: Leadership and Governance Challenges." *Intelligence and National Security* 35, no. 4 (2020): 586–602.

———. "Teaching Intelligence in the Twenty-First Century: Towards an Evidence-Based Approach for Curriculum Design." *Intelligence and National Security* 32, no. 7 (2017): 1005–21.

Warner, Michael. "Wanted: A Definition of 'Intelligence.'" *Studies in Intelligence* 46, no. 3 (2002): 15–22.

Warusfel, Bertrand. *Le renseignement français contemporain: Aspects politiques et juridiques.* Paris: L'Harmattan, 2003.

West, Richard F., Russell J. Meserve, and Keith E. Stanovich. "Cognitive Sophistication Does Not Attenuate the Bias Blind Spot." *Journal of Personality and Social Psychology* 103, no. 3 (2012): 506–19.

Whitesmith, Martha. "The Efficacy of ACH in Mitigating Serial Position Effects and Confirmation Bias in an Intelligence Analysis Scenario." *Intelligence and National Security* 34, no. 2 (2019): 225–42.

Wiers, Jochem. "Building a Bridge or Nurturing the Gap?" *Journal of Strategic Studies* 40, nos. 1–2 (2017): 283–86.

Wigell, Mikael. "Hybrid Interference as a Wedge Strategy: A Theory of External Interference in Liberal Democracy." *International Affairs* 95, no. 2 (March 2019): 255–75.

Wilensky, Harold L. *Organizational Intelligence: Knowledge and Policy in Government and Industry.* New York: Basic Books, 1967.

Willmetts, Simon. "The Cultural Turn in Intelligence Studies." *Intelligence and National Security* 34, no. 6 (2019): 800–817. https://doi.org/10.1080/02684527.2019.1615711.

Wiñazki, Nicolás. "La purga llegó a los camporistas de AFI, pero nadie los defendió." January 30, 2016. https://www.clarin.com/politica/gobierno-agencia_federal_de_inteligencia-la_campora-despidos-estado_0_BkajpaODXe.html.

Winks, Robin W. *Cloak and Gown: Scholars in the Secret War, 1939–1961.* New York: William Morrow, 1989.

Wintle, Bonnie C., Hannah Fraser, Ben C. Wills, Ann E. Nicholson, and Fiona Fidler. "Verbal Probabilities: *Very Likely* to Be *Somewhat* More Confusing Than Numbers." *PLoS ONE* 14, no. 4 (2019): e0213522. http://dx.doi.org/10.1371/journal.pone.0213522.

Wright, Robert. "Spies Used Top Academic to Monitor UK Campus Radicals, Files Reveal." *Financial Times*, July 18, 2019. https://www.ft.com/content/1e1cddca-a7b2-11e9-b6ee-3cdf3174eb89.

Young, Gerardo. *Código Stiuso.* Argentina: Planeta, 2015.

———. *SIDE: La Argentina secreta.* Argentina: Planeta, 2006.

Zambernardi, Lorenzo. "The Impotence of Power: Morgenthau's Critique of American Intervention in Vietnam." *Review of International Studies* 37, no. 3 (2011): 1335–56.

Zaretsky, Robert. *Catherine and Diderot: The Empress, the Philosopher and the Fate of the Enlightenment.* Cambridge, MA: Harvard University Press, 2019.

Zimmer, Louis B. *The Vietnam War Debate: Hans J. Morgenthau and the Attempt to Halt the Drift into Disaster.* Lanham, MD: Lexington Books, 2011.

Index

About the Contributors

Rubén Arcos is a senior lecturer in communication sciences at Universidad Rey Juan Carlos (URJC) in Madrid, Spain. He serves as program co-chair of the Intelligence Studies Section at the International Studies Association. He is a co-founder and co-director of the IntelHub—International Online Intelligence Hub, a joint initiative between the American Public University System, the University of Leicester in the United Kingdom, and URJC. He has been a freelance contributor of *Jane's Intelligence Review* and deputy editor of the *International Journal of Intelligence, Security, and Public Affairs*. Arcos is currently a researcher in the EU-HYBNET project— Empowering a Pan-European Network to Counter Hybrid Threats (a five-year-long project funded by the European Commission's Horizon 2020 Programme) and a member of the expert pool on information of the European Centre of Excellence for Countering Hybrid Threats. His main research interests are intelligence and intelligence analysis, strategic communication, foreign information manipulation, and hybrid threats. He is also the coeditor of *The Art of Intelligence: Simulations, Exercises, and Games* (2 vols.).

Michael J. Ard is the program director for the master of science in intelligence analysis program at Johns Hopkins University's Krieger School in Washington, DC. A former Central Intelligence Agency (CIA) analyst and manager, Dr. Ard specialized in Latin American and Middle Eastern issues. Part of his career included three years at the Office of the Director of National Intelligence, where he served as deputy national intelligence officer for the Western Hemisphere. In addition to his career in government, Dr. Ard worked in corporate security at Marathon Oil and as a consultant for a professional service firm focused on international risk. He was educated at the College of William & Mary and the University of Virginia, where in 2001 he earned his PhD in foreign affairs. He has written on a variety of issues, including Latin American politics, and in 2003 he published *An Eternal Struggle: How the National Action Party Transformed Mexican Politics*. Dr. Ard formerly was program director for intelligence studies at the American Public University System and taught international security in Rice University's master of global affairs program. Prior to his academic and intelligence careers, Dr. Ard served as an officer in the US Navy and is a veteran of the 1991 Gulf War.

James G. Breckenridge currently serves as the provost of the US Army War College. The provost serves as the chief academic officer of the college and focuses strategic direction in five principal areas: education, faculty, students, research, and support. Dr. Breckenridge previously served as the founding dean of the Ridge College of Intelligence Studies and Applied Sciences at Mercyhurst University, the largest private academic intelligence enterprise in the United States, and as executive director of the college's research arm, the Institute for Intelligence Studies, both in Erie, Pennsylvania.

Irena Chiru is a professor of intelligence studies at "Mihai Viteazul" National Intelligence Academy, Romania, and the chair of the International Association for Intelligence Education—European Chapter. She also serves as dean of the Faculty for Intelligence Studies with the "Mihai Viteazul" National Intelligence Academy. She is the author or coauthor of several books, chapters, and articles focused on strategic communication and its impact on intelligence organizations. She has also joined international research teams involved in research projects dedicated to security and intelligence.

Andrés de Castro García is a lecturer and researcher at the Faculty of Political Sciences and Sociology at UNED, Spain. He has been the head of the Department of International Relations at the Catholic University of Erbil in Northern Iraq. He earned his PhD in international security at the Instituto Universitario General Gutierrez Mellado (IUGM-UNED) in Madrid, and a law degree from the University of Salamanca, also in Spain. Dr. de Castro García specializes in intelligence and security studies.

Nicole K. Drumhiller currently serves as the associate dean for the School of Security and Global Studies at the American Public University System. She oversees the undergraduate- and graduate-level curriculums, ensuring their alignment with institutional learning objectives. Her published works cover topics such as intelligence, security studies, and political psychology. She also serves as an advisory board member for the Operative Intelligence

Research Center in Rome, Italy, and is a co-founder and co-director of the IntelHub, an online consortium for intelligence education and research.

Nicholas Dujmović is the founding director of the Intelligence Studies Program at The Catholic University of America. He served twenty-six years at the CIA as a Soviet analyst, speechwriter for the Director of Central Intelligence, editor of the *President's Daily Brief*, analytic manager, and deputy chief CIA historian. He received his PhD from the Fletcher School of Law and Diplomacy at Tufts University. As a staff historian, Dr. Dujmović worked on classified studies of CIA clandestine operations, including the hunt for bin Laden. His unclassified work on Agency operations and culture has appeared in several intelligence journals and anthologies. Dr. Dujmović has also taught at the US Coast Guard Academy and at American University's School of International Service. He is a deacon of the Orthodox Church in America.

Jan Goldman is professor of intelligence and security studies at The Citadel, The Military College of South Carolina. He is editor of the *International Journal of Intelligence and CounterIntelligence* and the founding editor of the Security Professional Intelligence Education Series at Rowman & Littlefield Publishing Group. He is the founding editor of the *International Journal of Intelligence and Ethics*, which is available for free at https://journals.flvc.org/ijie.

Rasmus Hindrén is the head of international relations at the European Centre of Excellence for Countering Hybrid Threats. Previously, he was the deputy head of the Unit for Defence Cooperation at the Ministry of Defence of Finland. He has served as Defense Counselor at the Embassy of Finland in Washington, DC, and as Defense Adviser at the Permanent Representation of Finland to the EU. He has held several positions in the Ministry of Defence and the Ministry for Foreign Affairs dealing with security policy, defense cooperation, and planning. Mr. Hindrén has a master's degree in international relations. He has authored several articles on security and defense policy.

Carolina Sancho Hirane currently works as a professor at ANEPE, developing research, teaching, and extension activities, and is the coordinator of the Chair on Security and Globalization at the University of Chile. In the public sector, she has served in the Office of the Comptroller General of the Republic, as well as in the Ministry of the Interior and Public Security as head of the Department of Organized Crime. She has also been a Chilean delegate at the Center for Strategic Studies (CEED) of the South American Defense Council

(CDS) of the Union of South American Nations (UNASUR) in Buenos Aires, Argentina.

Adrian-Liviu Ivan is the rector of "Mihai Viteazul" National Intelligence Academy and full professor at Babeş-Bolyai University in Cluj Napoca. He is the author of numerous books, articles, and scientific papers in the field of international relations, security studies, national and ethnic minorities in international relations, security policies, and European and international governance. He is also a member of various editorial boards of scientific journals. Professor Ivan's academic activity has been rewarded through various awards and distinctions received throughout his career.

Genevieve Lester is the De Serio Chair of Strategic Intelligence at the US Army War College. Prior to her position at the US Army War College, Dr. Lester was faculty at the National Defense University and Georgetown University, a fellow at the International Institute for Strategic Studies, and a Fulbright Scholar. She holds a PhD and MA from the University of California, Berkeley; an MA from the Johns Hopkins University, School of Advanced International Studies; and a BA in history from Carleton College.

David R. Mandel is a senior defense scientist with Defence Research and Development Canada and adjunct professor of psychology at York University. He publishes widely in peer-reviewed journals and has coauthored or coedited five books on reasoning, judgment, and decision making. Mandel was the chairman of the North Atlantic Treaty Organization (NATO) Research Technical Group on Assessment and Communication of Uncertainty in Intelligence to Support Decision Making, which received the NATO System Analysis and Studies Panel Excellence Award in 2020.

Professor **Sir David Omand** GCB is visiting professor in war studies, King's College London; PSIA Sciences Po in Paris; and the Norwegian Defence University in Oslo, where he teaches intelligence studies. Previously his posts in British government service included United Kingdom Security and Intelligence Coordinator in the Cabinet Office, Permanent Secretary of the Home Office, Director of Government Communications Headquarters, and Deputy UnderSecretary of State for Policy in the Ministry of Defence. He served for seven years on the Joint Intelligence Committee. He is the author of *Securing the State* (2010) and coauthor with Professor Mark Phythian of *Principled Spying: The Ethics of Secret Intelligence* (2018). His latest book is *How Spies Think: 10 Lessons from Intelligence* (2020).

José-Miguel Palacios led the Analysis Division in the EU Intelligence Analysis Centre (EU INTCEN) of the European External Action Service in Brussels between 2011 and 2015. He joined the EU Situation Centre (renamed EU INTCEN in 2012) in 2006 as an analyst, after having worked for the Spanish government since 1986 in several analytical roles. Currently, he is a visiting professor of intelligence studies at the College of Europe (Bruges, Belgium). He holds a PhD in political science.

Mark Phythian is the professor of politics in the School of History, Politics & International Relations at the University of Leicester. He is the author or editor of some fifteen books on intelligence and security topics, as well as numerous journal articles and book chapters. He is the co-editor of *Intelligence and National Security*, one of the editors of the Georgetown Studies in the History of Intelligence book series, and a Fellow of the UK Academy of Social Sciences.

Hanna Smith is Director of Research and Analysis at the European Centre of Excellence for Countering Hybrid Threats (Hybrid CoE) and visiting professor at the College of Europe, Brugge. Dr. Smith is an expert on hybrid threats, Russia and Eurasia, and great power identity. Her research interests include security studies, international relations and institutions, and regional and Nordic cooperation. Her latest publications are *Strategic Culture in Russia's Neighborhood: Change and Continuity in an In-Between Space* (Lexington, 2019), edited with Katalin Miklóssy; and "The Landscape of Hybrid Threats: A Conceptual Model" (European Commission, Ispra, 2020), edited with Georgios Giannopoulos and Marianthi Theocharidou. Prior to joining the Hybrid CoE, she worked at the University of Helsinki as research fellow and acted in several policy-relevant research projects as an expert. She has published numerous articles in books, academic journals, and newspapers and has taught courses at the University of Helsinki, at the University of Eastern Finland, and in Finnish national defense.

Col. Thomas Spahr teaches strategy, campaigning, and intelligence at the US Army War College. He served as a military intelligence officer in the US Army for twenty-three years before transitioning to his current position. Col. Spahr has a PhD in history from The Ohio State University and taught military history at West Point and the US Air Force Academy.

Damien Van Puyvelde is a lecturer in intelligence and international security at the University of Glasgow and a research fellow at the Institute for Strategic Research (IRSEM, French Ministry for Armed Forces). He chairs the Intelligence Studies Section of the International Studies Association and co-chairs the working group on intelligence of the Association pour les Etudes sur la Guerre et la Stratégie. His latest books include *Outsourcing US Intelligence: Contractors and Government Accountability* (2019), *Researching National Security Intelligence: Multidisciplinary Approaches* (2019), and *Cybersecurity: Politics, Governance and Conflict in Cyberspace* (2019).

Charles Vandepeer is a senior lecturer in intelligence and security studies at Charles Sturt University. His career has included service in the Royal Australian Air Force as an intelligence officer, serving in a number of roles and positions and gaining operational experience with deployments to the Middle East. Charles also worked as a civilian defense operations research scientist.

Troy Whitford is a senior lecturer in intelligence and security studies at the Australian Graduate School of Policing and Security, Charles Sturt University. He is course coordinator for the master's of intelligence analysis and program director for intelligence and security studies. Dr. Whitford has delivered tailored intelligence courses for Australian law enforcement and at the National Indian Police Academy in Hyderabad, India.

www.ingramcontent.com/pod-product-compliance
Lightning Source LLC
Chambersburg PA
CBHW021808270326
41932CB00007B/107